'At SEWA, we strongly believe that organizing
own cooperatives and micro-enterprises stre
ing power and generates sustainable employn
thereby reducing poverty. With the informal
welcome addition to the ongoing debates on
and rural economies of the Global South as well as the
the Global North.'

—*Reema Nanavaty, Director, SEWA, India and member of the
ILO Global Commission on the Future of Work*

'Through work, we create value and in good work, we find dignity and meaning. This book is an outstanding guide to the wealth of practice around the world
in which co-operative models of enterprise serve to make work a transformative
experience.'

—*Ed Mayo, Secretary General, Co-operatives UK*

COOPERATIVES AND THE WORLD OF WORK

As the world of work and jobs is more uncertain than ever because of various trends impacting it, including the rise of robotics and the gig economy, *Cooperatives and the World of Work* furthers the debate on the future of work, sustainable development, and the social and solidarity economy of which cooperatives are a fundamental component.

Throughout the book, the authors, who are experts in their respective fields, do not limit themselves to praising the advantages of the cooperative model. Rather, they challenge the narrow understanding of cooperatives as a mere business model and raise debate on the more fundamental role that cooperatives play in responding to social changes and in changing society itself. The book is unique in tracing the historical connection between cooperatives and the world of work since the end of the First World War and the recent shifts and restructuring in enterprise and the workplace.

This book is published in recognition of 100 years of the International Labour Organization, and gathers together research from leading experts who were brought together at an event co-hosted by the International Co-operative Alliance (ICA) and the International Labour Organization (ILO).

Bruno Roelants is the Director General of International Co-operative Alliance and was formerly Secretary General of CICOPA and of its regional organization, CECOP CICOPA-Europe.

Hyungsik Eum is the Data Analyst at CICOPA and Strategy and Statistics Coordinator of the International Co-operative Alliance.

Simel Eşim is the Head of the Cooperatives Unit of the International Labour Office in Geneva. Prior to this, she was a Senior Technical Specialist in the ILO's Regional Office for Arab States.

Sonja Novkovic is Chair of the Committee on Co-operative Research of the International Co-operative Alliance. She is also the Academic Director in the Co-operative Management Education program and Professor of Economics at Saint Mary's University in Halifax, Canada.

Waltteri Katajamäki works at the International Labour Office in Geneva as a Technical Officer on Rural Economy and previously worked at the ILO's Cooperatives Unit.

COOPERATIVES AND THE WORLD OF WORK

*Edited by Bruno Roelants, Hyungsik Eum,
Simel Eşim, Sonja Novkovic and
Waltteri Katajamäki*

Routledge
Taylor & Francis Group

LONDON AND NEW YORK

First published 2020
by Routledge
2 Park Square, Milton Park, Abingdon, Oxon OX14 4RN

and by Routledge
52 Vanderbilt Avenue, New York, NY 10017

Routledge is an imprint of the Taylor & Francis Group, an informa business

British Library Cataloguing-in-Publication Data
A catalogue record for this book is available from the British Library

Library of Congress Cataloging-in-Publication Data
A catalog record has been requested for this book

ISBN: 978-0-367-25084-3 (hbk)
ISBN: 978-0-367-25085-0 (pbk)
ISBN: 978-0-429-28593-6 (ebk)

Typeset in Bembo
by Swales & Willis Ltd, Exeter, Devon, UK

MIX
Paper from
responsible sources
FSC
www.fsc.org   FSC® C013985

Printed in the United Kingdom
by Henry Ling Limited

CONTENTS

FOREWORD

The recent economic crisis has had a profound effect also in the world of work. This has generated renewed interest of policy makers in the cooperative enterprise model as a pillar of the social and solidarity economy which focuses on work as either a form of reintegration of the marginalized people into economy and society, a mode to gain economies of scale for the self-employed, or as worker-owned and controlled enterprises.

The International Labour Organization (ILO) and the International Co-operative Alliance Committee on Co-operative Research (ICA CCR) organized a joint conference in Antalya, Turkey, in 2015 to identify, discuss and debate issues related to the changing landscape of the world of work, specifically focusing on the role of cooperatives in alleviating some of the pressures and in contributing to the achievement of decent work.

This book is a result of those conversations. The project began in mid-2016, out of a common effort of the ILO's Cooperatives Unit (ILO COOP), ICA CCR and the International Organisation of Industrial, Artisanal and Service Producers' Cooperatives (CICOPA), a sectoral organization of the ICA.

While in this volume we are only able to scratch the surface of this complex and diverse topic, it is becoming clear that cooperatives have a major role to play in self-defining work and working conditions as worker-members, but also as places to work, whether it is in consumer, producer, financial, or any other type of cooperative. It is increasingly evident that work is also about human dignity: it is about autonomy, creativity, self-determination and competence, among others.

As the world of work is undergoing major changes that will continue and intensify, efforts are under way to better understand and to respond effectively to these new challenges. We hope that this volume on cooperatives and the changing world of work contributes to those discussions, providing insights on the organization of work and production and the governance of work the cooperative way.

Simel Eşim (Head, Cooperatives Unit, ILO)
Sonja Novkovic (Chair, ICA Committee on Co-operative Research)

CONTRIBUTORS

Editors' biographies

Bruno Roelants has been director general of the International Co-operative Alliance since April 2018. He was Secretary General of CICOPA between 2002 and 2018 and of its regional organization CECOP CICOPA-Europe between 2002 and 2018. He worked on development projects in China, India and Central-Eastern Europe, and coordinated the cooperative negotiating group for the ILO Promotion of Cooperatives Recommendation 2002 (no. 193). He has a Master's in Labour Studies and has lectured on cooperatives in Italy.

Hyungsik Eum is Data Analyst of CICOPA and also Strategy and Statistics Coordinator of the International Co-operative Alliance. He finished his PhD programme in Sociology at the University of Liège, Belgium. He has worked mainly on work and employment in cooperatives, various models of worker and social cooperatives, institutionalization of social and solidarity economy, and statistics on cooperatives.

Simel Eşim is the Head of the Cooperatives Unit at the International Labour Office in Geneva. She obtained her PhD in Economics in 1997. In addition to cooperatives and social and solidarity economy, her research interests include informal economy, women's economic empowerment, and labour migration.

Sonja Novkovic is the Chair of the Committee on Co-operative Research of the International Co-operative Alliance. She is the Academic Director in the Co-operative Management Education Program and Professor of Economics at Saint Mary's University in Halifax, Canada. She has engaged in research and teaching on cooperative and self-managed firms, social economy, and comparative economic systems.

Waltteri Katajamäki works at the International Labour Office in Geneva as a Technical Officer on Rural Economy. He has a Master's in Development Studies from the University of Helsinki, Finland. Previously he has worked at the ILO's Cooperatives Unit, focusing on cooperative training, rural cooperatives, and cooperation in the future of work.

Contributors' biographies

Mélissa Boudes is an Associate Professor of Organization Behaviour at LITEM, Univ Evry, IMT-BS, Université Paris-Saclay. She obtained her PhD in Management from Paris Dauphine University in 2017. Her research interests include social economy, new forms of work, and digital social innovation.

Philippe Burny is a Professor of Agricultural Economics and Policy at the University of Liege, Belgium. He got his PhD at the Faculty of Agronomy of Gembloux and is involved in teaching activities at the master's level in Gembloux and other European universities and in research projects dealing with the impacts of the Common Agricultural Policy on farm income and with rural development. He is also Adjunct Research Associate Professor at the Babes-Bolyai University in Cluj-Napoca, Romania, and doctor honoris causa of the Ivan Turgueniev State University in Orel, Russia.

Sonia Maria Dias is a waste specialist at Women in Informal Employment Globalizing and Organizing (WIEGO), based in Brazil. She obtained her PhD in Political Science from the Federal University of Minas Gerais. She has worked in government, civil society organizations and research institutions. Her interests include participatory democracy, participatory research, gender, social inclusion and solid waste management.

Manuel García Jiménez is a Professor of Self-Employment and Social Economy, and Systems of Industrial Relations in the Department of Labour Law and Social Security, University of Córdoba, Spain. He is a Doctor in Legal and Business Sciences from the University of Córdoba. His research interests include self-management, labour relations in worker cooperatives, rights at work, and decent work. In these subjects, he has published books, book chapters, and articles for more than 20 years.

Kirsi Hokkila is a doctoral student at the Business School of the University of Eastern Finland, Finland. She is working on her PhD on Finnish worker cooperatives. She is interested in new worker cooperatives as a means of self-employment in the context of the new world of work and in relation to changing work values.

Sudha Kornginnaya is an Associate Professor in the Department of Commerce, Besant Women's College, affiliated to Mangalore University, Karnataka State, India. She obtained her PhD for the thesis entitled *Member Development in Cooperatives: A Study with Reference to Primary Level Initiatives* from Mangalore University. Her research interests include human resource development in third sector, gender studies, and social entrepreneurship.

Akira Kurimoto is a Professor of Institute for Solidarity-based Society, Hosei University, Tokyo, Japan. He is Chairperson of the ICA Asia-Pacific Research Committee and is the editor of several English/Japanese books. His research interests include comparative co-operative law, co-operative history, and social economy.

Philippe Lebailly is a Professor at the Department of Economics and Rural Development at Gembloux Agricultural University (ULg – GxABT). His academic career combines research and project experiences, especially in rural development and food security in EU member states as well as developing countries.

Deogratias Sebahire Mbonyinkebe is a former lecturer at the State University of Kinshasa (formerly Lovanium), Democratic Republic of Congo (DRC). He has also lectured at the University of Rwanda and Kigali Independent University, Rwanda. He holds his PhD in Social and Cultural Anthropology from the Catholic University of Louvain/Leuven, Belgium. His areas of interest are African thought and religions, medical anthropology, vulnerable groups and associative movement, governance and peace-building in the Great Lakes Region, and sociology and anthropology of genocide.

Ana Carolina Ogando is a Research Associate for WIEGO's Urban Policies Programme and is based in Belo Horizonte, Brazil. She obtained her PhD in Political Science from the Federal University of Minas Gerais in 2012. Her research interests include gender, feminist theory, social movements, and participatory methodologies.

Anu Puusa is a Professor in Management and Deputy Head of the Department at the Business School of the University of Eastern Finland and a Docent of Management and Co-operatives at LUT School of Business and Management, Lappeenranta University of Technology. Her research interest areas are cooperatives, organizational identity and change, and organization citizenship behaviour.

Claudia Sanchez Bajo has been a Visiting Professor at the University of Kassel, Faculty of Sociology, Germany. She is fellow researcher at the Faculty of Economics, University of Buenos Aires, and member of the ICA Committee of Cooperative Research. She obtained her PhD in Development Studies, on the political economy of business actors in regionalism, in 2001, from the International Institute of Social Studies in The Hague, which is part of the Erasmus University in Rotterdam. Her research interests include cooperatives and peacebuilding, history of cooperativism, entrepreneurship, and solidarity economy.

Nathan Schneider is an Assistant Professor of Media Studies at the University of Colorado Boulder, USA. His recent research has focused on adapting lessons from the cooperative business tradition for the challenges of the online economy.

Jürgen Schwettmann is a retired official of the International Labour Organization, where he served, inter alia, as Chief of the Cooperative Branch. Since his retirement in September 2015 he works as an independent consultant for various multilateral and bilateral organizations. He is also a visiting professor at the

Division of Economics of Agricultural Cooperatives of the Humboldt University, Berlin. He has considerable professional experience in cooperative development in Africa and other developing regions.

Guy Tchami works for the International Labour Office as a Cooperative Policy and Research Specialist. His area of expertise includes development cooperation projects on cooperatives and other social and solidarity economy enterprises. He holds a Master's in Development Economics from the University of Bordeaux-Montesquieu, France.

Marcelo Vieta is an Assistant Professor in the Program in Adult Education and Community Development at the Ontario Institute for Studies in Education of the University of Toronto, Canada. He obtained his PhD in Social and Political Thought from York University (Canada) and has published in several leading journals in labour studies, organizational studies, the social economy, and critical theory. His research interests include alternative economic organizations, economic democracy, and the social and solidarity economy, with a focus on worker cooperatives, *autogestión*, and the *empresas recuperadas* of Latin America.

Gisaro M. Ya-Bititi is a Senior Lecturer at the Department of Development Studies, University of Rwanda, Huye, Rwanda. He obtained his PhD in Economics and Rural Development from Gembloux Agro-Bio Tech, University of Liege, Belgium. His research interests include socio-economics, rural development, cooperatives management, and farm management.

FIGURES

TABLES

INTRODUCTION

Bruno Roelants and Hyungsik Eum

The world of work is undergoing one of its biggest transformations since the Industrial Revolution. That was also the time when cooperatives first emerged. Today, work in or within the framework of cooperatives represents at least 278 million people, and is adapting rapidly and profoundly to these changes, from integration of marginalized and informal economy workers to high-tech platforms.

It is under the backdrop of this big transformation of the world of work that Guy Ryder, Director-General of the International Labour Organization (ILO), launched in 2015 a worldwide debate on the *Future of Work*. A series of consultations and conferences have since then been organized. A Global Commission on the Future of Work was established in mid-2017, composed of policy makers, thinkers, advocates, researchers and social partners, including a representative from the cooperative movement. The Commission will give its conclusions by the end of 2018 and the process will culminate with the centenary of the organization in 2019. This book contributes to this wider global debate building on the trajectory of the cooperative movement – past and present.

Rethinking about work and employment in cooperatives

Before outlining the structure of the book, let us briefly review what work and employment in cooperatives means. As is well known, the current form of cooperatives was born as a child of the modern era characterized by industrialization and capitalism. All through the 20th century, capital has been at the centre of the economy and rights of ownership and control, including the right to profit, while 'work' has been considered a commodity sold by workers to capital owners. Workers have been obliged to sell their work, as the only asset they have been able to offer in order to gain access to tools for subsistence in the monetized economy. The status of wage-earner or employee has become the norm in this economic system, and its share among different forms of work has increased. Thanks to workers' collective actions and political struggles, various types of institutional provisions and tools have developed around this norm and, as a consequence, the status of employee has become an entry for accessing financial resources, social protection and rights as citizens. Other forms of work have been deemed secondary and destined to be marginalized, if not completely disappear. Together with the industrialization and marketization of the economy, this narrow sense of 'employment' has been perceived as a part of the 'modernity' of the economy, and as the most formal form of work into which other traditional or informal forms of work should be transformed.

With this *zeitgeist*, cooperatives have served people in several different ways. For those already employed, cooperatives have served to improve their well-being by reducing the cost of living and by promoting mutual aid and solidarity among workers. Some consumer cooperatives and credit unions have been organized by workers in individual companies or in industrial sectors, including with the initiative of trade unions. Worker cooperatives have evolved as an alternative way to reach an employment status for those who do not want to be subjected to the power of capital. The capacity of worker cooperatives for creating and maintaining jobs has received continuous attention, particularly when capital leaves the enterprise to seek higher profit and abandons the workers and the local economy. In addition to preservation of jobs at the level of the enterprise and the local economy, work integration for the disadvantaged and creating economies of scale for the self-employed remain key arguments for developing cooperatives. The worker cooperative model has also moved toward the multi-stakeholder cooperative form where the value of work as being deeply rooted in the local community is recognized. Particularly in developing countries, cooperatives have been set up to modernize economic activities in the primary sectors. Differently from for-profit enterprises, cooperatives have been able to develop modern economic activities that respect the local communities and their own ways of working and living. At the same time, cooperatives have enabled people suffering traditional forms of oppression and discrimination, in particular poor women, to learn about their rights, gain intellectual and material resources, and act together. In doing so, cooperatives have been important instruments of formalizing informal work and implementing the fundamental human rights and values of social justice, such as the principle of decent work, down to very small local communities. However, it should be noted that, in many countries, some cooperatives have also been utilized as a justifiable excuse to escape the work relations and social regime based on the traditional model of employment. This character has often been abused by hidden employers trying to avoid their legal duties as employers. Therefore, in those countries, cooperatives have been criticized by the labour movement as a tool to exploit workers and worsening working conditions.

However, a new trend is emerging: today's world of work is changing in its reality as well as in its conceptualization. The traditional 'employee' model of employment, and the social regime based on it, is being weakened by various economic trends, and in particular the one towards profit maximization. The development of technologies has also helped design different forms of work and control over work. Demographic changes have produced new needs and problems in the labour market. All these changes have gradually dismantled the social regime based on the traditional model of employment and, consequently, threatening the social cohesion of our society. New conceptualization has been needed and proposed in order to cover these new forms of work and employment. On the other hand, various forms of 'activities' which do not fit within the concept of employment have been gradually recognized to play a certain role in economic activities in a broader sense: activities for self-consumption, caring for others including household work, volunteering for the common good, mutual aid and non-monetary exchanges. This conceptual recognition of various forms of economies and activities has weakened the dominance of the salaried concept of employment and allowed to re-examine the whole set of activities and relations based on these forms, and in cooperatives in particular. With this conceptualization shift, the specificities of cooperatives which have not been sufficiently explained by the dominant concept of economy and employment should be revalued. Differently from for-profit enterprises and public organizations, economic activities in cooperatives are dependent not only on employees but also on members. In almost every cooperative, members' work in governance as well as in doing volunteering work are at the basis of economic activities conducted by or through the cooperative. This type of work has not been duly recognized, and has somehow been taken for granted. In addition, in new forms of cooperatives, such as social cooperatives and community cooperatives, the role of volunteers and ways of evaluating it have become increasingly important. The complexity caused by the combination of traditional forms of employment and different types of members' activities has now become one among key issues connected with democratic practices in cooperatives, such as professionalization and members' substantial participation.

The meaning of such changes is still controversial. They are often considered as weakening social protection and rights at work and encouraging the informalization of many economic activities. On the other hand, they are appreciated as providing more flexibility and autonomy to workers. Whereas some try to enlarge social protection and rights at work to include new forms of work and employment, others try to establish new regimes in order to promote these new forms. Some workers are obliged to accept the new forms of work not by choice, but by sheer necessity to survive. In other cases, workers seek new forms of work that they can combine with their main activity.

Within this wider framework, cooperatives can be considered as laboratories in shaping new forms of work, work relationships, and work communities based on them. As their history reveals, cooperatives have repeatedly designed and experimented organizational innovation in responding to members' needs but also their aspirations. This trend is no longer anecdotal, as some of these experiments have already been institutionalized, including through new specific legal forms of employment in the labour code, such as the 'wage-earning entrepreneur' (*entrepreneur-salarié*) in business and employment cooperatives in France.

Some cooperatives are able to innovate by accessing new institutional tools, such as social security schemes, while others by accessing technical tools, such as internet platforms. Cooperatives also innovate by redefining the meaning of working together as an open community of employees, members and volunteers, who join for specific projects. For such flexible communities, regulation based on the traditional wage-earning model can be perceived as an impediment to innovation and creativity.

Structure of the book

The book begins in a war-torn world in 1919, when the ILO was established. The following year a cooperative unit was set up in the organization, and it is still functioning today. The book finishes with a look towards the experiments around the cooperative platform economy, and what it may look like in the future. In between, it analyses conceptual issues around the changing world of work and the role of cooperatives; empirical cases illustrating the strength of cooperatives in empowering women; the relationship between cooperatives and workers; and new organizational experimentations in response to new challenges in the world of work. The chapters cover a wide range of cooperatives in geographical extension and types.

Conceptual and normative issues

The first five chapters provide a general orientation for the book by discussing conceptual and normative issues connected to the changing world of work and the role of cooperatives. Given that the meaning of work and employment has changed over the years, contemporary challenges around work and employment reveal that we are in the middle of a dramatic transformation. Whereas the Fundamental Principles and Rights at Work,[1] as set out by the ILO, are still unevenly implemented, new challenges caused by recent technological and demographic changes are undermining these principles and rights, making the future of work difficult to predict. As cooperatives have been among enterprises and organizations advancing decent work, it is expected that they will play a role in adhering to the principles of decent work and generating innovative solutions to respond to the challenges they are facing. However, cooperatives and the economies in which they function are very diverse, and their contributions need to be critically assessed with this in mind. As an organizational form which is not free from the constraints of institutional settings and market pressures, cooperatives may not always realize their positive potential, and at times suffer from abuses and distortions. The optimism embedded in these five chapters does not forget to remind of this risk. One of the plausible answers is to create and strengthen an 'epistemic community' around the issue of work and employment in cooperatives, with more analytical and critical tools and ideas for promoting the role of cooperatives in advancing decent work.

In her chapter 'Work and cooperatives: a century of ILO interaction with the cooperative movement', Claudia Sanchez Bajo discusses the interplay between work and cooperatives at the ILO, focusing on three major periods: (a) 1919 to the 1930s, corresponding to the first years of existence of the ILO at the end of the First World War and the role of the first ILO Director Albert Thomas, who had previously been closely linked to the cooperative movement; (b) 1945 to the late 1980s, with the *Co-operatives (Developing Countries) Recommendation*, 1966 (No. 127) as one of its main outcomes, in the midst of a 'developmentalist' period; and (c) 1990 to 2015, with the *Promotion of Cooperatives Recommendation*, 2002 (No. 193) as its main achievement. She emphasizes the continued existence of an epistemic community between the ILO and the cooperative movement, which was in great part made possible by the fact that the ILO's Cooperatives Unit has been in existence during this whole century. After examining the historical changes of the ILO's position on cooperatives and of the notion of work in relation to cooperatives, the author pinpoints that the ILO, with its present effort to include all forms of work, is returning to Albert Thomas's vision that comprised households, independent workers and families. Observing that the latest wave of globalization has brought about a long-lasting global crisis and higher inequality than the first period, the author wonders whether the increasingly conflictive tensions and the quest for peace and a sustainable future may be indicating a renewed call for both a strong cooperative community of knowledge and a strong cooperative movement.

After introducing the *Future of Work* initiative as part of the ILO Centenary Initiative, Jürgen Schwettmann's chapter, 'Cooperatives and the future of work', describes major trends affecting the world of work, in terms of demography, technology, economy and environment. The author assesses both positive and negative impacts of these trends on the world of work and provides examples of ways in which cooperatives can contribute to building a better future of work. The author emphasizes the distinct nature, characteristics, values, principles and governance structure of cooperatives and proposes that the global cooperative movement develops alternatives to the mainstream economic system, which has shown its drawbacks and limitations. Ultimately, cooperatives should be able to demonstrate that decent work for all is possible, even in a post-growth context. Bearing in mind those considerations, the author proposes to develop a pragmatic strategy of cooperative development in the context of the future of work, including cooperation beyond cooperatives, building alliances with likeminded movements, organizing cooperation along global supply chains and cooperatives formed in response to emerging trends.

In their chapter 'Cooperatives and fundamental principles and rights at work: natural disposition or commitment to action?', Simel Eşim, Waltteri Katajamäki and Guy Tchami highlight the role and responsibilities of cooperatives in advancing decent work in general and the Fundamental Principles and Rights at Work (FPRW) in particular. The chapter analyses what constitutes good employment practices among cooperatives in the different areas of FPRW, namely the fight against child labour and forced labour, non-discrimination at work, and freedom of association and right to collective bargaining. Cooperatives, the authors argue, can play a number of key roles in advancing FPRW. As critical players in some key global supply chains such as agriculture, they provide scale to smallholders, helping them access markets, information, technology and finance with conditions that they could not enjoy on their own. Furthermore, they can use their broad membership base to reach out to large numbers of producers and consumers, educating and raising awareness of their members and communities on FPRW as well as other topics, and providing a whole array of entrepreneurial services as well as extending social protection. Whereas cooperatives can promote FPRW, cooperative training and education infrastructures can disseminate awareness and information on FPRW and cooperative research institutions can conduct assessments of the relative performance of the cooperative model in advancing FPRW. Implementation and monitoring mechanisms need to be put in place at various levels in order to turn the potential of cooperatives in advancing FPRW into action.

In the chapter 'The autonomy or heteronomy of cooperative worker ownership', Manuel García Jiménez describes different ways of protecting workers and their rights. Whereas for salaried work labour law is an established mechanism for protecting labour from capital by guaranteeing certain inalienable workers' rights, the legal establishment of minimum working conditions in non-salaried work as the inalienable right of workers is still rejected on doctrinal grounds based on the defence of contractual freedom and autonomy. Worker ownership (namely the status of worker-member) as a specific form of work mainly found in worker cooperatives is, in a number of countries, also part of non-salaried work so that a tutelary application of labour law has not been deemed imperative; it is the workers themselves who manage their own businesses, adopt the most suitable mode of organization and share the results of their efforts in proportion to the work done by each person, and it is assumed that they will not harm their own interests. However, the central issue is that, when work is performed out of necessity, necessity itself is imbued with a dependency that compromises autonomy. In the case of workers in worker cooperatives, the need to survive may oblige them to accept less favourable conditions than conventional salaried workers, thereby compromising their autonomy and turning work into heteronomous work, paving the way to self-exploitation. Recourse to human rights and decent work as a means of limiting contractual freedom is used as a tool to counteract the loss of legal protection for wage-earning work in a labour market that is becoming increasingly deregulated. Although cooperatives are defined as independent and autonomous, they should also be subjected to human rights and decent work as universal norms. This double imperative is fully recognized in ILO Recommendation No. 193 and CICOPA's *World Declaration on Worker Cooperatives*. The author proposes that work in worker cooperatives is not autonomous but heteronomous so that labour law and international guidelines concerning labour should be applied to it.

In the Chapter 5, 'Work and employment in the informal economy and new forms of work: how can the cooperative model be an answer?', Hyungsik Eum argues that in the changing world of work, institutional frameworks for the rights and protection at work, mainly based on the employment relationship, have been weakened. The trend towards the informalization of employment over the last decades both in developing countries and industrialized ones has produced new forms of work and employment which are not sufficiently covered by existing formal arrangements. The cooperative model has been considered and used as an instrument to address problems related to informal employment as well as the current trend toward informalization. However, different kinds of contributions made by diverse types of cooperatives in various cases of informal employment have not yet been sufficiently analysed. As the concept of informal employment is complex and reflects diverse situations, the role of cooperatives in addressing problems related to it cannot be simply stated as evident. By focusing on different contributions of cooperatives, specifically regarding the possibility of providing rights and protection at work, which is directly related to the formalization of informal employment, the author argues that a better distinction between cooperative types would be useful to clarify different contributions of cooperatives to the world of work. He also argues that conceptual ambiguities between cooperative types, in particular the distinction between producers' cooperatives and worker cooperatives, should be communicated more effectively in order to help understand the role of cooperatives in the evolution of the world of work.

Cooperatives and empowerment of women

A significant part of the global population is still living in economically and socially vulnerable situations and does not benefit from the fruits of economic prosperity nor enjoy minimum human rights. It is particularly true for people in specific geographical regions as well as those suffering various types of discrimination due to gender, age, physical condition or social class, among others. Cooperatives have served people in vulnerable and disadvantaged situations by providing them with economic autonomy and social spaces that may empower them in struggling against discrimination and oppression. The following three chapters illustrate empirical cases of the role of cooperatives in empowering women in developing countries and in improving their work and life. However, they do not only show cooperatives' positive contributions, but also their limits and challenges.

In their chapter "'Coffee has given us power to act": coffee cooperatives and women's empowerment in Rwanda's rural areas', Gisaro M. Ya-Bititi, Philippe Lebailly, Deogratis Sebahire Mbonyinkebe and Philippe Burny examine the effects of coffee cooperatives as a tool for empowerment of women in Rwanda. The development of coffee cooperatives and coffee washing stations has acted as a source of employment and socio-economic empowerment for women, especially during the coffee harvesting and processing period. By enabling members to improve household income, coffee cooperatives have enhanced the socio-economic status and welfare of women. Cooperatives have also provided education to their members and thereby encourage them to engage in decision-making at family/household level. Coffee growers are also able to access credit through rotating funds, enabling them to participate in various socio-economic activities such as affording adequate shelter, accessing medical insurance, paying school fees for their children, undertaking entrepreneurial activities, saving income and gaining access to land.

Sudha Kornginnaya's chapter, 'The changing cooperative landscape in the world of work: a study of women's empowerment through participatory strategies in India', observes that women in the informal economy suffer multiple deprivations that have undermined their potential and marginalized and secluded them from the mainstream economy. Cooperatives have helped women organize and mobilize for joint action and achieve better bargaining power as buyers and sellers in the marketplace. The empowerment of women through cooperatives is found crucial to poverty reduction and human development, leading to enhanced productivity. The chapter presents the participatory strategies initiated by the district-level cooperatives in the banking and dairy sectors in Dakshina Kannada District in the Indian State of Karnataka and examines the diverse strategies undertaken by the cooperatives in terms of self-help group formation, provision of financial services, capacity-building measures and self-employment avenues.

In the chapter 'Waste cooperatives in Brazil: exploring links between cooperative ideals and raising gender awareness', Sonia Maria Dias and Ana Carolina Ogando argue that the cooperative values of self-help, equality and equity, as well as economic growth through cooperation and democratic processes within cooperatives are open to debate, and that gender equality in cooperatives cannot be taken for granted. They note that up until recently the gender inequality has been largely ignored by the cooperative movement of waste pickers in Brazil. Whereas there seem to be higher concentrations of women within cooperatives, this is neither indicative of gender equality nor of women's stronger presence in the higher echelons of the waste pickers' movement. The authors argue that efforts to uphold greater gender equality standards and to challenge the different forms of gender-based violence that pervade women waste pickers' lives are essential for bridging the cooperative movement's founding ideology with its practices, and that, when provided the proper training and discussion fora, the women waste pickers are becoming increasingly more vocal and assertive, presenting a clear challenge to the long-established barriers embedded in the movement's praxis and action. The authors argue that there is need for engagement with other social movements, such as the women's movement, and that a commitment to gender equality by the cooperative movement should be based on concrete, long-term action plans and strategies that confront the concerns brought forth by women waste pickers.

Cooperatives and workers

It is interesting to recall that the Rochdale Society of Equitable Pioneers, considered as the starting point of the modern cooperative movement, was initiated by workers engaged in the labour movement. An important number of cooperatives were developed by workers in an effort to improve their work and life conditions. Cooperatives have been organized to provide various kinds of goods and services to their members who were workers in the same factory, local community or industry.

We can also note that cooperative forms have been used by workers to claim owner-ship of their enterprises. Worker buyouts have been used as one of the final options through which workers have been attempting to save their jobs. The following two chapters present interesting experiences through which the cooperative model has served workers through consumer, financial and worker cooperatives. Beyond prac-tical benefits that cooperatives can provide to workers, these chapters illustrate how collaboration between cooperatives and the workers' movement might bring about a new synergy and institutional changes for a solidarity-based society.

Akira Kurimoto's chapter, 'Cooperatives and trade unions: from occasional partners to builders of a solidarity-based society', presents a long history of relations between cooperatives and trade unions in Japan. Consumer cooperatives and trade unions were born from common roots to improve the living and working condi-tions of workers, which had deteriorated in the wake of the Industrial Revolution. There were ample examples of mutual support between them in the past, but after the Second World War, they have followed different trajectories in adapting to the changing socio-economic context and resulted in institutional and political divide. Whereas Japanese consumer cooperatives today have more than 27.8 mil-lion members (around 49 per cent of all Japanese households), their political impact is marginal – the Japanese trade unions, whose membership has shrunk to 8 million workers (17.5 per cent of the total Japanese workforce), still have a strong presence with government and political parties. The author deems it imperative for trade unions and consumer cooperatives to build a common agenda and promote joint actions since they share basic values as mutual organizations and have a very close vision of a solidarity-based society.

In his chapter 'Saving jobs and businesses in times of crisis: the Italian road to creating worker cooperatives from worker buyouts', Marcelo Vieta focuses on the emergence of one of Europe's most promising paths for saving jobs and businesses in times of neoliberal crisis and austerity: Italy's Marcora Law legal and financial framework for worker buyouts (WBOs). He details the framework's main legal, financial, and policy dimensions for WBOs and reviews the most salient geo-graphic and firm lifespan trends for Italian WBOs. He identifies seven key factors that characterize the emergence of Italy's WBOs as: a strong policy and financing enabling environment; their surge during economic downturns; inter-firm and territorial networks; preponderance in labour-intensive sectors; their workers' ten-dencies for geographic and sectorial situatedness; intra-firm social networks; and their resilience. He ultimately argues that Italy's WBO phenomenon is exemplar and in ways unique because of Marcora Law framework's clear inclusion of three main stakeholders in the conversion of a workplace to a cooperative, namely the workers, the state and the cooperative movement.

Cooperatives as a laboratory for the future of work

The last four chapters introduce cooperatives as a new type of organizational experimentation in response to challenges raised by the changing world of work.

Today, many people underline that the technological changes have raised various issues related to work and employment. Among others, the growth of freelance work and the increasing importance of online platforms in creating new jobs have received particular attention over the last few years. These new phenomena allow people's aspiration towards autonomy to be realized but also bring them into a no man's land where classical regulations for protecting workers are not applied. As the history of cooperatives shows, people exposed to risk and challenges which do not fall under the existing institutional tools have organized into cooperatives in order to protect themselves against the excesses of the capitalist market logic, while maintaining their autonomy and flexibility. We can observe that their efforts were not so heroic but rather pragmatic in modifying and improving already available legal frameworks and institutional devices. However, new combinations of existing cooperative solutions have enabled them to generate new meanings to work and employment as well as a new sense of working together. We can also observe that to address the complexity of current challenges which are not limited to specific sectoral boundaries, different stakeholders who share a common interest or a common sense of social justice have been organized with a specific cooperative model, called multi-stakeholder cooperatives. As such, although these experimentations are still small in terms of numbers and impact, cooperatives serve as a laboratory for a more human, collaborative and innovative future of work.

Anu Puusa and Kirsi Hokkila in their chapter 'Cooperatives of independent workers in Finland: a unique forum for self-employment', present some specific cases of Finnish cooperatives of independent workers, with members who manage their own self-employed activities. Authors interpret self-employed members' motivation for choosing a cooperative as a business form for self-employment, by answering the question how a cooperative of independent workers meets the needs of the self-employed. Based on qualitative content analysis of interviews conducted with self-employed members in two multi-professional cooperatives and one cooperative specialized in media, art and education professionals, the authors identify six core motivational factors. Three of those factors reflect motivations concerning personal autonomy features (empowerment, self-management and freedom) and the remaining three concern communal features (security, diversity and communality). In taking into account the specificities of the Finnish model of cooperatives of independent workers, they propose that communal features which are unique features of the cooperative model offer various additional benefits to members compared with individual self-employed people. However, the authors also found that personal autonomy features and communal features might be in conflict and result in negative impact on cooperatives and members' activities. In analysing the sense which self-employed worker-members attribute to their motivation, this chapter highlights that cooperatives could be used by self-employed workers or freelancers whose numbers have been rapidly increasing.

In her chapter 'Labour transformation and institutional re-arrangement in France: a preliminary study of a business and employment cooperative', Mélissa Boudes focuses on a specific cooperative model born in France for freelancers, called business and employment cooperative (BEC). Using a neo-institutionalist approach with a welfare regime arrangement composed of three institutional orders related to labour – namely the state, the market and the social and solidarity economy and its destabilization – the author presents an analysis based on the case study of one BEC, Coopaname, showing how this cooperative has made selective coupling of diverse institutional building blocks from the three institutional orders so as to offer new solutions to what are called 'grey employment zones' comprising precarious forms of work between employment and entrepreneurship that do not benefit from genuine social protection. The Coopaname case also shows that, in order to overcome perverse effects of the selective coupling which might block the functioning of organization through increasing complexity and inconsistency, it is important to strengthen efforts towards education, training and information, and to create a meso-level institutional arrangement surrounding the cooperative.

Sonja Novkovic, in the chapter 'Multi-stakeholder cooperatives as a means for jobs creation and social transformation', offers a discussion of the multi-stakeholder cooperative (MSC) form, with particular attention given to MSCs with workers as one of the member categories (and therefore a role in decision-making), pointing out that MSCs are not a new phenomenon, and are much more widespread than would be suggested by exploring the existing specific MSC legal forms. The purpose of this chapter is to highlight the importance and raise some of the key relevant issues and research questions associated with the formation, purpose and governance of MSCs. It illustrates that there are cases of cooperatives with roots in social justice issues and labour emancipation that innovate to include other stakeholders when faced with complex problems such as those linked to community development.

In the last chapter, 'An internet of ownership: democratic design for the online economy', Nathan Schneider argues that the disappointments of the online economy, including systemic labour abuses, stem partly from its failures to meaningfully share ownership and governance with relevant stakeholders. Under the banner of 'platform cooperativism', an emerging network of cooperative developers, entrepreneurs, labour organizers, and scholars is developing an economic ecosystem that seeks to align the ownership and governance of enterprises with the people whose lives are most affected by them. This represents a radical critique of the existing online economy, but it is also a field of experimentation for alternative forms of ownership design. Drawing from published materials on websites and interviews with participants, the author introduces some of the design patterns that have so far arisen in the experimentation of platform cooperativism, in terms of work, data, finance and policy. He proposes that the two basic kinds of cooperative development paths, namely start-ups and conversions (or worker buyouts) might be applied to promote the ownership transition through platform cooperatives. According to his conclusion, despite the one-way determinism that often characterizes the tech culture's 'futurist' speculations, the rise of platform cooperativism may offer the corrective that a range of ownership designs is possible besides the presently dominant ones. These designs can result in better alignment between platforms and their users, as well as fairer distributions of value among those who create them and the communities that enable them to do so.

Throughout the chapters, the authors, experts in their respective fields, do not limit themselves to praising the advantages of the cooperative model. Rather, they challenge a narrow understanding of cooperatives as a mere business model and raise debates on the more fundamental role that cooperatives can play in responding to social changes and, beyond, in changing the society itself. The changing world of work is still evolving, bringing about fear and hesitation among the population, as well as in cooperatives. This book proposes to cooperators, political leaders and the public facing the uncertain future of work to dare to imagine a future with more sustainable, humane and decent work organized through the cooperative model.

Note

1 The four fundamental principles and rights at work include: effective abolition of child labour; elimination of all forms of forced and compulsory labour; elimination of discrimination in respect of employment and occupation; and freedom of association and collective bargaining.

1

WORK AND COOPERATIVES

A century of ILO interaction with the cooperative movement[1]

Claudia Sanchez Bajo

'By being a connoisseur of the old, you know the new.' (Confucius, Analects)

温古而知新 *(论语)*

Introduction

Since its creation in 1919, the International Labour Organization (ILO) has embraced cooperatives with strong interest. In 1920, it received an explicit mandate to work on cooperatives and has ever since had a unit specifically dedicated to them, currently called 'Cooperatives Unit' (ILO COOP). The ILO's relationship with the cooperative movement is stated in article 12 of the ILO Constitution, stipulating that the organization shall work 'with public international organizations having specialized responsibilities in related fields', and will consult 'as it may think desirable with recognized non-governmental international organizations, including international organizations of employers, workers, agriculturists and cooperators' who will 'participate without vote in its deliberations'.

Being the only United Nations (UN) organization to have issued a global normative instrument on cooperatives, the *Promotion of Cooperatives Recommendation, 2002* (No. 193), the ILO is also unique by being the longest lasting one (in 2019, it will celebrate a hundred years of existence), and by having a tripartite structure that gathers representatives of governments, employers and trade unions in the annual sessions of its International Labour Conference (ILC). On their side, cooperatives have shared a common set of norms worldwide called the Rochdale Principles, first written in 1844 by the Rochdale Society of Equitable Pioneers in Rochdale, England, and reviewed in 1937, 1966 and 1995. History can help understand change and persistence, through the broad range of human experience. The ILO is thus a unique place to analyse the history of how the concepts of cooperatives and work have interrelated in the international sphere.

The concept of 'epistemic community' is used to explain the ILO's work in relation to cooperatives, which includes the type of relationship that cooperatives have had with the ILO. In international organizations, concepts are normally rooted in epistemic communities, and article 12 mentioned above provides a legal foundation for this case, as a shared path between the organization (the ILO) and those creating economic activity and jobs in the real economy and society (cooperatives), from which the international institution receives information and expertise. By paying attention to an epistemic community, we can study how knowledge is co-produced through the interaction between society and institutions in a specific policy domain (Forsyth, 2002, pp. 53, 264; 2009, p. 180). Besides, conceptualizations do not appear in a vacuum and are also a function of the predominant socio-political environment and power structures in which language is performed (Bourdieu, 1991, p. 37). Thus, an epistemic community co-produces knowledge that is historically contextualized. This knowledge or 'network of knowledge-based experts' articulates 'cause-and-effect relationships of complex problems, helping . . . identify their interests, framing the issues for collective debate, proposing specific policies, and identifying salient points for negotiation' (Haas, 1992, p. 2), leading to interactive normative conceptualizations such as describing the scope of a document or setting out provisions, including recommendations, requirements and statements (permissions, possibilities and capabilities). ILO normative elements can be found in ILO recommendations and standards, except for the first period under ILO Director-General Albert Thomas's leadership, when the organization was just created.[2] Thus, to observe the conceptual evolution, both ILO key texts and definitions by the cooperative movement itself are linked to each other and placed in historical context.

When discussing the conceptual evolution in the interplay between work and cooperatives at the ILO in this chapter, we should keep in mind that the ILO has no mandate to work on the concept of enterprise as such, but has one on labour issues in the broadest sense. In view of the emergence of an international corpus on cooperatives in which the ILO has had an important role, it is appropriate to discuss this interrelation expressed in ILO texts by distinguishing three major periods: 1919 to the 1930s; 1945 to the 1980s; and 1990 to date. These three periods, analysed in the following three sections, coincide respectively with the creation of the ILO and the two major ILO documents focusing on cooperatives, as follows: (1) the first years of existence of the ILO at the end of the First World War and the role of the first ILO Director-General Albert Thomas, who was a 'cooperativist', or 'cooperator'; (2) the *Co-operatives (Developing Countries) Recommendation*, 1966 (No. 127) in the period post-Second World War; and (3) Recommendation No. 193 at the start of the 21st century.

First period: 1919 to the 1930s

The foundations of the epistemic community

The ILO was created by the Peace Treaty of Versailles just after the end of the First World War. After the war, Europe had millions of displaced refugees, poor and disabled soldiers. Production and supply of almost everything was disrupted. The Treaty gave two justifications to the ILO's existence: first, that 'peace can be established only if it is based upon social justice', since conditions of labour were so unjust, hard and causing privation as to produce unrest; second, there was an argument about unfair trade competition through a race to the bottom: 'Whereas also the failure of any nation to adopt humane conditions of labour is an obstacle in the way of other nations which desire to improve the conditions in their own countries' (Peace Treaty of Versailles, Part XIII, Section 1). From the start, the ILO was established as a permanent institution with a membership of nation-states (Peace Treaty of Versailles, art. 387) that would function on the basis of dialogue along interest representation (art. 393) to 'deal with questions of industry and employment' (art. 397), and of data collection and treatment of 'all subjects relating to the international adjustment of conditions of industrial life and labour . . . with a view to the conclusion of international conventions' (art. 396). Thus, the ILO came to enjoy two types of power: a soft persuasive one and a harder one through binding international conventions.

In March 1920, there was a unanimous decision by the ILO Executive Council:

> to monitor the cooperative movement . . . a mass movement . . . a movement of ideas . . . that moves towards the goals of fairness, order and worker emancipation . . . . The ILO . . . should harness this treasure of practical experiences that the cooperative movement represents . . . almost all general problems of labour concerning cooperation or involving solutions that cooperation can provide.
>
> *(Thomas, 1931b, p. 290)*

Albert Thomas, first Director-General of the ILO from 1919 to 1932, was also a French cooperator and had gathered extensive knowledge on the cooperative movement during his travels throughout Europe. He regarded cooperatives as one of the highest expressions of self-organized labour and assessed cooperatives in utilitarian fashion as a movement towards progress. Thomas 'opposed the original design in which the protection of labour is presented solely in terms of distribution of the wealth produced, in favour of considering . . . the place of work in the process of production itself' (Maupain, 2013, p. 68). His interest focused on the construction of the workplace in processes of production and distribution.[3] Cooperatives, in his view, were very important in this regard, and his leadership was essential to institutionalize the place of cooperatives within the ILO. Thomas personally reported twice to the international cooperative movement in 1921 and 1924, in Basel and Ghent, respectively. Besides, the first Head of the ILO COOP unit from 1921 to 1932, Georges Fauquet, was also a well-known French cooperative theorist and was part of the ICA from 1934 to 1953 (ILO, 2015a). Like Thomas, Fauquet upheld the role of cooperatives in national and international development. Maurice Colombain succeeded Fauquet from 1932 to 1947 as Chief of the ILO Cooperative unit, taking the first ILO step in providing policy advice on cooperatives to Morocco.

There were thus key ILO figures with a foot on both sides of the emerging cooperative epistemic community, who could innovate institutionally and set priorities. In 1923, Thomas set up an ILO Correspondence Committee on Co-operation, renamed in 1931 as the International Committee on Inter-Cooperative Relations. Its chairman was always the director of the ILO, and the secretariat ensured by the ILO Cooperative unit. The Committee, guaranteeing a direct connection between the ILO and the cooperative movement, as an official space for the epistemic community, was disbanded in 1938.

During this period, two of Thomas's speeches on cooperatives stand out. Written in French, they show the conceptualization of both work and cooperative under his mandate, in a world that had endured the First World War and the Great Depression.

In 1931, Albert Thomas gave a speech on the future organization of work (Thomas, 1931a) at the Consultative Chamber of the Producer Workers' Associations of the National Federation of Producer Cooperative Societies (namely worker cooperatives) of France and Colonies in Paris, at the height of the 1929 Great Depression. 'How! – they may ask us; can you talk of the "future organization of work" while an incredible crisis threatens the existence of the possibility to work?' he wrote. Comparing the crises of 1831 and 1931, he said, 'it was in 1831 that the workers' world had an idea of its own that would run across the entire nineteenth century: the thought of the Association.' Thomas recalled Buchez's idea of 1831, who drew from two currents that included Saint Simon and Fourier and delineated the 'workers' association' (as cooperatives were first called in France) that should include an indivisible capital reserve built on 25 or 20 per cent of net results aimed at bequeathing the undertaking onto future generations, with an inter-generational approach. It would give workers equal rights and would strive to organize all workers in the trade with the goal of transforming society. Thomas praised cooperatives as part of a trend towards a more articulated organization in the form of a large enterprise with workshops in only one site, where teams would work autonomously, just as he praised the Taylor Society, the Czech Bat'a[4] Company and the French National Printing-House *commandite* model.[5] Taylorism was perceived by Thomas as the rationalization of industrial production that could overcome the cycle of overproduction and undersupply. For him, salaries from work in one site and one employer were a sign of progress, as workers generally received uncertain and erratic payments for work executed at home or in small units, by unit of production and only when approved by the paymaster. Besides, Thomas mentioned, Taylor paid workers for five hours in a row and let them go to work on their family fields in the afternoon. The president of the French National Federation commented on Thomas's ideas, calling on cooperative worker-members to form cooperative groups to obtain guarantees and benefits to which they were entitled. Thomas's speech considered worker cooperatives as having the following capacities: they allowed workers to enjoy a better life, to transfer pay, to cover sick days and health care, to have decent food and housing, and to gather mutual funds to sustain industrial action. In this second speech, Albert Thomas mentions that the ILO had carried out studies on migrants' money transfers through cooperatives and on insurance and social welfare provided by both cooperatives and mutuals, and that he was interested in their work with the goal of promoting universal access to social welfare.

In the 1931 Preface to *Ten Years of the ILO* (Thomas, 1931b), Thomas underlined the importance of cooperatives in relation to three objectives: to pursue the general interest, to have an orderly economy that could avoid cyclical crisis, and to achieve social justice and peace. He mentioned five themes: cooperation and workers, the ILO's information endeavour, ILO studies, agriculture and consumer cooperatives, and other forms of cooperation. The cooperative movement was acknowledged as a social movement in favour of labour social progress because it showed both ideas and results (*ibid.*, p. 290). The ILO had a practical interest in cooperatives, and was to be regularly informed and inform workers about the international cooperative movement. Thomas clarified that this was of interest to salaried, independent and semi-independent workers, in both rural and urban classes, of all races, of all beliefs, of all economic and historical *milieus* (*ibid.*). Cooperatives covered the needs of housing, professional tools and supplies, product transformation and disposal, family and personal consumption, services including energy, irrigation, accounting, credit and insurance (*ibid.*). The ILO, in Thomas's view, should pay attention to some internal aspects: cooperative democracy, enterprise management, and the attitude that cooperatives have towards their own workers (including paid or salaried workers in consumer cooperatives) (*ibid.*).

Thomas mentioned that, under his mandate, the ILO had studied cooperatives, including their endeavour in improving all workers' conditions by organizing rural and urban households, and by providing all workers with affordable goods, leisure and recreation, culture and good health. In this sense, Thomas was prescient of the 21st-century debates on happiness and well-being. He added that, in addition, the ILO had studied cooperatives in insurance, cooperatives' promotion of workers' savings and safe migrant remittances back home, and above all cooperatives' role in preventing usury. It studied the Raiffeisen credit cooperatives as a best case for the needs of urban workers against usury and to improve workers' lives in colonies of urban extension, namely poor neighbourhoods in cities. It also studied worker cooperatives' enterprise organization and their contracts, although the main focus was on agricultural and consumer cooperatives.[6] Thomas mentioned other types of cooperatives – in fishing, arts and crafts, and those of small rural industries – because, he explained, they grouped independent workers that could not improve their condition unless they gathered their weak economic forces. 'Cooperation is for these workers the main and sometimes the only form of organization' (*ibid.*). His interest echoes the 21st-century concerns about informal economy and independent workers.

Thomas's speech also referred to cooperatives of producers and even value chains between producers and consumers that we would today term 'cooperative platforms'. Working jointly with the International Institute of Agriculture in 1924, the ILO examined how cooperatives' sales could allow producers to organize by themselves and control both the sales and disposal of their production;

how consumers could independently organize to access agricultural products; and how both consumers and agricultural producers' cooperatives could be connected through inter-cooperation. Besides, the ILO studied cooperatives producing seeds, cooperatives of *haras* (state stud) and cooperatives active in international trade of wheat and dairy products. *In fine*, he was interested in what would be the heart of the 21st-century globalization wave – standardization – and for him, cooperatives provided the means to the rational organization of the market. The ILO studied 'the original contribution that . . . (these) cooperatives offered to the elaboration of rational forms of distribution of products' (*ibid.*, p. 203) and the retail pricing of consumer cooperative societies (*ibid.*, p. 204). Last but not least, he underlined the importance of cooperative principles and of a moral basis for the economy, both of which should be expressed by a clear legislative framework.[7] The ILO published seven editions of its International Directory in its first ten years of existence. Whereas, in 1921, the first edition included 34 countries with 120 'central cooperative organizations' (namely federations and confederations), the 1930 edition covered 728 organizations in 48 countries. The ILO Cooperative unit had a *Bulletin on Cooperatives* with 12 to 15 issues per year.[8]

During this period, cooperatives were regarded by the ILO as independent entrepreneurial undertakings, and autonomy from others including governments was upheld as one of their key features. Thus, the treatment of Russian cooperatives under the Soviet regime was of concern to the ILO. Thomas drafted a thorough questionnaire[9] for a future mission to Russia ordered by the ILO Governing Body in January 1920, with an entire section on cooperatives. Russian cooperative organization Centrosoyuz had been a member of the ICA since 1903 (ILO, 2009) and there were 63,000 primary cooperatives in Russia from Tsarist times.[10] A meeting on 21 April 1920 with two Russian representatives, Krassine and Litvinoff, sent by Russia to negotiate with the West, were inconclusive. Although sent as a representative of cooperatives, Krassine affirmed that 'this has nothing to do with cooperatives. There are no more cooperatives here, it is the Soviet Government I represent.'[11] The ILO published without date their research under *Labour Conditions in Soviet Russia*, but the mission would not take place (ILO, n.d.). Its last small chapter on 'Russian cooperatives' explains how the new political regime came to control cooperatives after failing to dismantle them, while establishing communes. Without the existing cooperatives, the new regime could not ensure the country provisioning. In 1925, the ILO published *The Co-operative Movement in Soviet Russia* (ILO, 1925).[12] As we will see below, the conflating of the notion of cooperative with that of Russian commune may explain the shift that took place soon after Albert Thomas's death: cooperatives were displaced within the ILO organization, as observed in ILO organigrams.

Cooperatives' presence at the ILO during the first period

In the first years of existence of the ILO while Albert Thomas lived, namely between 1920 and 1932, cooperatives had the very same place within the ILO as workers and employers had, as shown in the ILO Yearly Organisational Books partners' pages. There were many written and personal exchanges between Albert Thomas and representatives of national cooperative movements and of the ICA, mainly with Europeans, both West and East, but also with the USA, the Joint Council of Cooperative Organisations in Tel Aviv, and later, Latin America.

David Mitrany, the father of functionalism, praised the 'whole activity of the ILO' (Mitrany, 1943, pp. 105, 109), based on functional relations through a network of agencies that would integrate nations in a ramified flexible manner. Transnational cooperation to solve common problems would bring about interdependence and peace (*ibid*.). Thomas spoke of 'cooperation' as experts and contact persons in the cooperative movement who had taken part in the 1927 International Economic Conference. This will turn out to be an epistemic community of experts with some representatives of cooperatives but also a community of knowledge internal to the organization that would contribute to the ILO's autonomy and specificity. During the first years under Thomas, a changing ILO relationship with cooperatives can be observed, from being considered a world social movement towards a focus on building an epistemic community with cooperatives' experts.

The ICA tried both to secure direct representation at the ILO among other international bodies and to assert cooperatives as a social movement. In 1919, then ICA General Secretary Henry May suggested to first ILO Director Albert Thomas that the ILO should have representatives of cooperatives 'to close a gap in the ILO's constitution' (Vocatch, 2015). Debates between the ICA and the International Federation of Trade Unions were reported to the ILO.[13] While the French and Italian representatives of cooperative movements tried to maintain the same treatment in the ILO that employers and workers had, others such as the UK showed less advocacy (Letter to Albert Thomas of 29 November 1922).

After Thomas passed away in 1932, his Deputy Director Harold Butler, from the UK, succeeded him with a different approach (Maupain, 2013, pp. 68–69). Butler continued building relations with countries outside Europe to provide them with technical assistance through missions to Latin America, Asia and the Middle East. Interestingly, the first ILO steps in 'international cooperation' took place in Latin America, where it helped set up producers' and consumers' cooperatives (Van Daele *et al.*, 2010, pp. 387–388).

Cooperatives disappeared from the *ILO Yearly Organizational Books* partners' pages, sent way down in the books as a 'special problem' from 1934 onwards, to never return to their original place. An ILO Overseas Section on 'special problems' included cooperatives, the agrarian question and indigenous peoples. Geopolitical considerations and the conflation of the word 'cooperative' with 'Russian commune' may have contributed to the change. The world was turning bipolar between the West and the East. In 1934, the ILO received a new member, the USA. Butler affirmed that the 'greatest single reinforcement that could be looked for was the entrance of the United States into the Organization'.[14] Cooperatives, from then on, provided information and expertise to the ILO Cooperative unit by working as an epistemic community.

Second period: 1945 to the 1980s

The epistemic community's shift to structural developmentalism

The period after the Second World War ushered in the 'glorious decades' under Keynesian thought. The ILO became a 'sister' organization within the newly established United Nations but maintained a key role for nation-states under the Keynesian approach, to build internal market demand through the goal of full employment, most noticeable in the *Employment Policy Recommendation*, 1964 (No. 122). In addition, the Cold War lent social policy a central role under two aspects: it raised social cohesion and state legitimacy on the one hand and it was a way to distinguish between two social systems on the other.

This was also a period of decolonization and of nation-state building, when international development cooperation came to existence. There was a belief in modernization and developmentalism conceived as a structuralist type of development in which a dual-sector economy should handle the transition from a handicraft rural-based cheap labour economy to industrialized city belts (Furtado, 1964; Lewis, 1954). Lewis's publication established development economics as a discipline and as a policy tool with which governments would drive growth through an engineered economic transformation. Labour in rural areas was thought of as unproductive, as a form of subsistence with no capacity for capital accumulation. Manufacturing and urban industrial enterprises were modelled as rational agents, with perfect information and unlimited capital formation. Fordism was replacing Taylorism. The bulk of employment was expected to take place in urban areas and in conventional investor-owned enterprises. In addition, concerns about rural movements and protests heightened the interest in organizing labour, which was considered as disarticulated.

Under ILO Director-General David Morse, elected in 1948 and re-elected for three consecutive terms until his resignation in 1970, the ILO turned towards standard-setting and technical assistance to developing countries with a focus on rural areas and the inclusion of a human rights-based approach. By moving away from its focus on Europe, the ILO would become 'the institutional nexus of embedded liberalism', in Ruggie's wording, where 'movement towards greater openness in the international economy is likely to be coupled with measures designed to cushion the domestic economy from external disruptions' (Ruggie, 1982, p. 405). According to Van Daele, Morse's shift to technical development assistance, '(which saw the ILO redefine itself as an agency of international development aid) . . . has to be seen first and foremost in the context of the looming Cold War and the first wave of decolonization in Asia' (Van Daele *et al.*, 2010, pp. 385–386). With the decolonization wave in Asia and Africa, the ILO worked primarily with former imperial powers in their ex-colonies' rural areas.

In 1964–65, the ILO had 80 experts on cooperatives in 40 countries, reaching the peak in 1969 when 15 per cent of total funds allocated by the UN Development Programme (UNDP) to the ILO went to projects on cooperatives.[15] The ILO focus appeared to be consumer cooperatives and credit unions in less developing countries. 1969 was also the year when the ILO received the Nobel Peace Prize.

In 1966, the 50th session of the ILC adopted Recommendation No. 127 *Concerning the role of co-operatives in the economic and social development of developing countries.* In Objectives II.2, the establishment and growth of cooperatives was to be a two-fold instrument: development and human advancement. Indeed, the objectives mention persons and members on the one hand and national resources, national income, export revenues and national employment on the other. Groups, communities, networks or local development do not appear, while improvement in working conditions and income appear related only to landless agricultural labourers. Recommendation No. 127 covered all types of cooperatives but was only destined to developing and newly decolonized countries, treating cooperatives as organizations, not as enterprises. However, the words autonomy and independence were part of it.[16] Besides, it raised the definition of legal frameworks on cooperatives to a priority.[17]

There are four main components in Recommendation No. 127: (a) the development of national law and the inclusion of cooperatives in national state planning and policies; (b) the assistance to cooperatives in various forms, including administrative, financial, supervision, and education and training; (c) international assistance through technical aid but also textbooks, material for drafting legislation, training, exchanges, grants, seminars and inter-cooperative exchange of goods and services among others; and (d) a long annex with key problems of interest that actually boiled down to one: agrarian reform. The fear of revolution was not far away. Cooperatives were seen as a form of pooling resources in land, labour and equipment for the objectives specified by the national government for rural areas, while

> consideration should also be given to the encouragement and development of other types of co-operative activities providing full- or part-time non-agricultural employment for members of farmers' families (for instance, crafts, home or cottage industries), adequate distribution of consumer goods, and social services which the State may not always be in a position to provide (for instance, health, education, culture, recreation or transport).
>
> *(Annex, point 13)*

The sentence refers to community and local or regional development without being explicit, but the attention remains focused on the individual farmer and the role of the state in national development.

Cooperatives' presence at the ILO during the second period

The ICA was granted Category A consultative status at the United Nations and thus also at the ILO in 1948. According to Rhodes, 'part of this success was due to its close work during the inter-war years with the cooperative branch of the ILO' (Rhodes, 2012, p. 289). But within the ILO, the view was that the cooperative movement was at a disadvantage without a formal constituency. 'Consultations never reached the status of those with the employers' and workers' organizations' (Fazzio and Ullrich, 1996).

The ILO also provided some opportunities for expert meetings (ILO, 2015a). Joe Fazzio, then Head of the ILO Cooperative unit, mentions a 1968 meeting of experts on the impact of Recommendation No. 127, without further meetings on the subject for the following 25 years, until 1993. The result of the 1968 meeting set the framework for the ILO's cooperative development projects but was otherwise inconclusive. 'Financed through various bilateral programmes with the Scandinavian countries, the Netherlands, Switzerland and later with Germany, France and Italy as well as through the UNDP, such projects assisted the creation of co-operative authorities, training and development centres' (Fazzio and Ullrich, 1996), to which the UK and the US should be added. Expertise was channelled through the ILO Cooperative unit.

Against the development in bilateral funding, and despite the 'several thousand expert missions' (von Muralt, 1994, p. 903) to implement Recommendation No. 127, 'the ILO publication "Cooperative Information" ceased, due to budget constraints caused by the temporary withdrawal of the US from membership in the organization' in 1978 (Vocatch, 2015). While the 'role of such expert meetings is to advise the Director General of the Office in the preparation of subjects relevant to the International Labour Conference . . . The disadvantage for co-operatives is that there is no formal constituency in the ILO bodies, and thus the lobbying has to take place via Governments', employers' and workers' representatives' (Fazzio and Ullrich, 1996).

Whereas the ILO strategy and policy frameworks were beyond discussion in this period, bilateral funding channelled through the ICA and the ILO gave way to joint technical assistance. In the early 1970s, the ICA created its own advisory groups on development cooperation, some funded by Sweden, which would consequently work with an ILO sister group to develop training material such as MATCOM – Training for the management of cooperatives, which started in 1978 (Fazzio and Ullrich, 1996; Rhodes, 2012, p. 299). Africa received special attention.[18] In 1971, upon a request of the 1968 UN General Assembly, the UN Joint Committee for the promotion of Agricultural Cooperatives was set up with representatives of agricultural workers and producers, the ICA, the ILO and the FAO, with a clear focus on rural areas, and in line with Recommendation No. 127. In 1989, this committee would become COPAC (Committee for the Promotion and Advancement of Cooperatives).[19] Besides, the ILO began to work with national institutions and NGOs interested in the new field of development cooperation.

Meanwhile, the ICA 23rd Congress in September 1966 in Vienna endorsed the *Statement of Co-operative Principles in a Modern Setting*.[20] In this period, new types of cooperatives renovated the landscape, such as the social cooperatives in Italy, the workers' buyouts through worker cooperatives, and the cooperatives of small and medium-sized enterprise (SME) owners such as bakeries in Germany and hairdressers in France. The idea of multi-stakeholder cooperatives with different types of stakeholder in the same enterprise (workers, other cooperatives, civil society organizations, local authorities, users of the cooperative services, foundations) slowly emerged.

Third period: 1990 to date

The epistemic community under globalization

Compared with the focus on development cooperation in the second period, the start of the 21st century brought about a variety of initiatives. This period may be compared with the first one, as characterized by a globalization process followed by peace and war concerns. Globalization was first considered to offer a large potential for good, but also leading to unbalanced outcomes both between and within countries.[21] At the same time, structural adjustment programmes (SAPs), under the so-called 'Washington Consensus', led to the rolling-back of the state through deregulation, privatization, and liberalization, with a negative impact on cooperatives.[22] To respond to the emerging challenges, the ILO institutionalized its concept of 'decent work' through one of its key texts, the ILO *Declaration on Social Justice for a Fair Globalization* of 2008.[23]

The ILO, after setting its new agenda based on decent work and its 1998 *Declaration on Fundamental Principles and Rights at Work*, has focused on four categories of labour standards.[24] The end of the Cold War could have allowed for a universal approach to rights, but economic and financial globalization set countries in competition against each other with a downward pressure on social rights and labour costs. At the same time, globalization began connecting regions far apart through supply and value chains. Emerging markets benefitted from the latter, leading to a multi-polar world, but entire sub-national regions and social and environmental externalities have been overlooked or assumed as silent fallouts. UN institutions are working with new actors active across and above nation-states, while transnational companies (TNCs) have set their own global standards. New trade treaties have been setting global rules without considering the gap in countries' levels of development. In practical terms, public policy finds itself hindered, democratic representation is in doubt and specialized information travels through segmented but interconnected supranational units. Still, managed trade would allegedly bring about development and social rights (Maupain, 2013, pp. 70–71).

While the ILO concentrated on its Decent Work Agenda in the face of globalization, the advent of the World Trade Organization (WTO) in 1994 and the multiplication of trade agreements with a labour clause have challenged the ILO's persuasive power and tripartite dialogue. Globalization runs through a de-structured workplace, with workers having different conditions and contracts for the same task in the same place. The 2015 ILO *Report on the World of Work* explains that work patterns are changing along value chains accompanied by government deregulation and technological change (ILO, 2015b), and that such changes lead to precariousness and inequality. The ILO strives for equal protection of workers in the so-called non-standard forms of employment. Active labour supply policies and social dialogue along value chains are two other favoured strategies, as well as promoting SME involvement in the chains.

As for cooperatives, in the 1990s, the ILO launched a host of interregional cooperative programmes with a focus on law, human resources, indigenous peoples, informal economy and fair trade.[25] In the mid-1990s, it engaged in an evaluation of Recommendation No. 127 with experts from the cooperative movement twice (1993 and 1995).[26]

Recommendation No. 193 was approved in 2002, replacing the previous one of 1966 and enlarging the scope to become global. This worldwide normative element entails both a set of policy recommendations and a prescription as it clarifies what a cooperative is. It describes the scope of the document as universal and sets out provisions in active tense (instead of passive tense). Recommendation No. 193 acknowledges the *Statement on the Cooperative Identity* in full, with its definition, seven principles and ten values, as adopted by the ICA in Manchester in 1995. It is the first time that a civil society organization's definition of identity and own standards are integrated into an ILO Recommendation voted by governments, employers and trade unions. It also mentions a long series of ILO standards, hugely contrasting with the previous Recommendation No. 127, which was not that rooted in ILO work.

Recommendation No. 193 affirms that cooperatives are autonomous enterprises of a certain form. They have, as 'enterprises and organizations inspired by solidarity, to respond to their members' needs and the needs of society, including those of disadvantaged groups in order to achieve their social inclusion' (Recommendation No. 193, I, art. 5). They are acknowledged to take part in all sectors and have goals that include income-generating activities, decent employment, human development, business potential, competitiveness, savings and investment, well-being, sustainable development, and the social and economic needs of the community (Recommendation No. 193, I, art. 4). The strengthening of the cooperative movement is included as well as the need for dialogue with trade unions and employers' organizations while representing their own at the international level (IV, art. 17).

Besides, during this period, the notion of 'work' has evolved from being a management term (see Blyton and Jenkins, 2008), to become an experience. The ILO's typology was previously based on (a) the labour market situation in terms of source of income and security, and (b) the work situation in terms of authority and control. The new approach integrates the various functions of work: as income, as meaning for the worker and as the production of goods and services with use-value (Goodwin, 2014). Already in the early 2000s, the UK had modified its socioeconomic classification integrating for the first time the category of self-employed (Noon *et al.*, 2013; Rose and Pevalin, 2001).

What kind of work and employment is cooperative concerned for the ILO? Jobs are categorized at the ILO Statistics Department according to the type of explicit or implicit employment contract of the person with other persons or organizations, the type of economic risk and the type of authority over establishments and other workers which the job incumbents have. In 2013, the 19th International Conference of Labour Statisticians adopted the *Resolution concerning statistics of work, employment and labour underutilization* and, accordingly, the ILO has worked on redefining the categories according to the type of work (not by type of authority or risk), including members of producer cooperatives (Hunter, 2015). Now under revision, the 1993 ILO International Classification of Status in Employment (ICSE-93) covers five groups: employees, employers, own-account workers, contributing family workers, and members of producers' cooperatives. The last four, including producers' cooperatives, are considered as self-employed. Members of producers' cooperatives are defined until now by the ILO as

> workers who hold a self-employment job in a cooperative producing goods and services, in which each member takes part on an equal footing with other members in determining the organization of production, sales and/or other work of the establishment, the investments and the distribution of the proceeds of the establishment amongst their members.
>
> *(ILO, 2006)*

Particular attention should be paid to conceptual confusion such as in the *2014 ILO Key indicators of the labour market* (ILO, 2014a). First, it talks of 'informal producer cooperatives', which is unacceptable, as cooperatives must be incorporated and registered to operate, or at least, have a certain formality in order to conduct economic activities on behalf of their members. At the end of the text, all 'producers' cooperatives' seem to be included under informal employment and informal jobs, which, again, is unfortunate.[27] However, on 12 January 2016, a few months after the *Transition from the Informal to the Formal Economy Recommendation*, 2016 (No. 204) approval, the ILO had to clarify its position regarding paragraph 3 of the Recommendation when speaking of informal economic units. Issued by the Director of the International Labour Standards Department of the ILO, explaining, 'the term "Cooperative" in Paragraph 3(c) of Recommendation 204 should be understood as referring to not formally established or not registered economic unit which are organized according to the cooperative principles and which operate in the informal economy.' These are units striving to become cooperatives but that are not yet so or not able to do it due to insufficient coverage of formal arrangements or to inefficiency of current systems discouraging formal registration. It does not refer to cooperatives as such but similar kind of initiatives of which problematic situations should be solved to become cooperatives at its own right.

The ILO has embarked in an ambitious restructuring and reflects upon upholding work as the key unit (not employment), and on integrating consumers and environmental representatives. Could the work form in which member-owners are both owners and workers become easier to accept? Roelants, Eum and Terrasi (2014, pp. 64–75) have analysed the logics of cooperative work in its various forms and the normative backgrounds that justify them. There is a third category of work where the two sides join in, provided member-owners have not only ownership but also control of their enterprise and labour, distinct from the 'Uber-type' dependence on the paymaster for working conditions, pay and work time (Pasquale, 2015). If, as the revision of ICSE-93 deals with, the door opens to diverse types of work and leads to categorization accordingly, what could the future look like?

Beyond issues around work and employment, now that cooperatives are conceptualized as enterprises at the ILO, we can observe the following areas of interest to the cooperative epistemic community: local development, SMEs, value chains and clusters, care services, the formalization of the informal economy towards employment and income-generation activities, post-conflict and post-crisis situations, and raising the quality of life for workers and their families. In 2015, ILO Director-General Guy Ryder identified in his report *The Future of Work Centenary Initiative* two areas of job growth, the green and the care economy (ILO, 2015c). To achieve such goals, the ILO should pay more attention to successful cooperatives in these areas. The ILO COOP unit has begun to consider these themes (ILO Cooperatives unit and Gender, Equality and Diversity Branch, 2016; ILO Cooperatives unit and Green jobs programme, 2013). Besides, ILO COOP has called upon cooperatives to work together (just as they have always done): to develop regulatory frameworks, to engage in education and training, and generate information and knowledge to build evidence-based data (ILO Cooperatives unit, 2017).

Cooperatives' presence at the ILO during the third period

In 2001 and 2002, the ILC worked on Recommendation No. 193. In the two years of negotiations of Recommendation No. 193 there were about 15 representatives of different national cooperative movements who worked strongly under the three tripartite sections of the ILC to make the instrument coherent and relevant (Roelants, 2003). These representatives came from Japan, Israel, Italy, Poland, Costa Rica, Uruguay, and Kenya, among others. Their success has been undeniable in terms of impact. However, most of them were not regular participants of the existing epistemic community and their impact was felt only once.

Trade unions at the ILO have made renewed efforts to listen to and work with cooperatives:

> Today, the Sustainable Enterprise Programme works with ILO constituents (governments, trade unions and employers' organizations) and representatives of cooperative organizations of all types and sizes to help cooperatives create and sustain employment and contribute to promoting decent work and social justice.
>
> *(ILO, 2014b)*

In 2003, an ILO Director-General was present at the ICA General Assembly for the first time since Albert Thomas. In 2004, the ILO and the ICA signed a Memorandum of Understanding to implement a 'Common Cooperative Agenda' aimed at creating decent jobs and reducing poverty. Thereafter, the ILO and the ICA made joint announcements and jointly launched several worldwide campaigns and initiatives, along three strands: first, within the UN policy framework and goals; second, on new challenges such as Europe and youth; and third, with a continuing focus on rural areas and the informal economy as in previous periods.[28] In 2014 and 2015, the ILO and ICA announced initiatives on sustainable development and equality, both along the UN wider framework of Sustainable Development Goals (SDGs), but also trying to respond to the challenges stemming from globalization and inequality.[29] These broad worldwide campaigns and initiatives are too recent to be assessed, but they show the need to work together as an epistemic community to share expertise and knowledge on the ground, to inform policy and to coordinate. At the same time, some of the emerging cooperative forms that had not reached the ILO in the previous period are finding other channels and voices, most notably, through the social and solidarity economy and the informal workers' movement. ILO COOP has funded a significant number of studies, some written by experts linked to the cooperative movement and, in particular, from developed countries and Africa.[30] Finally, the ILO has worked to bring cooperatives' voices into the post-2015 development agenda together with the ICA, the UN Research Institute for Social Development (UNRISD), FAO and UNDESA.

Conclusions

Between 1919 and 1932, cooperatives were on an equal footing with employers and workers at the ILO, and several ILO employees were dedicated to cooperatives. Not only the first Director-General but also other key figures were cooperators and had extensive knowledge of cooperatives and contacts with other cooperators across the world. The multiple exchanges between leading figures at this international organization and cooperators on the ground laid the foundation of an expert epistemic community on cooperatives. The cooperative movement sought to secure direct voice and representation at the institution but failed. Since then, the place of cooperatives within the ILO has been the result of three main factors: the external environment, institutional change (including leadership) and the cooperative movement itself. Particularly, it has relied on the cooperative epistemic community, which has been active to this date based, first and foremost, on factors built up by the two sides of the equation. On the side of the international organization, it seems due to its leadership as well as to the dedication of the successive ILO COOP unit's heads and staff. On the side of cooperatives, it is due to being self-defined through its own identity and standards as determined by the cooperative movement itself, to having built expertise in its own domain and having enjoyed representative and democratic legitimacy.

In the first period, first ILO Director-General Albert Thomas had looked at cooperatives in his quest for social justice, whereby economic development needed rational socio-economic organization requiring social peace as its foundation. Thomas spoke of cooperators as 'workers' as well as 'entrepreneurs'. Cooperatives were considered as business undertakings with their own specificities. The international organization valued cooperatives as solidarity in practice, through their relations, interconnections, services and general organization for mutual help, built by persons, families and communities in both rural and urban areas. Most of all, cooperatives offered inter-generational solidarity where newcomers and younger generations could take their place as older cooperators retired or left. ILO studies on cooperatives done by its Cooperative unit raised the ILO profile (Thomas, 1931b, p. 291) and provided it with direct contacts to the agricultural economy, the artisanal economy and the household economy (*ibid.*, p. 295). In the second period, the ILO influenced legal frameworks through labour standards and by assisting member states with cooperative law. The normative approach in Recommendation No. 127 was only for developing countries while, in the third period, Recommendation No. 193 is global. With the latter instrument, the understanding of cooperative is close to the one of the first period. In the third period, the ILO, by extending its coverage of forms of work, is returning to Thomas's vision that included households, independent workers and families, with cooperatives as an important means for a good life that include but also go beyond redistribution of income.

The cooperative epistemic community has provided technical expertise in every period. Whereas, in the second period, the community of expert knowledge strengthened their technical know-how and legislation capabilities, in the current period, the interest of the international organization in cooperatives' experience and new business and work forms has returned. Studies, as in the first period, are key to the epistemic community, by informing reflexivity, mutual dialogue and knowledge, and by raising awareness of history. Just like in the first period, the latest globalization process has brought about a long-lasting global crisis and higher inequality. It would not be a surprise if concerns about the increasingly conflictive tensions and the quest for both peace-building and a sustainable future accentuated the need for both a strong cooperative epistemic community and cooperative movement.

Notes

1 The author of this study would like to fully thank both the ILO Archive Albert Thomas for access to its documentation and the help and dedication of its staff in answering questions and requests, and the Cooperative unit for the interviews and material provided. During the visits to the ILO Albert Thomas Archive in Geneva, photos were taken of documents, letters and books.

2 For this reason, we consider texts and letters by Albert Thomas or between him and representatives of cooperatives as significant evidence for this period.

3 In a 1931 personal note, he wrote that a key word should be retained from a discussion in the Committee of Inter-Cooperative Relations: *la charnière coopérative*, namely the

cooperative pivotal role that constitutes 'the possibility of manoeuvre and action' (17 November 1931, Geneva, personal note by Albert Thomas).

4 The Bat'a Company was the largest shoe maker in Europe, with its first mass-market product in 1899 in Zlin, today Czech Republic. The founder learned from Taylor, but the Bat'a system had both horizontal and vertical integration (today we would call them clusters and value chains). Bat'a set up villages for the workers with schools and welfare. See information at Bat'a Heritage www.bata.com/about/ and www.bata.com/heritage/bata-story-begins/

5 On Taylorism and its diffusion by building an alliance with the ILO, see Bruce and Nyland (2013).

6 'The consumer cooperatives and the agricultural cooperatives are, first, the ones to retain the attention of the ILO,' Thomas wrote, 'because of the importance of their work-force, their high degree of federalization, the place they already have as producers or as consumers in the production and distribution of commodities of great interest, as agri-cultural workers and as industrial ones' (Thomas, 1931b, pp. 294–295).

7 Thomas spoke of the 'community of cooperative principles, expressed by the unity of legislation or by the reclamation of a common legislation', a convergence reinforcing moral links as well as organic and the economic relationships among cooperative organ-izations of various categories (mentioning those between consumer and agricultural cooperatives) (*ibid.*).

8 'The Cooperative Service of the International Labour Office publishes ... a bulle-tin ... appearing between 12 and 15 times a year ...' (Letter of 17th November 1926).

9 This 'systematic questionnaire published by the International Labour Office in 1920 for the mission of enquiry in Russia ... when the Russian Section was set up under ... Dr Pardo, one of its first tasks was to complete this preliminary bibliography and keep it up to date as being the most readily available instrument for the work of the Section. The publication was decided in response to many requests. But the practical difficulties involved in a work of this character have caused considerable delay, and the information refers only to the period preceding December 1921' (ILO, 1922).

10 The origins of the cooperative movement can be traced to the 1860s. By 1917 there were more than 63,000 primary cooperatives in Russia, with a total of 24 million members. There were consumers, credit, agricultural and industrial and production cooperatives (Salzman, 1982).

11 Memo of 21 April 1920, ILO, Conversation of 21 April with M. du Halgoet. 7, Seamore Place, Curzon Street, W.1. Original in French, translation by the author.

12 Terms used in texts and reports do not have to do with that of 'cooperative'. See ILO (1925). In brief, in Soviet Russia, collective farms appeared in 1918. A first decree also of 1918 imposed a Soviet director in each existing cooperative. See Italian documentation on cooperatives and social economy, available online at www.cooperazione.net/eng/paginaPrint.asp?uid=646&pid=648. A decree of 10 March 1919 ordered the predomi-nance of the party in all consumer cooperatives. On 27 January 1920, all cooperatives were forcefully merged into one Central Union by decree, seen from then on as consum-ers' communes or collectives and not cooperatives any more. The state created in 1921 the All-Russian Union of Villagers (*Sel'skosoiuz*) and in 1922 the All-Russian Union of Producers (*Vsekopromsoiuz*).

13 In a meeting of 9 December 1922, it was reported that the ICA requested (a) an '*entente*' and exchange of delegates; (b) joint propaganda demonstrating their economic interde-pendence and reciprocal action; (c) the promotion of 'consumers' councils' to oversee 'methods of production and supply in the interest of consumers'; (d) a joint committee to regularly discuss not only wages and labour conditions but also 'questions of peace, war, disarmament, free trade, protection, etc.'; and (e) 'joint action to secure direct represen-tation of both movements on international economic bodies, such as the International Labour Bureau, the economic section of the League of Nations, etc.' (Letter 9 December 1922, ILO Archive).

14 See Butler, at www.ilo.org/global/about-the-ilo/who-we-are/ilo-director-general/former-directors-general/WCMS_192709/lang--en/index.htm.

15 The ILO website upholds that 'ILO's 50th Anniversary in 1969 marks the golden age of ILO's technical cooperation in the field of cooperative promotion. Of all the funds allocated by the UNDP to the ILO, 15 percent was spent on assistance to cooperative projects. More than 120 ILO cooperative experts worked in nearly 70 countries in Africa, Asia, Latin America and the Middle East at this time.' Available online at www.ilo.org/global/topics/cooperatives/WCMS_483187/lang--en/index.htm. In 1953, there was an ILO Meeting of a Panel of Experts on the Action of the ILO as regards cooperation, particularly as regards its practical activities, followed by the 1955 ILO Recommendation No. 100 on *Protection of migrant workers in underdeveloped countries and territories* (para. 43 and 49), 1955, mentioning cooperatives as an option for the supply of consumer goods and of financial services for migrant workers. In 1962, a new ILO Cooperative Experts Meeting in Geneva reviewed the trends and developments of the cooperative movement, and in 1965, there was the first discussion of the Report *Role of cooperatives in the economic and social development of the developing countries* at the 49th Session of the ILC.

16 See *Co-operatives Recommendation* No. 127, Administrative Aid 26; II. 4 Objectives of Policy; C. 20 Aid to cooperatives financial aid and D. 28 Supervision.

17 *Ibid.*, Legislation.

18 The ILO included cooperatives by referring to Recommendation No. 127 in 'General Provisions' of Convention concerning *Organizations of rural workers and their role in economic and social development*, 1975 (No. 141) and its Recommendation No. 149. In terms of technical cooperation, the ILO concentrated mainly on Africa, with its training project Materials and Techniques for Cooperative Management (MATCOM) and a sub-regional project on Cooperative and Organizational Support to Grassroots Initiatives in Western Africa (ACOPAM). The 1988 ILO Africa Regional Conference deliberated on a report by the ILO Director-General on *Cooperatives in Africa*.

19 COPAC is a partnership between several UN organizations, the ICA and other non-governmental organizations (NGOs) to coordinate their action to realize the potential of cooperatives in economic and social development. In 1968, the United Nations requested the UN Economic and Social Council (ECOSOC) to consider the role of cooperatives in development. ECOSOC then asked the UN Secretary-General to collaborate with the Directors of the ILO, the Food and Agriculture Organization (FAO), the United Nations Industrial Development Organization (UNIDO), the ICA, and others, such as the International Federation of Agricultural Producers (IFAP), and the International Federation of Plantation, Agricultural and Allied Workers (IFPAAW). Available online at COPAC at www.copac.coop/about/.

20 Consideration of Cooperative Principles, Section 1 (1966), document made available by the International Co-operative Information Centre ICA-UWCC, available online at www.uwcc.wisc.edu/icic/orgs/ica/pubs/Other-ICA-Publications1/Report-of-the-ICA-Commission-on-Co-opera1/Part-II----Consideration-of-Co-operative2.html.

21 See *A fair globalization: Creating opportunities for all*, page X. Final Report of the World Commission on the Social Dimension of Globalization Report, February 2004. This Commission was established by the ILO.

22 For SAPs impact on cooperatives in Africa, see Lindenthal (1994). On African cooperatives and SAPs, see also Develtere, Pollet and Wanyama (2008).

23 The *ILO Declaration on Social Justice for a Fair Globalization* was adopted by the ILO on 10 June 2008 at its 97th Session in Geneva. In September 2015, the UN General Assembly made decent work and the four pillars of the Decent Work Agenda (employment creation, social protection, rights at work, and social dialogue) integral elements of the UN 2030 Agenda for Sustainable Development.

24 The four categories or pillars of the Decent Work Agenda are employment creation, social protection, rights at work, and social dialogue.

25 These ILO programmes were COOPREFORM on cooperative legislative reform, COOPNET on human resources development in cooperatives, INDISCO on cooperatives of indigenous and tribal people, SYNDICOOP on informal economy workers, and INTERCOOP on fair trade through cooperatives.

26 Apart from the 1993 Meeting of Experts on Cooperatives, held in the ILO Headquarters in Geneva, which included a point on the assessment of the impact of Recommendation No. 127, two other moments are noted. First, in 1994, ICA President Lars Markus addresses the ILO at its 75th anniversary conference mentioning the contributions of the ILO to cooperative development; and second, in 1995, there is a Meeting of Experts on Cooperative Law also held in ILO headquarters in Geneva, with further discussion on the impact of Recommendation No. 127.

27 See page 64 for 'producers' cooperatives' without the word 'informal', pp. 61 and 62 for 'informal producers' cooperatives', in ILO (2014a).

28 In the first strand, we find the 2004 joint ILO-ICA Peace and Cooperative Initiative as a commitment to peace and security, the joint ILO-ICA Forum of African Cooperatives was held during the Summit of the African Union Heads of State on Employment and Poverty Alleviation, and the 2005 joint ILO and ICA launching of a Global Campaign against Poverty, to advance the Millennium Development Goals (MDGs). In the second strand and third, we note the 2012 ILO and ICA agreement to focus on four areas: the European crisis and youth employment as new areas, while the informal economy and rural employment are areas of continuing collaboration.

29 The 2014 joint ILO and ICA initiative focuses on cooperatives and the post-2015 sustainable development framework. The 2015 joint ILO and the ICA initiative deals with cooperatives, gender equality and women empowerment.

30 See ILO list of publications on cooperatives, available online at www.ilo.org/global/topics/cooperatives/ publications/lang--en/index.htm

References

Blyton, Paul, and Jean Jenkins. *Key concepts in work*. London: Sage, 2008.

Bourdieu, Pierre. *Language and symbolic power*. Cambridge, MA: Harvard University Press, 1991.

Bruce, Kyle, and Chris Nyland. *Taylorism, the International Labour Organization and the diffusion of codetermination*, 2013. https://ssrn.com/abstract=2296758.

Develtere, Patrick, Ignace Pollet and Fredrick Wanyama, eds. *Cooperating out of poverty: The renaissance of the African cooperative movement*. Geneva: ILO, 2008.

Fazzio, Joe, and Gabriele Ullrich. The ILO: 75 years of co-operative service, *Review of International Co-operation* 89, no. 1 (July 1996): 52–60.

Forsyth, Tim. *Critical political ecology: The politics of environmental science*. London and New York: Routledge, 2002.

____. Democratizing environmental expertise about forests and climate. In *Environmental governance: Power and knowledge in a local-global world*, edited by Gabriela Kütting and Ronnie D. Lipschutz, 170–184. London and New York: Routledge, 2009.

Furtado, Celso. *Development and underdevelopment*. Berkeley and Los Angeles: University of California Press, 1964.

Goodwin, Neva. The new economy. In *Co-operatives in a post-growth era: Creating co-operative economics*, edited by Sonja Novkovic and Tom Webb, 49–50. London: Zed Books, 2014.

Haas, Peter M. Epistemic communities and international policy coordination, *International Organization* 46, no. 1 (Winter 1992): 1–35.

Hunter, David. *Issues to be addressed in the revision of the International Classification of Status in Employment (ICSE-93)*, Working Group for the Revision of the International

Classification of Status in Employment (ICSE-93) Discussion paper. Geneva: ILO Department of Statistics, 2015.

International Labour Office (ILO). *Bibliography of industrial and labour questions in Soviet Russia*, Geneva, 1922.

———. *The co-operative movement in Soviet Russia*, Studies and reports, Series H (Co-operation) no. 3. Geneva, 1925.

———. *Key indicators of the labour market*, Third edition, Geneva, 2006.

———. *Cooperative sector in Russia and the implementation of the ILO Recommendation No. 193 in the development of different Russian cooperative trends*, Moscow: ILO Subregional Office for Eastern Europe and Central Asia, 2009.

———. *Key indicators of the labour market*, Eighth edition, Geneva, 2014a.

———. *The cooperative way of doing business*, Geneva, 2014b.

———. *The story of the ILO's promotion of Cooperatives Recommendation, 2002 (No. 193) – A review of the process of making ILO Recommendation No. 193. Its implementation and its impact*, Geneva, 2015a.

———. *World employment and social outlook, the changing nature of jobs*, Geneva, 2015b.

———. *The future of work centenary initiative*, ILO Director-general report, Geneva, 2015c.

———. *Labour conditions in Soviet Russia, systematic questionnaire and bibliography prepared for the mission of enquiry in Russia*, London: Harrison and Sons, n.d.

ILO Cooperatives unit. *Cooperation in a changing world of work: Exploring the role of cooperatives in the future of work*, Cooperatives and the world of work no. 6. Geneva: ILO, 2017.

ILO Cooperatives unit and Green jobs programme. *Providing clean energy and energy access through cooperatives*. Geneva: ILO, 2013.

ILO Cooperatives unit and Gender, Equality and Diversity Branch. *Providing care through cooperatives*. Geneva: ILO, 2016.

Lewis, W. Arthur. Economic development with unlimited supplies of labor, *The Manchester School* no. 22 (1954): 139–191.

Lindenthal, Roland. *Structural adjustment and cooperatives in developing countries*. Geneva: ILO, 1994.

Maupain, Francis. *The future of the International Labour Organization in the global economy*. Oxford and Portland, Oregon: Hart Publishing, 2013.

Mitrany, David. *A working peace system: An argument for the functional development of international organization*. Reprinted in 1966 by Quadrangle Books. London: Royal Institute for International Affairs, 1943.

Noon, Mike, Paul Blyton and Kevin Morrell. *The realities of work, experiencing work and employment in contemporary society*. New York: Palgrave MacMillan, 2013.

Pasquale, Frank. *The unaccountable algorithm*. 2015. http://aeon.co/magazine/technology/judge-jury-and-executioner-the-unaccountable-algorithm/.

Rhodes, Rita. *Empire and co-operation: How the British Empire used co-operatives in its development strategies 1900–1970*. Edinburgh: Birlinn Ltd., 2012.

Roelants, Bruno. The first world standard on cooperatives and on their promotion, Recommendation 193 / 2002 of the International Labour Organisation, *RECMA Revue Internationale de l'Économie Sociale* no. 289 (July 2003): 20–29.

Roelants, Bruno, Hyungsik Eum and Elisa Terrasi. *Cooperatives and employment: A global report*. Brussels: CICOPA and Desjardins Group, 2014.

Rose, David, and David J. Pevalin. *The national statistics socio-economic classification: Unifying official and sociological approaches to the conceptualisation and measurement of social class*. ISER Working Papers, Issue Paper 2001-4, 2001.

Ruggie, John Gerard. International regimes, transactions, and change: Embedded liberalism in the postwar economic order, *International Organization* 36, no. 2 (Spring 1982): 379–415.

Salzman, Catherine. Consumer cooperative societies in Russia: Goals v. gains, 1900–1918, *Cahiers du monde russe et soviétique* 23, no. 3–4 (Juillet–Décembre 1982): 351–369.

Thomas, Albert. *The future organisation of work (Discourse by Albert Thomas at the Chamber of the Producer Workers' Associations, of the National Federation of Producer Cooperative Societies of France and Colonies).* Paris, 1931a.

___. *Dix Ans d'organisation internationale du travail (Ten years of the ILO).* Geneva: ILO, 1931b.

Treaty of Versailles. Organisation of labour. In *The Treaty of Peace between the Allied and Associated Powers and Germany.* Articles 387–399. Versailles: His Majesty's Stationery Office, London, 1919.

Van Daele, Jasmien, Magaly Rodríguez García, Geert van Goethem and Marcel van der Linden. (eds.) *ILO histories: Essays on the International Labour Organization and its impact on the world during the twentieth century,* Bern: Peter Lang AG, 2010.

Vocatch, Igor. *ILO timeline on ILO history and cooperatives.* mimeo (ed.). Geneva: ILO, 2015.

von Muralt, Jürgen. United Nations system and co-operatives. In *International handbook of cooperative organizations* edited by Eberhard Dulfer and Juhani Laurinkari. Göttingen: Vandenhoeck & Ruprecht, 1994.

2

COOPERATIVES AND THE FUTURE OF WORK

Jürgen Schwettmann

Foreword

This chapter relates to a 'Centenary Initiative' launched by the International Labour Organization (ILO) under the title *The Future of Work*; it is one of seven such initiatives introduced by ILO Director-General Guy Ryder in the run-up to the Organization's 100th anniversary in 2019. The broad contours of the Initiative were outlined in the Director-General's Report to the 104th International Labour Conference (ILO, 2015): the ILO has initiated four global conversations, as well as national dialogues in all ILO member states, on the future of work to explore the views of governments, workers, employers and civil society on the subject.[1] In August 2017, the ILO established a High Level Global Commission on the Future of Work to examine the output from the national dialogues and other input it may consider necessary. The Commission will publish a report and recommendations in the course of 2018. In the first half of 2019, all member states will be invited to organize events to mark the ILO's centenary and to discuss the Commission's report. The culmination of the *Future of Work* initiative will be the 2019 International Labour Conference, with the possible adoption of a Centenary Declaration (ILO, 2016a).

The future of work is a subject of major and growing global interest. Numerous books and research articles discuss the nature and purpose of work (in the broad sense) in the coming decades – some question that there will be much work left for humans at all. Authors may adopt different approaches and attitudes towards the future of work, but all agree that the nature, method, organization and location of work will change significantly in the not-so-distant future. The magnitude of the expected changes may be as profound as those caused by the information technology revolution. The World Wide Web, for example, is only about three decades old but has, within such a short period of time – and boosted by spectacular advances in mobile technology, computer processing speed and data storage capacity – radically changed the way we communicate, do business and gather and manage knowledge. The Internet makes it possible to work, produce and consume from anywhere; and whether desirable or not, today we could live much of our lives without interacting with any human being. The technology exists, and the capabilities of that technology are far from being fully exploited. And the Internet is just but one of the major developments of the last decades, not to mention those of the years to come.

Many articles about the future of work call for new models of work organization that would imply a greater degree of cooperation among workers, or between workers and management; such collaborative work arrangements could be temporary or permanent in nature. The new models would promote the collective use of resources, assets and services through the 'sharing economy' and various forms of collective entrepreneurship. Cooperatives and the wider social and solidarity economy have the potential to play a key role in establishing such new working arrangements. Clearly, the changing world of work will have a profound impact on cooperatives, on the role that cooperatives and similar economic organizations will play in society and the economy, and on the way cooperatives themselves will function and operate.

The present chapter[2] seeks to examine the relationship between the future of work and cooperatives in three stages:

- *The trends of the future*: an attempt to identify and briefly describe the major trends affecting the world of work in the broad sense;
- *The future of work*: an analysis of the impact of these changes on work, labour, employment and social dialogue;
- *The future of work and cooperatives*: a discussion around the possible role of cooperatives in relation to the future of work.[3]

Trends affecting the world of work

This section groups the tendencies that we were able to identify into four categories:

- demography
- technology
- economy
- environment.

Interestingly, several of these trends were already examined as far back as 1972, when the Club of Rome commissioned the *The Limits to Growth* study (Meadows *et al.*, 1972). The study, much criticized and even ridiculed at the time, argued that continued population growth, resource depletion, environmental degradation and industrialization would eventually cause the collapse of the earth's ecosystem. Recent research from the University of Melbourne has found that the book's forecasts were accurate, 40 years on; indeed, the early stages of global collapse could start appearing soon (Turner and Alexander, 2014).

Demographics

Within this category, three developments are likely to impact the world of work.

Population growth

According to the World Population Clock (WorldoMeters, retrieved 20 December 2016), there are currently about 7.5 billion people on earth. Figure 2.1, published by the United Nations, traces world population growth since 1950. It clearly shows that population growth continues unabated, albeit at a slightly lower rate than in the past. Yet, whereas in the 1960s (when the world was inhabited by a 'mere' 3 billion humans) the news was filled with alarming reports about the 'demographic explosion', it appears that today, when the world population has exceeded 7 billion, not many people seem to worry about population growth.

Population growth is unevenly spread between regions and continents, causing considerable changes in the demographic weight of the five continents: of particular significance is the rapid growth of the African population. The African continent, already plagued by widespread poverty, vulnerability and high degrees of informality, will have to create hundreds of millions of new jobs just to maintain the status quo.

Current demographic trends bring 40 million people to the labour market each year, meaning that between now and the year 2030, the world economy needs to create over 600 million new jobs.

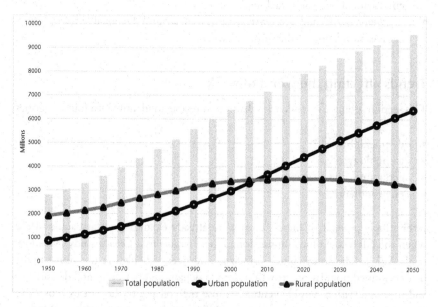

FIGURE 2.1 Urban and rural populations, 1950–2050

Source: Elaborated from United Nations (2012)

TABLE 2.1 World populations by major areas, 1950 and 2050

	World population 1950	World population 2050
Africa	9%	25%
Asia	55%	54%
America	13%	13%
Europe	22%	7%
Oceania	1%	1%

Source: Elaborated from United Nations (2012)

Ageing

Population ageing is a shift in the distribution of a country's population towards older ages, i.e., a declining proportion of the population composed of children, and a rise in the proportion of the population that is elderly. Population ageing is widespread across the world. It is most advanced in the most highly developed countries, but it is growing faster in less developed regions, which means that older persons will be increasingly concentrated in the less developed regions of the world. As people live longer they will have to work more years so that pension schemes remain affordable; this may have a negative effect on youth employment. Moreover, an ageing population entails higher medical, care and social expenditures.

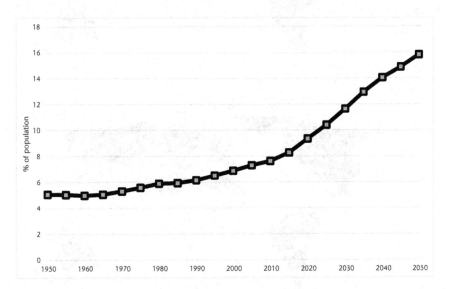

FIGURE 2.2 Percentage of the world population over 65, 1950–2050

Source: Elaborated from UN World Population Prospect (2017)

Urbanization

The population growth chart in Figure 2.1 shows that around the year 2005, the proportion of people living in cities has overtaken the rural population. It is predicted that by 2050 about 64 per cent of the developing world and 86 per cent of the developed world will be urbanized. Urbanization is often viewed as a negative trend, but there are positives in the reduction of expenses in commuting and transportation while improving opportunities for jobs, education, housing, and transportation. Living in cities permits individuals and families to take advantage of the opportunities of proximity and diversity. While cities have a greater variety of markets and goods than rural areas, infrastructure congestion, monopolization, high overhead costs, and the inconvenience of cross-town trips frequently combine to make marketplace competition harsher in cities than in rural areas. Moreover, urban citizens tend to abandon customary practices which are widespread in rural areas, such as mutual assistance and care for the elderly. This puts a further strain on governmental social protection systems.

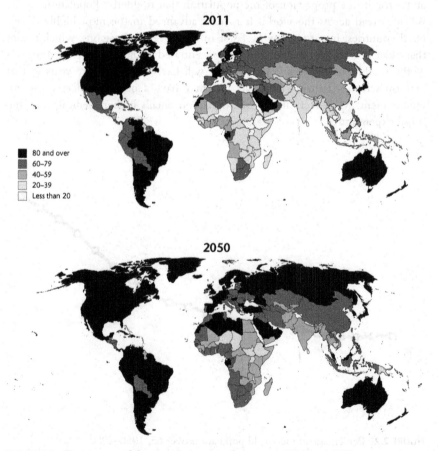

FIGURE 2.3 Percentage of the population in urban areas, 2011 and 2050

Source: United Nations (2012)

Technological trends

'Previous technological innovation has always delivered more long-run employment, not less. But things can change' (*The Economist*, January 2014). 'Technological unemployment . . . due to our discovery of means of economizing the use of labour outrunning the pace at which we can find new uses for labour' (Keynes, 1930). Indeed, a heated debate is taking place about whether or not the productivity gains resulting from automation and digitization will lead to greater unemployment. Most researchers agree, however, that it will lead to a greater polarization of the workforce between highly educated and low-skilled workers, cutting out the middle-level worker whose job may be performed by machines.

Automation

Automation refers to the use of computers and other automated machinery for the execution of business-related tasks. Automated machinery may range from simple sensing devices to robots and other sophisticated equipment. Automation may occur in different forms, such as:

- Automation of work processes through computers and algorithms, as well as self-service devices such as ATMs, self-service checkouts and boarding pass generators;[4]
- Automation of manufacturing and services through robots; this would also include 3-D printing technology, which makes it possible to decentralize industrial production;[5]
- Automation of transport through self-conducting or remote-controlled devices (drones, and self-driving cars, tanks and ships).

Concern about technological unemployment grew in 2013, due in part to a number of studies predicting substantially increased technological unemployment in forthcoming decades; concerns have included evidence showing worldwide falls in employment across sectors such as manufacturing, falls in pay for low- and medium-skilled workers stretching back several decades even as productivity continues to rise, and the occurrence of 'jobless recoveries' after recent recessions. The 21st century has seen a variety of skilled tasks partially taken over by machines, including translation, legal research, surgery and even low-level journalism. Care work, entertainment, and other tasks requiring empathy, previously thought safe from automation, have also begun to be performed by robots.

Communications and the Internet

The International Telecommunication Union (ITU, 2016) reports that, in 2016, some 3.5 billion people were using the Internet. While the growth in mobile-cellular subscriptions was slowing as the market reached saturation levels, mobile broadband remains the fastest growing market segment, with continuous double-digit growth rates and an estimated global penetration rate of 32 per cent. International

TABLE 2.2 Probability that computerization will lead to job losses within the next two decades (1=certain)

Occupation	Probability
Recreational Therapists	0.0028
Art Directors	0.023
Travel Guides	0.057
Financial Managers	0.069
Hairdressers, Hairstylists, and Cosmetologists	0.11
Electricians	0.15
Concierges	0.21
Geographers	0.25
Private Detectives and Investigators	0.31
Actors	0.37
Judicial Law Clerks	0.41
Police, Fire, and Ambulance Dispatchers	0.49
Audio and Video Equipment Technicians	0.55
Slaughterers and Meat Packers	0.6
Statistical Assistants	0.66
Maids and Housekeeping Cleaners	0.69
Archivists	0.76
Word Processors and Typists	0.81
Taxi Drivers and Chauffeurs	0.89
Telemarketers	0.99

Source: Elaborated from Frey and Osborne (2013)

bandwidth was also growing steeply, at 45 per cent annually between 2001 and 2013, and the developing countries' share of total international bandwidth increased from around 9 per cent in 2004 to almost 30 per cent in 2013.

Over the past two decades, the exponential growth of the Internet has led it to touch upon every aspect of modern life. From mobile entertainment to healthcare to the heart of enterprise, the Internet has become, in the words of Bill Gates, 'the town square for the global village of tomorrow'. One example of many is the production and sale of books, as illustrated in Figure 2.4 (produced by the author).

The Internet has not only changed the way we buy and read books; it has also made redundant entire sections of the industry, such as the production of reference books.

Internet-based commerce causes local shops to close down; e-banking reduces the traditional bank branch to a collection of man-less machines; we can expect

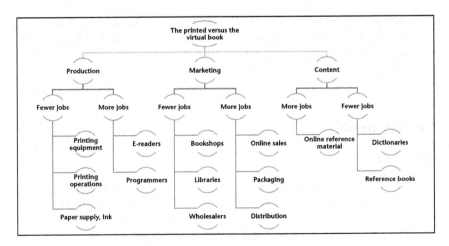

FIGURE 2.4 Jobs in the printed versus the virtual book

Source: Author's own elaboration

that travel agencies will disappear altogether. The next step consists of the 'Internet of Things': the network of physical objects or 'things' embedded with electronics, software, sensors, and network connectivity, which enables these objects to collect and exchange data. A much-cited example is the 'smart' fridge that orders fresh food supplies should certain food items run out.

Digitization

Closely related to the two phenomena above – automation and the Internet – the digital revolution has made it possible to collect, process and share an ever growing amount of data. Sound, text, data, speech, images and software are being produced, stored and transmitted in the same format, an endless combination of '0' and '1', which blurs the distinction between these different types of information. At the same time, the capacity of digital storage devices has grown exponentially. A miniscule USB stick now holds information equivalent to 100,000 floppy disks some 30 years ago. Processing speed has accelerated in a similar way: whereas in 1977 the fastest processor (a VAX-11/780) hardly performed 1 million instructions per second (MIPS), contemporary processors, such as the AMD-Ryzen 7, now exceed 300,000 MIPS – an increase of 30 million per cent in 40 years. Cheaper storage capacity and accelerating data processing speed provides the basis for the collection and analysis of 'big data', which is used to make citizens and consumers 'transparent'.

> In the IT field, for example, advances in microprocessors will support real-time speech recognition and translation, and artificial intelligence and robotics are likely to advance further. The use of more intelligent robotics in manufacturing will support the ability to quickly reconfigure machines to produce prototypes and new production runs, with implications for

manufacturing logistics and inventories. Further technological advances are expected to continue to increase demand for a highly skilled workforce, support higher productivity growth, *and change the organization of business and the nature of employment relationships.*

(Richards, 2013, emphasis added)

Economic trends

Globalization

Globalization is of course not a new phenomenon, and it is not confined to the economic sphere alone. Indeed, globalization has been defined as 'the process of international integration arising from the interchange of world views, products, ideas, and other aspects of culture' (Ioannou *et al.*, 2013). In the context of the present chapter, we focus on the economic aspects of globalization, in particular trade, finance and the global division of labour, and its impact on the future of work.

The advance of globalization is illustrated in Figure 2.5.

Since 1980, while world GDP has grown at just under 3.5 per cent annually, trade has been growing at about 5.7 per cent per year. The growth in trade is largely due to the international division of labour and the growing prominence of global supply chains. More than 60 per cent of global trade is dependent on contracts in supply chains sourced from different parts of the world. A typical manufacturing company uses inputs from more than 35 different contractors across the world. 'The integration of supply, production, transport, logistics, and services means all corporations are involved, and this is responsible for generating greater

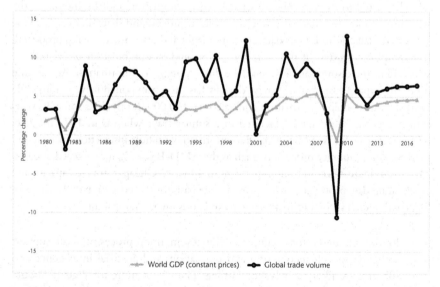

FIGURE 2.5 World GDP and global trade

Source: Elaborated from IMF World Economic Outlook (2012)

inequality along with massive poverty' (ITUC, 2014). Globalization has moved less sophisticated, low-paying jobs in manufacturing and services to developing countries, while the so-called 'industrialized' countries slowly but steadily de-industrialize. This trend has had a profound impact on the world of work in both developed and developing nations.

The growth of global financial flows has been even more spectacular, indicating that such flows are increasingly disconnected from the real economy; yet, the Global Financial Crisis of 2008 showed that any major disturbance of the global financial systems has immediate and drastic effects on the real economy, and on jobs and incomes.

Growing inequality

Many recent studies show that inequality is rising both within countries and between countries. We tend to equate 'inequality' with 'income inequality', since the latter is the most visible and can be measured through the Gini coefficient. But in many respects income inequality must be seen as just a symptom of more profound manifestations of inequality, such as:

- Inequality of *access*: to land, to markets, to finance, to jobs, to opportunities and resources in general;
- Inequality of *rights*: in terms of gender, race, religion, class, caste, etc.;
- Inequality of *participation*: in local and national decision-making, in elections, in governance structures, in social dialogue, in collective bargaining, etc.;
- Inequality of *protection*: by laws, by authorities, by social protection systems, etc.

Those different forms of inequality are more widespread in poorer nations and in countries governed by non-democratic regimes. Figure 2.6 shows the degree of income inequality in those countries for which data was available.

Even a market-friendly institution such as the IMF believes that widening inequality has significant implications for growth and macroeconomic stability, that it can concentrate political and decision-making power in the hands of a few, lead to a suboptimal use of human resources, cause investment-reducing political and economic instability (such as during the 'Arab Spring'), and elevate crisis risk. All of these factors have an impact on jobs, livelihoods and employment (Dabla-Norris et al., 2015).

The emergence of new economic powers

An emerging economy describes a nation's economy that is progressing toward becoming more advanced, usually by means of rapid growth and industrialization. These countries experience an expanding role both in the world economy and on the political frontier. Thirty-five years ago, the global economy was dominated by the members of the G7/G8 group; 35 years from now, only two of the G7 countries will make it to the top ten (Table 2.3).

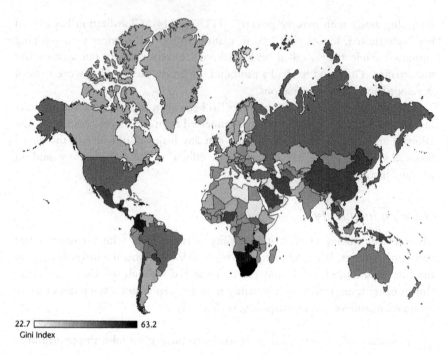

FIGURE 2.6 Degree of income inequality

Source: Elaborated from CIA (2009)

TABLE 2.3 The world's top ten economies, 1980, 2015 and 2050

The World's Top Ten Economies		
1980	**2015**	**2050**
US	US	China
USSR	China	US
Japan	Japan	India
Germany	Germany	Indonesia
France	UK	Japan
UK	France	Brazil
Italy	India	Germany
Canada	Italy	Mexico
China	Brazil	UK
Mexico	Canada	Russia

(Shaded: members of the G7/G8 group)

Source: Wikipedia, *List of countries by largest historical GDP*

It should be noted that Table 2.3 is based upon total GDP by country; the amounts of GDP per capita will remain significantly higher in the former 'First World' compared with the countries of the former 'Third World'.

Environmental trends

Climate change and global warming

Few people would argue that climate change (defined as a change in the statistical distribution of weather patterns lasting for an extended period of time) has become a reality. Ninety-seven per cent of climate scientists agree: climate-warming trends over the past century are very likely due to human activity. Climate change will affect different parts of the world differently, and unfortunately it is likely that the poorest countries, those that are least responsible for CO_2 emissions and that are equipped with the least coping ability, will be affected most (Center for Global Development, 2015).

It is estimated that by 2030, the cost of climate change and air pollution combined will rise to 3.2 per cent of global GDP, with the world's least developed countries forecast to bear the brunt, suffering losses of up to 11 per cent of their GDP (Harvey, 2012). Climate change will destroy millions of livelihoods in many parts of the world, such as lowlands prone to floods and regions affected by desertification, thus causing hunger, poverty and migration to less affected regions.

Resource depletion

Resource depletion was among the alarming factors that caused the Club of Rome in 1972 to call for a 'limit to growth'. Yet, since then, global GDP has quadrupled while GDP per capita has more than doubled (in constant 2005 USD terms). Certainly, growth has made it possible to significantly reduce the incidence of absolute poverty, but the growing number of middle-class consumers, mainly in Asia, will put a further strain on natural resources, and may accelerate global warming. And while demand for resources from an exploding and wealthier population soars, finding and extracting new sources of supply is becoming increasingly difficult and expensive. *The Limits to Growth: The Thirty Year Update* (Meadows *et al.*, 2004) shows the effects of resource depletion on industrial production, the availability of food, and pollution. In 2011 the United Nations Environment Programme reported that, if nothing changes, humanity will demand 140 billion tons of minerals, ores, fossil fuels and biomass every year by 2050 (UNEP, 2011). This is three times our current rate of resource consumption, and far beyond what the earth can supply. We therefore need to learn to decouple natural resource use and environmental impacts from economic growth. And we need to dissociate economic growth and job creation.

Global trends and the future of work

This section makes an attempt to assess the impact of demographic, economic, technological and environmental trends on the world of work. Such impact could

TABLE 2.4 Global trends and the future of work

Trend	Possible positive impact	Possible negative impact	Impact in emerging countries	Impact in developed countries
Population growth	Countries with low or negative population growth may be able to absorb labour migrants from other regions. More people = more demand = more job opportunities.	Growing unemployment, informalization of work, deteriorating working conditions as a result of competition for jobs; growing labour migration.	High, because of a strong correlation between low per capita income and high birth rates.	Low, except for the aspect of immigration.
Ageing	More job opportunities in the care industry and in industries producing goods for the elderly.	Strain on health and pension systems; need to extend the working life for all.	Low, but growing.	High and growing.
Urbanization	If economic growth exceeds the urbanization rate: employment levels maintained, living standards improving. Higher demand for rural products should benefit rural producers.	If the urbanization rate exceeds economic growth: deteriorating living conditions, more 'working poor'.	High.	Neutral (urbanization has peaked in most developed countries).
Automation	Creates well-paid jobs in highly sophisticated professions (engineering, software development, etc.).	Replaces manual work in services and industry. Will progressively take over more and more functions.	Low, because capital required to automate exceeds the cost of labour.	Very high
Information and communication technology	Creates mostly low-paid, unskilled jobs in online trade (transport, packaging, logistics), plus relatively few managerial and technical posts.	Massive job losses in the service industry (shops, banks, transport etc.). May lead to the isolation of workers (tele-working).	Low, slowly growing.	High and expanding.

Driver				
Digitization	New jobs in information and data management, processing and analysis.	Job losses affecting all functions that can be digitized.	Low, but growing.	High and expanding.
Globalization	Massive job creation in producing countries, job creation in the service industry in importing countries.	Rising inequality and deteriorating working conditions/job security in both importing and exporting countries.	The higher the more a country is open to the forces of globalization.	
Inequality	None.	Research shows that inequality (of income, of access, of rights) has negative effects on livelihoods of poorer segments of the population.	The amplitude of negative social outcomes is a function of the degree of inequality.	
Emergence of new economic powers	The transfer of industries and associated jobs from developed to emerging countries (as in Akamutsa's 'flying goose paradigm') and the subsequent restructuring of economies: less agriculture and more manufacturing in emerging nations, less manufacturing and more services in high-income countries.			
Climate change	New opportunities to create 'green jobs' in renewable energy, recycling, climate change adaptation, etc.	Massive job and income losses in countries most affected by climate change.	High in most developing countries.	Medium in most countries of the North.
Resource depletion		Job losses in resource-intensive industries and supply chains depending on them.	Impact depending on the ability and willingness of the world to switch to renewables.	

Source: Author's own elaboration

be positive (more jobs, better working conditions), negative (growing unemployment, deteriorating working conditions), neutral, or mixed. Moreover, the impact may differ from country to country and from region to region, or may affect different population groups in different ways.

The impact of the anticipated global changes will be felt not only on the number and quality of jobs in different countries, but also on the nature and quality of social dialogue, and on the application and enforcement of labour standards. The growth of global supply chains controlled by multinationals weakens national social dialogue mechanisms, which are further affected by the diminishing might and representativeness of worker and employer organizations.[6] We do not currently have institutions and mechanisms to organize social dialogue along global supply chains. Moreover, a global 'race to the bottom' in terms of labour costs will necessarily favour countries that do less to apply and enforce the fundamental principles and rights at work.

In addition, the progress of automation, digitization and information and communication technology is likely to have a significant impact on the way we will work in the future. Many of those tasks that are currently accomplished in offices and factories may require in the future nothing but a computer, an Internet connection and (in some cases) a decentralized production unit such as a 3-D-printer. More and more people will be able to work from home; this may offer advantages for some, but it will cause the alienation and social isolation of many. Wage earners may be forced to become pseudo-entrepreneurs, and standard employment relationships will turn into client–subcontracting relationships. This will diminish social security coverage, weaken social dialogue mechanisms and institutions, and accelerate the informalization of economies and societies.

Cooperatives and the future of work

When taking a holistic view of the trends above – a growing, ageing, and more urban population, growing global trade, escalating inequality, job losses through automation and digitization, and global warming, resource depletion and pollution – we must come to the conclusion that the current economic system is not sustainable. Yesterday, growth was the miracle recipe to cure all social and economic ills; today, growth has reached its limits because the natural resources that fuelled it in the past are disappearing. Capitalism has reached its peak. The world needs to reorganize national economies and the global economy to achieve social, economic and environmental sustainability. Sustainable production and consumption will entail greater equality, more justice, but also less comfort and diminishing wealth. The 2015 *Atlas of Globalization* (Le Monde Diplomatique, 2015) calls for a post-growth society whose progress would be measured by a more inclusive set of indicators than just GDP, and which would put greater emphasis on equality, sharing, recycling, voluntarism and community engagement. The *Atlas of Globalization*, however, also draws attention to the difficulties in building a bridge from capitalism to post-growth. Democratically elected governments with their limited time horizon – going not much beyond the next election – will hardly endeavour to implement the radical political changes required by such a transition.

Top–down change will succeed only under a dictatorship, or under the pressure of life-threatening catastrophes; to avoid both, dictators and catastrophes, the world must instead initiate reforms from 'bottom–up'.

The potential of cooperation

This brings us to the subject of the present volume: the potential role of cooperatives. Can cooperatives – or, put in a broader perspective, could an economic system built on the principles of cooperation, collaboration and sharing rather than driven by competition and profit maximization – provide answers to at least some of the problems highlighted in the previous sections? Let us recall the Statement on the Cooperative Identity (ICA, 1995), which states, *inter alia*, that: 'Cooperatives are based on the values of self-help, self-responsibility, democracy, equality, equity and solidarity. In the tradition of their founders, cooperative members believe in the ethical values of honesty, openness, social responsibility and caring for others.' Surely, such values, augmented by the seven cooperative principles, could provide the foundation for a fairer and more sustainable economic system. The ICA *Blueprint for a Cooperative Decade* reminds us that, 'By placing human need at their centre, rather than profit, co-operatives overcome short-termism and introduce real choice in how business is done.' Clearly, genuine cooperatives are people-centred, they promote equality and sustainability, they show concern for the community, and they look at the longer term. With these values and characteristics, cooperatives may indeed be more capable than other forms of business or social organization to alleviate the negative effects of global developments on jobs and livelihoods, and contribute to harnessing the positive forces of these trends. The Government of New Zealand states that 'there is a need to explore and promote other options and models for people to have job and/or employment security in the future work environment *such as cooperatives*' (Government of New Zealand, 2015, emphasis added).

Table 2.5 gives a few examples of how cooperatives and other social and solidarity economy units could contribute to building a better future of work.

Table 2.5 seems to indicate that indeed cooperatives could play a significant role in facilitating the transition towards a post-growth economy and society.

In addition, cooperatives may well play a key role in alleviating the negative effects of the alienation and social isolation of independent, home-based or itinerant 'pseudo-entrepreneurs'. Workers affected by these phenomena may be able to overcome their isolation, and lack of voice and bargaining power, through the formation of virtual cooperatives that use the Internet as a common bond.

Towards a cooperative future of work

When assessing the potential role of cooperatives in the future of work, we must remain realistic. Cooperatives are important players in the global economy, but their share of global GDP is easily dwarfed by mainstream businesses; cooperatives can show the way, give examples, shine a light; but they will not on their own be capable of solving all the problems mentioned above. Moreover, some

TABLE 2.5 Global trends and the potential of cooperation

Trend	Cooperatives supporting the positive impact on the future of work	Cooperatives alleviating the negative impact on the future of work
Population growth	Formation of migrant workers' cooperatives and self-help groups, including groups formed by returnees in their home countries.	Formation of informal economy associations and self-help groups to improve working conditions, protect rights, defend interests, increase bargaining power, and realize economies of scale.
Ageing	Promotion of community-based care-givers cooperatives as an alternative to commercial and state-run care provision.	Formation of workers' cooperatives of the elderly to generate income and maintain an active life (the Japanese model).
Urbanization	Formation of urban consumer cooperatives and networking with rural producer cooperatives.	As under 'Population growth'.
Automation	Automation is, by definition, 'machine-centred', and therefore an area of little relevance to people-centred cooperatives. An exception is shared-service cooperatives for the joint use of automated equipment.	
Communications	Formation of worker cooperatives in the online trade.	Formation of Internet-based collaborative platforms of tele-workers, software engineers, publishers, translators, journalists, etc.
Digitization	Shared service cooperatives for data-processing, cloud computing and information management (see DENIC [www.denic.de] and DATEV [www.datev.de], Germany); cooperative associations of open-source programmers (Mozilla, Linux, Wikipedia, etc.).	Self-help organizations or redundant workers?
Globalization	All types and forms of cooperation.	Social economy initiatives of local producers and consumers, fair trade, slow food, bio food, renewable energy, etc.

Inequality	–	Cooperatives are, by nature, governance structure and conviction, promoters of greater equality.
Emergence of new economic powers	Promotion of South–South cooperation involving cooperative movements from emerging economies, as well as North–South cooperative associations for the exchange of knowledge and experience.	
Climate change	Renewable energy generation and distribution cooperatives, recycling coops, etc.	Cooperatives as agents of climate change adaptation (example: green belt Sahel).
Resource depletion		Cooperatives as agents of conversion to resource-neutral production.

Source: Author's own elaboration

cooperatives, especially the larger ones, may be trapped in the same economic paradigm that causes the aberrations of the neoliberal market economy: the blind pursuit of growth, profits and shareholder value. And third, cooperatives, as member-based businesses, have so far been largely confined to national boundaries,[7] whereas global value chains, controlled by globally operating multinationals, transcend those borders and frontiers. Cooperatives must avoid the self-congratulatory tendencies that so often dominate congresses convened by like-minded organizations; cooperatives are not 'better' just because of their name or statute; they must prove their merits through tangible action.

During the past decade the international cooperative movement has invested considerable effort and energy in trying to convince the rest of the world that cooperatives, too, belong to the big players in the global economy; we all know the key figures: 1 billion members, almost 280 million livelihoods,[8] USD2.5 trillion in revenues for the largest 300.[9] However, on the one hand, the message has not found much resonance outside the cooperative universe; and on the other, it is doubtful whether the message is relevant to the future of work discussion. The true power of cooperatives does not only stem from their size or economic might, but from their distinct nature, characteristics, values, principles and governance structure. Rather than seeking recognition from the mainstream, neoliberal economic system, the global cooperative movement should develop alternatives to that system, which has shown its drawbacks and limitations. During the coming ten years, the international cooperative movement should focus on elaborating such alternatives, not doing business as usual but rather finding ways to doing business differently. Ultimately, cooperatives should be able to demonstrate that decent work for all is possible even in a post-growth context.

Bearing in mind those considerations, it should be possible to develop a pragmatic strategy of cooperative development in the context of the future of work. In addition to the examples mentioned in Table 2.5, four strategic directions would appear necessary.

Cooperation beyond cooperatives

The Cooperative Society Ltd., recognized by law and formally registered, is just but one manifestation of cooperation. The cooperative principles and values as defined by the ICA are not confined to formally registered and/or officially recognized cooperatives. We have, on the one hand, a great diversity of organizations, associations and enterprises belonging to the social and solidarity economy that share many of those principles and values without necessarily calling themselves 'cooperatives'. And we have, on the other hand, new manifestations of cooperation that have emerged as a result of new technologies, in particular mobile communications and the Internet. Open source projects such as Mozilla,[10] Linux and Wikipedia are implemented by people who are united by a common goal (the software project) without necessarily sharing a common bond, which is seen as essential in conventional cooperatives. The Internet has also boosted other forms of cooperation, such as the sharing economy[11] and 'collaborative consumption'.[12] While the largest and best-known of those ventures (such as eBay, AirBnB and Uber) are profit-oriented,[13] many others tend to operate partly according to cooperative principles. Beyond transport and temporary accommodation, several additional economic and social sectors could be of interest to the sharing economy: mutual education, health services, communication networks, energy generation and distribution, etc. In all those areas and others, cooperative ventures could play a key role. As we can see in Schneider's chapter in this volume (Chapter 14), new, Internet-based forms of cooperation may facilitate the transition from a future world of work characterized by unstable employment relationships, isolated workplaces (tele-working), greater informality, and lack of representation and protection towards one with more autonomous but also decent work. Such new forms of cooperation are not confined to the nation-state but will have a global outreach. New forms of cooperation will strengthen the capabilities of the individual, often isolated worker: the 'amplified individual' (Institute for the Future, 2007) of the future derives value and strength from their connection with the collective intelligence of others. Those individuals will rely on new technologies of cooperation, such as social networks. 'As social animals we are capable of cooperating more deeply than the existing social order envisions' (Sennet, 2012). Many believe that 'the Future of Work is all about collaboration', because new technologies have greatly facilitated collaboration between workers, even across continents and time zones (Haberman, 2015).

Building alliances with likeminded movements

As value-based organizations, cooperatives belong to a family whose members share a number of principles, such as the centrality of people and community, the quest for sustainability, equality and justice, and the values of mutuality and solidarity. Other members of that family include movements promoting fair trade, organic food production and consumption, 'slow food', mutual social protection, local sustainable development, environmental protection, recycling and reuse, employee-ownership, social entrepreneurship, etc. In addition, the global trade union movement, while pursuing its own objectives, recognizes many of the principles cherished by cooperatives; trade unions could become an ally as well. It would be in the interest of all to unite these movements under a common umbrella, with the aim of promoting a new economic model, and a better world of work. The International Cooperative Alliance, being the largest member of that family, could take the lead in building such an alliance to make the future of work cooperative.

Organizing cooperation along global supply chains

As mentioned earlier, traditional cooperatives are confined to the nation-state, whereas an increasing proportion of global economic activity and global trade and finance is linked in one way or another to global supply chains. Such global supply chains do create jobs but those are often of very low quality, and the most exploitative models of supply chains often involve forced labour, child labour and informal, unprotected work. Cooperatives do already play an important role in specific global supply chains, such as coffee and cocoa, where both producers and consumers (but not the enterprises involved between the two ends of the chain) are organized cooperatively (Sanchez Bajo and Silvestre, 2014). Would it be possible to extend this model to other supply chains, such as cotton and the garment industry? Can we envision a garment workers' cooperative in Bangladesh buying cotton from a marketing cooperative in India, and selling ready-made garments to a consumer cooperative in Japan? And would there be merit in involving other types of cooperatives, such as financial coops and shared-service coops, in such endeavours? These are just questions for the time being, but the growing economic importance of global supply chains, coupled with their often negative impact on the world of work and the environment, calls for a greater involvement of the international cooperative movement. The 2016 General Discussion on Decent Work in Global Supply Chains at the 2016 International Labour Conference called for 'specific measures targeted at [. . .] cooperatives and other entities of the social economy, to increase their productivity and promote decent work, including opportunities to formalize, further develop, upgrade and advance to higher segments of the supply chains' (ILO, 2016b).

Cooperatives formed in response to emerging trends

Some cooperative ventures have been or could be initiated in response to the trends introduced in this chapter. In the area of demographics, care-giver cooperatives and self-help groups of the elderly may alleviate some of the problems caused by ageing. In the technological area, 'virtual' cooperatives formed by independent, own-account workers could provide voice, representation, a greater degree of stability and security as well as economies of scale and scope. In the economic area, cooperatives formed to strengthen local economies and local communities could counter the negative effects of globalization. Shared service cooperatives could support SMEs in jointly acquiring and managing expensive digital, communications and automation equipment. And in the environmental area, recycling cooperatives, renewable energy generation cooperatives, plus the sharing economy and collaborative consumption, could contribute to creating jobs while protecting the planet. Could one envisage the cooperative management of the global commons? These are just a few examples of a broad range of possible collective endeavours towards a better future of work.

Notes

1 Those global conversations are being held under the headings 'Work and society', 'Decent work for all', 'The governance of work', and 'The organization of work and production'.
2 The sources used for the chapter are mostly extracted from the Internet, often relying on information provided by Wikipedia; those are not marked specifically. Other sources are listed in the References.
3 The chapter will not discuss the future of cooperatives since this has been the theme of a major ICA research conference held in April 2015 in Paris (ICA, 2015). But it will become evident in later sections of the chapter that cooperatives themselves will have to adapt to the emerging trends so as to remain relevant in a changing world of work.
4 In many cases, the automation of services simply means that certain functions are being transferred from a service provider to the consumer, thus increasing the provider's profits and reducing the consumer's free time.
5 Some authors believe that of all recent innovations, 3-D printing could have the greatest impact on jobs and the economy.
6 Today, just 7 per cent of the global labour force is organized in trade unions. And this number is shrinking in most countries.
7 In the European Union, however, the statute of the European Cooperative Society (SCE), adopted in 2003, is a legal form of a cooperative that facilitates cooperatives' cross-border and transnational activities. The members of an SCE cannot all be based in one country.
8 According to CICOPA *Cooperatives and Employment: Second Global Report* (Eum, 2017).
9 According to *World Co-operative Monitor 2016* (ICA-EURICSE, 2016).
10 Among the principles in *The Mozilla Manifesto*, these are notable in this regard: 'Free and open source software promotes the development of the internet as a public resource (Principle 7)' and 'Transparent community-based processes promote participation, accountability and trust (Principle 8)' (Mozilla Foundation, 2015).
11 A sharing economy provides individuals, corporations, non-profits and governments with information that enables the optimization of resources through the redistribution, sharing and reuse of excess capacity in goods and services.
12 Collaborative consumption as a phenomenon is a class of economic arrangements in which participants share access to products or services, rather than having individual ownership.
13 Those firms care little about sharing, mutual help and trust; they provide temporary access to goods and services between people that have no social relationship. Commercial share economy ventures may even contribute to deteriorating working conditions because they exclude the involvement of trade unions and destroy employment relationships (Metzger, 2015).

References

Center for Global Development. *Mapping the impact of climate change.* Accessed 22 October 2015. www.cgdev.org/page/mapping-impacts-climate-change.

CIA. *The world factbook.* 2009. www.cia.gov/library/publications/the-world-factbook/.

Dabla-Norris, Era, Kalpana Kochhar, Nujin Suphaphiphat, Frantisek Ricka, and Evridiki Tsounta. *Causes and consequences of income inequality: A global perspective,* IMF Staff Discussion Note. Washington, DC: IMF, 2015.

Eum, Hyungsik. *Cooperatives and employment: Second global report 2017.* Brussels: CICOPA, 2017.

Frey, Carl Benedikt and Michael A. Osborne, *The future of employment: How susceptible are jobs to computerisation?* Working paper, Oxford: Oxford Martin Programme on Technology and Employment, 2013.

Government of New Zealand. *The future of work.* The Future of Work Commission (Ministry of Labour, New Zealand). Accessed 31 October 2015. www.futureofwork. nz/security_job_and_employment_security.

Haberman, Michael. *The future of work is all about collaboration.* Society for Human Resource Management. Accessed 11 September 2015. blog.shrm.org/blog/future-friday-the-future-of-work-is-all-about-collaboration.

Harvey, Fiona. Climate change is already damaging global economy, report finds, *The Guardian,* 26 September 2012.

International Co-operative Alliance (ICA). Future of the cooperative model. In *ICA Research conference, Paris.* Accessed 20 December 2016. ica-paris2015.com/index.php/component/content/category/78-ica-research-conference.

ICA and EURICSE. *World co-operative monitor 2016,* Brussels: ICA, 2016.

Institute for the Future. *The future of work perspectives.* Palo Alto, CA: Institute for the Future, 2007.

International Monetary Fund (IMF). *World economic outlook.* 2012. www.imf.org/en/Publications/WEO/Issues/2016/12/31/Coping-with-High-Debt-and-Sluggish-Growth.

International Telecommunication Union (ITU). *Measuring the information society 2016.* Geneva, 2016.

International Trade Union Confederation (ITUC). *Building workers' power.* Brussels, 2014.

International Labour Office (ILO). *The future of work centenary initiative.* Geneva, 2015.

___. *The future of work centenary initiative.* Geneva, 2016a.

___. *Conclusions of the general discussion on decent work in global supply chains,* Geneva, 2016b.

Ioannou, Andriani, Enkeleint Aggelos Mechili, Aikaterini Kolokathi and Marianna Diomidous. Impacts of globalization in health, *Studies in Health Technology and Informatics* 190 (2013): 222–224.

Keynes, John Maynard. Economic possibilities for our grandchildren, *The Nation and Athenaeum* (1930).

Le Monde Diplomatique. *Atlas der Globalisierung - Weniger wird merh.* Berlin: Le Monde Diplomatique/TAZ, 2015.

Meadows, Donella H., Dennis L. Meadows, Jorgen Randers, and William W. Behrens III. *The limits to growth: A report for the Club of Rome's project on the predicament of mankind.* New York: Universe Books, 1972.

Meadows, Donella H., Jorgen Randers, and Dennis L. Meadows. *Limits to growth: The 30-year update.* London: Chelsea Green Publishing, 2004.

Metzger, Reiner. Teilen, die andere Oekonomie. In Le Monde Diplomatique, *Atlas der Globalisierung – Weniger wird merh.* 146–149. Berlin: Le Monde Diplomatique/TAZ, 2015.

Mozilla Foundation. *The Mozilla Manifesto.* Accessed 25 October 2015. www.mozilla.org/en-GB/about/manifesto/.

Richards, Hayden. The future trends that will shape work, *Intelligent HQ,* 2013. www.intelligenthq.com/intelligence/cipd-debatethe-future-trends-that-will-shape-work/.

Sanchez Bajo, Claudia, and Bruno Silvestre. Cooperatives in global value chains: Coffee in Guatemala and cooperatives. In *Congrès des Sciences Humaines* 2014, 2014.

Sennet, Richard. *Together: The rituals, pleasures and politics of cooperation.* London: Penguin Books, 2012.

The Economist. The future of jobs – The onrushing wave. 18 January 2014.

Turner, Graham, and Cathy Alexander. Limits to growth was right. New research shows we're nearing collapse, *The Guardian (Australia news)* 2 September 2014.

United Nations (UN). *World urbanization prospects: The 2011 revision.* New York, 2012.

____. *World population prospect.* 2017. https://population.un.org/wpp/Download/Standard/Population/.

United Nations Environment Programme (UNEP). *Assessing the environmental impacts of consumption and production.* Nairobi, 2011.

Wikipedia, *List of countries by largest historical GDP.* en.wikipedia.org/wiki/List_of_countries_by_largest_historical_GDP

WorldoMeters. World Population Clock, *WorldoMeters.* Accessed 20 December 2016. www.worldometers.info/world-population/.

3

COOPERATIVES AND FUNDAMENTAL PRINCIPLES AND RIGHTS AT WORK[*]

Natural disposition or commitment to action?

Simel Eşim, Waltteri Katajamäki and Guy Tchami

Introduction

Formed by producers, consumers, workers and businesses worldwide, cooperatives can and do create and consolidate employment opportunities, empower people, provide protection and alleviate poverty. They exist across all sectors of the economy. As enterprises they fulfil economic goals, and as social organizations they build social networks and strengthen voice and representation of their members. As service providers they improve the livelihoods of the communities through services in, e.g., education, health, water, energy, finance, retail and housing, while also generating employment, especially in areas that may be neglected by the state and investor-driven enterprises.[1]

Comparable data on the number of jobs created by cooperatives across time, sectors, countries and regions is not readily available, although concerted efforts are under way for improvements.[2] There is some evidence, however, that cooperatives are significant employers in many countries, globally involving at least 280 million people. Employment in or within the scope of cooperatives makes up almost 10 per cent of the world's employed population (Eum, 2017). In addition to salaried employment, cooperatives promote self-employment both directly, through producer-members getting their livelihood within their scope, and indirectly, by creating market opportunities and by improving market conditions as well as by providing loans and creating and reinforcing value chains through clients and providers.

Even less well known is the quality of work generated by cooperatives and whether this work respects the fundamental rights of workers in terms of remuneration, safe and healthy working conditions and equal employment opportunities.[3] In 1998, the International Labour Organization (ILO) adopted the *Declaration on Fundamental Principles and Rights at Work*, to support the safeguarding and promotion of respect for basic workers' rights (ILO, 1998). The fundamental principles and rights at work (FPRW) are those universal rights that apply to all people across all ILO member states, regardless of whether they have ratified the relevant Conventions or not.[4] As laid out in the Declaration, the FPRW are: freedom of association and the right to collective bargaining; elimination of forced or compulsory labour; abolition of child labour; and elimination of discrimination in respect of employment and occupation (*ibid.*). FPRW are means for achieving, among others, effective social dialogue, better conditions for workers, rising enterprise productivity, increased consumer demand, more and better jobs and social protection, and for formalizing the informal economy. Despite progress made in some countries, a rapid overview of the global picture relating to the four categories shows that the realization of FPRW remains a worldwide challenge.

Today over 200 million people globally are unemployed. There are an estimated 25 million people who are victims of forced labour, 4.3 million of whom are children (ILO *et al.*, 2017). Of the 152 million children in child labour, 73 million are in hazardous work, and 114 million are younger than 15 years old (ILO, 2017). On average, women are paid 23 per cent less than their male counterparts, and are much more likely to be in vulnerable employment (ILO, 2016b).

Discrimination in the world of work is widespread, with people suffering from discrimination because of the colour of their skin, their ethnicity or social origin, their religion or political beliefs, their age, gender, sexual identity or orientation, disability or because of their HIV status.

Despite the universality of the right to freedom of association, many workers are excluded from the right to associate in a significant number of countries. Exclusion, whether direct or indirect, disproportionately affects workers that are vulnerable to poor working conditions, such as agricultural workers, migrant workers, domestic workers and workers in non-standard forms of employment (ILO, 2012c).

FPRW are human rights,[5] and as such, respecting them is not only critical for achieving sustained economic growth but also for attaining sustainable development goals and objectives. Their violation contributes to the persistence of the cycle of poverty (*ibid.*).

In this chapter, the role and responsibilities of cooperatives in advancing decent work in general and FPRW in particular are explored. Because of data limitations, the analysis focuses on what constitutes good employment practices among cooperative enterprises in the different areas of FPRW. Highlights of cooperatives and their secondary and tertiary organizations, namely unions and federations, in advancing FPRW will be provided. The areas of action identified constitute a starting point for reflections on decent work and FPRW in the cooperative world.

WAYS COOPERATIVES CAN ENGAGE IN ADVANCING FUNDAMENTAL PRINCIPLES AND RIGHTS AT WORK

- Actively engage in and contribute toward actions to eliminate labour rights abuses in the four areas of FPRW in their business operations and supply chains they are involved in;

- Engage in community mobilization and awareness-raising campaigns among their members and within the communities where they operate on the four areas of FPRW;
- Provide guidance and community leadership, and contribute to the planning and delivery of health, educational and other basic social services in their communities on FPRW;
- Promote livelihood opportunities and the use of appropriate technologies as means of increasing income of their members within the guidelines of FPRW;
- Provide collective voice and negotiation power for their members with the public authorities in securing a range of economic and social rights, including FPRW; and
- Stimulate decent work opportunities through training and education programmes in all the four areas of FPRW.

Fundamental principles and rights at work: cooperative responsibility

Like any other business, cooperative enterprises need to comply with responsible labour practices. However, for cooperatives, which are based on a set of values and principles,[6] this is understood as being inherently built into their business model. Business practices that do not comply with FPRW are not aligned with cooperative values of equality, solidarity, social responsibility or caring for others, for example. The ILO's *Promotion of Cooperatives Recommendation*, 2002 (No. 193) recognizes the importance of the FPRW for the development of cooperatives, making a specific call for national policies to 'ensure that cooperatives are not set up for, or used for, non-compliance with labour law or used to establish disguised employment relationships, and combat pseudo cooperatives violating workers' rights, by ensuring that labour legislation is applied in all enterprises' (ILO, 2002).

Elements within the cooperative movement have been advancing toward decent work practices within their sectors and regions. The International Organization of Industrial, Artisanal and Service Producers' Cooperatives (CICOPA) is one of them.[7] CICOPA has adopted a *World Declaration on Worker Cooperatives*, which was approved by the International Co-operative Alliance (ICA) General Assembly in 2005, highlighting the role of worker cooperatives

> as actors in the solution of the problems of unemployment and social exclusion, and as proponents of one of the most advanced, fair and dignifying modalities of labour relations, generation and distribution of wealth, and democratization of ownership and of the economy.
>
> *(CICOPA, 2005)*

Close to 800 cooperative enterprises from around the world are signatories to the United Nations Global Compact initiative on sustainability and social responsibility principles for businesses. Four of the Global Compact Principles derive directly from the ILO *Declaration on Fundamental Principles and Rights at Work*.[8] Coop Italia was the first company in Europe, and among the first ten in the world, to get, in 1998, the Social Accountability SA8000 certification (ICA, 2015), which requires compliance with criteria related to child labour, occupational safety and health, discrimination, rights to collective bargaining, and working conditions.[9]

More recently declarations from two International Cooperative Summits in 2014 and 2016 included decent work elements in general and FPRW in particular among their commitments. The 2014 Declaration committed to 'work systematically to promote conditions that lead to decent work – job creation, labour rights, social protection, and social dialogue – in order to improve and better assess cooperatives' contribution to the means of production'.[10] The 2016 Declaration devoted a whole section on the topic of economic growth, employment and decent work.

DECENT WORK COMMITMENTS IN THE *DECLARATION OF THE INTERNATIONAL SUMMIT OF COOPERATIVES, 2016*[11]

- Promote and offer employment and decent work (job creation, labour rights, social protection, social dialogue) in accordance with the standards of the International Labour Organization, including the *Promotion of Cooperatives Recommendation*, 2002 (No. 193);
- Encourage collective entrepreneurship, particularly the active engagement of women, young people and indigenous people in cooperative start-ups;
- Empower women through their inclusion in management and governance, leading to the elimination of violence and discrimination towards them;
- Enable the most disadvantaged populations to gain access to decent work, in order to be able to accumulate assets, redistribute wealth and influence decision-making on issues of economic growth and development;
- Support the transition from informal to formal economy and employment through the cooperative model; and
- Fight inequalities, particularly through the cooperative principle of voluntary and open membership, and the principle of economic participation, ensuring an equitable redistribution of surplus among members and reinvestment in the cooperative's mission.

The advocates for the cooperative model insist that as democratic membership-based enterprises, cooperatives are well aligned with areas of decent work in general and FPRW in particular. However, the evidence on how cooperative principles and values manifest themselves in advancing these requires further analysis. In fact, there is a significant gap between the evidence on individual cooperatives' good employment practices and the declarations from the cooperative movement that needs to be filled.

Cooperatives and child labour

Child labour is understood as work that deprives children of their childhood, their potential and their dignity, and that is harmful to their physical and mental development. In its most extreme forms, child labour involves children being enslaved, separated from their families, exposed to serious hazards and illnesses and/or left to fend for themselves, often at a very early age. Agriculture remains the sector where most child labour is found: 107 million (71 per cent) of all working children are in agriculture. The problem is also particularly prevalent in services (26 million) and industry (18 million) – mostly within the informal economy (ILO, 2017).

The international community has identified the elimination of child labour as a fundamental human right at work, and in recent years there have been advances in its elimination. ILO estimates that in 2016 there were 94 million fewer children in child labour compared with 2000, while the number of children in hazardous work fell by more than half in the same period (*ibid.*).

As cooperatives have a significant presence in many countries, they can play a role in the elimination of child labour. They improve the livelihoods and well-being of people in rural areas, where over 3 billion continue to live, working mainly in agriculture, and where public services are often limited. Cooperatives are not only prominent in agriculture, fisheries, horticulture, forestry, transport and tourism, but also in a range of services from electricity, water and sanitation, to finance and social and community development (ILO, 2014b). They have extensive networks and strong presence in economic sectors where child labour is found. They address it in their own functions and in the communities where they operate by:

- *Improving the livelihoods of their members and people in the communities they serve*: A prominent example of cooperatives improving the quality of life of their members is through credit unions or savings and credit cooperatives that provide members with access to safe savings, affordable credits, and a chance to plan for the future. These cooperatives encourage regular savings of small amounts, helping their members address everyday financial challenges like school fees, medical expenses and transport (Amegashie-Viglo, 2014).
- *Actively engaging their members not to use child labour – directly or indirectly*: Child labour can often occur because of poverty, lack of education and limited knowledge of the risks. Cooperatives, including their secondary and tertiary unions and federations, carry out a number of training and education programmes for their members, elected representatives, managers, and employees. These can range from vocational and managerial training for their members and the members of the larger community to awareness-raising sessions from issues such as climate change and gender-based violence to HIV/AIDS prevention and child labour. Cooperatives in supply chains such as handicrafts, cotton, cocoa and tobacco have been training their members and communities in bringing down the numbers of child workers (ILO, 2009). When coupled with other measures these have proven effective.

- *Supporting the communities to eliminate the worst forms of child labour through educating children*: Lack of access to education is one of the reasons for the prominence of child labour in many rural communities, and the role of cooperatives as community-based enterprises is also to serve the wider community. For example, the Coopérative Agricole Kavokiva du Haut Sassandra (CAKHS) in Côte d'Ivoire is a cocoa and coffee marketing cooperative, which has since 2010 prevented and withdrawn over 1,800 children from hazardous child labour and provided them with basic education and vocational training. CAKHS has also set up kindergarten centres and school facilities hosting children withdrawn from hazardous child labour (ILO, 2014c).
- *Becoming involved in activities toward eliminating the worst forms of child labour in the global supply chains where they operate*: While it is likely to be more difficult for smaller cooperative enterprises to track and monitor as to whether the global supply chains where they operate are free of child labour or not, larger cooperatives and their organizations are likely to be better equipped. Regardless of size, cooperatives can and should adopt and implement codes of conduct to shift to more responsible policies and practices for supply chains free of child labour. In the Global North, particularly consumer cooperatives with large retail operations can use their economic leverage to actively engage in establishing child-labour-free supply chains (ILO, 2009).

A Germany-based cooperative online marketplace, Fairmondo, is owned and managed by its buyers, sellers, workers and investors. It sells ethically-sourced products from producers and small fair trade companies including cooperatives from around the world. As such it is an example of cooperative-to-cooperative trade and a fair trade alternative, providing users with transparent product sourcing. Other ethical trading initiatives involving cooperatives, such as Fairtrade, include criteria on child labour and other FPRW.[12]

Cooperatives and forced labour

Forced labour is work that is performed involuntarily and under the menace of penalty (ILO, 1930). It refers to situations in which persons are coerced to work through the use of violence or intimidation or by more subtle means such as manipulated debt, retention of identity papers or threats of denunciation to immigration authorities. Almost 25 million people are victims of forced labour – 15.6 million women and girls and 9.2 million men and boys. About 84 per cent of victims are exploited by private individuals or enterprises, while the remaining 16 per cent are in state-imposed forms of forced labour, or in rebel groups, for instance. Of those exploited by individuals or enterprises, 4.8 million are victims of forced sexual exploitation. Domestic work, agriculture, construction, manufacturing and entertainment are among the sectors most concerned (ILO et al., 2017). Migrant workers and indigenous people are particularly vulnerable to forced labour.

In order to assist enterprises, including cooperatives, in combatting forced labour and trafficking, the ILO has developed a set of principles to strengthen employers' activities against forced labour. While implementing and monitoring of these principles is the responsibility for all, including smaller cooperatives, secondary- and tertiary-level cooperative organizations (i.e. unions and federations) can play a crucial role reaching out to their members in reconfirming its importance and imparting tools (self-assessment checklists, guidelines and codes of conduct, etc.) and know-how that facilitate their change toward elimination of forced labour practices. In the United Kingdom, the Co-op Group has joined forces with a charity providing support to the victims of human trafficking. The scheme promotes the reintegration of trafficking victims in the society through offering job placements in Co-op Group's stores, while the charity provides them with longer-term support (Co-operative News, 2017).

TEN PRINCIPLES FOR BUSINESS LEADERS TO COMBAT FORCED LABOUR AND TRAFFICKING (ILO, N.D.)

- Have a clear and transparent company policy, setting out the measures taken to prevent forced labour and trafficking (applied to all enterprises in their product and supply chains);
- Train auditors, human resource and compliance officers to identify forced labour in practice, and seek appropriate remedies;
- Provide regular information to shareholders and potential investors, attracting them to products and services where there is a clear and sustainable commitment to ethical business practice, including prevention of forced labour;
- Promote agreements and codes of conduct by sector, identify and take appropriate measures in areas with risk of forced labour;
- Treat migrant workers fairly. Monitor carefully the agencies that provide contract labour, especially across borders, blacklisting those known to have used abusive practices and forced labour;
- Work towards securing written contracts for all workers, in a language they understand, specifying their rights on payment of wages, overtime, retention of identity documents, and other issues;
- Encourage events with business actors, sharing challenges and good practices;
- Contribute to programmes and projects to assist, through training and other appropriate measures, the victims of forced labour and trafficking;
- Build bridges between governments, workers, law enforcement agencies and labour inspectorates, promoting cooperation in action against forced labour and trafficking; and
- Find innovative means to reward good practice, along with the media.

The ILO estimates migrant workers accounted for 150 million of the world's approximately 232 million international migrants in 2013, of whom 44 per cent are women (ILO, 2015c). They contribute to growth and development in their countries of destination, while countries of origin greatly benefit from their remittances and the skills acquired during their migration experience. Yet, the migration process is mired with challenges. Restrictive migration policies, coupled with the continuing demand for low-skilled workers, often lead to an increased vulnerability of migrant workers to forced labour, trafficking and growth of irregular migration (ILO, 2010). Migrant workers have been establishing cooperatives to access formal labour markets, entrepreneurship opportunities, social protection and other services in the host countries. Their cooperatives range in services from finance and education to job placement (ILO, 2014a).

While migrant domestic workers constitute only a small segment of workers in forced labour, they comprise a significant part of migrant women's workforce and can often face terms and conditions of work that could lead to forced labour, including retention of identity papers, restriction of movement, physical and sexual violence, isolation, intimidation and threats (ILO, 2012b). Migrant domestic workers' cooperatives are emerging as alternatives to commercial employment agencies to negotiate better conditions of employment, including maternity protection and paid leave days, in countries as diverse as the Republic of Korea, Trinidad and Tobago, the USA, India and the Philippines (*ibid.*).

The results of a recent mapping exercise of over 40 cooperatives of domestic workers from around the world show that cooperatives of domestic workers help them with economies of scale, voice and representation, as well as a wide array of support services which help formalize their work. They provide their members with higher wages and better working conditions, member-controlled operations and decision-making processes, and greater bargaining power to leverage improved wages and conditions. They undertake job-matching, skills training, accountancy and awareness-raising to their members, among other services. There are no additional fees or costs charged to the worker-members, as the cooperative is not an outside intermediary, but one that is run by the worker-members for their own needs and interests (ILO, 2015b).

The all-women worker-owned cooperative Si Se Puede! (We can do it!) provides housecleaning services in New York City. It helps its members, who are largely immigrants, come out of situations that imply the risk of forced labour. The cooperative has secured wages at USD20 per hour, up from the USD7–8 per hour that most worker-members earned before. Si Se Puede! also provides members with educational and skills-building opportunities (ILO, 2014a).

The owners of these cooperatives are worker-members who take part in decision-making processes and aim to improve the labour conditions. This is a critical element in ensuring that they are not co-opted into pseudo-cooperatives, as has been the experience in some countries. While these cooperatives may not be able to remove all the elements of forced or compulsory labour, their governance structure reduces the vulnerability of workers and removes the moral hazards as well as its consequences, such as transfer of placement costs to workers, often found among other private recruitment service providers.

Cooperatives and non-discrimination at work

Hundreds of millions of people suffer from discrimination on the basis of race, colour, sex, religion, political opinion, national extraction, social origin or other grounds which are continuously emerging in the world of work. This not only violates most basic human rights, but has wider social and economic consequences, stifling opportunities, wasting the human talent needed for economic progress, and accentuating social tensions and inequalities. Certain population groups and categories of workers are clearly more exposed to such violations than others. This section focuses on discrimination faced by indigenous peoples and people living with disabilities as well as gender-based discrimination in the world of work, reflecting on how cooperatives can potentially be leveraged to assist populations who face discrimination to support themselves, their households and communities (ILO, 2014e).

Historically, indigenous peoples have long borne the weight of multiple forms of discrimination (ILO, 2013). It is estimated that although they constitute about 5 per cent of the world's population, they account for 15 per cent of the world's poor (ILO, 2016a). In Honduras, for example, an estimated 71 per cent of indigenous peoples live below the poverty line (IFAD, 2011). They are affected by issues that stem from a lack of directed attention, consultation and participation, as well as recognition and protection of culture and rights, especially rights to land, territories and resources. The livelihoods of indigenous peoples that are based on traditional and sustainable use of natural resources are also severely under threat by the impacts of climate change.

Cooperatives of indigenous peoples have served a number of purposes, including securing livelihoods, creating jobs and enabling access to market opportunities, and formalizing informal economic activities and protecting workers. In addition, they have supported preservation of traditional knowledge and environmental sustainability, while advancing gender equality and women's empowerment. Indigenous women's weaving cooperatives in Oaxaca, Mexico, not only foster economic empowerment, establishing them as independent artisans in global markets, but also assist them in gaining political and cultural rights in their communities (ILO, 2016a).

Worldwide, there are at least 785 million women and men of working age with disabilities. They often face enormous obstacles to equal opportunities in the world of work, ranging from attitudinal and physical to informational barriers. Disabled men and particularly disabled women experience higher rates of unemployment and economic inactivity than their non-disabled peers and they are also more vulnerable to discrimination in the workplace (WHO and World Bank, 2011).

Social cooperatives designed to promote the inclusion of women and men with disabilities into the workplace are emerging across the world. Increasingly, these cooperatives encourage the active involvement of people with disabilities in the management of their enterprises. Social cooperatives in Italy deliver services such as providing work integration for disadvantaged groups into society, including people with disabilities. Social cooperatives specializing in work integration must have at least 30 per cent of workers belong to disadvantaged groups according to the social cooperative law, which also foresees a reduction of the labour cost of these persons. Approximately 45,000 workers from disadvantaged groups work in social cooperatives in Italy (ILO, 2015a).

Despite commitments in many international agreements and treaties to the principle of gender equality, women worldwide continue to face oppression, discrimination and human rights violations. These take many forms, from violence, including harassment against women, to restricted access for women to education and health services. Compared with men, women continue to earn less, are more likely to partake in unpaid labour, and are more apt to be excluded from decent work and opportunities for advancement (ILO, 2014e).

The social and organizational nature of cooperatives can give them a comparative advantage relative to other types of enterprises in advancing gender equality. Women's participation in cooperatives seems to have increased over the past 20 years, together with growing attention to gender issues, increased access for women into leadership roles within cooperatives, and the rise of women-owned cooperatives. In addition, women's access to employment is facilitated by housing and care service cooperatives, providing them with affordable and accessible options that enable them to work outside their homes (ICA and ILO, 2015). Under-representation of women as members and leaders still persists in certain sectors of the cooperative movement, such as agriculture, where women form the majority of the workforce (ILO, 2012d).[13]

There are exceptions to this, however, with various manifestations of women leadership that can be observed across the cooperative movement. There is a strong presence of women members among worker cooperatives in Spain (49 per cent) and nearly 40 per cent of those women are in leadership positions (ILO, 2014b). According to the data from the International Cooperative and Mutual Insurance Federation, the number of women in leadership positions in cooperative insurers is larger than in other types of enterprises. Nine of the largest 100 cooperative and mutual insurers in the world have women CEOs, while only one of the top 100 stock company insurers globally is led by a woman. In countries such as Canada the figures are still higher for mutual and cooperative insurer CEOs, at 27 per cent (ICMIF, 2016).

Cooperatives and freedom of association and right to collective bargaining

Freedom of association is an enabling right to the enjoyment of all other FPRW, as it opens the door to participatory actions against forced labour, the protection of children from abuses, and responsive measures based on non-discrimination and equality (ILO, 2012a). The right of workers and employers to form and join organizations of their own choosing is an integral part of a free and open society. In many cases, workers' and employers' organizations have played a significant role in the development of their countries' democratic processes and institutions. Nevertheless, challenges in applying these principles persist: in some countries certain categories of workers are denied the right of association, workers' and employers' organizations are illegally suspended or interfered with, or threatened with violence, for example.[14]

As employers, cooperatives need to engage in effective labour relations and social dialogue with unions representing their workforce. As with any other enterprise, issues around freedom of association and the right to collective bargaining apply to cooperatives. While the majority of cooperatives are small and medium-sized enterprises, many of them grow into larger businesses. These exist particularly in sectors such as agriculture, retail, finance and housing, and while most of them have good labour relations, there are those that have faced labour disputes with regard to freedom of association and the right to collective bargaining among their workers. In addition, there are examples of workers establishing their own cooperatives and becoming owners as well as workers, insolvent enterprises transitioning to worker cooperatives, and trade unions forming cooperatives to provide services for their members.

The relationship between trade unions and cooperatives goes back a long way, and they have many similarities. Both are membership-based organizations, whose main objective is to protect and promote their members' economic and social interests. They share similar principles, such as voluntary adherence and resignation, democratic management and control, and a commitment to membership education and training.

Despite their common origins, joint history and common goals of fostering economic security and industrial democracy, genuine collaboration between trade unions and cooperatives has been rather limited in the past few decades (ILO, 2014f). Recently, however, a number of trade unions have started rediscovering cooperatives for their members, or extending their support for cooperatives among workers in the informal economy with the idea that economic activity based on more ethical and democratic principles can be possible.

Examples of solidarity between trade unions and cooperatives on a range of issues, such as curtailing the deterioration of worker rights, flexibilization of labour, loss of jobs and privatization, are expected to continue to grow as a response strategy to the changes that are taking place in the world of work. One of them is the Union Taxi in Denver, USA, a cooperative established by its 800 taxi driver worker-owners, which has a collective bargaining agreement through the support of a trade union (Peck, 2016).

Cooperatives can also promote a worker-owner governance model through, e.g., worker buyouts of failing enterprises in which workers buy firms with economic potential and transform them into worker ownership. A worker cooperative model does not always stem from enterprise failure, but may be attributable to the retirement of ageing owners as well, particularly where there is no clear plan for the future of the enterprise (Alperovitz, 2016).

Recent examples of worker buyouts include Brazil, where the metalworkers' union Sindicato dos Metalúrgicos do ABC (SMABC) successfully brought back Latin America's largest industrial forge, Conforja, renamed Uniforja, from bankruptcy more than ten years ago as a worker-owned business. It has built on this experience to help establish a new cooperative federation, Unisol. In Paraguay, an important ceramics business making roof tiles has been rescued by its workers and relaunched as the cooperative Cerro Guy (Orbaiceta, 2013). There are similar examples in other countries like Uruguay and Argentina.

In Europe, unions have also been actively engaged in such ventures. French trade unions have played a key role in several cases of business failure where the enterprise has been re-established under the SCOP (worker cooperative) legal framework. For the printing company Hélio-Corbeil, for example, the creation of a worker cooperative has successfully saved around 80 jobs. French textile firm Fontanille tells a similar story. After being run for 150 years as a family business, it was successfully saved from failure through its transformation to a cooperative. The workers helped recapitalize the business by investing their redundancy payments (Monaco and Pastorelli, 2013).

The growth of these enterprises continues, and while their productivity remains lower than their potential, the wages in these enterprises are above average in their respective sectors. The survival rate of the converted enterprises is relatively high – a trend that can be seen in other types of worker cooperatives as well (Pérotin, 2014). In addition, an increasing number of other countries have recently passed legislation that facilitates such enterprise restructuring, including Italy, Spain, Portugal, France, Brazil, Greece and Canada (ILO, 2014d).

Trade unions also have an important role in ensuring that democratic governance structures are established in the newly created cooperatives. Cooperatively run conversions of previously failed companies must operate successfully, both as businesses and as democratic bodies. If either of these is missing, failure may result. They should not, however, try to run the cooperatives themselves. After they help their members establish cooperatives, they should allow them to be managed independently.

Conclusions

It is not sufficient to conclude that cooperatives are 'better' employers just because of being based on values and principles.[15] Cooperatives are both responsible for respecting and promoting FPRW throughout their operations, and well placed to advance and advocate for their achievement through education, training, services and democratic decision-making processes, among others. Through their principles, values and governance structures, cooperatives can provide a model that allows for participation and inclusion of all stakeholders, including workers, in the management of the enterprise. They can bring in institutional infrastructure and economies of scale in disseminating the FPRW messages and practices. There are, however, many cooperatives that are not governed according to cooperative principles and values, either because of lack of knowledge and expertise – on account of not truly being cooperative enterprises – or finding themselves in a national environment that does not provide an adequate regulatory framework, including in terms of monitoring and sanctions. Even when they get their governance model to function effectively, they operate as enterprises in the logic of the market. Therefore, cooperatives need to find ways to bridge the gap between their ideals and the realities of the context, including the rapidly changing world of work on account of a series of factors, including technology, climate and demographics, to mention a few. This is why segments of the cooperative movement explore the links with the commons (e.g. platform cooperativism, see Schneider, Chapter 14 in this volume), ethical consumption, and equitable and fair trade (e.g. retail cooperatives that are serving users who seek goods and services that are produced with socially and environmentally conscious standards).

While the cooperative movement has started to recognize the need for increased engagement with global policy discussions, such as the Sustainable Development Goals, climate change and fair trade, more specific involvement on decent work platforms at the national, regional and international levels would be welcome. For instance, on the issue of equal pay, the cooperative movement could get involved and become active members in the ILO/UN-Women Equal Pay Coalition launched in 2017 in follow-up to the 61st session of the Commission on the Status of Women on women's economic empowerment in the changing world of work.

Cooperatives can play a number of key roles in advancing FPRW. As critical players in some key global supply chains such as agriculture, they provide scale to smallholders, helping them access markets, information, technology and finance with conditions that they could not enjoy on their own. Furthermore, cooperatives can use their broad membership base to reach out to large numbers of producers or consumers, educating and raising awareness of their members and communities on FPRW as well as other topics, and providing services such as financial services, vocational training, and extension of social protection. Organized in secondary- and tertiary-level organizations, cooperatives can encourage other private sector institutions as well as governments to adopt policies advancing FPRW. Through their training and education infrastructure, they can disseminate awareness and information on FPRW. Cooperative extension workers can be equipped with knowledge on FPRW to detect violations and relay messages. Cooperative and other research institutions can also conduct assessments of the cooperative model's performance compared with other types of enterprises in advancing FPRW.

Enterprise-level actions, such as codes of conduct, private certification schemes, or Global Compact and Fairtrade initiatives, are important in advancing FPRW in cooperatives. However, deepening their recognition of FPRW requires them to scale up from these enterprise-level actions to wider sectoral and regional-level commitment for sustainable and responsible business practices. At all these levels, implementation and monitoring mechanisms need to be put in place to turn their commitment into action. Good practices and emerging challenges on FPRW need to be better documented in order to generate a comparative database of cooperative practices compared with other types of enterprises. In order to fill gaps in understanding the performance and role of cooperatives in advancing FPRW, one practical step would be, for example, the development of guidelines and an assessment tool on FPRW and other decent work indicators. Such a move could help cooperatives play a stronger role in guaranteeing FPRW to enable, as outlined in the preamble to the 1998 Declaration, 'the persons concerned (. . .) to claim their fair share of the wealth which they have helped to generate, and to achieve fully their human potential' (ILO, 1998).

Notes

* Copyright © 2018 International Labour Organization. The responsibility for opinions expressed in the original article rests solely with its author, and publication does not constitute an endorsement by the International Labour Office of the opinions expressed in it.
1 A cooperative is 'an autonomous association of persons united voluntarily to meet their common economic, social, and cultural needs and aspirations through a jointly-owned and democratically-controlled enterprise'. The *Statement on the Cooperative Identity*, adopted by the General Assembly of the International Co-operative Alliance in 1995.
2 Among these efforts, ILO and COPAC are working on development of statistical definitions for the main concepts relevant to the identification and classification of cooperatives, and development of recommendations for data collection methods for collecting and producing statistics on cooperatives.
3 United Nations *International Covenant on Economic, Social and Cultural Rights*, 1966. https://treaties.un.org/Pages/ViewDetails.aspx?src=IND&mtdsg_no=IV-3&chapter=4&clang=_en
4 The eight Fundamental Conventions of the ILO are: *Freedom of Association and Protection of the Right to Organise Convention*, 1948 (No. 87), the *Right to Organise and Collective Bargaining Convention*, 1949 (No. 98); *Forced Labour Convention*, 1930 (No. 29), *Abolition of Forced Labour Convention*, 1957 (No. 105); *Minimum Age Convention*, 1973 (No. 138), *Worst Forms of Child Labour Convention*, 1999 (No. 182); *Equal Remuneration Convention*, 1951 (No. 100) and *Discrimination (Employment and Occupation) Convention*, 1958 (No. 111).
5 See *Universal Declaration of Human Rights*, 1948. www.un.org/en/universal-declaration-human-rights/. Apart from the abolition of child labour, all FPRW are found in the *Declaration of Human Rights*.
   Article 20: 'Everyone has the right to freedom of peaceful assembly and association.'
   Article 23: '(1) Everyone has the right to work, to free choice of employment, to just and favourable conditions of work and to protection against unemployment.
   (2) Everyone, without any discrimination, has the right to equal pay for equal work.
   (3) Everyone who works has the right to just and favourable remuneration ensuring for himself and his family an existence worthy of human dignity, and supplemented, if necessary, by other means of social protection.
   (4) Everyone has the right to form and to join trade unions for the protection of his interests.'
   Article 4: 'No one shall be held in slavery or servitude; slavery and the slave trade shall be prohibited in all their forms.'
6 The cooperative values and principles are defined in the *Statement of the Cooperative Identity* (1995), by International Co-operative Alliance. See http://ica.coop/en/what-co-operative for more information on these.
7 CICOPA is a sectoral organization of the ICA. See www.cicopa.coop/.
8 www.unglobalcompact.org/what-is-gc/mission/principles

9 SA8000 Social Accountability 8000 Standard is a global social accountability standard for decent working conditions, developed and overseen by Social Accountability International (SAI) www.sa-intl.org/index.cfm?fuseaction=page.viewpage&pageid=1689

10 2014 *Declaration of the International Summit of Cooperatives*, www.sommetinter.coop/sites/default/files/2014isc_declaration_en.pdf

11 2016 *Declaration of the International Summit of Cooperatives*, www.sommetinter.coop/en/2016-edition/2016-declaration

12 www.fairtrade.net/standards/aims-of-fairtrade-standards.html

13 See also Dias and Ogando, Chapter 8 in this volume.

14 ILO International Labour Standards on Freedom of Association, http://ilo.org/global/standards/subjects-covered-by-international-labour-standards/freedom-of-association/lang--en/index.htm.

15 See Schwettmann's chapter in this volume (Chapter 2).

References

Alperovitz, Gar. "6 ways we're already leading an economic revolution", *Yes! Magazine*, 7 September 2016. Accessed 6 February 2017. www.yesmagazine.org/new-economy/6-ways-were-already-leading-an-economic-revolution-20160907.

Amegashie-Viglo, Simon. Operation of credit union schemes as a strategy for meeting the financial expectations of the marginalised: The case of Ho municipality credit unions in Ghana, *Research Journal of Finance and Accounting* 5, no. 14, (2014): 20–34.

CICOPA. *World Declaration on Worker Cooperatives*, Approved by the ICA General Assembly in Cartagena, Colombia, on 23 September 2005. 2005.

Co-operative News. Co-op group offers paid work and a new life to victims of modern slave trade, *Co-operative News*, 1 March 2017. Accessed 2 March 2017. www.thenews.coop/114272/news/co-operatives/co-op-group-offers-paid-work-new-life-victims-modern-slave-trade/.

Eum, Hyungsik. *Cooperatives and employment: Second global report 2017*. Brussels: CICOPA, 2017.

International Co-operative Alliance (ICA). *Co-operatives and global supply chains*, Policy Brief. 2015.

International Co-operative Alliance (ICA) and International Labour Office (ILO). *Advancing gender equality: The co-operative way*. Geneva, 2015.

International Cooperative and Mutual Insurance Federation (ICMIF). *Cooperative and mutual insurance sector has significantly higher numbers of women CEOs than stock companies*, 2016. Accessed 2 March 2017. www.icmif.org/cooperative-and-mutual-insurance-sector-has-significantly-higher-numbers-women-ceos-stock-companies.

International Fund for Agricultural Development (IFAD). *Enabling poor rural people to overcome poverty in Honduras*. Rome, 2011.

International Labour Office (ILO). *Strengthening employers' activities against forced labour*. Geneva, n.d.

_____. *Forced Labour Convention, 1930 (No. 29)*. Geneva, 1930.

_____. *ILO Declaration on Fundamental Principles and Rights at Work and its follow-up*. Geneva, 1998.

_____. *Promotion of Cooperatives Recommendation, 2002 (No. 193)*. Geneva, 2002.

_____. *Cooperating out of child labour: Harnessing the untapped potential of cooperatives and the cooperative movement to eliminate child labour*. Geneva, 2009.

_____. *International labour migration: A rights-based approach*. Geneva, 2010.

_____. *General survey on the Fundamental Conventions concerning Right at Work in light of the ILO Declaration on Social Justice for a Fair Globalization, 2008*. Report III (Part 1B), International Labour Conference, 101st Session, Geneva, 2012. Geneva, 2012a.

____. *ILO Indicators of forced labour.* Geneva, 2012b.

____. *Fundamental principles and rights at work: From commitment to action. Recurrent discussion under the ILO Declaration on Social Justice for a Fair Globalization and the follow-up to the ILO Declaration on Fundamental Principles and Rights at Work,* Report VI, International Labour Conference, 101st Session, Geneva, 2012. Geneva, 2012c.

____. *How women fare in East African cooperatives: The case of Kenya, Tanzania and Uganda.* Dar es Salaam: ILO Office for Tanzania, Kenya, Rwanda and Uganda, 2012d.

____. *Understanding the Indigenous and Tribal Peoples Convention, 1989 (No. 169): Handbook for ILO Tripartite constituents.* Geneva, 2013.

____. *Cooperating out of isolation: Domestic workers' cooperatives.* Cooperatives and the World of Work Series No. 2. Geneva, 2014a.

____. *Cooperatives and the sustainable development goals: A contribution to the post-2015 development debate.* Geneva, 2014b.

____. *Cooperatives' considerable clout in the fight against child labour.* 2014c. Accessed 2 March 2017. www.ilo.org/global/about-the-ilo/newsroom/news/WCMS_249483/lang--en/index.htm.

____. *Job preservation through worker cooperatives: An overview of international experiences and strategies.* Geneva, 2014d.

____. *Leveraging the cooperative advantage for women's empowerment and gender equality.* Cooperatives and the World of Work Series No. 1. Geneva, 2014e.

____. *Rebuilding links: Trade unions and cooperatives get together again.* 2014f. Accessed 2 March 2017. www.ilo.org/global/about-the-ilo/newsroom/news/WCMS_243813/lang--en/index.htm.

____. *At work together: The cooperative advantage for people with disabilities.* Cooperatives and the World of Work Series No. 3. Geneva, 2015a.

____. *For many domestic workers, co-ops hold the key for decent work.* 2015b. Accessed 2 March 2017. https://iloblog.org/2015/07/03/for-many-domestic-workers-co-ops-hold-the-key-to-decent-work/.

____. *ILO Global estimates on migrant workers: Results and methodology.* Geneva, 2015c.

____. *Securing rights, creating jobs and ensuring sustainability: A cooperative way for empowering indigenous peoples.* Cooperatives and the World of Work Series No. 5. Geneva, 2016a.

____. *World employment social outlook: Trends 2016.* Geneva, 2016b.

____. *Global estimates of child labour: Results and trends, 2012-2016.* Geneva, 2017.

ILO, Walk Free Foundation and International Organization for Migration. *Global estimates of modern slavery: Forced labour and forced marriage.* Geneva, 2017.

Monaco, Marina, and Luca Pastorelli. Trade unions and worker cooperatives in Europe: A win-win relationship, *International Journal of Labour Research* 5, no. 2 (2013): 227–249.

Orbaiceta, José. Trade unions and cooperatives: The experience of CICOPA-Mercosur, *International Journal of Labour Research* 5, no. 2 (2013): 179–194.

Peck, Michael. Building the people's ownership economy through union co-ops. In *Ours to hack and to own: The rise of platform cooperativism, a new vision for the future of work and a fairer internet,* edited by Trebor Scholz and Nathan Schneider, 208–212. New York: OR Books, 2016.

Pérotin, Virginie. *What do we really know about worker co-operatives?* Manchester: Co-operatives UK, 2014.

World Health Organization (WHO) and World Bank. *World report on disability.* Geneva, WHO, 2011.

4

THE AUTONOMY OR HETERONOMY OF COOPERATIVE WORKER OWNERSHIP

Manuel García Jiménez

Introduction

In some parts of the world, members of worker-owned enterprises work in conditions which fail to comply not only with the basic standards applied to salaried employees in their country, but often with international regulation, thus constituting an infringement of their human rights.[1] They do so, not out of any voluntary wish for poor working conditions, but out of necessity; they are driven by the need to maintain their jobs. When contracting with other companies, or when selling their output on the open market at low prices (which also means that they are selling their labour below market rates), they are clearly engaging in unfair competition. This highlights the vulnerability of these enterprises, because, in these parts of the world, what is illegal in other companies is perfectly legal in worker-owned cooperatives, in that their work is deemed to lie outside the scope of labour law.

Labour law is an established mechanism for protecting labour from capital, by guaranteeing certain inalienable (non-traded) workers' rights. In return, workers yield to their employers the fruits of their work and submit to the power of management.

In worker cooperatives the scenario is different, at least in appearance. The capital in such entities belongs to the workers themselves, plays a subordinate economic role and has no influence on the distribution of power, because it operates on the democratic principle of one person, one vote.

In such circumstances, a tutelary application of labour law has not been deemed imperative, because it is the workers themselves who manage their own businesses, adopt the most suitable mode of organization and share the results of their work in proportion to the work done by each person, and it is assumed that they will not harm their own interests.

However, as in the case of the employment contract, which is theoretically a free agreement between equals before the law, the free will of a party is often compromised by the overriding need to survive, a situation that must be restored by applying protected rights; another consideration bearing upon cooperative work is that the same need to survive may oblige people to accept less favourable conditions than guaranteed-wage workers enjoy, to sell their labour, directly or indirectly, thereby compromising their autonomy and turning it into heteronomous work.

Moreover, this situation can be exploited by other companies or brokers of labour, distorting the labour market. Cooperatives in this way become a means of circumventing the protection afforded by labour legislation and pave the way to self-exploitation.

Labour law should embrace worker ownership, recognizing it as another mode of work and respecting its distinctive features; in accordance with the concept of decent work, the law should subsume the notion of rights at work under that of human rights, in accordance with the most recent international guidelines. Cooperative law and the statutes of each cooperative should also include a commitment to that aim.

The protection of work by labour legislation

The legal concept of a worker is constructed on the basis of those who, deprived of the means of production, are obliged to sell their labour or capacity to work in return for a salary.

> Capitalist production, therefore, of itself reproduces a separation between labour power and the means of labour. It thereby reproduces and perpetuates the condition for exploiting the labourer. It incessantly forces him to sell his labour-power in order to live, and enables the capitalist to purchase labour-power in order that he may enrich himself (. . .). His economic bondage is both brought about concealed by the periodic sale of himself, by his change of masters, and by the oscillations in the market-price of labour-power.
>
> *(Marx, 1990, p. 723)*

These workers, 'subject to employment contracts' (Montoya, 2014, p. 281), are accorded by the law, in their contractual relationship with the employer, certain rights that were gradually established over the course of the evolution of industrial society. Furthermore, in the early days of labour law (Martín, 1987), a need arises to give a political response to a new social reality (social issue), characterized by the generalization of dependent work, in which workers, in exchange for a salary, grant employers the fruits of their labour and submit themselves to their power of management, control and discipline.

Thus one of the fundamental characteristics of traditional labour relations is precisely the hierarchical power that employers exercise over workers, common to a whole range of countries and legal traditions, which combines three linked elements: (a) managerial power; (b) power of control; and (c) disciplinary power. So much is this the case that the presence of this hierarchical power, established by law and by jurisprudence, has become the element that distinguishes dependent work from independent work and, consequently, is the key to accessing worker protection legislation in the various jurisdictions. However, in order to avoid an unlimited expansion of the scope of labour relations, labour tribunals initially adopted a rigorous and strict interpretation, deeming management power to be present only in those cases in which the worker was subject to the control of management, exercised in organizational and disciplinary terms directly by the employer. This interpretation would entail a wide range of occupational activities being excluded from the scope of the work relation and the corresponding legal protection, despite being activities that would in fact benefit from such protection (Casale, 2011).

Meanwhile, legal protection for this dependent work has been designed on the basis of a collection of reciprocal and actionable rights and obligations between employers and employees (capital-labour), overseen by the state. This type of work has been distinguished from independent or autonomous work, which falls outside the set of rights mentioned earlier, since there is no one against whom such rights can be exercised; consequently, it has been left out of the legal-social sphere of protection, this also being the domain in which worker ownership (*trabajo asociado*) is usually located (Roelants *et al.*, 2014).

For these reasons, the concept of workers as limited to the sphere of subordinated work has been overtaken, almost since its origins, by the gradual emergence of new social realities and by the growing visibility of situations that already existed. Thus, for several decades, an increasingly large grey area has been apparent between dependent and independent work, which has made it ever more difficult to determine whether an employment relationship exists or not, since in many situations the respective rights and obligations of the interested parties are by no means clear. In other situations, however, the aim is to conceal the employment relationship, or exploiting the loopholes and shortcomings that exist in the legal framework, whether in its interpretation or in its application. Too frequently, vulnerable workers are those who most suffer in these situations (Casale, 2011, *Executive Summary*).

There is a need, then, to redefine the concept of the protectable worker, as well as the dependency or autonomy of work, something that the ILO is currently working on, leading the debate on the future of the employment relationship and its legal framework.[2] Cooperative work needs to be included as part of this debate.

Delineating the concepts of work and worker

In social and economic terms, the concepts of work and workers encompass much wider situations and realities than those narrowly defined in employment legislation. According to the Dictionary of the Spanish Language, *trabajador* (worker) refers to 'one who works', while the word *trabajar* (to work), among other meanings, is defined as: 'to occupy oneself in any type of physical or intellectual activity'; 'to have a remunerated occupation in a company, institution, etc.'; 'to practice a specific profession or trade'. Its meaning, depending on the context, may in general terms relate to an activity carried out for oneself or for others, whether for a third party (in a company or institution), or on one's own behalf (through the practice of a profession or trade).

Similarly, the *International Labour Organization Thesaurus* (ILO, 2014) defines work as the set of human activities, paid or unpaid, that produce goods or services in an economy, or supply the needs of a community, or provide a person's accustomed means of livelihood.

The word 'work' therefore refers to a category of human activity, which may be unpaid, to satisfy one's own needs, one's family's or those of the wider community; or if paid, to satisfy external needs via the marketplace. The latter is restricted, under the term 'employment', to a specific category, defined as 'work carried out in return for payment' (salary, wages, commission, tips, piecework payments or payments in kind). From a wider and more statistical perspective, employment 'also refers to the number of people in paid employment and self-employment', regardless of the dependency relationship (dependent-salaried, or independent self-employment).

From this perspective, therefore, paid work or employment includes the categories of both formal and informal work, work undertaken individually, as well as autonomous or independent work, or work carried out collectively, within an organization, for a third party and subject to the management of an employer, but also on one's own behalf, in a combined or self-managed way, in a cooperative for example.

In any event, however, all such employment-work shares a common distinctive feature, in that it is carried out for commercial exchange: workers work in order to make a living, to obtain for their work – whose fruit does not in itself have any direct utility – an income (remuneration) with which to buy everything that is needed and is produced by others (Gorz, 1989, p. 137).

From such perspective, it may be concluded that a worker is anyone who produces (goods or services), not for their own consumption, but for the market and in competition with other producers.

Autonomy and heteronomy in work

Just as in the early years of employment legislation, the legal establishment of minimum working conditions as the inalienable right of workers was rejected on doctrinal liberal grounds, citing the defence of contractual freedom: 'Attempting to ensure that workers are free in their contracts turns out to be absurd: can a choice between an inadequate working day and dying of hunger be called freedom?' (Canalejas, 1902); currently, one of the arguments most frequently used to oppose the legal establishment of minimum working conditions in non-salaried work is the safeguard of liberty and autonomy, and self-management in the case of cooperatives.

The central issue is that in both cases work is performed out of necessity, and the necessity is itself imbued with dependency, which compromises autonomy. As Marx (1993, p. 593) put it, 'the realm of freedom actually begins only where labour which is determined by necessity and mundane considerations ceases'. We are thus in the presence of the classic distinction between work done for pleasure and work done for necessity, between action undertaken for fun or leisure and 'productive work', depending on the aim that human effort has in view (Alonso, 1981, p. 25).

If the protection and guardianship of workers is justified by the unbreakable link between work and person and the need to work to make a living, it is clear that these cannot remain restricted to wage-earning and structured work, supported exclusively by arguments concerning their third-party nature and dependence, conceived under the formality of the employment contract, without questioning the frontiers of autonomy and independence.

As Gorz (1989, pp. 167) argues, 'autonomous activities' are those which constitute an end in themselves, which are used by individuals to experience their own sovereignty and realize themselves as persons. Commercial activities are by definition excluded: their end is commercial exchange, which relativizes and contaminates the intrinsic, unmeasurable value of the action or work concerned. All work undertaken with a view to exchange needs to be productive; it is governed by its efficiency and the latter is always measured in terms relative to the market in question. This calculation of economic rationality is what will determine the organization, the quantity and quality of the work and its rhythms, enabling a respectable living to be made, 'regardless of natural rhythms' (Gorz, 1989, p. 109).

In present-day societies, our needs are chiefly supplied by heteronomous work, that is to say by socially divided, specialized and professionalized work, carried out with one eye on its commercial value, and neither the exchange value of such work, nor the nature, nor the end, nor the significance can be freely determined by those who work:

> The heteronomy of a job *does not lie* merely in the fact that I must submit to the orders of a superior in the hierarchy, or, which amounts to the same thing, to the rhythm of a pre-programmed machine. Even if I control my own time schedule, rhythm of work and the way in which I complete a highly skilled, complex task, my work is still heteronomous when the objective or final product to which it contributes is outside my control. Heteronomous work is not necessarily completely devoid of autonomy: it may be heteronomous because the specialized, even complex activities involved, which require a considerable degree of technical autonomy of the workers, are pre-determined by a system (organization) to whose functioning they contribute as if they were the cogs in a machine.
>
> *(Gorz, 1989, p. 171, note 31, emphasis added)*

Economic activity, by definition, cannot be an end in itself, although it may include – when it is cooperative, self-organized and self-managed – certain aspects of autonomy that make it pleasurable and agreeable. 'Autonomy also stands opposed to necessity, not because all necessary activity is inevitably heteronomous (this is not the case at all), but because the autonomy of an activity dictated by necessity is condemned to remain purely formal' (Gorz, 1989, p. 166).

In many instances the hierarchical power is located outside the work organization, and does not involve direct participation in the management, control or discipline of the completion of specific tasks, but rather the imposition, often contractually binding, of certain results or prices, which must be accepted as a matter of vital necessity.[3] This is because necessity places the parties in unequal situations, a phenomenon that is present not only in the employment contract but, in general, in the contractual relationships between consumers and large corporations, which demand and frequently receive legal protection.

Labour rights in non-salaried work

The dependency of non-salaried work is slowly gaining visibility, highlighting the need to provide it with protection. This is the approach taken by the ILO, in recognizing that, owing to its origins, it has essentially focused its attention on the needs of wage-earning workers and companies in the structured sector, but that the world of work does not end there, nor is the ILO's mandate exhausted by advocating improvements in working conditions – rather it should take up the case of those who work on the margins of the structured labour market: unregulated wage-earners, the self-employed, and also the worker-members of worker cooperatives, domestic workers, etc. In short, all those who work have rights arising from their work, something that is reflected in the *Decent Work Agenda* (ILO, 2016a, 2016b).

The concept of decent work (ILO, 1999) is aimed at overcoming the limitations of the employment contract and formulating what ought to constitute, in the globalized world, a good job or decent employment, conceived of as that which lends dignity and enables the development of one's own capabilities. Work is not decent if it is carried out without respecting basic labour rights and principles, or does not allow an income that is fair and proportional to the effort invested, or suffers from sexual or any other type of discrimination, or is carried out without social protection, or excludes social dialogue (Sen, 2000).

Such proposals are rooted in the *Universal Declaration of Human Rights* (UN, 1948), article 23.1, which proclaims that everyone has the right to work and the free choice of one's work, which encompasses, according to article 6 of the *International Covenant on Economic, Social and Cultural Rights* (UN, 1966): 'the right of everyone to the opportunity to gain his living by work which he freely chooses', which in turn implies the possibility of freely participating in the activities of production, the provision of services to society and the enjoyment of the benefits obtained through these activities, but in such a way that these benefits enable an appropriate standard of living and conditions of life to be ensured.[4] Thus the right to work does not just mean the right to any occupation; rather, it is bolstered by others that underpin work as a universal right.

If such rights are considered as inherent to the person, inalienable in the sphere of the exercise of their activity, of their work, regardless of the formal role they play in the production process, then people who make their living in certain worker-owned cooperatives can in no way be regarded as being excluded from the international regulations relating to the protection and dignity of work and of the worker.

Recourse to human rights as a means of limiting contractual freedom is nowadays used as a tool to counteract the loss of legal protection for wage-earning work in a labour market that is becoming increasingly deregulated and that 'gives rise to various forms of dependent work with highly varying levels of protection, atypical forms of regulation, featuring a sector that is protected and grey areas with flexible relationships or entirely excluded from employment regulations'. In this context, the Spanish Constitutional Court[5] has ruled that the signing of a contract 'in no way entails the deprivation for one of the parties, the worker, of the rights that the Constitution bestows upon him as a citizen'. This has served to unequivocally sanction the idea of the efficacy of the fundamental rights of the person in dealings between private individuals, by virtue of their unassailability (Goñi, 2014, pp. 19–21).

If this idea assumes that fundamental rights bind everyone (not just public authorities) and must also be respected in the realm of work, the same reasoning can be extended to other types of contractual relationship, in which people's work is involved, as well as to cooperative labour relations, regardless of the legal classification they may receive. The same applies if labour rights as a whole are deemed to be human rights inherent to the person.

Autonomy and heteronomy in worker cooperatives

The democratic establishment of certain working conditions forms part of the autonomy and self-governing essence of worker cooperatives; however, just as many wage-earners are obliged by necessity to accept non-permitted working conditions, some cooperatives are obliged to accept contractual conditions that make it impossible to maintain 'decent' working conditions, respectful of labour rights, in this case unprotected by law, which regular businesses would not be able to take on because they would have to cover the costs of protected working conditions (García, 2014). This is also why recourse is frequently made to the cooperative formula in order to avoid the right to work (Cruz and Hernández, 2014; García and Valencia, 2012; Roelants *et al.*, 2014).

In such circumstances, can it be claimed that a worker cooperative is autonomous and independent? Is it really the case that the members freely decide to adopt certain working conditions that are inferior to basic standards, or are they forced by need, or are they used by other companies and business people?

Cooperative autonomy

Following the general and universally accepted concept in the *Statement on the Cooperative Identity* (ICA, 1995), referred to by Recommendation 193 *concerning Promotion of Cooperatives* (ILO, 2002),[6] cooperatives share three fundamental elements, even though their scope varies according to the legal and legislative arrangements of individual countries:

a.   *'Autonomous association of persons united voluntarily'*. The autonomous legal entity that arises is associative and personal in nature, not a function of capital inputs, and the existence of a voluntary and individual act of joining seems to entail the existence of a deed of partnership giving rise to obligations and rights;

b.   *'United (. . .) to meet common economic, social and cultural needs and aspirations'*. The aim of the association is to meet certain shared needs, which implies some kind of action (interaction), and an active membership, which enables the collective satisfaction of such needs;

c.   *'Through a jointly-owned and democratically-controlled enterprise'*. The objective expressed in paragraph b. above is brought about by means of an enterprise structure created for this end, to which it owes its existence. This enterprise is distinguished by the three features: it is not oriented towards a return on the capital invested, but rather to satisfying its members; it is the property of the users or recipients of its commercial purpose; and finally, management and control are democratic, which implies that they are egalitarian.

Based on the principles underlying the organization and operation of cooperatives, in terms of the various well-known components that constitute them,[7] it also follows that they are open and voluntary organizations, democratically managed by their members; they are autonomous and self-help entities, but with a social vocation reflected in the fact that they devote part of their resources to providing education, to strengthening the cooperative movement and to bringing about the sustainable development of their communities by means of policies approved by their members.

What most marks them out, however, as enterprises that meet the needs of their members, are three components that together constitute the principle of the 'economic participation of their members', related to questions of ownership, management and the distribution of economic results.

a.   The members contribute equal shares to their cooperative's capital as a condition of being a member, but they manage it democratically.

b.   The return on capital, if any, is limited.

c.   Profits are distributed to members in proportion to their transactions with the cooperative.

If the cooperative is a worker cooperative, the 'common needs and aspirations' that are to be 'jointly met', as laid down to in the ICA definition, focus on employment.

A worker cooperative is thus 'an autonomous association of persons united voluntarily to work through a jointly-owned and democratically-controlled enterprise'.

In cooperatives such as these, the member is linked to the organization by means of a deed of partnership in order to work in the cooperative, giving rise to rights and obligations both in the field of partnership and in the field of work. In the latter, the member gives the cooperative the fruits of their labour in exchange for an equitable share of the work carried out and submits to its managerial power, while participating democratically in its decisions.

In addition to this heteronomy or dependence of the member on their cooperative, the autonomy or independence of the cooperative itself may be jeopardized through its dealings with markets. This is highlighted by the ICA itself in its *Guidance Notes to the Co-operative Principles*:

> Autonomy and independence can be compromised by becoming over-dependent on supplying a single purchaser of a co-operative's product or services, and, equally, from over-reliance on dominant sources of supply. There are particular dangers to the autonomy and independence of newer and growing co-operative enterprises. Producer co-operatives can be attracted by the volume of contracts offered by a major buyer, but may inadvertently become over-dependent on such a contract and vulnerable if a major buyer subsequently seeks to inflict substantial price reductions.
>
> *(ICA, 2015, p. 53)*

International guidelines on cooperative work

The fact that worker ownership (*trabajo asociado*) cannot be regarded as falling outside the 'safety net' of fundamental rights, which 'have a life of their own and accompany the worker at all times, even when there is no contract, rather like a safety net' (Ojeda, 2006, p. 15), is evident from the ILO *Promotion of Cooperatives Recommendation, 2002* (No. 193), which, in guiding countries' policies on working conditions in cooperatives, sets out an eight-point global framework. National policies should:

'1.   Promote the ILO fundamental labour standards and the ILO *Declaration on Fundamental Principles and Rights at Work* (ILO, 1998), for all workers in cooperatives without distinction whatsoever;

2.   Ensure that cooperatives are not set up for, or used for, non-compliance with labour law or used to establish disguised employment relationships, and combat pseudo cooperatives violating workers' rights, by ensuring that labour legislation is applied in all enterprises;

3.   Promote gender equality in cooperatives and their work;

4.   Promote measures to ensure that best labour practices are followed in cooperatives, including access to relevant information;

5. Develop the technical and vocational skills, entrepreneurial and managerial abilities, knowledge of business potential and general economic and social policy skills of members, workers and managers, and improve their access to information and communication technologies;
6. Promote education and training in cooperative principles and practices, at all appropriate levels of the national education and training systems, and in the wider society;
7. Promote the adoption of measures that provide for health and safety in the workplace;
8. Provide for training and other forms of assistance to improve the level of productivity and competitiveness of cooperatives and the quality of goods and services they produce.'

With regard to the first point, concerning the application of fundamental labour standards and the ILO *Declaration on Fundamental Principles and Rights at Work* (ILO, 1998) in the context of cooperative workers, these are universal rights that apply to everyone in all countries, whether or not they have ratified the relevant accords, and regardless of their level of economic development. They comprise four categories set out in specific 'fundamental' conventions:

1. The freedom of association and the freedom to organize, and effective recognition of the right to collective bargaining;[8]
2. The elimination of all forms of forced or compulsory labour;[9]
3. The effective abolition of child labour;[10] and
4. The elimination of discrimination in employment and occupation.[11]

This general framework, while not particularly demanding, should be viewed from a global perspective of minimum standards, although a discriminatory outcome with respect to cooperative work is evident (García, 2014). Its lack of ambition is offset, however, by the provisions of the second point, where the requirement is subject to the degree of perfectionism in each country's labour legislation: 'Ensure that cooperatives are not set up for, or used for, non-compliance with labour law or used to establish disguised employment relationships, and combat pseudo cooperatives violating workers' rights, by ensuring that labour legislation is applied in all enterprises.'

Based on the content of the ICA *Statement of the Cooperative Identity* and the ILO's Recommendation 193, CICOPA, the International Organisation of Industrial, Artisanal and Service Producers' Cooperatives elaborated and endorsed the *World Declaration on Worker Cooperatives*, which sets out the following basic characters of worker cooperatives (CICOPA, 2005):

a. They have the objective of creating and maintaining sustainable jobs and generating wealth, in order to improve the quality of life of the worker-members, dignify human work, allow workers' democratic self-management and promote community and local development.

b. The free and voluntary membership of their members, in order to contribute with their personal work and economic resources, is conditioned by the existence of jobs.

c. As a general rule, work shall be carried out by the members. This implies that the majority of the workers in a given worker cooperative enterprise are members and vice versa.

d. The worker-members' relation with their cooperative shall be considered as different from that of conventional waged-based labour and from that of autonomous individual work.

e. Their internal regulation is formally defined by regimes that are democratically agreed upon and accepted by the worker-members.

f. They shall be autonomous and independent, before the state and third parties, in their labour relations and management, and in the usage and management of the means of production.

As far as their internal functioning is concerned, worker cooperatives must take into account the following rules. They shall:

a. Compensate the work of their members equitably, taking in consideration the function, the responsibility, the complexity and the specificity required by their positions, their productivity and the economic capacity of the enterprise, trying to reduce the difference between the highest and the lowest compensations.

b. Contribute to the capital increase and the appropriate growth of indivisible reserves and funds.

c. Provide the workplaces with physical and technical facilities aimed at achieving an appropriate functioning and a good organizational climate.

d. Protect the worker-members with appropriate systems of welfare, social security and occupational health, and abide by the standards of protection in force in the areas of maternity, childcare and minors of age at work.

e. Practise democracy in the decisive instances of the organization and in all the stages of the management process.

f. Ensure permanent education and training for capacity-building of members and information to the latter, in order to guarantee professional knowledge and the development of the worker cooperative model, and to stimulate innovation and good management.

g. Contribute to the improvement of the living conditions of the family nucleus and the sustainable development of the community.

h. Combat their being used as instruments aimed at making the labour conditions of wage-earning workers more flexible or precarious, and from acting as conventional intermediaries for jobs.

Among recent guidelines which may provide a future framework for worker ownership (*trabajo asociado*), attention is drawn to a Resolution passed by the United Nations General Assembly on 25 September 2015, entitled: *Transforming our World:*

The 2030 Agenda for Sustainable Development (UN, 2015), and more particularly to its 'Goal 8. Promote sustained, inclusive and sustainable economic growth, full and productive employment and decent work for all'. Specifically:

> 8.5 By 2030, achieve full and productive employment and decent work for all women and men, including for young people and persons with disabilities, and equal pay for work of equal value;
>
> 8.8 Protect labour rights and promote safe and secure working environments for all workers, including migrant workers, in particular women migrants, and those in precarious employment.

Decent work and the safeguarding of labour rights thus becomes a strategic goal for mankind as a whole, encompassing all people, and particularly those in precarious employment.

An attempt should be made to extend legal protection to all working people, and to ensure that, in practice, all enterprises or productive units, including cooperatives, are guaranteed social protection, decent working conditions and a minimum salary.

Heteronomy of cooperative worker ownership

Among the six basic characters of the *World Declaration on Worker Cooperatives* (CICOPA, 2005), in accordance with the aim of the present chapter, the following constitutive elements in labour relations within cooperatives are worth highlighting:

1. *The worker cooperative is an employer.* Its corporate purpose is to create and maintain jobs for its worker-members, who can also be employed as wage-earning workers. It is the cooperative – acting as an entity with a legal status distinct from that of its members – that creates and maintains the jobs.

   Free and voluntary membership is conditioned by the previous existence of jobs, and therefore also by compulsory dismissal. The fruits of the work belong to the cooperative, which subsequently sells them in the form of goods or services, in order to distribute the economic returns equitably among the members.

2. *A majority of worker-members.* The potential exists for the presence of non-member workers (wage-earners), in respect of whom the cooperative is, without a shadow of a doubt, an employer. This normally gives rise to working and protection conditions that are distinct from those of worker-members (Roelants et al., 2014).

3. *Worker-members' relations with their cooperative* should be considered as distinct from those of the conventional salaried worker and that of the individual self-employed worker. This should logically entail distinct and specific employment legislation (López, 2006, p. 586), in which rights and obligations, and social protection and guarantees are given legal recognition.

4. *Internal regulation democratically determined and accepted by the worker-members.* This acceptance entails submission to the cooperative's managerial, control and disciplinary powers, exercised by the persons designated for that purpose.

5. *Independent labour relations before the state.* Cooperative work differs from other types of work, and its principles and values should be respected. Here, the complete independence and autonomy of labour relations in worker-owned cooperatives would appear to eliminate the state's role in safeguarding rights which should be regarded as an indispensable element of any decent job (ILO, 2014), but which are occasionally compromised by external pressures or constraints (Cruz and Hernández, 2014; García and Valencia, 2012). These cooperatives would also appear to be excluded from government interventions relating to social protection, health and safety.

Since they are not subject to labour regulations, cooperatives are usually freed from the rigidities of the labour market and use the flexibility of working conditions as a competitive advantage. But sometimes this flexibility comes at the cost of the employment rights of the worker-members, who are legally vulnerable.

The case of Spain

In Spain, worker ownership (*trabajo asociado*) is to be found not only in the form of cooperatives but also in *Sociedades Laborales*,[12] companies in which over half the share capital is owned by the workers.

The major features of these companies are, briefly, as follows: (a) at least 51 per cent of the share capital is owned by workers, who receive a direct, personal salary in return for their labour, as laid down in an open-ended contract; (b) none of the company shareholders may hold more than a third of the share capital; (c) the number of hours per year worked by non-shareholder workers on open-ended contracts cannot exceed 49 per cent of the overall hours per year worked by shareholder workers. In practice, most of these are small companies. In many cases, all the shareholders are workers, and the share capital is often equally divided amongst the workers, giving rise to egalitarian (democratic) participation in the control of the enterprise and, indeed, to situations similar to those found in worker-owned cooperatives.

However, their employment status is very different. As can be inferred from the requisites indicated above, shareholder workers in *Sociedades Laborales* must be salaried workers for the company, and are bound to the company by a labour contract; as such, they are covered by the full extent of labour legislation. Thus, the law distinguishes between the status of shareholder as owner and shareholder as worker, thereby acknowledging a distinction between capital and labour.

In worker-owned cooperatives, this distinction between ownership and labour is not drawn; the two are seen as inseparably bound together in a single mixed status. So much so, that current legislation focuses on the associative nature (*nauraleza societaria*) of the worker's status, and in doing so deprives them of their labour rights and renders the subject to the provisions of cooperative law. As a result, jurisprudence has established that labour legislation is applicable to worker-owned cooperatives and their workers only when explicitly sanctioned by cooperative law or by the statutes of the cooperative itself.

Yet the real situation is somewhat more complex. Within the quasi-federal structure of the Spanish state, the 'Autonomous Communities' enjoy sole sovereign competence in all matters relating to cooperatives. As a result, there are currently 17 substantive Cooperative Laws (1 State law and 16 Autonomous Community laws, with a complex system of territorial implementation); each law provides its own definition of a cooperative, and establishes its principles and characteristics with no higher regulation of any kind to ensure harmonization which can only be provided by international or EU law.

Working conditions are thus regulated, *de facto*, by 17 different systems, although these can be grouped at various levels, ranging from those which draw fully on current labour legislation to those which grant cooperatives virtually total freedom in terms of labour rights.

In that respect, in order to ensure unified protection, it would suffice simply for labour legislation to recognize worker-members as workers.

It would be a different matter if cooperative law and international guidelines were to include workers' rights as cooperative rights. This would, to some extent, be tantamount to updating the original (Rochdale) principle of providing members with quality products, in this case 'quality labour'.

One of the recommendations in *Cooperatives and Employment: A Global Report* (Roelants *et al.*, 2014) is that cooperative organizations should enter into dialogue with trade unions and public authorities on the issue of working conditions (5.2.3. Labour standards, the transition towards the formal economy). Cooperatives cannot deal with current challenges such as precarious employment conditions, intermittent work patterns and low wages by themselves: these require systemic collaboration between all concerned actors at the national level.

Conclusions

The first conclusion is that the aims and guidelines set out by the ILO (2002, 2015) and CICOPA (2005) cannot be met in the absence of labour law, because the work of the cooperative members is not autonomous; nor, in certain circumstances, is the cooperative itself (even in terms of standardizing the conditions for competition). Otherwise, cooperatives run the risk of being relegated to residual employment, a refuge at times when formal employment is not available, rather than a model of organization and enhancement of work, for which the existence of certain inalienable legal rights, specifically providing protection in the marketplace, is no obstacle.

At the same time, while worker ownership is in many circumstances heteronomous, autonomy could be restored – however paradoxical this may appear – via the legal safeguard of labour rights; once minimum rights are guaranteed, further enhancements may be introduced when conditions are favourable.

The limits of cooperative autonomy lie in the rights of cooperative members. A consumer cooperative is not allowed to supply its members with defective or banned products, and is bound by health protection legislation. A housing cooperative – although one may argue that this is an internal matter, since the houses are intended for its members – is not allowed to build however it sees fit. So why is a worker-owned cooperative allowed to operate in conditions that would be illegal for any other company?

While acknowledging its principles and values, labour law should extend to cooperative worker ownership as simply one more form of work, and in accordance with the concept of decent work, furnish it with employment rights as human rights.

The argument would be reinforced if the labour rights of cooperative worker-members were considered, under cooperative law, as human rights enjoying the protection of international law.

Notes

1 This is true in countries where legal frameworks for worker-owned enterprises including worker cooperatives do not exist or do not provide appropriate legal status to worker-members. However, in other countries, it is also true that worker-members are sufficiently protected by labour laws or by cooperative laws, whether specific legal frameworks for worker-owned enterprises exist or not. Recently, as Brazilian worker cooperative law 2012 shows, there are increasing concerns for changing the former situations into the latter ones. Therefore, it should be explicitly noted that the situation of worker cooperatives addressed in this chapter is limited into the former situation.

2 Tripartite Meeting of Experts on Non-Standard Forms of Employment, Geneva. February 2015.

3 As in the case of the clothing industry cooperatives in Spain in the 1980s, backed by the large manufacturers, which supplied them with work and machinery, as well as access to finance, with an over-ambitious design that trapped the women involved into paying for the investments and forced them to accept the conditions imposed by the industry, which, using a pseudo contract between companies, thereby outsourced manpower, passing responsibilities on to the cooperative.

4 In specific terms, article 23 of the *Universal Declaration of Human Rights* (UN, 1948) proclaims the right to just and favourable conditions of work and to protection against unemployment, to equal pay for equal work, free of any discrimination. Everyone who works has the right to just and fair remuneration, ensuring for themselves and their family an existence worthy of human dignity and supplemented, if necessary, by other means of social protection. Everyone has the right to form and join trade unions for the protection of their interests. Furthermore, article 24 enshrines the right of everyone to rest and leisure, including reasonable limitation of working hours and periodic holidays with pay. These rights are developed and extended by the *International Covenant on Economic, Social and Cultural Rights* (UN, 1966).

5 SSTC 120/1983; 88/1985.

6 'A cooperative is an autonomous association of persons united voluntarily to meet their common economic, social, and cultural needs and aspirations through a jointly-owned and democratically-controlled enterprise.'

7 '1.Voluntary and open membership; 2. Democratic member control; 3. Member economic participation; 4. Autonomy and independence; 5. Education, training and information; 6. Cooperation among cooperatives; 7. Concern for community' (ICA, 1995).

8 *Freedom of Association and Protection of the Right to Organize Convention*, 1948 (No. 87); *Right to Organize and Collective Bargaining Convention*, 1949 (No. 98).

9 *Forced Labour Convention*, 1930 (No. 29); *Abolition of Forced Labour Convention*, 1957 (No. 105).
10 *Minimum Age Convention*, 1973 (no. 138); *Worst Forms of Child Labour Convention*, 1999 (No. 182).
11 *Equal Remuneration Convention*, 1951 (No. 100); *Discrimination (employment and occupation) Convention*, 1958 (No. 111).
12 Ley 44/2015, de 14 de octubre, de Sociedades Laborales y Participadas.

References

Alonso Olea, Manuel. *Introducción al derecho del trabajo*, 4th edition. Madrid: Edersa, 1981.

Canalejas, José. Discurso preliminar. In *El instituto del trabajo: Datos para la historia de la reforma social en España*, edited by Adolfo Buylla, Adolfo Posada and Luis Morote. I-CLX. Madrid: Ricardo Fé, 1902.

Casale, Giuseppe. *The employment relationship: A comparative overview*. Oxford: Hart Publishing. Executive summary of the Employment Relationship, 2011. Accessed 16 November 2016. www.ilo.org/global/publications/ilo-bookstore/order-online/books/WCMS_150013/lang--en/index.htm.

CICOPA. *World Declaration on Worker Cooperatives*. Approved by the ICA General Assembly in Cartagena, Colombia, on 23 September 2005.

Cruz Orejuela, Jaber and Ivan Hernández Villegas. *Las cooperativas de trabajo asociado como una herramienta para la vulneración del derecho laboral*. Santiago de Cali: Biblioteca digital, 2014. Accessed 16 November 2016. http://bibliotecadigital.usb.edu.co/handle/10819/1894.

García Jiménez, Manuel. El desamparo del trabajo asociado por la legislación laboral o el limbo del trabajo cooperativizado, *Revista General de Derecho del Trabajo y de la Seguridad Social* (2014): 105–123.

García López, Sara, and Daniela Valencia Cardona. *La vulneración al trabajo decente por parte de las cooperativas de trabajo asociado en Colombia, puesta en evidencia en el marco de la negociación del TLC entre Estados Unidos y Colombia*. Medellín: Universidad Eafit, 2012.

Goñi Sein, José Luis. Los derechos fundamentales inespecíficos en la relación laboral individual ¿necesidad de una reformulación? In *AEDTSS (XXIV Congreso Nacional de Derecho del Trabajo y de la Seguridad Social). Los derechos fundamentales inespecíficos en la relación laboral y en materia de protección social*. 17–81. Madrid: Cinca, 2014.

Gorz, André. *Critique of economic reason*. Translated by Gillian Handyside and Chris Turner. London: Verso, 1989.

International Co-operative Alliance (ICA) *Co-operative identity, values and principles*. 1995. Accessed 5 December 2016. http://ica.coop/es/node/1625.

____. *Guidance notes to the co-operative principles*. 2015. Accessed 27 May 2017. http://ica.coop/sites/default/files/publication-files/ica-guidance-notes-en-310629900.pdf.

International Labour Office (ILO). *ILO Declaration on Fundamental Principles and Rights at Work and its Follow-up* (Annex revised 15 June 2010). Geneva, 1998.

____. *Report of the Director-General: Decent Work*. International Labour Conference, 87th Session. Geneva, 1999.

____. *Promotion of Cooperatives Recommendation* (No.193). Geneva, 2002.

____. *International Labour Organization Thesaurus*. 2014. Accessed 17 November 2016. http://ilo.multites.net/

____. *Transition from the Informal to the Formal Economy Recommendation*, (No. 204). Geneva, 2015.

____. *Decent work agenda*. 2016a. Accessed 17 November 2016. http://ilo.org/global/topics/decent-work/lang--en/index.htm.

____. *Decent work, the key to the 2030 agenda for Sustainable Development*. 2016b. Accessed 17 November 2016. www.ilo.org/global/topics/sdg-2030/resources/WCMS_436923/lang--en/index.htm.

López Gandía, Juan. *Las cooperativas de trabajo asociado y la aplicación del derecho del trabajo*. Valencia: Tirant lo blanc, 2006.

Martín Valverde, Antonio. *La formación del derecho del trabajo en España*. Madrid: Congreso de los Diputados, 1987.

Marx, Karl. *Capital*, Vol. I. London: Penguin Books, 1990.

____. *Capital*, Vol. III. London: Penguin Books, 1993.

Montoya Melgar, Alfredo. *Derecho del trabajo*. Madrid: Tecnos, 2014.

Ojeda Avilés, Antonio. Equilibrio de interés y bloque constitucional personal en la empresa, *Revista de Derecho Social* 35 (2006): 11–33.

Roelants, Bruno, Hyungsik Eum and Elisa Terrasi. *Cooperatives and employment: A global report*. Brussels: CICOPA and Desjardins Group, 2014.

Sen, Amartya. Work and rights, *International Labour Review* 139, no. 2 (2000): 119–128.

United Nations (UN). *Universal Declaration of Human Rights*. New York, 1948.

____. *International Covenant on Economic, Social and Cultural Rights*. New York, 1966.

____. *Transforming our world: the 2030 Agenda for Sustainable Development – the outcome document of the United Nations summit for the adoption of the post-2015 development agenda*. 2015. Accessed 5 December 2016. www.un.org/Docs/asp/ws.asp?m=A/RES/70/1.

5

WORK AND EMPLOYMENT IN THE INFORMAL ECONOMY AND NEW FORMS OF WORK

How can the cooperative model be an answer?[1]

Hyungsik Eum

Introduction

For a long time, cooperatives have been considered as important tools to address social problems, such as poverty, unemployment and the informal economy. Recently, cooperatives have been formally acknowledged as part of the diverse private sector actors in the United Nations Sustainable Development Goals (SDGs)[2] and in the ILO *Transition from the Informal to the Formal Economy Recommendation, 2015 (No. 204)*.[3] While cooperatives are explicitly recognized as a form of entrepreneurship which can contribute to the SDGs as well as to the transition from the informal to the formal economy, the way in which cooperatives can contribute is not sufficiently clear. Are cooperatives just one among the private sector actors like other private enterprises? Or do they have specific features which would make them more relevant in addressing problems related to work and employment, particularly those caused by informality?

The concept of the informal economy has often been used to describe pre-modern or survivalist economic activities outside formal arrangements in developing countries. More recently, however, in industrialized countries, there has been growth in the numbers of self-employed workers, often called independent contractors or freelancers, of atypical forms of work in enterprises, as well as of new forms of work which are difficult to define and regulate with existing employment arrangements. Although stimulated by technological, social and economic changes and supposedly allowing people to work with more flexibility and independence, such forms of work raise concerns regarding the degradation of conditions of work and life, including the re-emergence of informal employment. Cooperatives are identified as one of the solutions to addressing the negative effects of these new phenomena, while preserving their technical, economic and social potential. The rapid development of informality, confusing concepts used in public debates and the absence of empirical data make it difficult to understand exactly what is happening and how the cooperative model can contribute to offering solutions.

This chapter aims to understand and clarify the specific contributions of cooperatives in addressing work and employment issues in the informal economy, which have been worsening substantially with informalization over recent decades, not only in developing countries but also, more recently, in industrialized ones (Birchall, 2001; ILO, 2012, 2013; Lund, 2009; Vanek *et al.*, 2014).

After identifying the main problems related to work and employment in the informal economy, the chapter examines various ways through which different types of cooperatives contribute to solving the problem. Based on current debates, a proposition on formalizing informal employment through the institutionalization of worker ownership will be raised.

What are the problems?

Informal economy and decent work deficits

The informal economy designates a broader phenomenon rather than an analytically distinguishable reality. Debates on the informal economy centre on the concern for reducing problems caused by the absence or weakness of formal arrangements related to people's economic activities. In the International Labour Conference (ILC) Resolution *Concerning decent work and the informal economy*, the concept of informal economy was introduced in referring to 'all economic activities by workers and economic units that are – in law or in practice – not covered or insufficiently covered by formal arrangements' (paragraph 3 of the 90th ILC Resolution, 2002).

Whereas informal economy actors suffer from insufficient social protection granted to workers and from a lack of efficiency as economic entities, it is also true that the reality in the informal economy is not always negative. The informal economy generates jobs and income, often for the poorer segments of the population who cannot find them elsewhere. Therefore, instead of considering the formality and informality themselves as 'good' or 'bad', a more solution-oriented approach is needed in order to address the problems and to find appropriate solutions. The concept of 'decent work' and its four pillars (employment generation, social protection, rights at work, and social dialogue) proposed by the ILO provides us with an orientation. In the 2002 ILC Resolution and related discussions, the ILO recognized that decent work deficits are more common in the informal economy and among those working in it. Within the framework of the Decent Work Agenda, decent work deficits are defined as: (1) the absence of sufficient employment opportunities for quality employment; (2) inadequate social protection; (3) the denial of workers' rights and benefits; and (4) the exclusion from social dialogue. Reducing these means reducing the employment gap, improving the rights at work, providing social protection and increasing the voice of the workers (Becker, 2004). The 2002 ILC Resolution emphasized the critical need for an integrated and comprehensive approach. The ultimate objective is to support the transition to formality by bringing the informal economy gradually into formal channels of protection and support, while seeking to preserve existing dynamic potentials.[4] This orientation was reaffirmed in ILO *Transition from Informal to Formal Economy Recommendation*, 2015 (No. 204).

Informalization of the economy and employment

Today, deterioration of existing social rights and protection granted to workers and a consequent tendency towards informalization is drawing more people away from formal employment arrangements. Over recent decades, the informal economy in developing countries has come to stay, while in the industrialized countries atypical forms of work inappropriately covered by existing social security systems and stemming from within the formal economy have been increasing. Empirical research shows that, since the 1980s, the informal economy has been continuously on the rise (ILO, 2012, Brief 3.1). A short period of moderate decline was observed between 2000 and 2007, but this was surprisingly modest considering the strong economic growth of the time. While the precise impact of the recent global financial crises on the size of the informal economy in different countries is not yet clear, new forms of informality, often related to new technological development, have drawn attention particularly in the most industrialized countries as well as in emerging economies such as India, China, Brazil and Indonesia (Eum, 2017).

Informalization causes a number of problems which need urgent interventions but also raises questions about the classical social protection model based on the hypotheses of dominance of wage labour. From the early 1980s onwards, the neo-liberal economic model started being adopted in industrialized countries, and then disseminated to many developing countries through the international development programmes of the IMF and the World Bank, in a global policy known as the 'Washington Consensus'. It emphasized tight monetary policy to keep inflation low, free trade, financial liberalization, market deregulation, privatization, more flexible labour markets accompanying increasing outsourcing production and the growth of temporary and casualized forms of work (ILO, 2012, Brief 3.1). The model resulted in economic growth coupled with a low level of employment growth and the deterioration of working conditions, as well as the informalization of employment. The increase of unemployment through massive lay-offs and structural adjustment programmes forced people to choose atypical jobs with poorer working conditions or to look for economic activities outside the formal economy. The globalization of the economy, the development of technology and demographic changes of labour markets such as the increase of women, the youth, the elderly and migrants in them also contributed to informalization. Finally, the successive economic crises (Asian countries in the late 1990s, Argentina in the early 2000s, the global financial crisis in the late 2000s) created new pressures on formal employment and often resulted in the expansion of the informal economy. The so-called 'sharing economy' is partly the result of the financial crisis which has pushed people to trade their own houses, cars, time and work through newly created online platforms in order to get additional or, increasingly, substantial income, and for consumers to save money. The most recent development of informalization is symbolically expressed as the emergence of the 'gig economy'.

The informal economy and employment, and increasing decent work deficits are not a done deal. These phenomena have triggered people's resistance around the world. Not only by enlarging the coverage of workers' rights and social protection but also by developing new frameworks for emerging forms of work, a number of measures have been carried out by diverse stakeholders. While immediate interventions to formalize the informal economy have been difficult, public authorities, trade unions and civil society actors, including the cooperative movement, have tried to improve working conditions and the quality of life of those working in the informal economy. Cooperatives have been recognized as a tool for addressing the problems caused by the informal economy as well as informalization. The ILO's *Promotion of Cooperatives Recommendation*, 2002 (No. 193) states that 'Governments should promote the important role of cooperatives in transforming what are often marginal survival activities (sometimes referred to as the "informal economy") into legally protected work, fully integrated into mainstream economic life' (paragraph 9). The section below examines how cooperatives are concretely contributing and can contribute to addressing problems related to work and employment in the informal economy.

Contribution of cooperatives to addressing problems related to work and employment in the informal economy

Cooperatives on their own are not a panacea to counter these challenges, but they can be part of the solution in the integrated approach. As a complex socio-economic phenomenon, the informal economy and its problems need to be addressed using an integrated approach in which various stakeholders participate and contribute. In some cases, cooperatives are just one among several instruments used by trade unions or local governments for their own efforts. In other cases, the cooperative movement itself is the outcome of self-help efforts of people working in the informal economy. Through appropriate legal frameworks, cooperatives themselves can provide an alternative which allows informal economy actors to formalize economic activities and obtain rights and protection. After briefly examining the general contribution of cooperatives in addressing various problems of people working in the informal economy, this section focuses more specifically on direct contributions of cooperatives to the issues of employment.

General contributions

By definition, those working in informal arrangements lack partially or totally formal status to carry out their economic activities. Whether they conduct these economic activities by choice or by necessity, they are often excluded from rights and protection provided through formal arrangements. By joining various types of cooperatives, such as savings and credit cooperatives, mutual insurance, multipurpose cooperatives and consumer cooperatives, they can benefit from certain formal or semi-formal services and be connected to formal arrangements for at least some of their economic activities. Cooperatives have provided workers in the informal economy, who are normally very poor, with easier access to credit, education and training, affordable goods and services to meet their basic needs and a certain level of social protection based on solidarity and mutual help (Birchall, 2001, 2003; Co-operative College, 2014).

However, more substantially, cooperatives have been created to support and strengthen economic activities of self-employed producers or entrepreneurs, through various forms of shared services. Since the beginning, cooperatives have been recognized as an important tool for organizing and supporting self-employed producers and entrepreneurs whose economic activities were situated in a disadvantaged position compared with private enterprises, which tried to prevail on the market by mobilizing the power of capital. Agricultural cooperatives, fishery cooperatives, artisans' cooperatives, retailers' cooperatives and SME cooperatives have been organized by and for self-employed producers and entrepreneurs who were often in the informal arrangements at the initial stages. Whereas they are often titled according to 'who are members', they are also commonly called 'shared service cooperatives' according to their functions. Whereas finance and insurance are often part of the services, their main activities consist of upstream and downstream services in support of members' economic activities: marketing of members' products including joint advertisement and development of common brands; collective purchasing of raw materials, retail goods, equipment or machinery; and provision of premises, technical information, research and development, training and consulting. Whereas these cooperatives cannot provide a stable legal status or formal social protection to their members, they contribute to raising and stabilizing members' incomes, increasing the performance and competitiveness of members' business, and making members' voices heard collectively. In this fashion, self-employed producers and entrepreneurs in the informal economy can enjoy various services which were not available to them due to the small size of their business and lack of applicable formal arrangements. Furthermore, they can adapt quickly to changing economic conditions rather than become victims of them. Practising horizontal integration and, thereby, reaching economies of scale and a higher bargaining power is a key strategy of shared service cooperatives.

In the debates on the problems in the informal economy related to work and employment, several categories of workers who are in vulnerable situations have drawn special attention: these include waste pickers, domestic workers, migrant workers, street and market vendors, transport workers and home-based workers. Many studies and reports show that shared service cooperatives can play an important role in organizing, supporting and representing these workers, by providing them a formal framework through which their economic activities can be recognized as real businesses and members can negotiate with public authorities in order to introduce appropriate social security and protection schemes (Birchall and Simmons, 2009; Co-operative College, 2014; ILO, 2012; Schwettmann, 1997, 2001; Smith, 2006; Wanyama, 2014).

Specific contributions

Beyond their general contributions in improving life and economic activities of people working in the informal economy, cooperatives can play a direct role in formalizing informal employment and, thereby, in providing people with social protection and rights at work. This is drawing more and more attention, not only because of the informalization of employment, but also because of the increasing number of new forms of work which are somewhere between wage employment and self-employment. Many recent studies suggest that cooperatives can be alternative workplaces for self-employed workers[5] and freelancers (Conaty et al., 2016; Scholz, 2016). Particularly, recent discussions about platform cooperativism have stimulated the idea that cooperatives could provide alternative employment models which could address problems caused by the 'uberization' of work and employment.[6] However, in preserving the dynamics, enthusiasm and diversity that have erupted in this field, it seems necessary to clarify this idea on cooperatives as alternative workplaces for self-employed workers and freelancers in terms of different modalities provided by different cooperative types.

Shared service cooperatives specialized in providing work opportunity

Many cooperatives where members have a legal status as self-employed reflect an almost similar model to the shared service cooperatives which we examined above. Although these cooperatives can provide members with various services, more income and more work opportunities, as well as a sense of community, it is clear that they cannot provide a definitive solution to the informal employment arrangements. For example, due to the lack of an appropriate legal framework, specificities of business models or members' specific situations, some worker cooperatives have chosen the shared service cooperative model rather than the traditional worker cooperative model, which provides direct employment to worker-members. This is often found in worker cooperatives providing care services or domestic work. In administrative or statistical terms, the worker-members might be classified as self-employed. However, when these cooperatives have a solid orientation as worker cooperatives, it seems that the meaning of work and the practical relationship between cooperatives and their members is clearly different from that existing in shared service cooperatives with which self-employed producers and entrepreneurs are content with using the services provided but hardly share a collective identity or the sense of working together.

One of these models is a cooperative that functions as an 'employment agency': indeed, while not providing a direct employment contract to members, some cooperatives can mainly provide work-finding services. Therefore, it is reasonable to classify them as shared service cooperatives rather than worker cooperatives, despite the existence of borderline cases. When work is arranged through the cooperative, employment contracts are individually signed between the work-seeker who is a member of the cooperative and an external employer. In the sense that these cooperatives can help self-employed workers not to be abused by private interim enterprises or middlemen, this model has its advantages and contributes to addressing certain problems related to the informal economy. An example is actors' cooperative agencies and the Co-operative Personal Management Association (CPMA) in the UK. Working closely with Equity, the trade union for actors, stage managers and models, each actors' cooperative is a kind of employment agency, ranging typically in size from 20 to 35 members. Not only providing work-finding services, CPMA provides regular inputs in negotiating Equity's collective agreements and consultations on industrial issues (Conaty et al., 2016).

The labour cooperative model

There are cases where the cooperative provides an employment contract with members and has a contract with a large factory or workplace, to supply a certain number of their members per day or carry out certain tasks. This form of work, called 'contract labour', is one of the atypical forms which are increasingly used by enterprises to avoid employers' obligations. However, it has also been argued that if workers could form a cooperative and bid for the contract directly, they could ensure transparency and exclude possible exploitation of private contractors (Smith, 2006). This kind of cooperative is called a 'labour cooperative' in English and has developed mainly in South Asia and, under the 'worker cooperative' (*cooperativa de trabajo / cooperativa de trabalho*) denomination, in Latin America as well. The expected effect of labour cooperatives on employment is the creation of jobs and distribution of available labour demand that is as regular as possible, so that workers' employment opportunities are as steady as possible throughout the year. In some countries like India, labour cooperatives have been promoted as a tool to generate jobs for the unemployed and the poor, and are entitled to easily get contracts for public works,[7] e.g. in construction, civil engineering, cleaning, landscaping services, forestry works, dock works, etc. This model has also been used in industrialized countries as a way to help unemployed people be trained and find a job in other enterprises (e.g. in Finland, see Birchall, 2003, Seacare cooperative for displaced seamen in Singapore, see Kui, 2001).

This model has also been the object of many debates. Where legal frameworks do not apply workers' rights and protection to members in considering them as self-employed, labour cooperatives can be used as a tool for a distorted form of outsourcing which hides the real subordinate relationship between workers and the true employers. It also allows employers to shift all risk and costs of employment to workers through cooperatives. In Colombia and Brazil during the 1980s and 1990s, a number of such cooperatives were set up partly as a result of neoliberal policies.

They were created to carry out work outsourced from factories and administrations where workers had worked previously, but this time under much worse conditions for the workers, who no longer enjoyed their former employment rights and became treated as self-employed. Many labour cooperatives were also completely dependent on one entity for their contracts (Co-operative College, 2014; Smith, 2006). Recently, a series of new laws (Brazil) or public policies (Colombia) have been introduced in order to reduce these bogus labour cooperatives and to limit their practices.[8]

New initiatives focusing on provision of formal employment contracts

Whereas labour cooperatives aim at creating jobs for members, sometimes at all costs, there are also cooperatives that focus on retaining or accessing the highest possible level of rights and protection, usually that of employees.[9] Whereas for some uncertainty can mean risk and vulnerability, for others it can mean an inevitable cost to be paid for freedom and autonomy. More people, particularly among millennials, prefer to accept uncertainty and fluctuation as a new norm in order to keep the self-determination and self-management of their work and life. For them, reducing uncertainty in keeping their flexibility and independence is a prime need to be met. Cooperatives aiming at addressing this specific need have been organized over the last two decades and have used existing institutional frameworks in an innovative way, or even created new ones by introducing new legislation and public policies.

An emblematic example of this phenomenon is the business and employment cooperative (*coopérative d'activité et d'emploi*) in France. Business and employment cooperatives were originally designed as a specific form of worker cooperative with the aim of providing people who plan to develop their own business project with full-fledged rights and protection as employees during a test period (6–18 months), as well as various back-office services. After legal recognition through the 2014 law on social and solidarity economy, they have now been recognized as a particular form of cooperative, not only for persons who are creating their business, but also for those who have completed their test period and have their own business and clients, like most freelancers, by allowing them to have full-fledged rights and protection as employees and also as members of cooperatives. For this purpose, a new status of 'employee-entrepreneur' (*entrepreneur-salarié*), which reflects the specificities of independent workers and applies only to business and employment cooperatives, was introduced in the French labour code. This legal status is characterized by a higher level of rights and protection, compared with similar legal statuses introduced for flexible forms of work, such as auto-entrepreneurs and umbrella companies (*portage salarial*).[10]

Another example is SMart Belgium, which was converted into a cooperative in 2016 (www.smartbe.be). Established in 1998 as a non-profit association specializing in offering contract management services, insurance services, legal and consulting services, information and training, co-work spaces and mutual financial tools mainly to artists, and, more recently, it has opened to freelancers and people working in the so-called sharing economy, SMart Belgium has organized a process for converting itself into a multi-stakeholder cooperative mainly based on worker-members. This is possible thanks to the capacity of SMart Belgium to combine diverse institutional tools, such as a well-designed employment and social security system in Belgium and special legal treatment for artists and certain professions.[11] Differently from the case of French business and employment cooperatives, which now have a specific legal status for employee-entrepreneurs but no distinction between employee-entrepreneur-members and permanent staff members, in SMart Belgium all workers, namely both independent workers using the services provided (75,000 persons) and the permanent staff (165 persons), have the same legal status as employees but correspond to distinct member categories in order to balance votes in the governance structure, which *de facto* results in a multi-stakeholder cooperative form.

Interestingly, we can find that all these cooperatives are organized to respond to specific needs of people working, whether by choice or by necessity, as self-employed workers or in sectors where this type of work form prevails. Their common needs are mainly to have more and better work and income, to avoid possible exploitation by intermediaries and attain formal employment arrangements aimed at enjoying rights and protection while easing the administrative burden. Therefore, cooperatives commonly provide a wide range of services, such as marketing, advertising, provision of information and training, administrative services including bookkeeping and invoicing, sometimes more sector-specific services and, in some cases, collective bargaining or political representation. Indeed, these functions are very similar to those carried out by back-office services. However, differently from employment agencies or personal service companies, whose main purpose is to maximize profits for shareholders to the detriment of workers' interest, in cooperatives these services are controlled and managed by and for the workers themselves. In a sense, these cooperatives look like shared service cooperatives or users' cooperatives in which members use the services provided by cooperatives. But in another sense, since members are workers and since the main purpose of the cooperative is to create and maintain members' jobs, they also offer similarities with worker cooperatives.

Worker cooperatives as a direct solution to formalize informal employment, but when conditions are met

The primary aim of worker cooperatives is to provide formal and decent employment to their members. This is well illustrated by the fact that they tend to maintain better employment for their workers, even during economic recessions, compared with the average of enterprises and even with other types of cooperatives. This comes from the basic DNA of worker cooperatives, whose owners are the workers themselves. Worker cooperatives are enterprises trading on the market with other economic actors, because their economic activities cannot be dependent on internal transactions among members, as is the case for, e.g., consumer cooperatives. Even when they are micro-size enterprises with limited capacity for formal arrangements, they must have the basic level of formality required by enterprises, such as written rules, formal governance structures and bookkeeping. If an economic entity claiming to be a worker cooperative does not have these formal tools, it cannot be considered to be a cooperative whatsoever. As a formal enterprise, worker cooperatives have to establish formal employment contracts or their equivalents with workers, whether these are members or not. Therefore, worker cooperatives could be recognized as a direct solution to providing formal employment to people (Co-operative College, 2014; ILO, 1992, 2012; Levin, 2002).

How can worker cooperatives help workers in the informal economy? Above all, by creating worker cooperatives, workers who need to work but cannot find jobs in the formal economy can have an opportunity to work through formal arrangements. This is the main hypothesis used by a number of government public policies and development projects that aim at promoting worker cooperatives. Second, by taking over companies in difficulty or in crisis where they work, workers facing unemployment or forced to find a job in worse conditions can maintain their jobs. This preventive role of worker cooperatives has been noted in the literature, in citing anecdotal episodes, such as the case of 'recovered factories' (*fábricas recuperadas*) in Argentina in the early 2000s (ILO, 2012, Brief 5.4) and the cooperativization of former public enterprises during the enterprise reform period of the late 1990s in China (Roelants, 2001).[12]

This being said, are worker cooperatives a feasible solution for people working in the informal economy, who are often vulnerable in terms of social and economic conditions? First of all, except for some countries where there is no available legal framework, establishing worker cooperatives does not differ much from establishing other types of cooperatives. It is even easier than creating consumer cooperatives or banking cooperatives, which generally require a significant number of members or amounts of capital from the outset. The real challenge lies in how they can survive and succeed in the market. Moreover, when members are mainly people in vulnerable conditions, it is even more difficult for them to be competitive in the market. Therefore, whereas worker cooperatives do have a great potential to address problems related to work and employment in the informal economy, it should also be pointed out that their development is very difficult and challenging. Since worker cooperatives, unlike other types of cooperatives, do not establish commercial transactions among members but provide them with a workplace and an income, the risk is higher. Thus, far more attention should be paid to the creation of favourable conditions for their development, such as indivisible reserves, financial tools managed by cooperative movements, horizontal integration (groups, consortia, federations) and favourable institutional frameworks which allow for and promote these factors.[13]

Even when they enjoy a conducive environment for their success, if there is no appropriate legal framework regarding worker-members, the worker cooperative model can also be abused to worsen problems rather than solving them. In countries where the cooperative legal framework emphasizes the legal status of worker-members as owners, resulting from civil contracts among members as the basis of the work relationship, worker-members are often regarded as self-employed who are not covered by any rights or protection granted to employees. This approach can produce significant damage to the worker cooperative movement. As the above-mentioned cases of cooperatives involved in labour intermediation in Colombia and Brazil have shown, bogus worker cooperatives that on the surface are formal enterprises can restrict and suppress workers' rights and protection by self-exploitation forced by market pressure or by dominant buyers who are hidden employers profiting from outsourcing works (ILO, 1992; Lindenthal, 1994; Schwettmann, 1997).[14]

Experience shows that an appropriate and tailored legal framework for worker cooperatives, guided by the cooperative principles as well as the values of decent work, can solve many of these problems in a pragmatic fashion, and even strengthen the role of worker cooperatives as a solution to the informal economy.

In the countries where the relationship between worker-members and the worker cooperative is based on an employee contract, clear distinctions in the legal framework for worker cooperatives within the cooperative law can be used by case law to properly combine worker-members' double relationship with the cooperative, namely an employment relationship and a member-owner relationship. For example, French worker cooperatives are recognized as a specific type of cooperative, while the worker-members' legal status as employees with full-fledged rights and protection is maintained (Espagne, 2007).

Another way is to fully apply the universal norms of decent work enshrined in the fundamental conventions of the ILO to worker cooperatives through cooperative laws by explicitly dealing with the legal status of worker-members and worker cooperatives. In Spain, worker-members' labour relationship is not covered by labour law as an employment relationship but constitutes a specific type of labour relationship regulated by the cooperative law. The latter explicitly regulates a minimum level of rights and protection for worker-members so that worker cooperatives as enterprises do not violate the basic rights and protection against their worker-members, even though the enterprise is constituted by the worker-members themselves. Furthermore, Spanish worker cooperatives can choose between two social security regimes: the 'general regime', which is the same as the scheme for salaried workers in other types of enterprises; and the scheme for self-employed workers without, however, providing the same level of coverage. The new legislation on worker cooperatives in Brazil defines that worker-members in worker cooperatives should be treated as workers in terms of social protection and labour rights, which includes a minimum wage, annual leave, paid weekly rest, working time limits, and worker insurance (Co-operative College, 2014). It is expected that this new law could improve the role of worker cooperatives in delivering formal employment and decent work to workers by removing bogus cooperatives which provide only formal employment without decent work. Although there are some concerns that strengthening rights and protection for workers could bring additional costs to worker cooperatives and that cooperatives could lose their competitiveness, the position of this chapter is that cooperative solutions should be pragmatic but also normative as proposed by the ICA's *Statement on the Cooperative Identity*, the ILO Recommendation No. 193 and CICOPA's *World Declaration on Worker Cooperatives*.

Formalizing informal employment through the institutionalization of worker ownership

The analysis above reveals that there are some conceptual ambiguities in the worker cooperative model concerning their roles in addressing employment issues and that the promotion of formal arrangements, in the fields of legal coverage in labour law, social security coverage, right to organize into trade unions *de jure* and *de facto*, etc., should be addressed at the regulatory level, through debates and through a better cooperation between cooperative organizations and trade unions.[15]

Among other issues, the extent to which cooperatives should be responsible for their members' employment has become more important not only for cooperatives but also in the wider debates on the flexibilization and informalization of employment. In the majority of cases, members of producers' cooperatives, particularly agricultural and fishery cooperatives, are real self-employed producers who use shared services provided by cooperatives for their own production activities. However, in producers' cooperatives in industrial and service sectors, it is not always clear whether producer-members are real self-employed producers: we can find cases where producer-members significantly depend on their cooperative for their jobs and production activities and where producers' cooperatives retain all necessary control over members' work rather than simply provide shared services, thereby playing to a large extent the *de facto* role of an employer.[16] There have been many warnings on the misuse or abuse of this kind of practice by unscrupulous employers to bypass labour regulations and shift all costs of employment to individual workers (Co-operative College, 2014; Lindenthal, 1994; Smith, 2006). It should be pointed out that, in many cases, national labour legal frameworks, market practices in certain economic sectors such as transportation services and personal services, or specific forms of work organization like 'piece-rate worker' among home-based workers[17] (Roever et al., 2011), might force this kind of practice not only onto cooperatives but also other forms of enterprises. In effect, in considering this kind of labour practice as part of the phenomenon called the informalization of employment, various initiatives have been carried out by governments, trade unions, NGOs as well as cooperatives in order to reduce their negative effects and, in addition, to reclassify them into a classical employment relationship which could provide appropriate rights and protection to workers.

Therefore, from a more normative perspective, producer cooperatives that have a substantial role as employers beyond being simple providers of shared services, should perhaps be reclassified as worker cooperatives and, thereby, should provide strengthened rights and protection to their producer-members. This reorientation is more necessary than ever, because, in developing countries as well as new emerging economies, as the role of cooperatives in industrial and service sectors is growing, the cooperative business model should be modernized beyond simple cooperation for survival, in order to compete with other enterprises. In the same line of reasoning, some worker cooperative models which consider worker-members as self-employed and do not grant any rights or protection to workers should improve worker-members' rights and protection.

However, does this normative approach mean that producer-members should give up their freedom and rights as owners of cooperatives to gain rights and protection as employees? If producer-members claim their rights as employees in resorting to labour laws without assuming their responsibility as owners, how can cooperatives manage it? This point is what the concept of 'worker ownership' proposed by CICOPA tries to address. Worker ownership is one of the three basic modalities for undertaking occupational activities together with the self-employed and wage-earners. In this form of work, 'work and management are carried out jointly without the typical limitations of individual work, nor exclusively under the rules of conventional wage-based labour. Among the modalities of worker ownership, the one being organized through worker cooperatives has attained the highest level of development and importance at present' (CICOPA, 2005). Since its origin, the worker cooperative model has kept atypical forms of employment which aim at reconciling the self-determination as owners with protection for workers, through the collective and democratic governance of cooperatives. The concept of worker ownership is not a fixed one but a dynamic and pragmatic approach which is completely in accordance with the universal cooperative definition, operational principles and underlying values enshrined in the *Statement on the Cooperative Identity*, agreed upon within the framework of the ICA, and incorporated in ILO Recommendation No. 193 and, through the latter, also with the fundamental labour standards and rights at work enshrined in ILO conventions.

In many countries, including the French, Spanish and Brazilian cases examined above, this core characteristic has been institutionalized through legal frameworks or substantially recognized through case law or public policies. As such, some legal frameworks for worker-members in worker cooperatives have opened a third form of work, beyond the traditional dichotomy dating from the 19th century between employees and self-employed. Given that the changing world of work calls for more pragmatic approaches allowing new forms of work and employment that would combine flexibility and independence with rights and protection, the concept of worker ownership might be a pragmatic model enabling workers to fully enjoy both self-determination and protection through cooperative methods. Furthermore, the institutionalization of worker ownership and the promotion of worker cooperatives as its realized form might be one of the most effective strategies for addressing the mounting problems caused by the informalization of employment and formalizing informal employment through a new form of decent employment.

Conclusion

This chapter aimed at examining various contributions of cooperatives to address problems related to work and employment in the informal economy. Instead of considering the informal economy itself as 'good' or 'bad', we focused on the decent work deficits faced by people working in the informal economy and tried to identify the actual and potential contribution of cooperatives.

In recognizing the importance of the integrated approach based on multi-stakeholders' involvement, this chapter proposed that cooperatives be part of an integrated solution in various ways: as an instrument used by trade unions or local governments within the framework of their own efforts, as self-help efforts of people in the informal economy for improving their economic and social situations, and as an alternative model allowing informal economy actors to formalize their economic activities and to obtain rights and protection at work. It also proposed to envisage the institutionalization of 'worker ownership' as an important solution to the informal economy and informal employment. Why don't we dare to imagine a better world of work through various cooperative models?

Notes

1 This chapter is a reformulated version of a part of *Cooperatives and employment: Second global report* (Eum, 2017) published by CICOPA.
2 '44. We acknowledge the role of the diverse private sector, ranging from micro-enterprises to cooperatives to multinationals, and that of civil society organizations and philanthropic organizations in the implementation of the New Agenda' (UN Resolution 70/1, *Transforming our World: The 2030 Agenda for Sustainable Development*).
3 '11. This integrated policy framework should address: (. . .) (g) the promotion of entrepreneurship, micro, small and medium-sized enterprises, and other forms of business models and economic units, such as cooperatives and other social and solidarity economy units' (ILO Recommendation No. 204).
4 Article 13 of the 2002 ILC Resolution states that 'To promote decent work, it is necessary to eliminate the negative aspects of informality while at the same time ensuring that opportunities for livelihood and entrepreneurship are not destroyed, and promoting the protection and incorporation of workers and economic units in the informal economy into the mainstream economy. Continued progress towards recognised, protected decent work will only be possible by identifying and addressing the underlying causes of informality and the barriers to entry into the economic and social mainstream.'
5 Differently from self-employed producers or entrepreneurs, self-employed workers offer their labour to work suppliers or a succession of them, with whom workers only have short-term or fixed-term contracts. However, while they work with a temporary employer, they are subjected to the latter's control. Conaty *et al.* suggest in their report *Not Alone* that 'worker is a broader category in law than employee'. According to them, 'a worker is any individual who works for an employer, whether under a contract of employment, or any other contract' (Conaty *et al.*, 2016). Following this argument, workers should be entitled to core rights and protection related to their work, regardless of their contract form. The concept of 'self-employed worker', which we recapture from *Not Alone*, represents this line of argument.
6 See Nathan Schneider's chapter in this volume (Chapter 14).
7 It should be noted that the concept of 'contract labour' itself is very ambiguous. For example, when the concept is used for public works, labour cooperatives supposedly undertake these works as 'contractor'. At least as far as public works are concerned, we

can consider that the role of labour cooperatives is not to provide workforce to other enterprises, but to undertake project contracts. This should be further clarified in the case of labour contract cooperatives in India, which work mainly for public work contracts. For a more detailed description of Indian labour contract cooperatives, see Prasad (2001) and Isaac and Williams (2017).

8 CICOPA has been very active in struggling against them. The rapid expansion of bogus labour cooperatives was one of the main motivations for elaborating the World Declaration on Worker Cooperatives, which was approved by the General Assembly of the ICA in 2005 and clearly excludes bogus labour cooperatives from the definition of worker cooperative. 'In their internal operations, worker cooperatives must take into account the following rules. They shall . . . Combat their being instruments aimed at making the labour conditions of wage-earning workers more flexible or precarious, and from acting as conventional intermediaries for jobs' (CICOPA, 2005).

9 This is well explained by SMart Belgium. 'Our mission is to invent exactly the opposite of uberization which aims to transform subordinate work (to algorithm and platforms) into so-called self-employment. Smartization is the reverse: we allow self-employed workers to retain or access social protection corresponding to that of wage-earners' (SMart Belgium, 2016).

10 See also Mélissa Boudes' chapter in this volume (Chapter 12).

11 Interview with financial director of SMart Belgium (22 July 2016).

12 Also, for Italian cases, see Vieta's chapter in this volume (Chapter 10).

13 See more in detail Roelants *et al.* (2012 and 2014).

14 See also García Jiménez's chapter in this volume (Chapter 4).

15 See also Eşim, Katajamäki and Tchami's chapter in this volume (Chapter 3).

16 Although the debate on the criteria that define the nature of labour contracts – juridical subordination or economic dependence – was settled in favour of juridical subordination in the early 20th century, the recent increase of new forms of work which are legally independent but economically dependent, and thus characterized by substantial subordination imposed by economic dependency, has reactivated the debate (Conseil national du numérique, 2016). For example, in the US context, during the debates about the legal status of workers working through online platforms, which are actually considered by online platform companies to be independent contractors, one important classifying criterion on which judges' and regulators' decisions will depend is whether the workers themselves are overall in control of their own work or are generally subject to the enterprise's instructions about when, where and how to work (Singer, 2015). Another point is, according to the regulatory guidance of the US Department of Labour, whether a worker is economically dependent on the employer or is in business for themselves (*New York Times*, 18 July 2015). Other more concrete criteria can be used according to different national legal frameworks, such as whether there are instructions, provision of tools, training, regular remuneration, financial risk, work control, integration of the worker in the enterprise, entitlements, work done mainly for another, work done within specific hours, a specific time or at a specific location, work carried out personally, etc. (ILO, 2012, Brief 4.a.3). These questions could be taken into account in order to reclassify certain producers' cooperatives into worker cooperatives.

17 According to Roever *et al.* (2011), within the group of home-based workers, a further distinction can be made between 'piece-rate workers' and 'own-account workers'. Piece-rate workers can be contracted by a firm, an individual entrepreneur, traders, subcontractors or other intermediaries, are usually given the raw materials and are paid a stated amount per piece produced. These workers do not have any direct contact with the markets for the goods they produce. Own-account workers are those who are generally in direct contact with the market and buy their own raw material (*ibid.*). Among producers' cooperatives, producer-members in some handicraft cooperatives or handloom weavers' cooperatives are piece-rate workers.

References

Becker, Kristina Flodman. *The informal economy.* Stockholm: Sida, 2004.

Birchall, Johnston. *Organizing workers in the informal sector: A strategy for trade union-cooperative action.* Geneva: ILO, 2001.

____. *Rediscovering the cooperative advantage: Poverty reduction through self-help.* Geneva: ILO, 2003.

Birchall, Johnston and Richard Simmons. *Co-operatives and poverty reduction: Evidence from Sri Lanka and Tanzania.* Manchester: Co-operative College, 2009.

CICOPA, *World Declaration on Worker Cooperatives*, Approved by the ICA General Assembly in Cartagena, Colombia, on 23 September 2005. 2005.

Conaty, Pat, Alex Bird and Philip Ross. *Not alone: Trade union and co-operative solutions for self-employed workers*, Unity Trust Bank, Wales Co-operative Centre and Co-operatives UK, 2016.

Conseil National du Numérique. *Travail, emploi, numérique – Les nouvelles trajectoires.* Paris, 2016.

Co-operative College. *Co-operatives and workers in the informal economy: Possibilities and challenges.* Cambridge, MA: WIEGO, 2014.

Eum, Hyungsik. *Cooperatives and employment: Second global report.* Brussels: CICOPA, 2017.

Espagne, François. *Les différentes formes de travail associé dans les sociétés coopératives ouvrières de production en Europe.* 2007. Accessed 1 December 2016. www.les-scop.coop/export/sites/default/fr/_media/documents/travail-associe-europe.pdf.

International Labour Organization (ILO). *Le rôle des coopératives en matière de promotion de l'emploi et des revenus dans les secteurs rural et non structuré*, Réunion d'experts en coopératives. Geneva, 1992.

____. *The informal economy and decent work: A policy resource guide – Supporting transitions to formality.* Geneva, 2012.

____. *Measuring informality: A statistical manual on the informal sector and informal employment.* Geneva, 2013.

Isaac, T. M. Thomas, and Michelle Williams. *Building alternatives*, New Delhi: LeftWord, 2017.

Kui, Leow Peng. Case study: Singapore National Cooperative Federation. In the final report of *Regional Conference on Employment Creation through Cooperatives and Small Enterprises*, 47–50. Bangkok, Thailand, 16–18 May 2001.

Levin, Mark. Cooperatives and unions: Joint action for informal workers, *Labour Education 2*, no. 127 (2002): 28–32.

Lindenthal, Roland. *Cooperatives and employment in developing countries.* Geneva: ILO, 1994.

Lund, Francie. Social protection and the informal economy: Linkages and good practices for poverty reduction and empowerment. In *Promoting pro-poor growth: Social protection.* 69–88. Paris: OECD, 2009.

Prasad, Bhagwati. Case study: Labour-contracting cooperatives, India. In the final report of *Regional Conference on Employment Creation through Cooperatives and Small Enterprises*, 51–60. Bangkok, Thailand, 16–18 May 2001.

Roelants, Bruno. Case study: Activities in Asia of the International Organization of Industrial, Artisanal and Service Producers' Co-operatives (CICOPA). In the final report of *Regional Conference on Employment Creation through Cooperatives and Small Enterprises*, 76–88. Bangkok, Thailand, 16–18 May 2001.

Roelants, Bruno, Diana Dovgan, Hyungsik Eum and Elisa Terrasi. *The resilience of the cooperative model: How worker cooperatives, social cooperatives and other worker-owned enterprises respond to the crisis and its consequences.* Brussels: CECOP-CICOPA Europe, 2012.

Roelants, Bruno, Hyungsik Eum and Elisa Terrasi. *Cooperatives and employment: A global report*. Brussels: CICOPA and Desjardins Group, 2014.

Roever, Sally, Shalini Sinha and Sonia Dias. *AAPS Planning education toolkit: The informal economy – Appendix A: Informal economic sector livelihood profiles*. AAPS, 2011.

Scholz, Trebor. *Platform cooperativism: Challenging the corporate sharing economy*. New York: Rosa Luxemburg Stiftung, New York Office, 2016.

SMart. *Rapport d'activité 2015 – Perspectives 2016*. Brussels, 2016.

Schwettmann, Jürgen. *Cooperatives and employment in Africa*, Occasional Discussion Paper 97-1. Geneva: ILO, 1997.

____. Case study: Presentation on shared services cooperatives. In the final report of *Regional Conference on Employment Creation through Cooperatives and Small Enterprises*, 108–121. Bangkok, Thailand, 16–18 May 2001.

Singer, Natasha. Twisting words to make 'sharing' apps seem selfless, *New York Times*, 8 August 2015.

Smith, Stirling. *Let's organize! A SYNDICOOP Handbook for trade unions and cooperatives about organizing workers in the informal economy*. ILO, ICA and ICFTU, 2006.

Vanek, Joann, Martha Alter Chen, Françoise Carré, James Heintz and Ralf Hussmanns. *Statistics on the informal economy: Definitions, regional estimates & challenges*. Cambridge, MA.: WIEGO, 2014.

The Editorial Board. Defining 'employee' in the gig economy, *New York Times*, 18 July 2015.

Wanyama, Frederick O. *Cooperatives and the sustainable development goals: A contribution to the post-2015 development debate*. Geneva: ILO, 2014.

6

'COFFEE HAS GIVEN US POWER TO ACT'

Coffee cooperatives and women's empowerment in Rwanda's rural areas: a case study of Karaba coffee cooperative

Gisaro M. Ya-Bititi, Philippe Lebailly, Deogratias Sebahire Mbonyinkebe and Philippe Burny

Introduction

Cooperatives bring socio-economic benefits to their members through combining forces with others. Worldwide, it is estimated that there are around 800,000 cooperatives which provide affordable products and services and access to resources (UNDESA, 2014). Cooperatives create opportunities and promote income-generating activities for many communities by providing goods and services through their daily activities. They provide medical care, access to markets, and job creation. Apart from enabling their members to access economies of scale, cooperatives help to enhance the status of their members to voice their needs and challenges in the community.

Access to resources helps cooperative members to improve the quality of life by enhancing social and economic empowerment of women. It is in this context that Karaba coffee farmers joined their organization in order to address their social and economic problems. Cooperatives have empowered their members by creating jobs and other advantages. The potential contribution of women empowerment in development and poverty reduction is supported by global institutions such as the World Bank and other development practitioners. Cooperatives are used as engines of development in homesteads and agricultural activities (Gibson, 2005; UNDESA, 2012). Rwanda's paid labour force employed as casual workers in the agriculture sector and other informal sectors constitutes 97.3 per cent of active persons with very low salaries (Ansoms, 2008; Birchall, 2003). In addition to housework, most of the women in Rwanda's coffee-producing zones are involved in coffee production. The major concern of this study is to assess the role of cooperatives in empowering rural women in Karaba. The study aims at answering the following questions: (1) To what extent has the Karaba coffee cooperative contributed to social and economic empowerment of women? (2) What is the impact of women's empowerment on Rwanda's rural households?

Methods

Data were collected during a field survey in the Karaba coffee cooperative located in Huye District in Southern Province from April to July 2015, especially from female members. Both primary and secondary data were collected. Primary data were collected using interviews, questionnaires and focus-group discussions. Interviews were administered to key informants drawn especially from the management teams of Karaba Coffee Washing Stations (CWSs) and the cooperative. A survey was conducted of 48 purposefully sampled women informants drawn from 6 coffee zones in Karaba, each of which was represented by 8 women. They were sampled on the basis of a set of criteria that included the following: (i) each respondent had to be a coffee grower owning between 500 and 1,000 coffee trees with an experience of more than five years in the field; (ii) she had to occupy a position of seniority for at least three years in cooperative management; (iii) at least three active persons had to work under her at the time of the investigations; (iv) the respondent had to demonstrate evidence of active involvement in cooperative business, such as delivering coffee beans to the nearest CWS; (v) she should have borrowed more than 100,000 Rwandan Francs (USD121.95) as credit, and should have repaid it without difficulty and was supposed to have made some savings for the household.

The selected women respondents were chosen from a list of all members provided by the chairperson of the cooperative. Primary data was supplemented with secondary data from Koakaka coffee cooperative, another coffee cooperative in Karaba. The collected data were analysed using descriptive statistics such as mean and percentage counts with regard to different socio-economic indicators and benchmarks provided by the cooperative and its two CWSs. Both quantitative and qualitative analyses were carried out to assess the impacts of the coffee cooperative scheme in improving the social and economic empowerment of women. During the exploratory phase, observations and semi-structured interviews were conducted to identify the effects of coffee farmers on women's empowerment. Coffee producers were asked to identify the impacts of CWSs and cooperatives on women's empowerment. They were also asked to give their opinion on whether they thought that cooperatives improved their members' socio-economic welfare.

Results and discussion

This section is divided into two parts, namely the economic and social empowerment of women.

Economic empowerment

Coffee cooperative and job creation/satisfaction for women

The coffee growers were asked to describe how their interests were protected by the cooperative and whether their needs were satisfied: 89.7 per cent of them responded that they have attained better conditions such as monetary advantages and various other services; 67.3 per cent of the informants reported obtaining facilities of agricultural inputs offered by the cooperative; and 96.3 per cent wished to acquire more strength and the necessary synergy to improve the well-being of the members. It was found that the establishment of CWSs had led to job creation through employing permanent staff and engaging technical and logistical support staff, mainly during harvest seasons. The CWS manpower teams participated in conducting coffee campaigns on activities related to coffee picking and trans-portation, coffee sorting, treatment, drying, storage and marketing. The findings showed that women were more engaged in coffee production than men, especially during coffee harvesting and processing activities at the stations. The created jobs contributed to sustainable income and future perspectives for them (women). The results also showed that 98.7 per cent of the respondents were vulnerable groups, especially widows, who were among the most marginalized populations. On the other hand, 98.4 per cent of the informants were identified as vulnerable groups as well as victims of discrimination who did not have access to jobs in the agriculture sector before the introduction of the cooperative. The processing of coffee beans in CWSs has improved the lives of women in Karaba. The activity has helped empower women members economically and socially and create sustainable rural employment through equitable business models. CWSs and cooperatives have also demonstrated some evidence of gender mainstreaming in daily tasks, especially during the coffee growing campaigns. During such campaigns (from March to July), Karaba cooperative employs more than 260 occasional workers, who receive a daily income of RWF1,500 (USD1.83). The majority of these are girls and women, while men are employed to handle cooperative machinery and other services where heavy physical energy is required.

In Rwanda, '29.1 per cent of the work force involved in coffee produc-tion is composed of men compared to women who represent 71.9 per cent of the work force involved in proactive coffee farming activities' (NAEB,[1] 2014). However, men tend to monopolize the income from coffee sales, which, like cow ownership, is a major item that culturally belongs to men. Women tend to be marginalized in the management of family income from cash crops. Through the cooperative movement, men and women are trained to share income equally; thus, coffee revenue is shared by all family members. In this context, the coop-erative movement has empowered women by giving them a chance to think about the progress of the entire family by enjoying sales from coffee. In addition, women are taught how to save and invest money from coffee. The majority of the cooperative members have opened bank accounts, keeping and withdrawing money whenever they wish.

This is demonstrated by one of the respondents, who testified:

> Coffee has opened our eyes; we do not ask our husbands to buy salt, soap, body lotion and cloth for us on Christmas and during Easter holidays. Our children and us have new dresses because coffee has provided money for us, there is no more problem.

This study found that men and women jointly discuss their problems and look for joint solutions by identifying family priorities during and after coffee harvests. As a result, husbands are no longer the exclusive and unchallenged heads of families to make family decisions or to consume beer alone in bars during evening hours. Coffee cooperatives have therefore empowered women in family decision-making, thereby becoming joint participants in the development process of households – as confirmed by 76.4 per cent of the respondents interviewed.

Coffee income and the improvement of women's independence

The original goal of Karaba cooperative was to improve women's income and reduce their dependence on men. In this context, the women of Karaba coopera- tive no longer depend on their husbands' income: 58.1 per cent of the respondents said that women had acquired financial autonomy and independence as a result of their involvement in the cooperative. They reported that through the coffee coop- erative, women had been emancipated and had acquired financial independence from their husbands. However, this independence does not mean that women are completely free and self-sufficient. The results also reveal that the woman's role is complementary to that of their husbands, although there is still much to be desired in this respect. Compared with men, women can now use their income on more constructive things like buying food, paying for children's education and health care (79.1 per cent).

According to one respondent, it was noted that: 'When men get income, many of them spend it on drinking local beer, leaving women to take care of the family members.' Other respondents revealed that women use bigger portions of their earnings on family and domestic expenses, consequently their income had a greater impact on family welfare (Birchall, 2003; Gisaro, 2013). Coffee growing has led to the empowerment of rural women because cooperatives have enabled them to exchange ideas, leading to a rapprochement with their husbands. This has reduced conflicts, discrimination and gender-based violence against women because Rwanda's men and women can now participate together in income-generating activities within the household. Men can no longer impose their decisions on the use of money, as was the case before. Instead, income allocation is now a joint deci- sion that concerns the two parties. This was confirmed by one of the respondents, who said that: 'Coffee has empowered women through cooperatives; it has given them pride and self-esteem.' In Karaba cooperative, women have managed to find money. Cooperatives are viewed as an important 'tutor for resilience' because they not only deal with their psychological problems but they also promote the development of economic activities that enable women to gain income for social and economic development (Gisaro, 2013; Sibelet and Montzieux, 2012). Socio- economic resilience has been made possible thanks to cooperatives, which have become promoters of better socio-economic conditions for women. Through the system of working together and sharing experience, cooperatives have helped their members to mobilize funds for income-generating projects.

Cooperative participation and women empowerment

Coffee agricultural practices require sufficient time in order to be fully accomplished. These include: ploughing, weeding, mulching and post-harvest activities, which involve washing, treatment, drying, transportation and search for markets. Women are mostly engaged in more different stages of coffee production than men. According to the men interviewed, coffee sorting is a task reserved for women, the reason being that women tend to concentrate on their work and that they are patient and enduring while performing such tasks every day. At Karaba cooperative, coffee has changed the lives of women. Ever since the CWS was established in 2003, women have been earning RWF1,500 per day (around USD2). They can now solve their financial problems. A total of 98.7 percent of the workforce are engaged in coffee processing activities and have been able to fulfil their family duties: they buy food, pay medical bills and school fees for their children. They have bought cattle and rehabilitated their homes (57.6 per cent). Women's participation in economic activities has made them regain confidence and esteem in their home by giving them economic autonomy, which has increased their bargaining power vis-à-vis their husbands.

Women's participation in coffee activities has also led to improvement in social status for them (67.8 per cent). They have gained business skills (58.1 per cent). Agricultural ventures have enabled them to improve their livelihoods, thus reducing their socio-economic vulnerability. Women are now actively engaged in agricultural ventures in which they never traditionally participated. In general, Karaba coffee cooperative has played a pivotal role in empowering women at the grassroots level (69.2 per cent).

Cooperatives and women's access to micro-credit

Women's accessibility to, and utilization of, micro-credit is an important sign of economic empowerment. The results of this study confirm that coffee cooperatives have had a positive impact on poverty reduction in Karaba, which was among the poorest regions of Rwanda. The cooperative has made remarkable progress in producing impressive results for women. Through its well-planned credit and saving programmes, cooperatives have improved the capacity of women by providing self-employment. The poorest women of Karaba cooperative have been taught how to make savings, how to invest and how to stand on their own. According to the findings of this survey, 23.6 per cent of the credit is used to buy livestock, while 26.4 per cent goes to small businesses, 42.3 per cent to agriculture, and the remaining 7.7 per cent to personal uses.

The use of micro-credit has economically empowered women through their involvement in economic activities, which was never the case before. Through the cooperative movement, a saving culture has therefore been developed among Rwandan women. They have now joined savings and internal lending communities (SILCs), known locally as 'Ibimina'. This is a rotating community-based credit scheme where members borrow money at low interest rates, and earn bonuses (returns) at the end of the year.

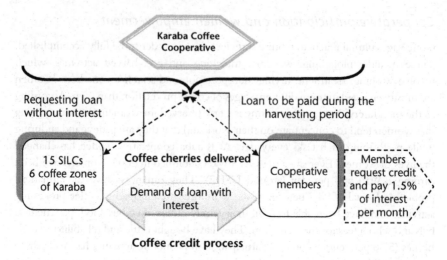

Coffee credit process

FIGURE 6.1 Channels of demand and credit repayment in Karaba coffee cooperative

Source: Authors' own elaboration

The functioning of the SILCs is summarized in Figure 6.1.

SILCs impart skills and techniques to women on handling their coffee and managing their financial activities. Through the loans obtained, members pay 1.5 per cent interest monthly, even if upon acknowledgment of delays, they may be asked to pay the following month. Penalties range from RWF100–200. Normally, a SILC group is composed of 15 to 30 members who are known to one other. The cooperative's members must be of good conduct and must attend monthly meetings; the solidarity and mutual relationship between members provide a kind of collateral for accessing loans. The cooperative acts as an intermediary between farmers and financial institutions. Coffee serves as a guarantor in terms of collateral for agricultural loans to buy chemical fertilizers and pesticides. Members also borrow some cash to buy inputs for mulching young coffee seedlings and transporting coffee beans to the nearest CWSs or selling points. Financial transactions among members are hinged on mutual trust and confidence. The cooperative assists members to use the loan efficiently in order to reduce risks.

According to the cooperative report of 2015, the loans were well used by borrowers. The same report reveals that after the coffee selling process, the cooperative management distributed bonuses to the active members. The results of this study have revealed that there is a high level commitment by women who have enhanced the care and welfare of their husbands, children and even relatives. The money earned has helped many of them run and expand small-scale businesses, such as hair salons, livestock, animal husbandry, canteens and restaurants. Families can now afford to pay for telephone costs, buying solar energy equipment, local beer, cassava flowers, fruits and vegetables. Through the income generated from coffee, rural farmers in Rwanda can also afford small-scale equipment used in milling produce and tailoring. All these activities have empowered women.

This was expressed by a 57-year-old widow:

> We as members of Karaba cooperative have opened a bank account at the Popular Bank of Karambi; no one can be paid without it. When we earn money, we save a small amount which supports us during bumper harvests when we do not have jobs. In fact, the cooperative has been fruitful and generated income and has enabled us to improve our health and shelter.

Coffee washing stations and women's empowerment

Karaba CWSs are funded and constructed by a USAID[2] project in order to enhance Rwanda's rural development by increasing the quality of coffee. This has helped to market coffee at competitive prices. CWSs have extended coffee innovation facilities through training programmes offered to members. They provide advantages to farmers which include: (i) reduction in labour demand required in coffee processing for vulnerable groups, especially households headed by children, widows and aged people; (ii) creation of jobs, especially for women; (iii) access to micro-credit institutions; (iv) access to electricity and safe water in rural areas, and provision of agricultural inputs. In addition, CWSs have provided a certain degree of autonomy for women in rural areas who were originally marginalized and abused by their husbands. Work in CWSs requires a lot of physical strength that necessitates the support of men, who are fully engaged in washing coffee while women and children help in carrying coffee beans, drying and storing them. With the construction of CWSs in Karaba, both women and men can now participate in coffee processing, which traditionally was done by men. With the presence of CWSs in rural areas, the work burden for women and children has been reduced and in some instances removed.

Women and the burdensome activities after the coffee season

Coffee is a perennial crop that produces beans once a year from March to July. After the harvest season, farmers experience difficulties in finding other sources of revenue to meet their daily needs. After this season, farmers are faced with the difficulty of getting money. To solve this problem, the USAID project has initiated other sources of income for producers. Among these is the production of mushrooms. Mushrooms can now be sold or bought at local markets. The production of mushrooms does not require much capital, space or time. A kilogram of mushrooms is sold at RWF1,200 (USD1.46). A widow and genocide survivor had this to say:

> Once I joined Karaba coffee cooperative and started supplementing diet with the mushrooms, my health has greatly improved. Earnings from mushrooms have enabled me to rebuild and repair my house, which was destroyed during the genocide. It has also enabled me to rear some chickens for eggs and rabbits for sale. All these activities have increased my monthly income, which helped me to cover daily family expenses.

In addition to mushrooms, female members have been initiated in weaving hand-craft baskets known as '*Agaseke*'. These are made of sisal and stiff fibre. The *Agaseke* is in high demand in the US and European markets. This has created an opportunity for Rwandan women to exchange ideas about their future. Thus, women have acquired new knowledge about circumventing the unemployment that comes after the coffee harvest and this has reduced poverty within families and communities. Cooperatives have enabled Rwandan women to build a network of mutual support to overcome cultural restrictions that are an impediment to progress and development. In 2011, through the cooperative movement, active members received bicycles on credit from the USA worth RWF100,000 (USD121.95). The main purpose of this credit was to relieve peasants from the hardships associated with transporting coffee to washing stations.

Social empowerment

Training as a tool for empowering women

Training and information have an important role to play in increasing women's involvement in cooperatives. During the interviews, members explained how work groups promote knowledge and skills, especially among female farmers. The exchange of experience has enabled women to increase farm output and coffee quality, which in turn has increased the production in general. Through different training sessions, cooperatives have popularized the concept of women's empowerment in the rural community: 69.3 per cent of the respondents said that through training, they have learned skills of reading, writing and counting. This has increased their skills and provided knowledge in the management of their resources. Members have also benefited from other advantages provided by the cooperative: they have learned bio-intensive farming techniques, which have helped them to increase production and acquire more skills by visiting other cooperatives in the country and region. Members have also been trained to handle health matters –6 per cent of their children were originally malnourished (Gisaro, 2013). As a measure to fight malnutrition, the cooperative has provided training sessions on family planning, HIV-AIDS, use of soya milk and tofu (called soya meat), eating a balanced diet and fruit production. According to one agricultural extension officer who was interviewed, the above practices have significantly reduced malnutrition and increased revenue.

Social advantages from the cooperative

Karaba cooperative has created strong social ties which constitute dependable social capital for its members in general and women in particular. Cooperatives offer networks for mutual support and solidarity that allow women members to improve their self-reliance. Karaba cooperative has enabled its members to acquire a voice in decision-making (FAO, 2011). It has also helped members to strengthen and extend ties of solidarity to members outside the family. The cooperative spirit has reinforced unity and reconciliation between members who were torn apart and divided by the 1994 genocide against the Tutsi. Many coffee growers in Karaba testified that hatred and divisions no longer existed among them. The cooperative spirit has taught them to forgive one another and this has reinforced unity and reconciliation. As a result of women's empowerment, women and widows have gained access to land titles and can now earn income of their own. This has improved the family diet, thus enabling children to attend school regularly.

Women and environmental protection

The two CWSs were established and funded by USAID and PDCRE projects in 2003 in implementing Rwandan government policy of having fully washed coffee. These tools of coffee quality have improved environmental conditions. In relation to soil degradation, planting coffee trees has brought better cover to the soils and has helped to fight against soil erosion. However, the waste water released after coffee fermentation has created a problem of environmental pollution. The solid organic matter from the coffee pulp decomposes in designed pits. After decomposition, the pulp can be turned into manure, rich in minerals, as demonstrated in Karaba. Women are mostly involved in maintaining coffee plantations. They are trained in environmental protection through the use of coffee pulp as fertilizers for their crops. In addition, since women spend most of their time working on farms, they have learned more about soil management and how to plant trees to protect the environment. Through the USAID project, women have been trained to use 'rondereza', or a firewood stove, which uses less firewood in order to protect the environment. Under this framework, they have also been taught how to treat water by boiling it before use in families, and by so doing, they have learned to protect water sources in their areas. Women have also been trained to make compost manure from other crops.

Apart from the benefits coffee has brought to the rural communities, it has also become a liability. Many social costs from CWSs, such as disease, water and air pollution, have been witnessed. As coffee waste is stored in pits before being recycled, these pits produce stinky water, which enters the water table of River Kibingo, running cross the CWS of Karambi. This river water is consumed by the neighbouring population. Despite this problem, the cooperative has embarked on recycling the waste and raising worms to digest the coffee pulp. The results are significant in terms of essential compost manure for agriculture.

Women and land inheritance in Karaba cooperative

Historically and culturally, land ownership in Rwanda was based on a patriarchal land system. Only boys had the automatic right to inherit land after the death of the family head. Women and girls were completely excluded from this affair. This was traditionally known as '*Kuzungura*'. As a result, land issues in Rwanda have been a source of conflict since time immemorial, with violence and divorce becoming frequent in the country. It was only in 2006 that the inheritance law was enacted, thus enabling girls, boys, women and men to have equal rights to inherit land. After joining Karaba cooperative, members have been trained by USAID and the cooperative management team on women's rights and the fight against gender-based violence, among others. The results of this study reveal that cooperatives offer the best channel through which families can acquire knowledge on land acquisition without causing friction and conflict among couples. According to the cooperative system, land does not belong to the husband alone but it is for both husband and wife, who enjoy equal rights. They can all use their land as collateral to apply for credit in times of financial crisis or to use the credit facility to invest in small-scale income-generating ventures. None of the two parties (husband or wife) has exclusive rights to sell land without informing the other. Thus, women have acquired significant bargaining power within their households and are protected against gender-based violence. For all these reasons, property and inheritance rights have created an enabling environment in empowering Rwanda's women, thus strengthening their rights in Rwanda. However, gender equality within the cooperative has posed a challenge regarding land inheritance issues. Obstacles to women's active participation are often structural and are mostly rooted in socio-cultural norms at community and household levels.

Karaba cooperative and leadership skills for women

Cooperatives offer an opportunity for women to have their voice heard and to access leadership roles that would otherwise not have been extended to women. Women participated in all activities of the cooperative, especially in the process of coffee production and washing. However, they do not participate more in the major decisions affecting the cooperative than men. Women were found to be actively involved in coffee growing, while men were simultaneously involved in many other activities. Karaba cooperative organizes sessions to enhance members' reading and counting skills and other activities, such as making savings and initiating micro-projects for income-generation, intended to empower mainly women. The coffee cooperatives have also provided a unique platform for women producers to be integrated into the decision-making process within the family. This has enabled them to be courageous and become part of the community leadership dynamics through participation in local government activities, especially for community development. These activities involve community work known as '*Umuganda*', local judicial courts '*Gacaca*' and '*Abunzi*', management of Umurenge Saving and Credit Cooperatives (SACCO), and Village Umurenge Development Programme (VUP). It is through such activities that Karaba coffee cooperative has communicated political messages from government to the grassroots. Cooperatives have become a tool for promoting women's empowerment in rural areas.

Conclusion

The study has shown that coffee cooperatives render invaluable services to their members, especially to women, by empowering them. It has revealed that Rwandan rural women are now recognized in society; they enjoy economic independence in the family, contrary to what used to happen before the introduction of the cooperatives, when their husbands had absolute control over family income. The coffee washing stations have helped to reduce the wage costs of coffee producers while valorising women's activity and encouraging the integration of vulnerable groups. The cooperative spirit has opened new perspectives for women's employment to fight against poverty as well as rural–urban migration. Besides, coffee has become a source of income, providing revenue to women, and this has led to dialogue between husband and wife, who jointly solve household problems. Women have become participants in family decision-making on income matters. This has given women the opportunity to share with their husbands and children on income distribution. Such joint discussions brought about by Karaba cooperative have reduced conflicts and violence; they have created peace in many families. Cooperatives have succeeded in enabling women to access agricultural facilities, livestock and credit from the bank. Through the income and coffee-credit system, coffee farmers (women in particular) have succeeded in paying for the education of their children, subscribing to the health insurance scheme, making house repairs for the family and developing a spirit of entrepreneurship among rural women. Coffee farmers have benefited from many socio-economic advantages and services, such as new agricultural techniques, developing an entrepreneurial culture, opening bank accounts, etc. The findings of this study have shown that cooperatives have had far-reaching socio-economic benefits for women. They contribute to women's employment, reduce discrimination against women, and lead to exchange of experiences. However, the low level of education and cultural barriers still pose a big challenge for the development of Rwandan rural women in the areas of land-and income-sharing within households (Bayisenge, 2014).

Notes

1 NAEB: National Agricultural Export Development Board.
2 US Agency for International Development.

References

Ansoms, An. Striving for growth, bypassing the poor? A critical review of Rwanda's rural sector policies, *Journal of Modern African Studies* 46, no. 1 (2008): 1–32.
Bayisenge, Jeannette. *Changing gender relations? Women's experiences of land rights in the case of the Land Tenure Reform Program in Rwanda.* PhD thesis, University of Gothenburg, Sweden, 2014.
Birchall, Johnston. *Re-discovering the co-operative advantage: Poverty reduction through self-help.* Geneva: ILO, 2003.

Food and Agriculture Organization (FAO). *Agricultural cooperative: Paving the way for food security and rural development factsheet*. Rome: FAO, IFAD, WFP, 2011.

Gibson, Ryan. *The role of cooperatives in community economic development*, RDI Working Paper 2005-3, 2005.

Gisaro, M. Ya-Bititi. *La structuration du monde paysan au Rwanda: cas des stations et des coopératives caféicoles de Maraba et de Karaba, District de Huye, Rwanda*. Thèse de Doctorat, Université de Liège, Gembloux Agro Bio-Tech, Belgium, 2013.

National Agricultural Export Development (NAEB) Board, *Annual report*. Kigali: NAEB, 2014.

Sibelet, Nicole and Mathilde Montzieux. Les facteurs de résilience de la caféiculture au Kenya: de la sécurisation alimentaire à la retraite, *Cahiers Agricultures* 21, no. 2–3 (2012): 179–191.

United Nations Department of Economic and Social Affairs (UN DESA). *Role of cooperatives in poverty elimination*. New York: UNDESA, 2012. Accessed 14 September 2017. www. un.org/en/development/desa/news/social/role-of-cooperatives-eliminate-poverty. html.

____. *Measuring the size and scope of cooperatives economy: Results of the 2014 Global census on co-operatives*. New York: UNDESA, 2014. Accessed 17 September 2017. www.un.org/ esa/socdev/documents/2014/coopsegm/grace.pdf.

7

THE CHANGING COOPERATIVE LANDSCAPE IN THE WORLD OF WORK

A study of women's empowerment through participatory strategies in India

Sudha Kornginnaya

Introduction

In India, more than 94 per cent of the women in the labour force are in the informal sector, working under conditions of poverty and its multiple disadvantages, such as lack of health, sanitation and education, impairing their work productivity (GOI, 2014). They often lack access to information and support services that are needed to directly increase their income (Ahluwalia, 1990). However, the economic pressures and changing socio-cultural attitudes towards women have necessitated their participation through collective action in the labour market. Women have opted for the cooperative model because it helps women organize and support themselves, their families and society (ICA, 1997; ILO, 2014). Cooperatives help women achieve better bargaining power as buyers and sellers in the marketplace and to negotiate needs and concerns vis-à-vis markets, state and community collectively, which they would not be able to do on their own individually (Dash, 2007; Jhabvala, 2013).

Cooperatives have been a democratic frame for millions of women workers in India who are either excluded due to the vicissitudes of the market or social constraints (Taimni, 1993). They have mobilized women for collective entrepreneurship in production, marketing, banking, services and other entrepreneurial activities in India. They have provided women workers an economic platform for their income-generation and livelihood activities along with social safety nets. Financial services offered to women members have increased their participation in paid work and engagement in diversified economic options contributing directly to family welfare, health and education of the children. Cooperatives have addressed the issues related to poverty, discrimination, vulnerability and social exclusion that the women face, reflecting on their physical mobility, political participation and gender equality (ILO, 2015; Kabeer, 2005; Kornginnaya, 2015).

Cooperatives have also provided equality of opportunities to many women workers to leverage their potential to assume leadership roles, to actively participate in the decision-making process and governance. Being enterprises based on values and principles, cooperatives can be considered to be apt instruments for advancing women's empowerment (ICA, 1997; ILO, 2015; Sudha, 2005).

In view of the above, this chapter outlines the participatory strategies initiated by the district-level cooperatives in the banking and dairy sectors in Dakshina Kannada District in the State of Karnataka in India. It also delineates the impact of participation of women members in such initiatives, leading to their sustainable empowerment. This study is descriptive and exploratory in nature and is based on empirical work conducted between 2012 to 2014, confined to two district-level cooperatives – South Canara District Central Cooperative Bank (SCDCC Bank) and Dakshina Kannada Cooperative Milk Producers Union Ltd (D.K. Milk Union) in Dakshina Kannada (D.K.) District in the State of Karnataka in India. Both primary and secondary sources of data were used in the study. Primary data from both the organizations and 200 women beneficiary members were collected through semi-structured interviews and informal discussion. A cross-section sample of 100 women beneficiary members were selected at random from each of the two district-level cooperatives from among the members who had participated in the activities initiated for women's empowerment. Thus a total of 200 women members constituted the sample of respondents for the study. In addition, organizational data of SCDDC Bank and D.K. Milk Union relating to empowerment strategies are also collected from official records that include annual reports, balance sheets, bye-laws, manuals, newsletters and magazines.

This chapter is organized as follows. In the next two sections, participatory strategies of SCDCC Bank and D.K. Milk Union are described respectively. In the fourth section, based on interviews with 200 women beneficiary members who participated in the initiatives taken by two cooperatives, factors impacting empowerment of women members are analysed in terms of economic, political and social empowerment. After examining challenges to be dealt with further, some recommendations are proposed as a conclusion.

Participatory strategies of South Canara District Central Cooperative Bank Ltd (SCDCC Bank)

This cooperative bank has operated in South Canara and Udupi District of Karnataka in India since 1914. The bank has given priority to financing the agricultural sector by providing timely and adequate finance through 902 cooperative societies at the grassroots level. The bank has a total business of INR33.91 billion, with deposits worth INR22.94 billion and returns to members of 10.5 per cent as of 2014, showing the growth rate of 28 per cent as compared with the previous year. The bank has computerized all its branches and introduced innovative customer services, such as a single window system for integrated service delivery, any-branch banking, 12 hours' banking in the head office branch, *Rupay Kisan* credit cards, banking on wheels, and the formation of *Navodaya* (Upstart) self-help groups (SHGs). SCDCC Bank has been awarded as the best District Central Cooperative Bank by Karnataka State Cooperative Apex Bank, Bangalore for the last 15 years. The bank's success in completing 100 years of fruitful service in the wake of stiff competition in the banking sector is mainly attributed to its customer-centred policies, which have been greatly beneficial to the farming community and the population of the district (SCDCC Bank, 2015).

SCDCC Bank's initiatives toward empowerment of women

The bank set up *Navodaya Grama Vikasa* (Upstart Village Development) Charitable Trust (NGVCT), Mangalore, in 2004 and formed *Navodaya* SHG for the socio-economic empowerment of the rural poor, particularly rural women. With the help of the trust, the bank has made a silent revolution in rural upliftment by promoting and financing 41,143 SHGs. Micro-finance is provided to the rural mass in a most simplified manner. They have mobilized a total savings of INR1.51 billion from 283,276 members, of which more than 67.23 per cent, namely 190,446 persons, are women members, and 32,971 groups are credit linked with INR17.91 billion advanced to them.

Programmes for SHGs consist of basic orientation to members for the formation of groups, maintenance of books of accounts, credit management and capacity-building. NGVCT imparts training for production, provides financial assistance and marketing guidance for the self-employment of SHG members and helps all committed members to achieve economic progress. The project organizes marketing fairs and exhibitions every year to market their products and to build the brand image. Outstanding women entrepreneurs are also honoured on the World Women's Day. The trust organizes conferences for SHG members that help them build their leadership capabilities, managerial competencies and livelihood skills.

To promote self-employment of the rural youth, NGVCT conducts the Rural Entrepreneurship Development Program (REDP) in collaboration and under the guidance of the National Bank for Agriculture and Rural Development (NABARD) in the area of agriculture and allied activities, such as dairy farming, bee keeping, horticulture, mushroom cultivation, screen printing and other activities. It also organizes micro-entrepreneurship development programmes (MEDPs) for SHG women members that include tailoring, food and fruit processing, fashion design, home products and office file making. The SCDCC Bank, through the trust, has endeavoured to achieve 100 per cent financial inclusion in the district, for which it received appreciation from the Government of India.

Besides, it provides social safety nets in terms of *chaithanya* (life) insurance schemes (CIS) and financial help to poor patients suffering from cancer, cardiac problems and renal failure. Free health check-up camps were organized, benefitting more than 8,000 rural poor people. Under CIS, for the nominal premium amount of INR250 per year, the insured will get the benefit of INR6,000 for medical treatment, INR25,000 as insurance compensation for accidental death and INR10,000 as maternity benefits for women members. Women welfare programmes of the government are optimally utilized for leveraging the competencies of poor women, with an impact on their empowerment. In the case of death of a SHG member, 'Navodaya Santhwana' (console) amount of INR1,000 will be given to the dependant of a deceased member. This scheme was implemented in 2012 and 310 dependants of SHG members have received a total amount of INR310,000 as of December 2013. The trust also provides life coverage to their members through micro-insurance called *Jeevan Madhur* (good life) in collaboration with the Life Insurance Corporation of India.

NGVCT has introduced educational institutions for the higher education of rural poor children and has set up job-oriented training centres for rural unemployed youth. Rural sports and cultural events are organized to promote rural sports and conserve the spirit of folk culture among rural youth. *Navodaya* trophy is bestowed to the outstanding performers in folk arts and games as an encouragement initiative. On the eve of the centenary celebration of the cooperative movement, meritorious scholarships were given to 1,000 poor and needy students of Dakshina Kannada and Udupi Districts.

In view of the commendable service and the achievement of the NGVCT, it was conferred a coveted award from NABARD for the best management of Self-Help Groups in the Karnataka State. The bank has received this award for the past 13 years (NGVCT, 2015; SCDCC Bank, 2015).

Participatory strategies of Dakshina Kannada Cooperative Milk Producers Union Ltd. (D.K. Milk Union)

Dakshina Kannada Co-op Milk Producers' Union is an ISO 22000:2005 certified organization having jurisdiction in Dakshina Kannada and Udupi coastal districts. The union has 119,774 farmer members, of whom 33,290 are women members. It is one of the leading milk unions in the state of Karnataka and was conferred the Best Cooperative Milk Union Award during the All India Cooperative Week. At the time of registration in 1986, the union's initial procurement was 4,500 kilograms per day. Now the union is procuring 0.4 million kilograms of milk per day, average sale is 339,688 litres per day, and it markets 12 value-added products. It has 1,397 active dealers, 10 franchisees and 18 milk parlours. The union has 671 member dairy cooperative societies, which consists of 179 women dairy cooperative societies (WDCSs) in its jurisdiction, out of which 137 WDCSs are under the Support to Training and Employment Programme (STEP) of the Government of India. D.K. Milk Union has been rendering integrated services in production, procurement, processing, assured marketing, scientific pricing, provision of technical services and other related extension activities. The union has organized women into SHGs at the village level, who have floated their dairy cooperatives and also formed their federation at the district level (DKMUL, 2014).

Strategies for women's empowerment

Support to Training and Employment Programme (STEP)

D.K. Milk Union has successfully implemented the STEP in seven different phases (1997–2014) initiated through the Karnataka Milk Federation at the state level. It was a central government sponsored programme under the Ministry of Women and Child Development. It promoted an integrated package of inputs for the self-reliance and empowerment of women by enhancing their productivity and enabling them to take up sustainable income-generation activities. The STEP aims to make a significant impact by upgrading skills and providing employment to women on a project basis by mobilizing women into viable groups to form women's dairy cooperative societies. The programme also includes provisions for margin money, imparting skills, arranging for productive assets and support services, creation of backward and forward linkages, visiting the Amul cooperative groups in Anand, Gujarat, providing access to credit and awareness generation programmes in gender awareness-raising, nutrition education, legal literacy and awareness-raising of project staff.

The ultimate endeavour of the project is to develop the group to thrive on a self-sustaining basis in the marketplace with minimal government support and intervention after the completion of the project period. The target group includes the marginalized, asset-less rural women and urban poor, such as wage labourers, unpaid daily workers, female-headed households, migrant labourers, tribal and other dispossessed groups and families below the poverty line. Each WDCS gets a grant of approximately INR0.25–0.30 million for establishment, management and for granting interest-free loans for the purchase of livestock. Both the Government of India and the implementing agency share the financial responsibilities in the order of 90 per cent and 10 per cent, respectively.

Ksheera Sanjeevini

This strategy is a part of the *Sanjeevini* Project initiated by the National Rural Livelihoods Mission (NRLM), launched in 2011 by the Ministry of Rural Development (MoRD) of the Government of India, through the Karnataka State Rural Livelihood Promotion Society (KSRLPS). It was implemented by the union in 2014 with the twin goals of achieving women's empowerment and poverty reduction through the promotion of entrepreneurship development activities and self-employment opportunities in dairy farming for dispossessed and marginalized rural poor. It envisages enhancing the net income of women by providing direct employment to women, securing them a guaranteed livelihood. The project cost per beneficiary was INR17,100; each WDCS received grants of approximately INR0.455 million for management, training, and awareness programmes, and for purchasing and insurance of the livestock. The activities of the project consist of mobilizing women into WDCSs through SHGs, provision of margin money, computer and managerial training, dairy farming management, visit to Amul Dairy, general awareness programmes, organic manure unit, installation of fodder production machine, solar green energy and fodder processing unit in WDCSs (KMF, 2015).

The total fund granted under NRLM was INR3.4 million, of which INR2.4 million was utilized for the various activities mentioned above. In total, 27 SHGs were formed, 72 livestocks were purchased, seven vermicompost units were established, 485 general awareness and training programmes were organized for the SHG members, management committee members, women resource persons and dairy farmers.

Factors impacting empowerment of women members

The participatory interventions initiated by both district-level cooperatives have paid good returns to members in terms of increased deposits from SHGs, enhanced client base, better financial inclusion coverage, more income-generating activities, viable business and social propositions, realized both economic enterprise and association goals, improved community outreach, institutional networking, enhanced the organizational identity and brand image. However, how are these initiatives perceived by the beneficiary women themselves?

Data collected through the interview schedules and open discussions with the beneficiary women respondents have helped in understanding the efficacy of the above-mentioned participatory strategies as perceived by them.

Economic empowerment

The study uncovered the fact that the majority of the women trained under empowerment initiatives of the SCDCC Bank and D.K. Milk Union, who were once in the margins, now found themselves bankable and able to mainstream their economic trajectory. They opined that the work itself is life, as it supports their right to live and acts as a panacea for the concomitant ills of poverty. There has been a paradigm shift from the economic dependency due to unpaid and unaccounted household work to economic sustainability reflected in women's involvement in economic activities, better choice for spending and the consequent self-respect gained in their houses. Expressing the sense of satisfaction, they asserted that they were capable of meeting their wants out of their earnings, have increased the power of resilience and standard of living, which were imperceptible before joining the cooperatives.

The four Ds, namely – Desire to work, Determination to empower, Development of the family, and Dedication to collective action – have galvanized women to choose the participatory model of cooperatives. Women asserted that the integrated approach of gainful work and micro-finance, coupled with capacity-building measures and infrastructure facilities provided through their collectives have been instrumental for their upward economic mobility. Their economic prowess and social solidarity are testified in the way they organized into SHGs to set up WDCSs or other allied activities, leading to secured livelihoods and financial independence. They also conduct tailoring, computer training and other diversified activities to get an additional income.

The business acumen and experiential learning gained over the years by the WDCS women members led to the floating of a multi-purpose cooperative in Handattu and cooperative bank in Hemmadi regions to meet their diverse financial needs and deepen their financial inclusion. The proliferation of developmental initiatives has promoted cooperatives in other sectors, attracted localization of economic activities and self-employment opportunities in the region, resulting in better living culture and rural regeneration. Thus, through the cooperative efforts women have been the catalysts of socio-economic change for themselves and for the local community.

The self-help group members who were trained under entrepreneurship development programmes initiated by NGVCT wing of SCDCC Bank have been successful social entrepreneurs, creating full-time occupations for many wage-earners in the study area. They run micro-enterprises in the domains of tailoring, home products, food and fish processing, fashion design, candle and file making, horticulture and floriculture, poultry farming and vermicompost. Their main thrust is to fulfil the goals of self-actualization and socio-economic well-being of group and family members. The collective entrepreneurship ensured equality of ownership and equitable distribution of income and risks. It has given a direct access to the market, strengthened their bargaining power and increased their business networking. They have eschewed an asymmetry in access to entrepreneurial resources, which is a common trend in the labour market. However, inadequate forward and backward linkages, marketing and logistic facilities hinder the supply chain and economic returns. Though these start-ups have high significance in terms of their economic contributions and job creation, they are invisible and unaccounted for in the growth process when compared with corporate start-ups.

The survey showed that, given the financial literacy to the poor, their labour has economic value when they work in groups. It has enhanced their financial decision-making power in the management of their personal finance and households, transforming them from the state of utter illiterates to functional literates. Illiterate women members are now capable of handling the banking transactions independently and are confident to take good decisions for their secured future. The stable income and peer pressure have promoted them to save and improve their investment potential. They have invested their discretionary income, which they get after meeting the family necessities, in the form of deposits in financial institutions, gold ornaments, land, renovation and purchase of their houses, durable consumer goods and for the education of their children. This has increased their capital assets and improved their standards of living.

The micro-finance has been the life blood of 32 per cent of the agricultural women worker respondents in the survey, as it has helped them repay old debts to banks and recover collateral security. It has served as a hedge against the agrarian crisis and acted as a lubricant for the agriculture wheel moving. The repayment compulsion has enabled women to shift from mono-cropping to multiple cropping, animal husbandry and other allied activities, perpetuating their economic engagement and hence increasing their purchasing power.

Dairying is perceived as a way of life and a homestead subsidiary occupation by many farming women. Eighty per cent of women found it more lucrative in terms of assured market for the milk and processed products, nutritional food, increased marginal household income and free manure for agriculture. In their view, it provides security in terms of work, income, food, saving, nutrition, health and livestock. Survey respondents opined that investment by cooperatives in dairy farming has solved the problems of malnutrition, energy deficiency and deforestation due to the access to affordable bio-gas, leading to their improved work productivity. Permanki WDCS is a unique cooperative model and epitomizes women's empowerment. This is exemplified in the diverse labour-intensive job opportunities created for the rural poor, which serve as a revenue spinner for them and cooperatives. They include community fodder grass cultivation in barren leased land, selling saplings, installation of a cattle feed preparation unit and a vermicompost unit. They have envisaged to set up a mechanized feed preparation unit using the areca nut leaves, generating more jobs and income to SHG members. It is an exemplary cooperative for its communal harmony and unity, as it demonstrated that it could transcend all castes, religions, political interests, classes and status rigidities.

Political empowerment

Work influences the family, local community, social system and the cultural process. 'The nature and arrangement of work often signals the relationship in society' (Jhabvala, 2013, p. 383). Decent work, exposure to weekly meetings, discussion of problems, lending operations, decision-making, entrepreneurial activities – all these have sharpened their latent talent and boosted their confidence, helping them meet any kind of challenge. They were able to consolidate their voice and articulate their concerns against obdurate behaviour and intractable structural inequalities that persist in the labour market. Women, who were circumvented only to a domestic role, are now found active in outdoor activities for the purpose of banking, marketing, micro-enterprising and community-oriented activities. The enhanced functional awareness has made them assertive, responsive and responsible, both at work and in the domestic sphere.

Half of the office-bearers of WDCSs are proud of their position and affirmed that they could disprove that politics is a world of men for which the women have neither an attitude nor the knowledge and are circumscribed only to the domestic realms. Some of them have contested for local government bodies and participated in community development projects in the study area. By exercising political power and through their collective effort, they were able to get access to basic resources such as drinking water, roads, electricity, primary health care centres and schools. Thus, through the assertion of the rights and articulation of their identities, the women could get the legitimate demands and citizenship-based rights fulfilled,proving the cooperative precept of 'all for each and each for all'.

Women's representation on boards enhanced their decision-making ability, governance skills, lobbying and networking capabilities, leading to the strategizing of more pro-poor and pro-women initiatives. Besides gaining political identity, they are emboldened to voice against governance deficits, systemic aberration and corrupt practices. They were not hesitant in apprising the government officials of their problems. They are bolstered to challenge and change the age-old ideologies that have relegated them to social exclusion. Deprived women respondents were motivated to deliberate in the meetings and contest for the elections. However, establishing equality of opportunities, changing the existing power relationship and mitigating the social barriers are an uphill task for the women leaders, particularly in the rural areas.

Social empowerment

The study revealed the fact that women gain their social status and play their social role well when they are economically independent. They affirmed that their active involvement in SHGs has helped them to get identity and visibility in both the family and society. The group cohesion and solidarity among women have transformed their status from dependence on men to interdependence on the group members and cooperatives. Sharing of their work responsibility in times of exigencies testifies to their sense of mutuality and caring, which are the essence of cooperation. Women supplement the family income as equal economic partners in addition to the shared care work and family responsibilities, promoting gender parity, both in the family and the community. Never-schooled women are able to educate their daughters in higher education institutions. Awareness of and information about the social safety nets to the poor are vital to reduce their debt and poverty (Ahluwalia, 1990). The access to safety nets in terms of micro health insurance and medical facilities has also impacted positively on work productivity and efficiency, decreased morbidity, arresting their downward slide into health crisis and the poverty trap. However, it is insufficient in terms of value and coverage, particularly for the extreme poor.

Although poverty eradication remains the central agenda of cooperatives, the latter seek to achieve it through a dual process of inclusion and promoting grass-roots leadership. Whereas the group liability approach of SHGs inculcated the spirit of thrift, the skill development initiatives ignited the spirit of 'I can do it' that has driven them to come out of the confines of their houses and engage in their choice of livelihood activities, resulting in increased household incomes and economic independence. Besides, it has transformed their lifestyles from the state of irrational spending to financial prudence. Marginalized women deemed cooperatives as an institutional option to organize and a learning centre for participatory democracy – both are imperative for their leadership development. The innate needs of the women that have affected them kindled their leadership ability and ignited their sense of involvement in cooperatives. Realizing the need to develop, all the women office-bearers strived very hard to acquire land and construct their own building for their WDCS, multi-purpose cooperative and cooperative bank, mobilized capital and women's support, leading to their self-sustenance.

Challenges

Participation of members, as the essence of cooperative democracy, is gaining more significance in the cooperative circles compared with before. With the approval and release of the ICA *Blueprint for a Cooperative Decade*, 'enhancing participation has become a critical mandate and a must-do agenda', highlighting its urgency, relevance and importance while moving towards Vision 2020 (ICA, 2013, p. 8). Inclusive participation of members is an opening for women's integration into cooperatives, but it may not be perceived as a basic value of cooperation among the leaders of the cooperatives, staff of cooperative departments and cooperative development agencies (Taimni, 1993). Cooperatives in general neither have any educational initiatives for the disadvantaged members on the cooperative basics nor provide any practical exposure to the management to enrich their experience. So women's involvement is circumvented either to the trade terms or to be the recipients of the benefits of the government programmes.

In this regard, the study shows that even in these cooperatives, there are still significant challenges. A third of the respondent members under study articulated that lack of awareness of cooperative functions and its potential have deterred them from assuming a leadership role. Half of the members stated that the patriarchal system, social culture and gender discrimination in the family have rendered them susceptible to subordination. Forty per cent of the sample respondents opined that their low economic status made them vulnerable to passivity and timidity, retarding their managerial ability. Consequently, active participation of women in decision-making and governance processes in their cooperatives was found inadequate. Even women who were found active in SHG-related activities as they directly impact their livelihood were characterized by a lack of quantitative and qualitative participation in annual general meetings and cooperative administrative affairs. Member communication and information was insufficient to keep member proximity, which is vital for participatory democracy at the grassroots level. Lack of decentralization in governance structures and member-led committees has also hindered the enlightened involvement of women. So the interest of members was limited only to the benefit they derive from the cooperatives. They expressed that the cooperatives should regularly conduct women leadership development activities and capacity-building initiatives that perpetuate constructive member engagement with their cooperatives.

To counter the systemic paralysis and democratic vacuum in cooperatives, participatory strategies are paramount. Membership of a cooperative per se is not a panacea to the problems of poverty, discrimination and inequalities. So there arises the need for informed participation that is based on the agency of the women, rather than depending on one institutional form or another (Müncker, 2002).

Efficacious and motivational strategies that ignite the latent potential of the poor towards self-reliance with self-esteem are the need of the hour.

More capacity-building in cooperative principles, values and governance is needed in rural areas in India, where there is inadequate and weak infrastructure for human resources, and where women are more likely to face poverty, illiteracy and societal restrictions (Kumar and Singh, 1992). Moreover, work insecurity fraught by the unbridled market forces have necessitated cooperatives to devise effective interventions that give women access to information, inclusion, opportunity, security and human development. This will go a long way in winning the lifelong allegiance of poor women for cooperatives.

Conclusion

This chapter outlines the role of cooperatives in empowering women and the need for participatory strategies for their active participation in India. Based on survey data, it examines the diverse strategies in self-help group formation, micro-finance, micro-insurance, capacity-building measures, and self-employment avenues initiated by SCDCC Bank and D.K. Milk Union for espousing the cause of women's empowerment. It also analyses the three factors explaining the impact of participatory strategies on the empowerment of women in terms of economic empowerment, political empowerment and social empowerment. The empowerment dimensions are reflective of the efficacy of women's participation that effect socio-economic change in their lives.

The policy implications of the findings include the need for collaboration between the government and the cooperative movement for devising a favourable regulatory framework, structural reorganization and a policy mandate for integrating and internalizing the women's empowerment agenda into cooperatives. Supportive legal reforms and administrative provisions are vital for organizing deprived women into cooperatives voluntarily. Necessary social protection and legal entitlements need to be extended by the state to poor women organized under cooperatives. District- and state-level federations need to provide support in terms of finance, human resources, infrastructure and technology to the resource-scant primary cooperatives for the effective implementation of women's empowerment programmes. Concerted efforts of the state government, Cooperative Department, state- and district-level federations through policies, investment and programmes oriented towards the empowerment of women in varied dimensions are paramount for mainstreaming women on the inclusive growth trajectory.

References

Ahluwalia, Montek S. Policies for poverty alleviation, *Asian Development Review* 8, no. 7 (1990): 111–132.

Dakshina Kannada Co-operative Milk Producers Union Ltd. Accessed 5 December 2014. www.dkmul.com/index.html.

Dash, Bishnu Mohan. Entrepreneurship through cooperatives: An ideal vehicle for women's sustainable development, *Women's Link* 13, no. 2 (April–June 2007): 7–9.

Government of India. *Statistical profile on women labour 2012–2013.* Chandigarh/Shimla: Labour Bureau, Ministry of Labour and Employment, 2014.

International Co-operative Alliance (ICA). *Cooperative leadership training for women*, Report of the Regional Preparatory Workshop, Kuala Lumpur, Malaysia, 9–11 December 1997. New Delhi: ICAROAP, 1997.

____. *Blueprint for a cooperative decade*, 2013. Accessed 10 January 2015. http://ica.coop/en/publications/ blueprint-co-operative-decade.

International Labour Office (ILO). *Leveraging the cooperative advantage for women's empowerment and gender equality.* Geneva, 2014.

____. *Advancing gender equality: The cooperative way.* Geneva, 2015.

Jhabvala, Renana. Informal workers and economy, *Indian Journal of Industrial Relations: A Review of Economic and Social Development* 48, no. 3 (2013): 373–386.

Kabeer, Naila. Is microfinance a 'magic bullet' for women empowerment? Analysis of findings from South Asia, *Economic and Political Weekly* 40, no. 44–45 (2005): 4709–4718.

Karnataka Milk Federation. Accessed 3 March 2015. www.kmfnandini.coop.

Kornginnaya, Sudha. Women in leadership for effective governance: Issues and challenges. In *The 10th ICA Asia-Pacific Regional Research Conference on Governance of Co-operatives: Issues and Challenges*, VAMNICOM, Pune, India, 5–6 November 2015.

Kumar, Prem and Bhawdeep Singh. *Managing human resources in rural sector.* New Delhi: Akashdeep Publishing House, 1992.

Münker, Hans-H. *The supportive environment for cooperatives in the context of current political, economic, social, demographic and ecological environment.* A paper for the Expert Group Meeting on Supportive Environment for Cooperatives: A Stakeholder Dialogue on Definitions, Prerequisites and Process of Creation, cited in *Cooperatives and rural financial development: Great opportunities and surmountable difficulties.* Rabobank: Nederland, 2002.

Navodaya Grama Vikas Charitable Trust (NGVCT). *Annual report.* 2015.

South Canara District Central Cooperative Bank Ltd. (SCDCC Bank). *Annual report.* 2015.

Sudha, K. Micro initiatives: An effective member relationship management strategy in cooperatives in India, *Review of International Cooperation.* 98, no. 1 (2005): 90–98.

Taimni, K.K. *Cooperative development: The next phase*, New Delhi: ICA-DOMUS Trust, 1993.

8

WASTE COOPERATIVES IN BRAZIL

Exploring links between cooperative ideals and raising gender awareness

Sonia Maria Dias and Ana Carolina Ogando

Introduction

Despite the growing number of studies on solid waste management, gender dynamics in the sector is understudied. Moreover, gender inequality has been, up until recently, largely ignored by the cooperative movement of waste pickers (Dias and Ogando, 2015),[1] as well as supporting non-governmental organizations (NGOs), in Brazil. Although there seem to be higher concentrations of women in Brazilian waste pickers' cooperatives in comparison with men, this is neither indicative of gender equality nor of women's stronger presence in the higher echelons of the waste pickers' national movement (*Movimento Nacional de Catadores de Materiais Recicláveis*, MNCR). Recent national studies have documented conflicts arising from the sexual division of labour in waste pickers' cooperatives (Goulart and Lima, 2012; Wirth, 2010), while others have looked at women's leadership and management positions at the local cooperative level versus the national movement (Dias *et al.*, 2013). Adopting a gendered approach to waste picking is, therefore, one of the current key challenges for the Brazilian waste pickers' cooperative movement. Our core argument is that efforts to critically reflect on gender equality and to challenge the different forms of gender-based violence that pervade women waste pickers' lives are essential for bridging the cooperative movement's founding ideology with its practices.

Such an approach within the context of the waste picking sector and cooperative environment may constitute, among other elements, the identification of impediments to women's access to knowledge and information, the valorisation of both productive and reproductive roles and how they relate to women's economic empowerment, and the guarantee of equal representation in different levels and spaces of decision-making. More broadly, this also entails recognizing two important dimensions that impact gender relations. First, that the interconnection among these elements cannot be overlooked since each sustains practices and structures that reproduce gender inequalities. Second, that women experience gender injustices differently as a result of complex identity markers, including race, sexuality, age, disability, ethnicity, and others.

Identifying the above-mentioned inequalities, as well as others, within waste pickers' cooperatives and the national movement[2] reveals some of the day-to-day challenges women waste pickers experience. Moreover, it prompts a reflection on how the ideals of the cooperative movement have been upheld, including in terms of promoting gender equality. Initially, waste pickers' cooperatives in Brazil were founded on the principles of mutual help, solidarity, and democratic relations. One of the main objectives of the cooperative model is to strengthen the economic and social inclusion of groups of vulnerable informal workers. Stemming from this context, our reflections here seek to understand how the expressions of gender inequalities within waste picker cooperatives and the MNCR in Brazil present a contradiction to the very ideals from which they originated and thus hinder the broader pursuit for social justice.

The first section of this chapter will reflect on some of the national historical and political elements that established the waste pickers' cooperative movement. The second section considers some of the gender dynamics within the sector based on findings from the feminist participatory action research project with women waste pickers in Minas Gerais, Brazil. These findings reinforce the belief that raising gender awareness is part of a long-term process with concrete actions that seek to promote gender quality. In the last section, we argue that calling attention to gender inequalities in local cooperatives and the MNCR can be one path to promoting more democratic and inclusive relations, while also contributing to strengthening collective action and revitalizing the cooperative movement of waste pickers in Brazil.

The genesis of the waste pickers' cooperative movement in Brazil

Although organizing is fundamental for the 'emancipation of the marginalized' (Bhowmik, 2006), informal workers face numerous challenges in their organizing efforts. Some practical challenges include falling outside a legal framework for formal employers, working in individualized or mobile workplaces, and ultimately attempting to secure their livelihoods, which overshadow efforts to enable a sense of collective identity (Bonner and Spooner, 2011). In addition, daily struggles for survival and security, coupled with social stigma and internalized racial and gender norms, present other barriers (Kabeer et al., 2013). In the waste picking sector, though studies have traced different models such as associations (some operating under the cooperative model), unions, community-based organizations, micro-enterprises and cooperatives (Dias and Alves, 2008; Moreno et al., 1997; Samson, 2009), concrete obstacles remain and can directly impact on the possibilities to organize according to the existing contextual dynamics.

In Brazil, the cooperative model has been a popular mode of organization among waste pickers. This choice can be partly explained by three interconnecting factors that coincide with the political and economic context of the country from the 1980s through to the early 1990s. On one level, and related to the economic recession of the period, we can identify efforts to map out and consolidate theoretical discussions on solidarity economy, with the cooperative model emerging as a challenge to capitalist and exclusionary modes of production. On another level, the end of the military regime and beginning of the country's re-democratization paved the path for the effervescence of social movements and civil society demands for social justice. Aligned with these demands are the efforts of Catholic NGOs working with marginalized communities and unorganized waste pickers. It is also in this political context that municipal governments, primarily associated with the Workers Party (PT), would begin incorporating demands for economic and social justice in their discourse and agenda. In this sense, there was some convergence between civil society and municipal governments' attention to the growing rates of poverty and exclusion. Finally, on a third level, it is important to consider how the legislative and policy context also encouraged the creation of cooperatives, particularly with the rise of the PT to the federal government in 2003. While a comprehensive account[3] of the genesis of the national waste pickers' movements, guided by the cooperative model, is still needed, a framework that considers theoretical, political, and legislative/policy contexts provides insights on the organizing processes involving informal recyclers in Brazil.

Accounts of the first cooperatives in Brazil date as far back as the end of the 19th century in the southeast region of the country and were largely influenced by European immigrants (Silva et al., 2003). Studies point to the diverse types of cooperatives established across the country based on the political, social, and economic specificities of each region (de Morais et al., 2011; Silva et al., 2003). It is, however, amidst the high levels of unemployment and adoption of neoliberal policies of the late 1980s and 1990s that cooperatives emerge as a strategy for survival. Far from aiming to systematically review theoretical debates on solidarity economy, our purpose is to show how these discussions were important for reflecting on the emancipatory potential of cooperatives for marginalized populations and connected various civil society actors – academia, NGOs, social movements, trade unions – engaged in their own initiatives to tackle poverty and organize workers (Singer, 2009).

The values associated with cooperatives and linked to solidarity economy serve as an entry point for our analysis because they cast light on the association between the precarious nature of the work done by waste pickers and the emphasis on equality and democratic management. In this sense, cooperatives break from the capitalist logic of competition and focus on setting the grounds for mutual help and equality of opportunity (Birchall, 2001), despite the fact that there are numerous debates centring on the fact that the model cannot be entirely disassociated from a market logic. Cooperatives, nevertheless, establish an organizational process that attempts 'to bridge the calculative and power rationality (found in the Market and the State) and the goal or communicative rationality (driving social movements and found in the spheres of reproduction)' (Develtere, 1993).

Associated to this broader and underlying theoretical discussion that impacted the choice of cooperative models for organizing waste pickers in Brazil, it is also worth highlighting the political context and the role of both civil society and the state. In the 1980s in Brazil, informal recyclers were largely working in an autonomous and isolated manner in open dumps or collecting on the streets. In some cases, family units worked together. Organizing efforts were scarce and, as a result, these individuals were subject to exploitation by middlemen and exposure to hazardous work environments (Dias and Alves, 2008). However, by the early 1990s, Catholic NGOs began pioneering work by facilitating the first organizing processes among street dwellers, particularly noting those who collected recyclable materials on a regular basis to sustain their livelihoods. These Catholic NGOs identified the potential for these groups to organize themselves around labour demands (Dias, 2002). Sister Cristina Bove,[4] one of the leading supporters of the waste pickers' organizing movement in Brazil and a member of the Catholic NGO Pastoral da Rua, acknowledges that given how atomized street dwellers and waste pickers were at the time, a model of organization based on strong cooperative principles would be better suited to galvanize the organizing efforts of these groups. These cooperatives were thus influenced by international models, such as the strong housing cooperative movement in Uruguay, and national dynamics emerging from the progressive sector of the Catholic Church, which emphasized communitarian ideology and practices. Along with Catholic NGOs, it is worth noting that other NGOs, social movements, and international development agencies were key supporters in organizing waste pickers.

During this incipient phase of organizing, both civil society and municipal governments played important roles. By the late 1980s, municipal governments headed by the PT were fundamental in calling attention to the role waste pickers played in cities such as São Paulo,[5] Porto Alegre and Belo Horizonte. Ultimately, these cities, all governed by PT mayors, became national references for including waste picker cooperatives as partners and service providers in their solid waste management systems (Dias and Alves, 2008). The integration of these cooperatives resulted from the willingness of the first municipalities to meet waste pickers' demands and the party's high responsiveness to claims for social inclusion and participation coming from Brazilian social movements (Alvarez et al., 1998; Heller, 2001).

The experiences of integrating cooperatives in waste systems also inspired the creation of a national stakeholders' platform called the National Waste and Citizenship Forum (*Forúm Nacional de Lixo e Cidadania*, FNLC), whose main goal was to promote better environmental standards in solid waste management, as well as social and economic recognition of recyclers (Dias, 2009). This visibility had a nationwide impact, inspiring other groups of waste pickers to get organized. It also served as a catalyst for social activism among workers that led to the creation of the MNCR during the First Congress of Brazilian Waste Pickers held in Brasília in 2001.

With the advent of the PT to the federal government in 2003, the policy and legislative environment became more favourable for further implementing and supporting waste picker cooperatives throughout the country. One example of this is how federal government policies were influenced particularly through the institutionalization of the National Secretariat for Solidarity Economy (*Secretaria Nacional de Economia Solidária*, Senaes). In her review of the organizing process in the waste sector, Samson (2009) affirms that there is a clear link between the policy and legislative context and the choices for organizing waste pickers, including the goals workers establish afterward. The choice of how to organize is related to existing laws that may induce one type of organization over the other. For instance, some countries may forbid informal workers to organize into unions and/or as cooperatives, while others may encourage workers to organize under one specific model by creating incentives to do so. An example is how Brazil's current national solid waste policy (Law No. 12.305/2010) establishes cooperatives as the preferential partners of source segregation schemes. Ultimately, workers need to take into consideration the legal and regulatory environment, as well as the registry and tax systems when evaluating strategies and formats for organizing.

The theoretical debates, political context, and policy/legislative incentives show that despite the economic stalemate of the late 1980s, there was a political opportunity for consolidating the organizing process as a result of the synergy between civil society and municipal governments. While the scenario presented above paints a favourable picture of the process, the challenges to upholding cooperative ideals should not be overlooked. One of the main challenges for cooperatives is ensuring that democratic relations, accountability, respect, and equal opportunities prevail within the work environments. In this sense, cooperatives face the tension of whether or not they are capable of steering away from hierarchical structures that reproduce inequalities and create problems for communication feedback loops between leaders and cooperative members. With regard to inclusive recycling schemes, waste picker cooperatives also face challenges related to the fact that they need to present themselves as service providers and thus need to abide by the specific demands from both the political and/or economic sectors. As a result, waste picker cooperatives not only have to represent the ideals of the social movement and meet demands from the market, they must also meet public health service standards and understand the rules involved in many political negotiating arenas that compose urban solid waste systems. The demands placed on cooperatives result from recognizing the multiple roles they play in contemporary urban systems. This involves understanding how cooperatives (1) play a central social role in the socio-economic inclusion of waste pickers (the livelihood dimension), (2) carry out a public health and environmental service for urban solid waste systems (the service dimension), and (3) are important actors in the recycling chain (the economic dimension) (Dias, 2009).

Overview of the National Waste Pickers' Movement (MNCR)

The National Waste Pickers' Movement is a social movement committed to organizing waste pickers and to advancing workers' collective demands. The cooperatives and associations affiliated with the MNCR abide by guiding principles such as the following: worker control of the organization by waste pickers; direct action; autonomy from political parties, governments, and private sector; class solidarity; direct democracy; and collective decision-making.

These informal workers have fought for recognition as environmental agents and as service providers in solid waste systems, a collective worker's identity primarily based on a class identity, collective rights for waste pickers, and public policies that strengthen their economic and social inclusion (Dias, 2009; Samson, 2009). These multiple demands have been directed at both governments and industries as recyclers push for inclusion in urban and political landscapes.

In many ways this represents essential pillars of a social movement's objectives. As Munck (1995) argues, a 'social movement's orientation towards change can only be realized by conjoining its identity, its vision of change, to an appropriate strategy, the means to effectively bring about change'. The MNCR has asserted its identity as a social movement representing workers' demands and simultaneously acts in two arenas: civil society and the state. First, it has focused on its strategies and repertoires by mobilizing protests, social marches, and other activities associated with social activism. These actions are part of conventional repertoires of social movements, once they are recognized by political elites and society in general, and may facilitate the process of having demands met (Tarrow, 1998). Second, it established direct links with the political-institutional arena given the political opportunity of the re-democratization phase, where leftist governments and key actors such as the Church supported the claims from various social movements, including those of the poor. As a result, the MNCR participated in committees, working groups, and forums that involved actors from the government and private sector.[6] These actions were geared towards the MNCR's objective of including waste pickers as relevant actors in solid waste management by grounding their demands on a class identity given the material injustices waste pickers face. However, the MNCR has been committed to revealing how the injustices waste pickers experience are rooted not only in a politics of redistribution, but one of recognition and representation as well (Dias 2009, 2014).

In spite of the many challenges that still need to be addressed, Brazil has gradually introduced inclusive policies that give legal backing to redistributive measures and establish grounds for the social recognition of waste pickers' cooperatives, including the recognition of waste picking as a professional category in the National Classification of Occupation (Dias, 2011, 2014; Dias and Alves, 2008).

According to the data from the National Solid Waste Diagnostic, there are 1,200 cooperatives or associations that are similar to cooperatives of waste pickers in Brazil (IPEA, 2012). Other data show that women comprise 56 per cent of the members of these cooperatives and associations, whereas men make up

44 per cent (INSEA, 2007). However, when looking at numbers available from the official data system (PNAD) for 2006, only 28 per cent of 14,029 waste pickers were women (Crivellari *et al.*, 2008). Gender distribution nationwide for the same year shows 67 per cent male pickers and 33 per cent female (*ibid.*). PNAD figures capture information from both cooperative and autonomous waste pickers. What these figures may point to is the fact that women waste pickers prefer to work in cooperatives, rather than as non-organized workers who may work at middlemen deposits. This may also be attributed to the fact that cooperatives allow women more flexibility given their double and triple work shifts.

However, as mentioned previously, higher concentrations of women waste pickers in cooperatives are not necessarily indicative of gender equality. In the next section, we examine the gender dynamics and inequalities within the waste sector and then provide an overview of the participatory action research project with cooperatives in Brazil.

Reflections on building gender awareness in cooperatives

A gendered approach to waste picking recognizes the need to address the multiple dimensions of gender inequalities that result from a cultural and social naturalization of stereotypical gender roles, the manifestation of the sexual division of labour, and processes of invisibility associated with working with waste, often exacerbated by the intersections of class and race, among other identity markers. A gendered lens also explores how the aforementioned dimensions affect women's economic autonomy and experiences of political participation, thus sustaining structures of exploitation and marginalization.

In capitalist societies, gender exploitation at the workplace and at home can involve tasks that require 'typically feminine' activities that are often unnoticed and undercompensated (Young, 1990). Marginalization not only involves matters of distributive justice, but also entails the 'deprivation of cultural, practical, and institutionalized conditions for exercising capacities in a context of recognition and interaction' (*ibid.*). These oppressive structures coupled with feelings of powerlessness and experiences of violence are a direct extension of the social division of labour in capitalist societies, but may also result in the sexual division of labour.

At the workplace, women waste pickers experience oppression in at least three different ways in a national context. First, women might not be allowed access to recyclables with the highest value (Dias and Fernandez, 2012), therefore negatively impacting their earnings when compared with men. The emerging literature on gender reveals that there is a clear division of labour in most recycling cooperatives in Brazil, whereby men work in collection, transport, and processing activities such as weighing and compressing materials. These activities may involve more physical strength in comparison with the activities women are involved in that require greater dexterity, such as the sorting of recyclables (Goulart and Lima, 2012; Wirth, 2010). Sorting is one of the most time-consuming activities for waste pickers, yet it is essential because it adds more value to recyclables, enabling workers to sell to specific markets. Yet, this activity is deemed less important in some cooperatives. Goulart and Lima's (2012) small-scale study of cooperatives in the state of Minas Gerais illustrates how gender can be a source of conflict among workers, since men and women attribute different value to each other's tasks and accuse each other of not being responsible enough with collective duties. In addition, the study highlights how in some cooperatives, women are allowed to work flexible hours to meet their domestic demands, creating another source of conflict with men. The sexual division of labour, as exemplified in these cases, reinforces the idea that certain tasks are given more value in detriment of others (Young, 1990).

Second, it is important to recognize that both women and men are exposed to several health risks while working with waste materials. National studies with women waste pickers reinforce these findings and show that women often minimize the risks and accidents at the workplace without taking into consideration the long-term impacts on their health (Coelho *et al.*, 2016a). Precarious work environments and interpersonal problems also impact waste pickers' emotional well-being (Bleck and Wettberg, 2012; Coelho *et al.*, 2016a, 2016b; Gutberlet and Baeder, 2008).

Finally, women waste pickers have claimed that when they occupy leadership positions within cooperatives or the MNCR in Brazil, they may not be as respected as their male counterparts. In addition, women's participation seems to be higher at the community and local level, with stronger impediments for participation at the national level. Stereotypical assumptions regarding women's use of emotion and different communicative patterns contribute to women waste pickers being ignored or silenced in group meetings or formal settings. It is interesting to note that when focusing on the dynamics within the MNCR, women leaders in Brazil have demanded the need for equal representation in national levels of the movement (Dias *et al.*, 2013; Van Zeeland, 2014). Nevertheless, this visibility, considered here as a dimension of their agency, has only recently emerged.

Beyond the workplace, women waste pickers also confront gender inequalities in the private sphere, including experiences of gender violence. Furthermore, asymmetrical power relations at the household level affect women's abilities to make important decisions, as well as take part in public committees or to exercise leadership within their representative organizations. This can be attributed to the fact that women are responsible for raising children and fulfilling most (if not all) reproductive activities, ultimately limiting their time and energy for taking up leadership opportunities.

A close examination of the gender dynamics in Brazilian cooperatives help illuminate how raising gender awareness in the sector can serve as a catalyst for encouraging cooperative ideals of internal democracy and equality.

Hence, the discussion here poses several questions that can guide future debates on strengthening gender equality in waste picking cooperatives. What are the consequences of reproducing multiple dimensions of gender inequality within the cooperatives and the waste pickers' movement in light of the ideals of the cooperative model? Can gender awareness contribute to renewing these cooperative ideals? How can gender awareness be introduced in a waste pickers' movement and local cooperatives where sexism is deeply entrenched and reproduced on various levels? How can gender inequalities beyond the workplace and movement, including the home, be addressed? While these are complex questions, they are nonetheless of value in an effort to begin challenging different gender inequalities. One path for doing so is providing women waste pickers with the tools they need to enhance their role as economic and political actors. As part of this objective, an exploratory research-action process – the Gender and Waste Project – was created in the state of Minas Gerais, Brazil, so as to strengthen women's capacities and voices. The project proposal was designed as a 'bottom–up' participatory process,[7] originating from demands made by Brazilian women waste picker leaders, who, along with the support of Women in Informal Employment Globalizing and Organizing (WIEGO) and in a partnership with the MNCR, the Centre for Women Studies of the Federal University of Minas Gerais (NEPEM/UFMG), and the NGO Instituto Nenuca de Desenvolvimento Sustentável (INSEA), organized workshops to discuss the forms of discrimination women waste pickers experience.

The project was divided into distinct phases, beginning with a learning stage in 2012. By 2013, four exploratory workshops[8] were conducted in Minas Gerais, Brazil. The one-day workshops focused on issues related to women's autonomy in a multidimensional perspective, including sexuality, the sexual division of labour, and gender roles in the home. In addition, the workshops sought to identify the problems women face with regard to their empowerment as women and leaders in both the cooperatives and the national waste pickers' movement. In 2015, a general workshop with waste pickers from across Brazil and Latin America was held to share learnings from the project. As part of the process of identifying women's practical needs, a group of women waste picker leaders also participated in individual coaching sessions to improve their communication and management skills within cooperatives.

Project findings: women waste pickers' perceptions on gender inequalities

The findings from the project cast light on what women identify as barriers to gender equality, as well as the strategies they have used to overcome challenges in their work places and the MNCR.

Women waste pickers recognized that gender equality, for them, is primarily linked to having economic autonomy. For these workers, attaining economic autonomy has come primarily through their membership in cooperatives. A young waste picker reinforced this belief in the following statement: 'I gained independence through waste picking. This means paying my own bills.' Others associated their economic autonomy with the pride they feel as waste pickers. Some participants also reflected on the fact that cooperatives have been a way to include economically marginalized groups, while offering a different mode of production: 'I'm free, I can arrive [at the cooperative] and work without somebody telling me what to do.' A similar sentiment was expressed by a waste picker leader:

> I found my autonomy in my organization. It's being able to manage my business, my livelihood. It's being able to pay my bills. I found myself in the cooperative, because outside I felt exploited by the powerful. There are employers who simply do not care, you have to punch a time card, you have to follow operation hours, but in the cooperative, we are the owners of our business, we set our times because we know we need them for things to work out.

Interestingly enough, it has also been within the cooperative setting that some women waste pickers have improved their leadership skills. Women claimed they have gained confidence in 'managing and giving opinions' in their cooperatives.

Despite the positive perceptions on the cooperative environment, women waste pickers noted several challenges they face as a result of gender inequalities. The most recurrent problem mentioned was how the sexual division of labour reproduces a different set of valorisation in terms of work activities. Most women waste pickers emphasized that they are capable of taking on the multiple roles required of them within the sorting warehouse, but the same cannot be said of the men, who either refuse to sort materials or who prefer to concentrate on only one activity, such as collecting materials on the streets or from businesses. As one waste picker claimed: 'Men are all timid when it comes to sorting [materials], they think this is something feminine.' Another complaint was the fact that women are often responsible for the cleaning duties in the cooperative for the same reason. Examples of the sexual division of labour led women waste pickers to critically reflect on the need for male colleagues within the workplace to not only recognize the work women typically carry out, but also to take part in other activities so that women are not consistently overburdened. A second problem addressed by the participants referred to the lack of respect and authority women waste pickers face on cooperative boards, even when they have acquired leadership status. For one of the participants, this can only happen if women support each other: 'When men sit on the cooperative board, women are rarely recognized . . . We need self-esteem.' Lastly, women pointed to the different forms of violence they experience within cooperatives and at home, including bullying, sexual harassment and even physical aggression. In many of these cases, women reported feeling oppressed by the psychological, verbal and physical abuse they face. However, being able to share experiences and stories of overcoming violence during the workshops has been an important outlet for women, especially in terms of supporting co-workers who experience violence.

Workshops permitted women waste pickers to reflect on the naturalization of gender roles in the cooperatives, as well as to problematize how different identity markers, such as race and sexuality, also shape experiences of oppression. Participants called attention to the fact that many waste pickers across the country are black and the stigma and exclusion they have experienced is a result of Brazil's history of racial discrimination. Others highlighted the need to confront homophobia and transphobia within cooperatives, so that the work environment can uphold its commitment to respecting differences. As a worker stated: 'It's recognizing that a lesbian [in the cooperative] faces discrimination, that a young gay man may not be accepted, [but] people need to be respected because we are all humans. We need to openly discuss these issues.' While such discussions on the intersectionalities of race and sexuality were not as predominant as others in the workshops, participants found it relevant to bring to light such tensions and learn from cooperatives that have started to tackle such issues.

When participants considered gender inequalities in the national movement, women addressed the need for more recognition from male colleagues. A waste picker leader emphasized how many women have gained more voice in their base organizations, but this has not necessarily been the case in the MNCR. According to her:

> Waste picking has been a huge achievement [for us], [but] today we need to improve many things, we need to have autonomy within the movement, we [as women] need to talk more, we need to be more recognized, we need to conquer this space because it is still weak in the national movement.

She gave the example of how male leaders do not always create a fair environment in decision-making spaces: 'Sometimes [when] we are in a group discussion, there is no technical staff around [and] men will cut off women speaking.' Or in other moments, women waste pickers are criticized by male colleagues for taking on leadership positions. These examples represent many women leaders' concern with democratizing all decision-making spheres and levels from the base organizations to the national movement.

It seems clear that women waste pickers take pride in their work and, in general, feel safe within their cooperatives despite the aforementioned problems. During the workshops, women identified strategies for challenging gender inequalities and for creating a more gender-just and democratic environment within the workplaces. Some of these strategies refer back to the originating ideals of the cooperative movement, including the need for strengthening transparency and communication processes among leaders and cooperative members. Women also stressed the need to support other women leaders or those interested in taking on leadership positions. One path identified for encouraging leadership is through more solidarity and capacity-building courses that target the practical skills women waste pickers need.

One insight from the workshops is that women waste pickers individually and collectively constructed their own understandings of the forms of gender inequalities that affect them. The project recognized, however, that establishing a platform for collectively building gender awareness would not automatically produce structural changes within cooperatives or the MNCR. Notwithstanding, the collective opportunity to share experiences brought visibility to forms of oppression that have been historically and culturally designated as unimportant. By fostering an outlet for women waste pickers' demands to be heard, permitting women to deepen their understanding and analysis of gender roles, and providing women with the opportunity to develop their demands, the project sought to facilitate the creation of new alliances, as well as new attitudes and behaviours in the process (Mitlin, 2012). In this sense, the emphasis on engaging key actors, including male waste picker leaders, gender and waste experts, and supporting NGOs, was one way to build support and commitment to future and long-term gender-awareness discussions.

Can engendering waste revitalize the cooperative movement in Brazil?

Historically, leftist social movements have had difficulties in incorporating gender equality in their own practices and structures once their primary struggles are directed at class injustices (Alvarez, 1990), overshadowing other injustices. Hence, it may be that social movements reproduce patriarchal practices and structures despite an ideology based on equality, democratic management and social justice. In many ways, the project findings bring to the surface the varied forms of gender inequalities experienced by women waste pickers and reveal a disjuncture between what social movement studies have highlighted as three mutually reinforcing dimensions of a social movement: ideology, praxis, and organization (Gerard and Martens, 1987, cited in Develtere, 1993).

As mentioned previously, the MNCR's ideology for organizing cooperatives included the ideals of mutual help, democratic practices such as direct democracy and direct actions, and self-management. These formed the basis of the cooperative model that worked to include groups facing social stigma and economic oppression. Our argument is that the notion of upholding gender equality should not be disassociated from the very principles that shaped the establishment of cooperatives and the MNCR. The challenge lies in the actions taken by the MNCR in effectively working towards ensuring democratic practices at the local and national levels. Some authors argue that cooperatives are well positioned to answer claims for gender equality since they are 'rooted in values of self-help, equality, and equity, as well as economic growth through cooperation and democratic processes' (McMurtry and McMurtry, 2015). The extent to which these values truly represent the dynamics and organizing capacity and culture within cooperatives is open to contestation, which is why raising gender awareness cannot be taken for granted. For instance, Wirth's (2010) study of gender relations in recycling cooperatives in Brazil reveals tensions given certain hierarchies in the management process that do not necessarily reflect solidarity or a more democratic management.

For these reasons, raising gender awareness can be one step towards revitalizing cooperatives and the MNCR, since it targets deeply rooted structures and practices that are not, in theory, aligned with the principles and ideals of the cooperative model. Nevertheless, aims to challenge such norms are often met with resistance or even a degree of backlash. With this in mind, the project's approach to raising gender awareness was to open spaces for dialogue on the experiences of gender inequalities. The process was not construed as an end in itself, but a first step in placing gender equality on the agenda. As Cornwall and Edwards note (2010), projects that aim to empower women should consider how and to what extent are power relations being targeted and what kind of perspectives and voices are paving possibilities for change. In other words, there is an explicit understanding that there are no detailed road maps for raising gender awareness. Nevertheless, the process, at once dynamic and open to setbacks, must enable the strengthening of relationships, as well as individual and collective understandings of how gender shapes the very lives of women and men waste pickers.

This reinforces popular education beliefs that any NGOs supporting such complex processes should steer from top-to-bottom initiatives. Raising gender awareness can only be successful as an initial step in a concrete gender equality action plan if all involved commit to a collaborative and non-hierarchical process, which especially entails guaranteeing the respect for waste pickers' own learning pace on the subject matter. In order to do this, a strategic message in all stages of the project centred on countering notions that discussing gender relations in the cooperatives and the MNCR would not establish divisions, but would rather foster critical reflections on what may be needed to democratize relations and practices among workers.

More concretely, the project served two initial purposes. First, it sought to bridge understandings on how gender shapes relations among waste pickers. This was primarily due to the fact that this is a theme which has not emerged as a priority in the cooperatives and the MNCR. Second, it encouraged both men and women waste pickers to envision practices that could promote more mutual respect and equality in different decision-making spheres, as a way to strengthen cooperative principles.

Clearly, these processes involve the time and the willingness of the leaders and the MNCR. Sharing experiences and understanding of gender inequality among waste pickers can ultimately pave the way towards concrete action plans to deal with the sexual division of labour in cooperatives, to ensure parity of representation and transparency in the cooperatives and the MNCR, and even to establish a commitment against gender violence. Ultimately, as the theme gains visibility among cooperative members and the MNCR, the goal is for waste pickers themselves to claim this discussion as their own and demand strategies to address gender inequalities. Furthermore, undertaking such a long-term action plan is critical for attaining any kind of transformative potential with regard to gender equality.

What is undeniable is that the women waste pickers are becoming increasingly more vocal and assertive, presenting a clear challenge to the long-established barriers embedded in the movement's praxis. For example, the MNCR historically had a male waste picker representative sit on the Interministerial Committee for the Social Inclusion of Waste Pickers (CISS).[9] In 2013, women leaders demanded gender representation and sent a formal request to then President Dilma Rousseff, who incorporated the demand to establish gender parity within the committee. Another important example is that in the last three years, gender panels were part of the formal agenda of the MNCR national event, *Expocatadores*. These panels were important outlets for sharing experiences of raising gender awareness across the country, as well as for discussing women's health issues, needs related to basic public services, race issues, and women's political participation. At a more local level, women leaders who participated in the project have taken an interest in participating in university conferences, events on women in solidarity economy, and in courses offered by the state public defender's office on access to justice. While these observations do not represent a comprehensive and long-term action plan on gender equality, they nonetheless point to how the issue has impacted behaviours and practices in local cooperatives and within the MNCR.

Conclusion

By incorporating the demands for gender equality, both men and women waste pickers will admittedly be working alongside each other against common structures and practices that oppress not only women in the sector, but men as well. The idea of a common struggle among equals reflects back to the notion of mutual help, one of the pillars of the cooperative movement's ideology.

Efforts to raise gender awareness have unravelled the ways in which the movement and dynamics in waste picker cooperatives reproduce sexism. The visibility given to feminist struggles in contemporary Brazil have also facilitated a process by which men and women identify inequality and mistreatment of women on a daily basis. According to Klatch (2001), not only do social movements have to recognize the inequality women face, but they must also work on articulating how these injustices must be rejected even in traditionally male-dominated spaces. This involves framing these gender injustices as part of a social condition that entails political action (*ibid.*) in the same way class-based demands do. In other words, working towards gender equality does not diminish class struggles, but is connected to broader struggles for social justice.

These initial reflections attempt to illustrate how building gender awareness is aligned with the ideals of the cooperative movement precisely because it exposes how forms of power and injustice undermine workers' capacities to improve their livelihoods. It also calls for a collective debate among waste pickers with regard to their roles in sustaining an inclusive, transparent, and democratic organizational culture and movement. One of the main points to be emphasized is that our exploratory findings can serve to encourage future dissemination projects in Brazil, Latin America, and elsewhere. When it comes to envisioning more gender-fair relations within the cooperative movement, two critical strategies become evident. First, there should be stronger engagements with other collective feminist struggles and social movements. Second, a commitment to gender equality by the cooperative movement should be based on concrete, long-term action plans that confront the concerns brought forth by women waste pickers. Therefore, tackling the lack of equal representation and respect, as well as gender-based vulnerabilities, must stem from the combined efforts of men and women waste pickers.

Notes

1 The term waste picker is used in this text to abide by the provisional agreement reached in the 2008 World Conference of Waste Pickers. In Brazil, informal workers mainly collect recyclables since municipalities are responsible for household waste collection. Informal workers fill in the gap in source segregation, not in refuse collection.
2 The text will refer to two different, but complementary, units of analysis. Waste pickers' cooperatives are primary organizations and the MNCR is a social movement composed of organized cooperatives.
3 For overviews of the waste pickers' movement, see Dias (2002) and Teodósio et al. (2013). Future research agendas could include an analysis of the MNCR's foundation, main strategies, achievements, challenges, and influence from external organizations and actors.
4 In a 2015 interview with Dias, Sister Cristina Bove attests to the fact that during her talks with left-wing unionists in the 1980s, in attempts to seek support for the work with street dwellers and waste pickers, she often heard these two groups would never be able to form organizations as they were part of the lumpen proletariat. Resulting from these tensions, efforts were made to organize through cooperatives.
5 Luiza Erundina (PT) was the mayor of São Paulo from 1989–1992, Olivio Dutra (PT) was the mayor of Porto Alegre from 1989–1993, and Patrus Ananias (PT) was the mayor of Belo Horizonte from 1993–1996.
6 Social movements experience a permanent tension between two arenas of action: the social and the political-institutional. One of the greatest challenges for any social movement is to establish a balance between fulfilling its role as a strategic actor that engages in formal political arenas and its role as a mobilizing agent that represents the demands of its own bases. With regard to the latter, this is crucial for social movements to maintain their dissenting and critical identity. In many ways, the waste pickers' movement in Brazil has been able to achieve this balance thus far.
7 According to Moser (1993), the entry point for any kind of gender training will have implications with regards to the structure set-up. For more on the methodological underpinnings of the project, see Dias and Ogando (2015).
8 The workshops were held with 12–22 women, who represented 41 cooperatives in the state.
9 CIISC is an inter-ministerial committee created by former President Lula to coordinate the integration of waste pickers within solid waste systems. With President Rousseff's impeachment and under the administration of President Temer, the committee has been abolished.

References

Alvarez, Sonia E. *Engendering democracy in Brazil: Women's movements in transition politics.* Princeton: Princeton University Press, 1990.

Alvarez, Sonia E., Evelina Dagnino and Arturo Escobar. Cultura e política nos movimentos sociais latino-americanos. In *Cultura e política nos movimentos sociais latino-americanos: Novas leituras*, edited by Sonia E. Alvarez, Evelina Dagnino and Arturo Escobar, 15–61. Belo Horizonte: Editora UFMG, 1998.

Bleck, Daniela and Wieland Wettberg. Waste collection in developing countries: Tackling occupational safety and health hazards at their source, *Waste Management* 32, no.11 (2012): 2009–2017.

Bhowmik, Sharit. Cooperatives and the emancipation of the marginalized: Case studies from two cities in India. In *Another production is possible: Beyond the capitalist canon*, edited by Boaventura de Sousa Santos, 70–94. London: Verso, 2006.

Birchall, Johnston. *Organizing workers in the informal sector: A strategy for trade union-cooperative action*, ILO Working Paper 01-1. Geneva: ILO, 2001.

Bonner, Christine and Dave Spooner. Organizing in the informal economy: A challenge for trade unions, *International Politics and Society* 2 (2011): 87–105.

Coelho, Alexa Pupiara Flores, Carmem Lucia Colomé Beck, Marcelo Nunes da Silva Fernandes, Natiellen Quatrin Freitas, Francine Cassol Prestes and Juliana Zancan Tonel. Mulheres catadoras de materiais recicláveis: condições de vida, trabalho e saúde, *Revista Gaúcha de Enfermagem* 37, no. 3 (2016a): 1–8.

Coelho, Alexa Pupiara Flores, Carmem Lucia Colomé Beck, Marcelo Nunes da Silva Fernandes, Francine Cassol Prestes and Rosângela Marion da Silva. Risco de adoecimento relacionado ao trabalho e estratégias defensivas de mulheres catadoras de materiais recicláveis, *Escola Anna Nery* 20, no. 3 (Jul–Sep 2016b).

Cornwall, Andrea and Jenny Edwards. (2010) Introduction: Negotiating Empowerment, *IDS Bulletin* 41, no. 2 (2010): 1–9.

Crivellari, Helena Maria Tarchi, Sonia Maria Dias and André de Souza. (2008) Informação e trabalho: uma leitura sobre os catadores de material reciclável a partir das bases públicas de dados. In *Catadores na cena urbana: Construção de políticas socioambientais*, edited by Helena Maria Tarchi Crivellari and Valéria Heloisa Kemp, 299–324. Brazil: Grupo Autêntico, 2008.

de Morais, Edson Elias, Fabio Lanza, Luis Miguel Luzio dos Santos and Silvia Schroeder Pelanda. Propriedades coletivas, cooperativismo e economia solidária no Brasil, *Serviço Social e Sociedade*, no. 105 (2011): 67–88.

Develtere, Patrick. Cooperative movements in the developing countries: Old and new orientations, *Annals of Public and Cooperative Economics* 64, no. 2 (1993): 179–208.

Dias, Sonia Maria. *Construindo a cidadania: Avanços e limites do projeto de coleta seletiva de Belo Horizonte em parceria com a asmare*. Master's dissertation, Department of Geography, Federal University of Minas Gerais, Brazil, 2002.

____. *Trajetórias e memórias dos fóruns lixo e cidadania no Brasil: Experimentos singulares de justiça social e governança participativa*. PhD thesis, Department of Political Science, Federal University of Minas Gerais, Brazil, 2009.

____. *Statistics on waste pickers in Brazil*, WIEGO Statistical Brief No. 2. Cambridge: WIEGO, 2011.

____. Waste and citizenship forum's trajectories: Achievements and challenges. In *IPSA Congress Proceedings*, Montreal, Canada, 2014.

Dias, Sonia Maria and Fabio Cidrin Gama Alves. Integration of the informal recycling sector in solid waste management in Brazil. Study prepared for GIZ's sector project *Promotion of concepts for pro-poor and environmentally friendly closed-loop approaches in solid waste management*. Eschborn: GIZ, 2008.

Dias, Sonia Maria and Lucia Fernandez. Waste pickers: A gendered perspective. In *Powerful synergies: Gender equality, economic development and environmental sustainability*. 153–155. New York: UNDP, 2012.

Dias, Sonia Maria and Ana Carolina Ogando. Rethinking gender and waste: Exploratory findings from participatory action research in Brazil, *Work Organisation, Labour and Globalisation* 9, no. 2 (2015): 51–63.

Dias, Sonia Maria, Marlise Matos and Ana Carolina Ogando. Mujeres 'catadoras': Construyendo una agenda de gênero em las organizaciones catadoras. In *Genero, pobreza et medio ambiente*. Madrid: The Spanish Foundation IPADE, 2013.

Goulart de Oliveira, Fabiana and Francisco de Paula Antunes Lima. *Eficiência e solidariedade nas associações de catadores de materiais recicláveis*, WIEGO Working Paper no. 22. Cambridge: WIEGO, 2012.

Gutberlet, Jutta and Angela M. Baeder. Informal recycling and occupational health in Santo André, Brazil, *International Journal of Environmental Health Research* 18, no. 1 (2008): 1–15.

Instituto Nenuca de Desenvolvimento Sustentável (INSEA). *Perfil sócio-econômico dos catadores da rede CATAUNIDOS*, Internal Research Report. Belo Horizonte: INSEA/Federal University of Minas Gerais/Waste and Citizenship State Forum, 2007.

Instituto de Pesquisa Econômica Aplicada (IPEA). *Diagnóstico sobre os catadores de materiais recicláveis*, Research Report. Brasília: IPEA, 2012.

Heller, Patrick. Moving the state: The politics of democratic decentralization in Kerala, South Africa, and Porto Alegre, *Politics and Society* 29, no. 1 (2001): 131–163.

Kabeer, Naila, Kirsty Milward and Ratna Sudarshan. Organising women workers in the informal economy, *Gender and Development* 21, no. 2 (2013): 249–263.

Klatch, Rebecca E. The formation of feminist consciousness among left-and right-wing activists of the 1960s, *Gender and Society* 15, no. 6 (2001): 791–815.

McMurtry, Lisa Schincariol and J.J. McMurtry. *Advancing gender equality: The co-operative way*. Geneva, ILO, 2015.

Mitlin, Diana. From aid to empowerment, *Reflect and Act*. London: International Institute for Environment and Development, July 2012.

Moreno, Jorge, Francisco Rivas Rios and Inge Lardinois. *La gestión de residuos sólidos em América Latina: El caso de las pequenas y microempresas y cooperativas*, Urban Waste Series 5, Lima: IPES/ACEPESA/WASTE, 1997.

Moser, Caroline. *Gender planning and development: Theory, practice and training*. New York: Routledge, 1993.

Munck, Gerardo L. Actor formation, social co-ordination, and political strategy: Some conceptual problems in the study of social movements, *Sociology* 29, no. 4 (1995): 667–685.

Samson, Melanie. *Refusing to be cast aside: Waste pickers organising around the world*. Cambridge: WIEGO, 2009.

Silva, Emanuel Sampaio, Inessa L. Salomão, Jimmy Peixe McIntyre, Joao Guerreiro, Maria Luiza Lins e Silva Pires, Paulo Peixoto Albuquerque, Sandra S.S Bergonsi and Sidney da Conceiçao Vaz. Panorama do cooperativismo brasileiro: História, cenários e tendências, *Rede de Universidades das Américas para Estudos Cooperativos e Associativos-UNIRCOOP* 1, no. 2 (2003): 75–102.

Singer, Paul. Políticas públicas da Secretaria Nacional de Economia Solidária do Ministério do Trabalho e Emprego, *Boletim Mercado de Trabalho*, no. 39. 43–48. Brasília: IPEA, 2009.

Tarrow, Sidney. *Power in movement: Social movements, collective action and mass politics in the modern state*. Cambridge: Cambridge University Press, 1998.

Teodósio, Armindo dos Santos, Sylmara Lopes Francelino Gonçalves-Dias, Patricia Maria Emerenciano de Mendonça and Maria Cecilia Loschiavo dos Santos. Waste pickers movement and right to the city: The impacts in the homeless lives in Brazil, *CESContexto – Debates* 2 (2013): 443–475.

Van Zeeland, Angelique. *The interaction between popular economy, social movements and public policies*, Occasional Paper 11 for Project on *Potential and Limits of Social and Solidarity Economy*. Geneva: UNRISD, 2014.

Wirth, Ioli Gewehr. *As relações de gênero em cooperativas populares do segmento de reciclagem: um caminha para a constituição da autogestão?* Master's dissertation. Department of Education, State University of Campinas, São Paulo, Brazil, 2010.

Young, Iris Marion. *Justice and the politics of difference*. Princeton: Princeton University Press, 1990.

9

COOPERATIVES AND TRADE UNIONS

From occasional partners to builders of a solidarity-based society

Akira Kurimoto

Introduction

As found across the world, cooperatives and trade unions have appeared to respond to social problems and injustice caused by the development of the modern capitalist system. However, whereas the relationship between cooperatives and trade unions has been considered as collaborative in general, it is also true that in reality, there have been tensions, conflict, competition as well as indifference. The history of their relationship in Japan illustrates a history of close collaboration but with diverted trajectories. In tandem with the Industrial Revolution in Japan, cooperatives and trade unions were founded to improve living conditions of workers and farmers since the late 19th century. They had reached a stage of development in the early 20th century; however, they were crushed by governments or integrated into state organs during the Second World War.

During the 1950s consumer cooperatives and trade unions developed a variety of worker-oriented cooperatives with mixed results. The labour banks and insurance cooperatives established themselves as financial institutions while housing cooperatives could not take roots. On the other hand, cooperatives and trade unions took diverted trajectories since the 1960s when rapid economic growth brought about a socio-economic shift and ecological consumerism. Cooperatives started to grow from housewives' buying clubs to businesses and took part in consumer and environmental campaigns, while trade unions concentrated on the 'Spring Labour Offensive' for wage increases. This evolution also reflected the shift in organizational culture in cooperatives (from a worker culture to a consumer one) and trade unions (from class struggle to material gains).

This chapter aims at examining historical development of the relationship between consumer cooperatives and trade unions. Beginning with the early history of consumer cooperatives and trade unions in the formative Japanese capitalism, it then explains the socio-economic context of development of these organizations after the Second World War. It describes how worker-oriented cooperatives had emerged in the 1950s and why cooperatives and trade unions took diverted trajectories from the mid-1960s. Finally, it showcases some areas of collaboration and suggests the future policy direction.

Emergence of cooperatives and trade unions after the Meiji Restoration

Japanese consumer cooperatives can trace their history back to the late 19th century. After the Meiji Restoration in 1868, the knowledge on consumer cooperatives had been imported in conjunction with modern economics. In 1878, Takeyoshi Baba published an article on the establishment of cooperative shops in a newspaper, *Yubin Hochi*, widely introducing the Rochdale Society of Equitable Pioneers in the UK. The first cooperative shops based on the Rochdale model were set up in Tokyo, Osaka and Kobe in 1879–80.[1] These pioneering cooperatives had been supported by elites such as bureaucrats, business and media leaders, but they disappeared in a few years because of a lack of wider social support. At the turn of the century, several trials and errors had been made in the course of industrialization that generated the working class. '*Rodo Kumiai Kiseikai*' (Trade Union Society) was set up by Fusataro Takano in 1897 to establish trade unions and helped organize trade unions of mechanics and railway workers, which opened *kyodoten* (cooperative shops) as their subsidiaries. In 1900, the Public Order Police Act was passed to make organizing difficult, while the Industrial Cooperative Act was enacted in the same year following the Raiffeisen model.[2] These unions had been oppressed by the police, while *Kyodoten* was succeeded by worker-oriented consumer cooperatives in the 1920s. After these short-lived cooperative shops, the workplace cooperatives were created by the benevolent owners of factories and mines, while some cooperatives were organized by middle-class people such as civil servants and teachers. Thus, three types of consumer cooperatives emerged around 1920: (1) worker-oriented cooperatives associated with the labour movement, (2) cooperatives attached to companies/factories serving their employees, and (3) citizen cooperatives organized by middle-class people (Okutani, 1935). These streams were deeply split along different ideologies: Marxism, paternalism, and liberalism. They were all small-sized and short-lived because of the lack of institutional backing and support structure in the Meiji era.

In the wake of 'Taisho democracy' in the interwar period, a series of citizen cooperatives were set up to protect consumers' purchasing power against inflation. They were called '*Sinko Shohi Kumiai*' (emerging consumer cooperatives) and often encouraged by local governments. Katei Co-op, founded in Tokyo in 1919, was chaired by Sakuzo Yoshino, a proponent of '*Minponshugi*' (politics of the people), and grew to be the largest cooperative with 20,000 members in 1941. Kobe Co-op and Nada Co-op[3] were established under the influence of Toyohiko Kagawa and Zenji Nasu in 1921.[4] They grew as major cooperatives in

Kobe and introduced women's organizations called *kateikai* to support cooperatives and enhance women's consciousness in 1924 following the model of the British Co-operative Women's Guild. Other citizen cooperatives were set up in Osaka, Kyoto and Tokyo in this period, while a number of student consumer cooperatives were set up in Tokyo and Kyoto. Outside Japan, the South Manchuria Railway Co. Ltd., as a spearhead of the Japanese colonial rule in north-eastern China, helped set up a consumer cooperative for its employees in 1919. These cooperatives operated retail shops or *goyoukiki* home delivery.[5]

The worker-oriented cooperatives established the Kanto Consumer Cooperative Federation in 1926, while many cooperatives linked to citizens and companies/factories that were affiliated to the Central Union of Industrial Cooperatives set up the National Consumer Cooperative Association in 1931. The former designated itself as a wing of the proletarian class movement and some affiliated cooperatives in Tokyo started to organize *Han* groups for joint purchase and communication among members in 1929 (Yamamoto, 1982).[6]

When the Second World War ended, most consumer cooperatives were destroyed; the left-wing cooperatives had been liquidated by the military government while citizens' cooperatives were deprived of trading licences by the Staple Food Control Act of 1942, and their facilities were largely destroyed by air raids. Needless to say, cooperatives had to start from scratch, although the legacy of the cooperative movement was inherited through pre-war leaders. Trade unions had also been dissolved and integrated into the Patriotic Industrial Service Federation, aiming to mobilize workers during the war regime.

Socio-economic contexts after the Second World War

In 1945, the General Headquarters of the Supreme Commander for the Allied Powers (GHQ-SCAP) declared five major reforms (abolishment of the secret police, encouragement of trade unions, liberation of women, liberalization of education, and democratization of the economy) to dismantle Japanese militarism. These reforms were crystallized in the new 1946 constitution with fundamental principles of popular sovereignty, pacifism and basic human rights. The Anti-Monopoly Act was enacted to dissolve industrial/financial business conglomerates called *Zaibatsu*, while the Agrarian Reform was carried out to curtail the landlords' power and create owner-farmers. Basic labour legislation (Labour Standard Act, Trade Union Act and Labour Relations Adjustment Act) were enacted between 1945 and 1947.

Under such circumstances, the labour and other social movements had rapidly expanded under the heavy shortage of food and daily necessities. The newly legalized trade unions had already organized 56 per cent of workers in 1949, while the coalition government headed by socialist Katayama was established in 1947. However, under intensified tension in American–Soviet relations, the GHQ took a 'reverse course' to oppress left-wing unionism by banning public workers' strikes and implementing a wide range of 'red purges'. The General Council of Trade Unions of Japan was set up to consolidate right-wing and neutral unions in 1950, while the All Japan Trade Union Congress was founded by right-wing unions to limit the General Council of Trade Unions' 'turn to the left' in 1954. In this period, several radical unions went on strikes that often ended with organizational split on political and ideological grounds. The surge and defeat in the labour disputes over Mitsui mines and the political campaigns against the Japan–US Security Pact in 1959–60 urged trade unions to concentrate on economic improvement by obtaining a larger share of the high economic growth while a new social movement for consumerism, ecology and peace emerged to tackle inflation, hazardous products and environmental deterioration as side effects of such growth. The unions' competition for hegemony continued among civil servants while enterprise unions became a dominant form, often supported by employers.

Also after the end of the Second World War, consumer cooperatives joined the labour movement to cope with serious shortages of food through campaigns for revelation and fair distribution of hidden goods and petitioning for democratic control of daily necessities. Thousands of small consumer cooperatives were organized in communities and workplaces aiming to procure scarce food. These 'food buying cooperatives' had mushroomed throughout the country and reached approximately 6,000 in 1946. The Cooperative League of Japan (CLJ) was set up by Toyohiko Kagawa and cooperative leaders with different ideologies in 1945 seeking to become a federation embracing all types of cooperatives. However, the Agricultural Cooperative Act was enacted in 1947 to protect numerous smallholders who had emerged as a result of agrarian reform. Thereafter separate cooperative legislation in line with the industrial policies became the norm. The Japanese Consumers Co-operative Union (JCCU) was founded in 1951 based on the Consumer Cooperative Act of 1948. In the post-war period, agricultural cooperatives and consumer cooperatives underwent a very different evolution in relation to public policies and political parties. The former had been promoted under the protectionist agricultural policy backed by a coalition of the Liberal Democratic Party, Ministry of Agriculture, Forestry and Fisheries, and *Zenchu* (Central Union of Agricultural Cooperatives), while the latter had been hampered by the protectionist commercial policy and anti-cooperative campaigns often staged by small retailers' associations, which saw consumer cooperatives as competitors and political opponents since a large number of cooperatives had been close to opposition parties. Such a divided institutional setting made it difficult for cooperatives to cultivate a sense of identity and promote a common agenda, although direct transactions between consumers and farmers had been encouraged by consumer cooperatives and later by agricultural cooperatives as well.

Emergence of worker-oriented cooperatives in the 1950s

In the 1950s, trade unionism greatly expanded and took on the role of promoting 'workers' welfare businesses' to supplement its main function of collective bargaining. Trade unions and consumer cooperatives worked together to set up worker-oriented cooperatives such as *Rokin* (labour banks), *Rosai* (workers' insurance cooperatives) and *Kinjukyo* (workers' housing associations).

The first labour bank was set up in Okayama Prefecture by the Okayama Consumer Cooperative Union, while the second one was founded in Hyogo Prefecture (Kobe) under the trade union's initiative in the same year. Both banks were incorporated under the Urban Credit Cooperative Act. JCCU's Managing Director Sadao Nakabayashi served as CEO (and later vice president) of the National Association of Labour Banks between 1953 and 1963 and contributed to the enactment of the Labour Bank Act in 1953, while JCCU's office was located in the *Rokin* Building in Tokyo between 1958 and 1964.

JCCU also helped set up workers' insurance cooperatives and their federation *Rosairen* (National Federation of Workers and Consumers Insurance Cooperatives) in 1957, which was consolidated with primary cooperatives and renamed as *Zenrosai* in 1976. When the Niigata Insurance Cooperative faced a great fire in Niigata City in 1955, just five months after its inception, it had not accumulated sufficient premiums to pay insurance benefits. The Niigata Labour Bank offered urgent loans backed by funds which major trade unions in the prefecture had accumulated. Such an action of solidarity rescued the insurance cooperative from insolvency and raised workers' confidence in it.

To promote joint actions between trade unions and consumer cooperatives, the Central Council for Trade Unions' Welfare Businesses, later renamed the Central Council for Workers' Welfare, was set up by trade union confederations with different backgrounds and the CLJ in 1950. It sought to coordinate welfare activities of *Tansan*,[7] enhance welfare through activating mutual help functions, establish social security systems, and promote public policies for solving workers' livelihood problems, transcending different *Tansan* and trade union confederations. The prefectural councils for Trade Unions' Welfare Businesses were organized throughout the country in 1951–53.

In this period, worker-oriented retail cooperatives were created under the sponsorship of trade unions and often with the support of local governments' labour offices. They undertook economic activities to meet various workers' needs and brought about the second period of consumer cooperatives' growth. In particular, they opened relatively large stores in comparison with the small retailers who prevailed at that time, providing a wide variety of food and consumer goods in local cities prior to the advent of supermarkets. They earned quick success by automatically enrolling unionists as cooperative members and attracting a wide range of consumers, which triggered strong reaction from retailers and led to intense anti-cooperative campaigns. However, the success of these cooperatives was short-lived due to lack of management skills and member education. In particular, they failed to compete with the emerging supermarkets introduced by more progressive retailers in the late 1950s. Learning from their failure, some of these cooperatives transformed themselves to citizen cooperatives by adopting consumer-oriented policies. For example, Tsuruoka Co-op started organizing housewives in *Han* groups to disseminate information on how to use the self-service system in 1956.[8]

On the other hand, workplace cooperatives were founded under the initiative of trade unions, often under the personnel and in-kind support from employers (e.g. seconded managers/employees and rented premises for canteens/stores with

TABLE 9.1 Organizational relationship between trade unions and consumer cooperatives

Institution/company	Trade unions	Consumer cooperatives
Governments	Ministry/prefectural/ municipal workers' unions	Ministry/prefectural/municipal workers' cooperatives
Schools	Teachers' union	School teachers' cooperatives
Mines	Miners' unions	Miners' cooperatives
Seamen	Seamen's union	Seamen's Co-op
Toyota Motor Corp.	Toyota Workers' Union	Toyota Co-op
Japan Airlines	JAL trade unions	JAL Co-op (JALOP)

Source: Author's own elaboration

no or nominal fees). They were widely set up by public workers' unions at municipal, prefectural and national government levels, school teachers of primary and secondary schools, coal miners and seamen, while they were sponsored by trade unions to cater for unions' needs in daily necessities (Table 9.1). When they faced unions' strikes and ensuing organizational splits, a number of difficulties arose. In many cases, they tried to maintain neutrality towards the divided unions but tended to serve the majority unions often supported by employers while severing relations with the minority unions.

The relationship with employers had been an important issue in promoting worker-oriented cooperatives. The employers in large companies had introduced a beneficial treatment to their employees to retain them in times of high demand for workforce accompanied by a rapidly growing economy. They offered company housing, staff canteens or special benefits, including high-interest deposits or low-interest loans, aimed at strengthening a sense of belonging and loyalty to companies, stabilizing labour relations and raising labour productivity. Workers' organizations contrasted this enterprise-based benevolent welfare with workers' autonomous welfare, which was promoted by and for workers. On the other hand, coal mine owners often set up staff canteens or shops for their employees. Miners' unions had opposed these arrangements as 'a truck system' or the second exploitation on top of low wages and mounted campaigns to transform them into miners' cooperatives. As a result, a majority of them were transformed into facilities owned and run by miners' cooperatives.

Diverted trajectories since the 1960s

Rapid economic expansion started in the late 1950s through large-scale investment in infrastructure (highways, rapid trains, airports, etc.) and the development of heavy industries for domestic consumption and export. This process was accompanied by the energy shift from coal to oil and nuclear power, causing environmental degradation and major labour disputes in abandoned mines. Japan became the second largest industrial state in terms of GDP in 1968. The economic boom had drastically enhanced the population's standard of living and brought a massive migration of people from villages to large cities. Industrialization and urbanization were accompanied by revolutionary changes in production, distribution and consumption patterns. Manufacturers developed a system of mass production and distribution of packaged food for mass consumption by utilizing chemicals as food additives. Even fresh food was produced increasingly in an industrialized way, making wide use of pesticides and antibiotics. Consumers were concerned by the use of chemicals, as well as high inflation, misleading labelling and air/water pollution. With the oil shock of 1973, the Japanese economy experienced negative growth for the first time since the Second World War and shifted from rapid to moderate growth (from 9.1 per cent per annum in 1956–73 to 4.2 per cent in 1974–90). Japan suffered from a wild price spiral of land and commodities while a drastic export drive of cars and consumer electronics caused trade conflicts with the USA. The Plaza Accord of 1985 caused a sharp appreciation of the Japanese yen and prompted the government to adopt a large spending and low interest policy, which resulted in an economic bubble. During that period, the Japanese-style management, characterized by lifelong employment, seniority-based wage system, enterprise labour unions and the convoy system (ministries–industries coalition), was often praised as a world-class practice (Vogel, 1979).

The rapid economic expansion generated a range of by-products such as consumer and environmental problems. The arsenic-contained milk or PCB-contaminated edible oil caused serious damages to human bodies, while thalidomide brought about deformed babies. Such circumstances gave momentum to consumerism seeking safer food, consumer rights and a better environment. In the 1960s and 1970s, massive consumer campaigns were organized against food additives, controlled prices, misleading labelling, water pollution and skin eczema caused by detergent, air pollution, etc. Inspired housewives started the 10 yen milk movement by organizing buying clubs in many places to secure unadulterated pure milk for their families, particularly children. They formed *Han* groups for ordering and receiving milk. From these buying clubs emerged citizen cooperatives from the mid-1960s, with members of various backgrounds; university cooperatives assisted housewives in creating and running consumer cooperatives by providing staff and expertise in Sapporo, Saitama, Nagoya and Kyoto, while trade unions helped organize Seikatsu Club Cooperatives in Tokyo and Yokohama. The existing cooperatives also joined them; Co-op Kobe shifted from *goyoukiki* delivery system[9] to joint buying in 1977, while worker-oriented Yokohama Co-op adopted *Han* groups in the 1960s and joined with other cooperatives to create the Kanagawa Co-op in 1975. Tsuruoka Co-op involved housewives in addition to unionists and initiated *Han* groups. Until 1985, citizens' cooperatives were operating in all the prefectural capitals. JCCU developed alternative products reflecting consumer campaigns: CO-OP brand milk to promote the 10 yen milk movement, CO-OP detergent/soap to reduce impacts to water and health, CO-OP colour television sets to help consumer campaigns against controlled price. In this process,

the Japanese-style consumer cooperatives were generated with common characteristics of predominant female membership, joint purchase through *Han* groups
and a strong dimension of social movement for consumerism, ecology and peace.
Their membership continued to grow; 27.8 million in 2014, equivalent to 49.3 per
cent of total households. This means they are the largest civil society force in Japan.

Trade unions held campaigns for wage hikes and better working conditions
through annual 'Spring Labourer Offensives' from the mid-1950s. This was
intended to contribute to the overall improvement of working conditions through
a spill-over effect in that the higher pay achieved by forerunning powerful unions
could provide a positive impact in other industries and SMEs. During the high
economic growth period, it worked well and the wage level rose through sta-
bilized labour relations, while the emphasis shifted to safeguarding employment
after the oil shocks in the 1970s. However, the changing industrial structure from
manufacturing to services and the shift of production of the heavy industries to
overseas had a negative impact on union membership consisting of full-time workers. The rate of unionized workers decreased to reach 30 per cent in 1983. The
Japanese Trade Union Confederation (JTUC-*Rengo*) was formed in 1989 by merging four national confederations, while the left-wing unions set up the National
Confederation of Trade Unions (*Zenroren*) and the National Trade Union Council
(*Zenrokyo*).[10] Because of the prolonged economic downturn and industrial restructuring from 1990, formal employment that constituted a hard core of unions has
been restrained, while non-unionized informal employment has sharply increased.
As a result, the union membership ratio came down to 17.5 per cent in 2014.[11]

As such, consumer cooperatives and trade unions have followed diverted trajectories since the 1960s and created different organizational cultures. Such evolution
can be seen in other industrialized countries, but the interface between them has
been weakened to the extent that both parties had very little concern for each
other, with a few exceptions. To some extent, it reflects the shift of dominant
cultures from worker culture to consumer culture, but it also seems to reflect a
gender bias. Women account for 32.3 per cent of trade union membership and
9.3 per cent of their leaders (in the case of JTUC-*Rengo*), while they account for
95 per cent of consumer cooperative members and a majority of board members.
It mirrors the division of labour in which male workers earn money for households while their wives work as part-timers or housewives, bearing the major
responsibilities of caring for children and the elderly. Such a single bread-winner
family model had even been intensified by the taxation and social security system.
However, it is now facing a serious challenge of rapid ageing combined with lower
birth rates and increased difficulties for young people to form families, weakening
the safety net function of families and communities.

Such diverted trajectories can be seen in statistics as well. The ratio of trade
union members to the total workforce has declined over recent decades, while that
of consumer cooperative members to total households has grown since the 1970s
and reached a plateau in the 2000s.

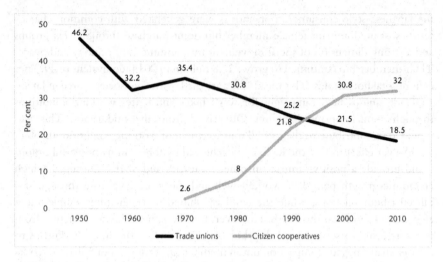

FIGURE 9.1 Organizational ratio of trade unions and citizen cooperatives

Source: Author's own elaboration from MHLW's Basic survey on trade unions and JCCU's Statistics on consumer cooperatives.

* Organization ratio of trade unions means the percentage of union membership out of the total workforce, while that of citizen cooperatives stands for the percentage of cooperative membership out of the total of households.

Typology of consumer cooperatives and link with trade unions

Consumer cooperatives are classified by industries/functions and locations. The industries/functions range from retailing, insurance, banking and housing to health/social care. The locations are local communities, workplaces and universities. The dominant citizen cooperatives operate in local communities and serve

TABLE 9.2 Typology of consumer cooperatives

Industry/ function	Location		
	Communities	*Workplaces*	*Universities*
Retailing	Citizen cooperatives	Workplace cooperatives	University cooperatives
Insurance	*Rosai*, JCIF	*Rosai, Tansan kyosai*	University *kyosai* cooperatives
Banking	Labour banks	Labour banks	
Housing	Housing cooperatives		
Health and social care	Health/social cooperatives		

Source: Author's own elaboration.

residents/consumers living therein, while workplace cooperatives operate in the companies' premises or government offices and serve employees. There is a hybrid type called 'extended workplace cooperative' that serves both employees and residents.[12] University cooperatives operate in university/college campuses and serve all constituencies, including students and faculty members.

The majority of Japanese trade unions are organized as enterprise unions (in-house unions) embracing all employees in enterprises or government offices while they form industry-based federations called *Tansan*. There are occupational unions such as school teachers' unions and seamen's unions, while general unions are organized by independent workers regardless of their employers. They are federated at local, prefectural and national levels.

Both the labour banks and the workers' insurance cooperatives are organizations based on trade unions and consumer cooperatives, but they are different in some respects (Table 9.3). The former only have corporate members such as trade unions and consumer cooperatives, while the latter have individual members such as workers and consumers. Thirteen labour banks are affiliated to the National Federation of Labour Banks and sought further consolidation into a nationwide Labour Bank, but that was not allowed by the Financial Service Agency. *Zenrosai* accomplished the national consolidation with 46 prefectural workers' insurance cooperatives (except for Niigata Sogo Co-op) in 1976, while it integrated the businesses of four out of eight *Tansan kyosai*, which were organized by *Tansan*, covering several prefectures.[13]

As mentioned earlier, the first labour bank had been founded by consumer cooperatives in Okayama, while the ensuing ones were set up by trade unions' initiatives. Today they are fundamentally owned and controlled by trade unions. In contrast, consumer cooperatives have a marginal presence in deposits and

TABLE 9.3 Comparison between labour banks and insurance cooperatives

	Labour banks (Rokin)	*Insurance cooperatives* (Rosai)
Regulation	Labour Bank Act of 1953	Consumer Cooperative Act of 1948
Supervising agency	Financial Services Agency (FCA) plus Ministry of Health, Labour and Welfare	Ministry of Health, Labour and Welfare
Membership	Trade unions and consumer cooperatives (corporate members only)	Workers and consumers
National federation	National Federation of Labour Banks (with 13 labour banks)	*Zenrosai* with 47 prefectural *Rosai* and 8 *Tansan Kyosai*
Business consolidation	No consolidation allowed	46 prefectural *Rosai* and 4 *Tansan Kyosai*

Source: Author's own elaboration

loans of labour banks, while they deal with other financial institutions, including mega banks and local banks. The boards of labour banks are mostly composed of representatives of affiliated trade unions. Such characteristics of labour banks as trade-union-led banks are often referred to as a union-based approach, where individual workers are treated as an indirect constituency. In view of potential conflicts of interests between unions' and workers' interests, the labour banks need to listen to the voice of individual savers/borrowers. The labour banks promote distinct activities such as consultation on revising loan repayment plans, awareness-raising on excessive debt problems, and support loans to non-profit and community organizations (Ikezaki, 2012).

Collaboration between cooperatives and trade unions[14]

Consumer cooperatives and trade unions are supporting labour banks and workers' insurance cooperatives while these cooperatives are affiliated to the Central Council for Workers' Welfare, a network of organizations that seeks to promote workers' welfare. They also collaborate in some areas such as lobbying aimed to improve the social security system, tackling social exclusion and assisting victims of natural disasters.

Since 2005, JTUC-*Rengo*, the Central Council for Workers' Welfare, the labour banks and the workers' insurance cooperatives at the prefectural level set up local 'life support centres' (LSCs) to provide one-stop counselling for working people on issues ranging from employment and pensions to social services and legal matters. 120 LSCs have been set up throughout the country; for example, in Shizuoka Prefecture, three LSCs and two satellite offices are in operation linking more than 100 organizations. Each LSC is staffed with full-time or part-time advisers who listen to visitors and give advice to solve problems linking those constituting organizations and channelling to public agencies, non-profits and specialists as required. After ten years of operation, they seek to expand services to a wider scope of people, including retirees and housewives.

The initiatives for assisting victims of natural disasters, both in rescue and rehabilitation phases, have been the most prominent area of collaboration. When the Kobe earthquake hit the Kansai area in 1995, cooperatives and trade unions sent tens of thousands of volunteers to assist the victims in order to save and rehabilitate lives in the affected area. Co-op Kobe initiated a campaign for the enactment of new legislation to help rehabilitate victims' lives. Then JCCU, *Zenrosai* and JTUC-*Rengo* joined and collected more than 24 million signatures, which accounted for half of the total households. Such a campaign resulted in the enactment of the Act for Assisting Rehabilitation of Victims' Lives in 1998, breaking the bureaucrats' opposition to public spending for private properties. Since 2000, the Tokyo Consumer Co-op Union, JTUC-*Rengo* Tokyo and other civic organizations continued to raise funds and send volunteers to Miyake Island, located 175 kilometres south of Tokyo, after the volcano erupted and all the residents had evacuated.

There are some business links among consumer cooperatives, workers' insurance cooperatives and labour banks. *Zenrosai* is affiliated to JCCU, while Japan CO-OP Insurance Consumer Co-operative Federation (JCIF), as a spin-off of JCCU, sells fire insurance products of the former. *Zenrosai* also sells its fire insurance for housing loans through labour bank branches based on a partnership agreement since 2009. However, opportunities of cross-marketing need to be explored to meet stiff competition in the financial industry. Iwate Consumer Credit Co-op was approved under the Consumer Cooperative Act in 1969 to provide a safety net for multiple debtors through consultation and small loans. It has been supported by *Rokin*'s matching loans to local governments' loans since its inception. It expanded to the neighbouring Aomori Prefecture in 2011 while it became a model of government policy to tackle problems associated with heavy debtors.

The worker cooperatives have been emerging from two origins since the 1970s. The All Japan Construction Workers Union organized daily workers who conducted public works (cleaning, garbage recycling, etc.), financed by a municipal relief work project. It launched worker cooperatives from the late 1970s when governments quit relief work projects on the ground, which was inefficient and tended to maintain workers in a precarious status. On the other hand, Tokyu Railways Workers' Union helped set up the Seikatsu Club Consumer Cooperative from which 'workers' collectives' were organized by dominant female members as a spin-off from the 1980s. As such, both streams were created by trade unions but had quite different constituencies and organizational culture; the former were made up of aged male workers who wished to earn full salary to feed their families, while the latter were made up of female workers who wanted to supplement household income. Today they seek to enact a new supportive legislation to legitimate and promote workers' cooperatives as a whole.

Conclusion: search for solidarity-based society

Consumer cooperatives and trade unions were born from common roots to improve the living and working conditions of workers, which had deteriorated in the wake of the Industrial Revolution. There are many examples of mutual support between them; the former supported the latter in strikes, while the latter assisted in organizing the former. However, after the Second World War, they have followed different trajectories in adapting to the changing socio-economic context, resulting in institutional and political divides.

Today consumer cooperatives have more than 27.8 million members, or approximately 49 per cent of all Japanese households, but their impact on politics is marginal. Trade unions maintain a strong presence in relation to governments and political parties, but their membership has shrunk to 8 million, or 17.5 per cent of the total workforce. The labour banks and the workers' insurance cooperatives have established themselves as workers' welfare businesses, but their linkage with unions is diluting both in their businesses' and members' consciousness. It is imperative for these organizations and consumer cooperatives to have a common agenda and promote joint actions since they share basic values as mutual interest organizations and have a very close vision for a solidarity-based society.[15]

To promote collaboration among worker-related organizations, inter alia to develop future leaders and cadres, JTUC-*Rengo* took the initiative in 2010 to create a graduate school granting a master's degree. Together with *Rokin, Rosai* and JCCU, it launched the Institute for Solidarity-based Society at Hosei University (ISS-HU), Tokyo in April 2015. ISS-HU provides higher education for future leaders, bridging political science and public policy schools, and conducts studies to categorize the Solidarity-based Society and promote the social and solidarity economy. It is not an easy task given that the current government dedicates very little attention to the social and solidarity economy, but cooperatives and trade unions are expected to create policies that can offer effective alternatives to the neoliberal agenda and demonstrate their capacity to implement them.

Notes

1   *Kyoritsu Shosha* and *Doekisha* in Tokyo, Osaka *Kyoritsu Shoten* and Kobe *Shogisha Kyoritsu Shoten* were set up.
2   This can be comparable with Bismarck's policy combining labour-protecting social policy and anti-socialist laws as a carrot-and-stick approach, but these legislations in 1900 had targeted different groups, such as workers and farmers/SMEs.
3   Kobe Co-op and Nada Co-op grew steadily and became the largest consumer cooperative in Japan. They merged into Nada Kobe Co-op in 1962, which was renamed as Co-op Kobe in 1991 when it reached 1 million members.
4   Toyohiko Kagawa, a Christian social reformer, founded Kansai Labour League (*Kansai Rodo Domeikai*) in 1919 and led historical industrial disputes against Mitsubishi and Kawasaki Shipyards in 1921 with a serious defeat. He also founded a number of cooperatives to improve workers' and farmers' lives. His book *Brotherhood Economics* in 1936 became a best-seller and widely contributed to the dissemination of the cooperative idea worldwide. He was a founding president of the JCCU. Zenji Nasu succeeded him as a business leader in Osaka and founded Nada Co-op together with Kagawa.
5   *Goyoukiki* is a kind of home delivery system in which rounds men regularly visit patrons to take orders and deliver goods or services. A coop employee visited each member's home every morning to take orders and then delivered the ordered items in the evening.
6   *Han* means a small unit of organization. The cooperative *Han* group was organized by several members living in the proximity. *Kyodo konyu* means joint buying by members who place and receive orders in *Han* groups. From the coop's viewpoint, it is an arrangement of product delivery to *Han* groups.
7   *Tansan* means the industry-based federation of enterprise unions and not the industrial unions. For example, the Federation of All Toyota Workers' Union, the Federation of All Nissan Workers' Union, etc., are affiliated to the Confederation of Japan Automobile Workers' Unions.
8   Tsuruoka Co-op's President Hideo Sato took the idea of *Han* groups from the *Consumer Coop Guidebook* published in 1949, which described practices initiated by cooperatives in the 1920s (Kurimoto, 2005).
9   See note 5.
10 JTUC-*Rengo* had 33,940 unions with 6,507,000 members in 2005, while *Zenroren* had 7,351 unions with 730,000 members and *Zenrokyo* had 1,625 unions with 158,000 members.

11 The organization ratio of unions in the large companies with more than 1,000 employees decreased to 45 per cent in 2013, while that in the SME with 100–999 employees was 13 per cent and that in small companies with less than 99 employees was 1 per cent. In contrast, that of part-time workers grew from 2 per cent to 7.6 per cent between 1990 and 2013. Public sector workers shrank from 3.6 million to 1.5 million between 1981 and 2013, mainly due to staff cuts, privatization, outsourcing and replacement by informal workers.

12 For instance, Toyota Co-op was founded as a workplace cooperative for employees of Toyota Motor Corp. but later extended its services to residents in the neighbouring areas.

13 *Kyosai* cooperatives in All Japan Prefectural and Municipal Workers' Union, National Forest Workers' Union, Japan Tobacco Workers' Union, and National Water Supply Workers' Union are integrated, while those in Japan Teachers' Union, Japan Post Workers' Union, Japan Communication Workers' Union and National Transport Workers' Union are not integrated.

14 There exist both successful and failed examples of collaboration in the world. In Singapore, the National Trade Union Congress (NTUC) developed union-based consumer and insurance cooperatives; the NTUC Fair Price commands more than half of the retailing, while NTUC Income has a dominant position in the insurance sector. They enjoy preferable treatment by the government. On the other hand, German trade unions sponsored labour-oriented enterprises (so-called *Gemeinwirtschaft*) such as BfG bank, Volksfürsolge insurance, Coop AG retail giant, Neue Heimat housing and GUT travel agent since the 1960s, but they were all bankrupted or sold to the private sector in the 1980s. The Confederation of German Trade Unions (DGB) announced that it would not be involved in business operations any more.

15 JCCU's 2020 Vision 'To build a new society where people link together, feel happiness and trust prevails', *Rengo*'s Proposal in 2010 'Toward a secure society based on work', and *Rofukukyo*'s 2020 Vision 'To build a secure and symbiotic welfare society through solidarity and cooperation' share a common idea toward a solidarity-based society.

References

Ikezaki, Shoko. *ROKIN Bank: The story of workers' organizations that successfully promote financial inclusion*, Geneva: ILO, 2012.

Kurimoto, Akira. (1992) Japan's consumer co-operative movement: A comparative review. In *Robert Owen and the world of co-operation*, edited by Chishichi Tsuzuki, 223–237. Tokyo: University of Tokyo Press, 1992.

____. The institutional change and consumer co-operation: Japanese vs European models. In *Consumerism versus capitalism?* 53–75. Ghent: Amsab-Institute of Social History, 2005.

Okutani, Matsuji. *Nihon Shohi Kumiaishi* (History of Japanese consumer cooperatives). Tokyo: Koyo Shoin, 1935.

Vogel, Ezra F. *Japan as number one: Lessons for America*. Cambridge, MA: Harvard University Press, 1979.

Yamamoto, Osamu. *Nihon Seikatsu Kyodo Kumiai Undoshi* (History of Japanese consumer co-operative movement). Tokyo: Nihon Hyoronsha, 1982.

10

SAVING JOBS AND BUSINESSES IN TIMES OF CRISIS

The Italian road to creating worker cooperatives from worker buyouts

Marcelo Vieta

Introduction

It is no coincidence that we have witnessed in recent years spikes in new worker cooperatives in countries hard hit by the global economic crisis, particularly where there are also established cooperative and labour movements (Birchall and Hammond Ketilson, 2009; EURICSE, 2015; Zevi *et al.*, 2011). Indeed, the literature on labour-managed firms (LMFs) suggests that worker cooperatives are more robust than conventional investor-owned firms during economic downturns (Bentivogli and Viviano, 2012; Smith and Rothbaum, 2014; Zanotti, 2011) as they protect jobs (Estrin, 1985; Pérotin, 2006, 2014) and encourage worker and community well-being (CECOP CICOPA-Europe, 2012, 2013; Erdal, 2012; Estrin, 1989; Oakeshott, 2000; Theorell, 2003). One source for this recent growth in worker cooperatives has been the conversion of conventional businesses via worker buyouts (WBOs) – employee-led acquisitions or rescues of companies in trouble or with succession issues that are converted to some form of worker-ownership and management (Quarter and Brown, 1992; Jensen, 2011; Vieta, 2016). The robustness of worker cooperatives has particularly been reflected in the increased interest in and rising number of business conversions to cooperatives across the world in recent years, particularly in Latin America and Southern Europe (Vieta *et al.*, 2017; Zevi *et al.*, 2011). In Southern Europe, for instance, France, Spain, and Italy have witnessed over the last decade a growth in new worker cooperatives and other LMFs emanating from WBOs of troubled companies (Jensen, 2011; Soulage, 2011; Zanotti, 2011). While perhaps less storied than their South American cousins, the *empresas recuperadas por sus trabajadores* (ERTs) (Chedid Henriques, 2014; Ruggeri and Vieta, 2015), Southern Europe's WBOs have been equally promising for saving jobs, businesses, and local communities from further depletion in the aftermath of economic crises.

In this chapter we focus on the emergence of one of Europe's most promising paths for saving jobs and businesses in times of neoliberal crisis and austerity: Italy's

Legge Marcora (hereafter, Marcora Law) legal and financial framework for WBOs. In the following pages we draw on key findings from a qualitative, quantitative, and documentary research project that the author led exploring Italy's WBOs and published in full in the report *The Italian Road to Recuperating Enterprises and the Legge Marcora Framework: Italy's Worker Buyouts in Times of Crisis* (Vieta *et al.*, 2017).[1]

The chapter is organized as follows: first, we discuss the historical and macro-economic conditions undergirding Italy's WBOs and supporting Marcora Law framework. Second, we detail the framework's main legal, financial, and policy dimensions for WBO creation. Third, we review the most salient geographic and firm lifespan (i.e., demographic) trends for Italian WBOs. We conclude the chapter with a discussion of seven main trends that characterize the emergence of Italy's WBOs: (1) a strong policy and financing enabling environment, (2) their surge during economic downturns, (3) their inter-firm and territorial networks, (4) their preponderance in labour-intensive sectors, (5) their workers' tendencies for geographic and sectoral situatedness, (6) their intra-firm social networks, and (7) their resilience. Italy's WBO phenomenon, we ultimately argue, is exemplar and in ways unique because of its worker-recuperated firms' resilience in times of crisis, in no small part secured by the Marcora Law framework's clear inclusion of three main stakeholders in the conversion of a workplace to a cooperative, namely: *workers, the state,* and *the cooperative movement.*

The emergence of Italy's worker buyouts

The pattern of WBO emergence in Italy is indicative of the socio-economic and socio-political conditions that reduce the barriers and opportunity costs for workers contemplating starting a worker cooperative from conversions. That is, WBOs tend to emerge in national contexts where there has been a general decline of economic circumstances merging with a country's historical and material particularities, including an established and supportive cooperative movement, traditions of workers' activism and strong unions, and various forms (to a greater or lesser extent) of institutionalized assistance mechanisms. In these contexts, as Johnston Birchall alludes to, workers have historically 'set up workers' cooperatives that took over failing firms or parts of firms that were still viable' (Birchall, 2003, p. 48). As Avner Ben-Ner further articulates, in a comprehensive study comparing the conversion of capitalist firms (CFs) with worker-owned firms (WOFs):

> Declining economic conditions . . . reduce the obstacles present to WOF formation. . . . The buyout of a CF entails particularly low formation obstacles because the firm is already in existence and because the cost of purchasing capital that lacks alternative uses is lower. Thus industrial decline and recessions simultaneously increase the demand for WOFs and lower the obstacles to their entry, increasing the probability of WOF formation. Governments and other organizations may accentuate the trend of WOF formation if they realize that WOFs constitute a comparatively inexpensive measure to combat loss of

employment and unemployment. . . . As relatively large numbers of WOFs are established they become more widely known, and the recurrence of recessions or decline of industries prompts even larger waves of WOF formation.

(Ben-Ner, 1988, p. 23)

An overview of Italy's WBOs

Since the early 1980s in Italy, the recuperation and conversion of businesses to cooperatives have mostly emerged from WBOs. Almost all have arisen from the conversion of conventional small- and medium-sized enterprises (SMEs) in crisis or, to a lesser extent, with succession issues. While present throughout the national territory (see Table 10.1), these conversions have particularly taken root in the centre and the northeast, in the 'Made in Italy' regions where the majority of the country's speciality-based manufacturing industry consisting of intricately connected SMEs is located.[2] Since the mid-1980s and the passing of Law 49/1985 – officially 'Provisions for credit to cooperation and urgent measures to safeguard employment levels,'[3] known more commonly as Marcora Law after the Minister of Industry who sponsored it, Giovanni Marcora – Italy's WBO framework has promoted and assisted both the conversion of firms into worker cooperatives and the consolidation, refurbishing, and start-up of employment-generating cooperatives. The most recent surge in WBOs in Italy took place starting in 2008 with the lingering negative effects of the global economic crisis and subsequent austerity measures on Italy's GDP and labour markets, and the overall shrinking of its SME-based manufacturing sectors over the past 25 years (Sforzi, 2007; Triglia and Burroni, 2009; Tridico, 2012). As we will see, Italy's Marcora Law framework has been an especially promising WBO-generating mechanism during times of crisis, saving local jobs and businesses.[4]

As Figure 10.1 shows, Italy's contemporary WBOs emerged with some regularity between 1982 and 1995, during the key years leading up to and following the establishment of the Marcora Law. During a time of economic downturn, high unemployment, and market instability, our research tracked a total of 155 WBOs that entered during this 14-year period, averaging almost 12 converted firm openings per year. WBOs began to witness a net deficit of entries when compared with exits between 1996 and 2007. Addressed below, these 12 years include the period when the Marcora Law framework was contested by the European Union (EU), and a period of time with relative stability in the Italian political economy, thus making WBO projects less compelling for workers. Since 2008 and the aftermath of the global economic crisis and continuing austerity, WBO solutions have again become an option for private sector workers in Italy facing possible job loss from business closures. Between 2008 and 2014, there was a consistently sharp rise in new WBOs, paralleling the presence of persistent economic crisis in Italy in recent years. In total, 76 new WBO projects were recorded by our research between 2008 and 2014, with only 29 confirmed closures, most of which were older WBOs closing in recent years. In 2013 and 2014 alone, there were 34 new WBO entries and only 11 closures, again mostly of older WBOs.

TABLE 10.1 Regional distribution of WBOs, by Marcora Law period (1979–2014)[6]

Region	Pre-L. Marcora and Marcora I WBOs (1979–2001)		L. Marcora II WBOs (2002–14)		Total WBOs in Italy	
	n.	% of total WBOs	n.	% of total WBOs	n.	% of total WBOs
Nord-Est (and totals)	46	17.90%	30	11.67%	76	29.57%
Emilia-Romagna	20	7.78%	21	8.17%	41	15.95%
Friulia-Venezia Giulia	2	0.78%	3	1.17%	5	1.95%
Trentino-Alto Adige[5]	11	4.28%	0	0.00%	11	4.28%
Veneto	13	5.06%	6	2.33%	19	7.39%
Nord-Ovest (and totals)	25	9.73%	9	3.50%	34	13.23%
Liguria	6	2.33%	0	0.00%	6	2.33%
Lombardia	12	4.67%	8	3.11%	20	7.78%
Piemonte	7	2.72%	1	0.39%	8	3.11%
Val d'Aosta	0	0.00%	0	0.00%	0	0.00%
Centro (and totals)	89	34.63%	26	10.12%	115	44.75%
Lazio	10	3.89%	5	1.95%	15	5.84%
Marche	21	8.17%	3	1.17%	24	9.34%
Toscana	42	16.34%	13	5.06%	55	21.40%
Umbria	16	6.23%	5	1.95%	21	8.17%
Sud (and totals)	16	6.23%	7	2.72%	23	8.95%
Abruzzo	3	1.17%	1	0.39%	4	1.56%
Basilicata	0	0.00%	1	0.39%	1	0.39%
Calabria	2	0.78%	0	0.00%	2	0.78%
Campania	5	1.95%	5	1.95%	10	3.89%
Molise	0	0.00%	0	0.00%	0	0.00%
Puglia	6	2.33%	0	0.00%	6	2.33%
Isole (and totals)	0	0.00%	9	3.50%	9	3.50%
Sardegna	0	0.00%	2	0.78%	2	0.78%
Sicilia	0	0.00%	7	2.72%	7	2.72%
Totals	176	64.48%	81	31.52%	257	100.00%

Column percentages calculated on total WBOs in Italy (n=257).

Taking into account all WBOs with known opening and closure years over the 25-year period spanning 1990 (the first year of recorded WBO closures in our database) to 2014 (the last year of WBO formation in our database), the average birth or entry rate of Italian WBOs was 5.08 per cent, the average death or closure

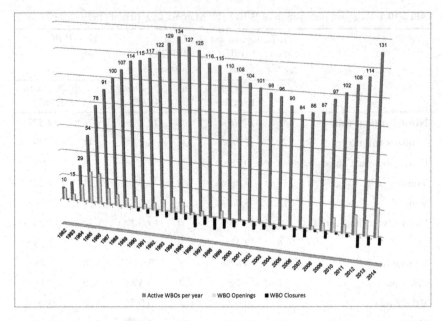

FIGURE 10.1   Active WBOs per year compared with WBO openings and closings per year during the Marcora Law era

n = 248 WBOs with complete opening and closing dates as of 31 December 2014, inclusive of one WBO in database that emerged prior to 1982.

rate was 4.27 per cent, and the average growth rate was +0.96 per cent. In the 17 years covering 1990–99 and 2008–14 (when WBOs were also forming and not only closing and when the Marcora Law framework was in full effect), Italy's WBOs had an average birth rate of 7.71 per cent compared with an average death rate of 4.18 per cent, with an average growth rate of +3.73 per cent. While this slightly exceeds the average birth rate of all Italian manufacturing firms in recent years, which is around 7.5 per cent, this death rate is much less than the average death rate of all Italian firms at roughly 6.5 per cent (OECD, 2010).[7] These numbers point to very favourable survival rates and highlight further the possibilities of the WBO model for saving jobs and firms during times of crisis and austerity.

Historical and macro-economic contexts

Worker-led occupations and recuperations of firms had already been known in Italy since the early part of the 20th century (i.e., the *Bienno Rosso* of 1919–20), re-emerging again during Italy's reconstruction after the Second World War and during the years of social and labour strife in the 1960s and 1970s. As with most cases of workplace conversions to worker cooperatives around the world, Italy's WBOs of the last three and a half decades – during what we can call the 'Marcora Law era of WBOs' – have had a pattern of development following closely the country's macro- and micro-economic ebbs and flows, such as the rate of unemployment

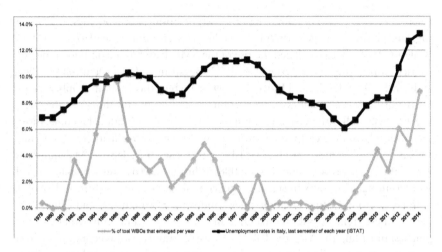

FIGURE 10.2 The emergence of WBOs in Italy compared with unemployment rates during the Marcora Law era

(Figure 10.2), the GDP rate, and increasing closures of conventional businesses, particularly in the manufacturing sector (Figure 10.3).

Specifically, the phenomenon of workplace conversions to worker cooperatives began to re-emerge in Italy in the early 1980s (Figures 10.1 and 10.2) as workers'

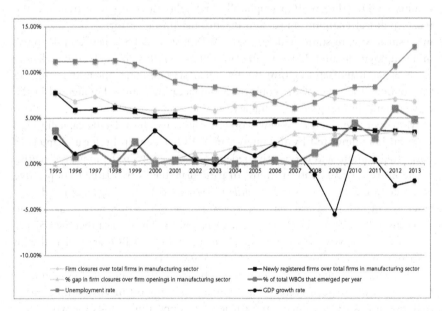

FIGURE 10.3 Various socio-economic indicators and the emergence of WBOs in Italy (1995–2013)

Sources: Firm closures, Newly registered firms, Total active firms (InfoCamere-Movimprese, 2014, Jul.). GDP growth rate (World Bank, 2014, Nov.; Eurostat, 2014, Nov.). Unemployment rates (ISTAT, 2014, Aug.). Percentage of total WBOs emerging per year (Vieta *et al.*, 2017, Chapter 2).

responses to the rise in unemployment caused by business downsizings, restructurings, and closures of large parts of Italy's industrial sector during the 1970s and 1980s (Gallino, 2003). This paralleled the rise of the SME-based 'Made in Italy' industrial districts during these years (Bagnasco, 1977; Becattini and Dei Ottati, 2006; Piore and Sabel, 1984; Triglia and Burroni, 2009). Much of this economic upheaval and restructuring was also due to the recessions caused by the oil shocks of the 1970s and 1980s, as well as the increased competition that Italy's traditional manufacturing sector faced from developing countries with cheaper labour markets (i.e., China, India, Turkey) or more productive labour processes (i.e., Japan) (Malanima and Zamagni, 2010; Morone and Testa, 2008; Whitford, 2001). Subsequently, at-risk workers in Italy began to engage in workplace takeovers, conversions, and buyouts as responses to escalating unemployment, industrial restructuring, and failing businesses. These trends would ultimately lead to the creation of employment-related policies, including the Marcora Law, as a way to stimulate local economic revival, prevent further business closures, and promote workers' *autoimprenditorialità* (literally, self-entrepreneurialism, capacity to do business via workers' self-management) (Dandolo, 2009). WBOs would see a new resurgence in the early-to-mid-1990s with the new wave of business restructurings and privatizations of the era, lingering structural unemployment, neoliberal reforms of labour legislation, the early stages of the shrinking of Italy's SME-based manufacturing sector, negative rates of business openings to closures, and the concurrent erratic ebbs and flows of the country's GDP.[8] Figure 10.3 graphically highlights three negative trends in the Italian political economy impacting the manufacturing sector, trends that have, in no small way, re-stimulated the rise of WBOs since 2008: a new and sharp rise in unemployment after 2007–08, the fall of Italy's GDP since 2007, the widening gap between manufacturing firm closures versus start-ups since the mid-1990s, and the continued decline of the country's manufacturing base as highlighted in the concomitant shrinking of the manufacturing sector.[9]

Moreover, the creation of new worker cooperatives from failing capitalist ones were further stimulated by the interest in WBOs taken up by local chapters of Italy's trade unions and cooperative federations, especially in the industrial centres of the northeast and centre regions. In particular, Italy's two largest cooperative confederations, the *Lega Nazionale delle Cooperative e Mutue* (Legacoop) and, to a lesser extent, the *Confederazione Cooperative Italiane* (Confcooperative), have been supporting the WBO solution in recent years, reflected in the fact that over 57 per cent of Italy's new worker cooperatives emerging from WBOs are affiliated with Legacoop and over 18 per cent with Confcooperative.[10]

This general decline of economic circumstances, together with the country's long history of cooperativism and its Marcora Law support mechanism, has made Italy ripe for WBOs, reducing the barriers and opportunity costs for workers to attempt to start new worker cooperatives in particularly conducive areas of Italy, such as the Made in Italy regions.

We can summarize the historical roots of and macro-economic conditions undergirding Italy's WBOs in: (1) the general decline of its SME-based manufacturing sectors; (2) lingering high rates of unemployment; (3) the militant position of some of its local trade union chapters and the long-standing Italian tradition of bottom–up shop floor organizing (Piore and Sabel, 1984); (4) workers' links to tight local social networks and associations that preserve connections to local and regional chapters of the country's trade unions and cooperative federations; (5) well-established cooperative and WBO legislation and financial support mechanisms; (6) and a long-standing tradition of cooperativism for local economic development (Salvatori, 2012; Menzani and Zamagni, 2010; Zamagni and Zamagni, 2010).

Italy's Marcora Law framework: a collaborative approach to worker buyouts

The Italian method of converting conventional businesses to worker cooperatives is, in the main, a negotiated WBO process with a unique set of supportive policies and financing mechanisms that facilitate a collaborative approach.[11] In this section we map out what has been called the 'Italian road' to worker-recuperated enterprises (Vieta *et al.*, 2017). This road merges the Marcora Law framework with other complementary cooperative, labour, and business legislation and norms, mapping out a concerted WBO development approach between the following stakeholders: workers, the state, and the cooperative movement, the latter including institutional investors that become temporary and partial members of the subsequent worker cooperative.

Workers

Under the Marcora Law, employees facing losing their jobs due to the closure of the firm that employs them have a priority right (*diritto de prelazione*) to buy out the firm before final bankruptcy is declared or before the firm is sold off to another group of investors. Employees in Italy can begin a WBO process in any of the following scenarios: (1) the imminent closure of a firm; (2) if part of or all of a firm is offered to employees by its owners (such as in a succession conversion); (3) if a group of employees has been or will be laid off due to the closing of a business;[12] or (4) after a group of workers from the closing company regroup into a new worker cooperative or other associative business form.[13] Employees at risk of facing unemployment will most often discover the WBO possibility after consulting with their local unions, the regional offices of one of Italy's cooperative federations, from local business experts, or from other contacts in their social networks. Once employees form into a worker cooperative they can begin the process of acquiring part or all of the target company via share capital (*capitale sociale*) contributions financed by their personal savings, severance pay,[14] or from advances of their cash transfer-based unemployment insurance benefits, an innovation of the Marcora Law framework.[15] Workers can also pursue debt capital (*capitale di debito*) financing from either the cooperative sector or an institutional investor, which we will discuss shortly. If they do so, the funds can be secured by projections on future revenues of the worker cooperative and/or by the collateral offered from the acquired assets of the target company.

The minimum contribution per worker to the start-up capital of the WBO can be no less than €4,000 (€1,000 if starting a social cooperative, which is also permitted by the Marcora Law provisions). Moreover, virtually all WBOs in Italy convert firms into limited liability cooperatives, thus protecting participating workers from risking personal assets should the venture fail.

The state

Complemented by numerous laws and provisions guiding Italian cooperative societies, the Italian state, via the Marcora Law and its subsequent amendments and reforms, has made available two funds for the start-up, development, or consolidation of work-generating cooperatives in order to promote and secure levels of employment in times of crisis and for the conversion of businesses in crisis into cooperatives. Title I of the Marcora Law sets out the provisions for a 'rotating loan fund for the promotion and development of cooperativism'.[16] Also known as Foncooper, this is a rotating fund consisting of soft loans. Title II of L. 49/1985 details the 'special fund for initiatives to protect occupational levels',[17] or the 'Special Fund', a risk-capital fund dedicated to the development of work-generating cooperatives. The Special Fund is made available to the institutional investors (see below) that are mandated to subsequently carry out investments in employment-generating cooperatives.

Foncooper has been used extensively to, among other objectives, 'increase productivity or employment' via cooperatives and for the 'restructuring and conversion of firms' to cooperatives. Over the years, Foncooper has been managed by the *Banca Nazionale del Lavoro*'s (BNL) 'Special Section for Credit to Cooperation'[18] (Zevi, 1990) and, in recent years, Italy's administrative regions[19] in collaboration with financial institutions such as, among others, BNL, UniCredit Banca SpA, regionally based banks (e.g. *Banca Popolare dell'Emilia Romagna, Banca Popolare di Verona e Novara*, etc.), and Cooperfidi Italia (an institution that facilitates favourable credit to cooperatives through accessible terms of repayment and loan guarantees). In turn, the Special Fund is distinguished in that 'the financial institutions [i.e., institutional investors] able to [deploy] its resources' and assist new cooperatives 'in fact, share in the corporate capital of the worker cooperatives in proportion . . . to the amount their worker-members invest' (Zevi, 1990, p. 358). Differentiating the purposes of each fund, while Foncooper is offered as debt-capital financing to new and established work-generating cooperatives, the Special Fund contributes risk-capital financing to cooperatives by institutional investors that take on a temporary stake (or shares) in the cooperative as a financial member. And while both funds are initially provisioned from the state budget, they have been set up to minimize burdens on state coffers by placing the onus for repayment and fair return on investments on the beneficiary cooperatives. Moreover, Marcora Law financing contributes to the capitalization of a new cooperative in proportion with workers' initial start-up or capital investments (Zevi, 2012). These two funds, the backbone of the Marcora Law framework and Italy's enabling environment for WBOs and other forms of employment-generating cooperative creation, are ultimately regulated by the Ministry of Economic Development (*Ministero dello Sviluppo Economico*) in agreement with the Ministry of the Economy and Finance (*Ministero dell'Economia e delle Finanze*) and the Ministry of Labour and Social Policy (*Ministero del Lavoro e delle Politiche Sociale*) (as per Article 7 of the law).

The cooperative movement

Employees involved in a WBO most often will eventually also work with one of the Italian cooperative confederations, most usually with Legacoop or Confcooperative, but in some cases with one of the other smaller confederations. The members of the new worker cooperative can access technical assistance and know-how and/or secure financing from the confederations' portion of the cooperative movement's mutualistic fund (*fondo mutualistico*). The mutualistic fund is a national fund for cooperative development made up of 3 per cent of all Italian cooperatives' yearly net income that, by legislation, must be contributed to the fund on an annual basis (most of the remaining proceeds from dissolved Italian cooperatives also go to this fund) (Fici, 2010, 2013). The entities that control the mutualistic fund are arm's length agencies responsible for autonomously managing each confederation's fund, such as Legacoop's Coopfond and Confcooperative's Fondosviluppo.

Institutional investors

Much of the Marcora Law framework for WBOs has been managed by two national institutional investors: *Cooperazione Finanza Imprese* (CFI) and, to a much lesser extent, *Società Finanza Cooperazione* (SOFICOOP). Both CFI and SOFICOOP have been mandated by the Italian state, via the auspices of the Ministry of Economic Development, to coordinate the Marcora Law framework's financing of cooperative start-ups and WBOs. Most often, institutional investors such as CFI and SOFICOOP will temporarily 'participate' in the new worker cooperative as a financial member (*socio finanziatore*) as allowed by Italian legislation after reforms to cooperative law in 1992 and the Civil Code in 2003 (see next section). The task of these institutions is not only to provide financing to employment-generating cooperative societies in the form of share or debt capital, but also to ensure the sustainability of the investments in new cooperative projects and, additionally, to carry out technical, economic, and financial consulting and oversight.

CFI, the larger of the two institutional investors and at the vanguard of financing and supporting Italy's WBOs, is a limited liability second-tier cooperative formed in 1986 as an initiative of Italy's three largest cooperative confederations (Legacoop, Confcooperative, and AGCI), together with Italy's three major trade union confederations (CGIL, CSIL, and UIL). As a second-tier cooperative, CFI's members include the Ministry of Economic Development, Invitalia SpA (an agency of the Ministry of the Economy and Finance that was established to promote the development of enterprises in Italy), and 270 cooperatives (including some of the cooperatives they have helped fund). As of 31 December 2014, CFI had intervened in over three-quarters of the 257 Italian WBOs tracked by our research. CFI also partners 'in pool' with a plethora of social economy organizations and economic development authorities, agencies, and financial institutions, such as: Coopfond and Fondosviluppo (Italy's two major mutualistic funds that we already mentioned), workers' representative unions, local authorities, and various national and regional consortia that finance and support new cooperatives and WBOs. Providing technical assistance, SWOT-type business analysis, feasibility studies, and participating with risk-capital or debt-capital financing of WBOs, CFI works closely with the worker-members of its beneficiary cooperatives, local labour and business representatives, cooperative associations and consortia, and other 'territorial experts' before deciding to invest in or assist in the start-up or further consolidation of its WBO and cooperative development projects.

Reforms to the Marcora Law framework in 2001

Controversially, the Marcora Law framework was suspended in the mid-to-late 1990s due to an infraction ruling by the EU shortly before Italy entered the Eurozone. The ruling by the EU's Commission stipulated that the Marcora Law scheme was in contravention of EU competition rules because, it claimed, the Italian state was giving unfair competitive advantage to cooperatives. This was particularly so, the Commission deemed, since the Marcora Law provisions at the time made it possible for the state to invest up to three times' workers' contributions to their cooperative project – that is, on a 3:1 ratio to workers' share-capital investments (Zevi, 2012). Because of this ruling, a reform of the Marcora Law was passed in March 2001 with L. 57/2001. Article 12 of L. 57/2001 now reforms or omits several articles of the original L. 49/1985 and has impacted the way the Marcora Law provisions are carried out in practice while, at the same time, making it more flexible for financing other forms of work-generating cooperatives. Most obviously, the 2001 reforms to the Marcora Law now limit institutional investors' contributions to worker cooperatives to a 1:1 ratio with workers' contributions. Further, financing from the Special Fund was changed from a grants-based financing model to a risk-capital model, where institutional investors drawing on the state-provisioned Special Fund must now guarantee a 'fair rate of return' on investments at reasonable rates that are meant to balance the capitalization needs of cooperatives while minimizing 'undue burdens' to the Italian state budget. In addition, there are now clearer rules for institutional investors' interventions with beneficiary cooperatives. For instance, institutional investors can take on the status of a financing member (*socio finanziatore*), effectively becoming a member of the cooperative for the duration of their investment (usually seven to ten years). With some exceptions, financing members can be any legal person or other entity with 'financial interests' in the cooperative. This alternative type of cooperative membership comes with some restrictions in order to preserve the 'mutualistic' core of Italian cooperatives; for instance, the total share of votes of all financing members of a cooperative in the assembly cannot exceed a third of the membership base. This form of investor-member in Italian cooperatives was made possible in Italy after the 1992 cooperative law reforms (Articles 4 and 5 of L. 59/1992) and the 2003 Civil Code reforms, and was originally focused on the 'subsidizing member' (*socio sovventore*).[20] In sum, the financing member status permits entities such as CFI to participate in some decision-making and administrative rights in funded cooperatives for a period of time (Fici, 2010, 2013).

Between the late 1990s and the mid-2000s, while Marcora Law reforms were being worked out and consolidated with the EU ruling, there were only a handful of new WBOs (see Figures 10.1 and 10.2). During this period, institutional investors such as CFI continued to provide technical consulting with already-existing WBOs but did not invest in new WBOs.[21]

The geographic spread and resilience of Italy's worker buyouts

As Table 10.1 illustrates, Italy's WBOs have taken off mainly in the regions of the centre – particularly in Tuscany (the region with the most WBOs in our database), Umbria, and Marche, but also in Lazio – and the northeast – especially in Emilia-Romagna (the region with the second-highest number of WBOs in our database) and Veneto. Not surprisingly, as we have already discussed, these are the regions where the majority of Italy's specialty and SME-based 'Made in Italy' manufacturing industry is located.[22]

What we also see from Table 10.1 when comparing the Marcora Law II period (2002–present) from earlier WBOs is: a marked reduction in new WBOs in the centre and northeast regions, and a new phenomenon in the Marcora Law II period of WBOs in Sicily and Sardinia (the island regions). These findings are related to the increased use of the Marcora Law framework for funding the development of Italy's *Mezzogiorno* (south and islands) at the expense, to some degree, of the traditional regions where worker cooperatives have historically been strong (i.e., Emilia-Romagna and Tuscany). Moreover, the Marcora Law framework is also increasingly being used in the Italian state's programme of ceding businesses confiscated from the proceeds of mafia activity to employees or the community, also explaining to some degree the surge of WBOs in the *Mezzogiorno*. Overall, the use of the Marcora Law framework for supporting development in the *Mezzogiorno* is linked to the Italian state's wider policies focusing on underwriting cooperatives to spur development in Italy's more economically challenged regions.

However, despite the increased use of Marcora Law provisions for the development of other areas of Italy, WBOs are still predominant in the centre and the northeast regions. Indeed, almost three-quarters of Italy's WBOs have emerged in the Made in Italy geographic area. Given that the Marcora Law framework was designed to lessen unemployment by bolstering, in the main, its SME-based manufacturing sectors via the worker cooperative model, and given that most of Italy's manufacturing and supporting economic activities takes place in SMEs located in the Made in Italy regions, we can understand why 68.52 per cent of Italy's WBOs, as we can see in Figure 10.4, consist of manufacturing firms. Moreover, most of the remaining WBOs are in SME-based business support services and related activities, such as rental, travel and other business services; commercial (wholesale and retail); information and communication; and transport and storage.

Figure 10.5 offers a more detailed breakdown of the manufacturing sub-sectors where Italian WBOs are found. Noteworthy are several sectors that are quite ubiquitous in the Made in Italy regions as well as in pockets in other regions, with each sub-sector following the general pattern of development of economic activity in particular localities in each region. Of particular note is the preponderance of WBO-generated firms in the metallurgical and machinery production sectors, particularly present with WBOs in Veneto and Lombardy; furniture manufacturing, particularly prevalent in Tuscany and Marche; cement, ceramics, and glassware, predominant in Tuscany and Emilia-Romagna; clothing manufacturing and textiles (including leather attire and shoes), prevalent in Marche, but also in Emilia-Romagna; and shipbuilding and repairs, mostly in Tuscany, but also in Veneto, Liguria, and Campania (Vieta *et al.*, 2017, Chapter 2).

From the 'Total' column in Table 10.2, we more clearly see that Italy's contemporary WBOs have been almost entirely SMEs, consisting mostly of small enterprises of 10–49 employees (68.38 per cent), medium-sized enterprises of 50–249

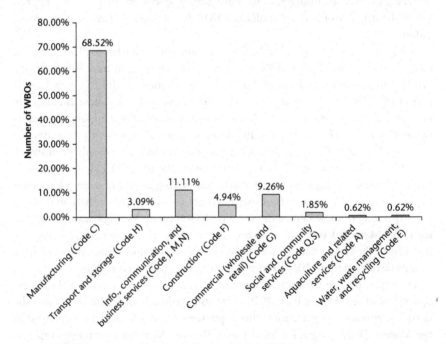

FIGURE 10.4 Economic sector breakdown of Italy's WBOs

n=159 WBOs with available ATECO2007 economic activity data[23] as of 31 December 2014.

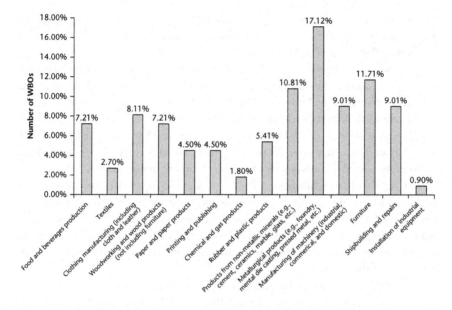

FIGURE 10.5 Breakdown of WBOs in the manufacturing sector

n=111 WBOs in the manufacturing sector with known ATECO2007 'Code C' economic activity data as of 31 December 2014.

employees (almost 22 per cent), and micro-enterprises of fewer than ten employees (almost 9 per cent), with only two enterprises consisting of over 250 employees in our database. The average size of WBOs in Italy is, at 36 workers, technically a small enterprise (Lazerson and Lorenzoni, 1999; Morone and Testa, 2008). While much larger than the average Italian firm – which is predominantly a micro-enterprise averaging four employees (Amatori *et al.*, 2011) – the average size of Italy's WBOs are not uncommon for firms in the Made in Italy regions (Unioncamera-Tagliacarne, 2010).[24]

TABLE 10.2 Size of Italy's WBOs, by number of workers (members and hired workers) during the Marcora Law era (1979–2014)[25]

Size of firm	Pre and L. Marcora I WBOs (1979–2001)		L. Marcora II WBOs (2002–14)		Total	
	n.	%	n	%	n	%
<10 employees	8	4.76%	13	20.00%	21	8.97%
10–49 employees	119	70.83%	41	63.08%	160	68.38%
50–249 employees	39	23.21%	12	16.92%	51	21.79%
> 250 employees	2	1.19%	0	0.00%	2	0.85%
Total	**168**	**100.00%**	**66**	**100.00%**	**234**	**100.00%**

n=234 WBOs with known employee data, including members and non-members of the cooperative.

These firm sizes also seem to be typical for WBOs in other conjunctures, suggesting they might be appropriate for conversions to worker cooperatives (Jensen, 2012; Ruggeri, 2010; Ruggeri and Vieta, 2015).

As Figure 10.6 depicts, by 31 December 2014, Italian WBOs in our database were either young firms – almost 33 per cent of all WBOs (active and inactive) had existed for five years or less – or older, established worker cooperatives – almost 27 per cent of all WBOs (active and inactive) had existed for over 20 years. Looking at only active firms as of 31 December 2014, almost 25 per cent had existed for five years or less, while over 20 per cent had existed for over 20 years. Perhaps surprisingly initially, slightly over 1 per cent of still-active WBOs fell into the '11–15 years' cohort, while almost 7 per cent were in the '6–10 years' and '16–20 years' cohorts (3.23 per cent and 3.63 per cent, respectively). The small number of active WBOs that were 6–20 years of age was indicative of the small number of new WBOs emerging between 1996 and up to the mid-to-late 2000s, encompassing the years when the Marcora Law framework was in dispute at the EU and before the beginning of the global economic crisis.

Our research also found that Italian WBOs are quite resilient.

The average age of still-active Italian WBOs as of 31 December 2014 was 13.9, and 11.9 years for closed (i.e., inactive) WBOs. When taking into account all still-active and inactive WBOs that had existed in Italy in our database up to 31 December 2014, their average lifespan was 13 years. While this overall average age fell short of the average age of all Italian cooperatives at slightly over 17 years, it

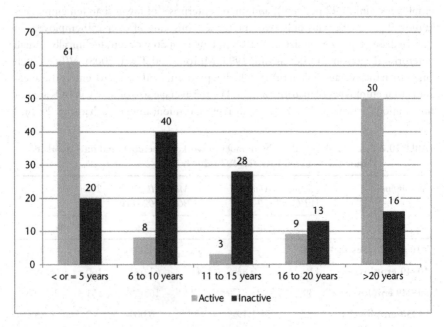

FIGURE 10.6 Lifespans of WBOs in Italy during the Marcora Law era (1979–2014)

n=248 WBOs with known opening and closing dates (131 actives and 117 inactives)

TABLE 10.3 Geographic distribution of all active and inactive WBOs in Italy, by the Marcora Law period

Geographic Distribution	Pre-L. Marcora I and L. Marcora I WBOs (1979–2001)				L. Marcora II WBOs (2002–14)			
	Inactive		Active		Inactive		Active	
	n.	%	n.	%	n.	%	n.	%
Nord–Est	30	25.86%	16	26.67%	1	10.00%	29	40.85%
Nord–Ovest	19	16.38%	6	10.00%	1	10.00%	8	11.27%
Centro	56	48.28%	33	55.00%	6	60.00%	20	28.17%
Sud	11	9.48%	5	8.33%	2	20.00%	5	7.04%
Isole	0	0.00%	0	0.00%	0	0.00%	9	12.68%
Totals	116	100.00%	60	100.00%	10	100.00%	71	100.00%
	Total in period	176			Total in period	81		

n=257 WBOs known to be active or inactive. Column percentages calculated on total WBOs per the Marcora Law period.

is almost equal to the average lifespan of all Italian firms at 13.5 years (Unioncamere-Tagliacarne, 2010). Moreover, a good number of Italian WBOs, as Table 10.3 shows, had been in existence for far longer than this average lifespan. For instance, the average age of the oldest WBOs in our database (that is, for those over 20 years of age) was 27.7 years.

From Table 10.3 we learn that just over 34 per cent of the oldest WBO-generated cooperatives (60 firms) were still active as of 31 December 2014, equalling over 23 per cent of the 257 WBOs in our database. In other words, at least 60 WBOs in existence by the end of 2014 emerged during the 20-year period leading up to the reforms to the Marcora Law in 2001, and many of these did so over 25 years ago. Moreover, from Table 10.3, we also note that 66 WBOs (active and inactive), or 26.21 per cent of all WBO firms in our database, had existed for over 20 years. Indeed, when we dig deeper into the total WBOs in existence for 25 or more years (active and inactive) in our database, we can count 54 WBOs, or 21.8 per cent of the 248 WBOs with known opening and closing dates, with only ten of these oldest WBOs having closed by 31 December 2014. The resilience of Italy's WBOs is further underscored when we consider that almost 88 per cent of Italy's newest WBOs emerging after the 2001 reforms were still active as of 31 December 2014 (71 out of 81 cooperatives).

Discussion: main trends in the emergence of Italy's worker buyouts

In this final section we summarize the main points of this chapter, which also reviews the most relevant findings from our study of Italy's WBOs (Vieta et al., 2017).

We group these findings into seven major trends that characterize the emergence of Italy's WBOs. These seven trends begin to crystallize the socio-political and socio-economic contexts that seem to have made Italy ripe for WBOs in recent decades.

Italy's WBOs are rooted in a strong policy and financing enabling environment

Perhaps the main factor driving the emergence of Italy's WBOs is the country's strong enabling environment for creating new cooperatives from conversions, grounded in its Marcora Law framework. This framework spearheads a robust policy and financing ecosystem for supporting business conversions of troubled firms to cooperatives. This ecosystem also rests on a broader base of complementary cooperative, business, and labour legislation, such as favourable tax treatment of cooperatives, a robust unemployment insurance scheme, and various cooperative development funds that can be used for WBO projects. Without such an enabling environment, the record shows that there will be much less propensity for the widespread take-up of the WBO solution. Notable for its collaborative approach between workers, the state, and the cooperative sector, the Marcora Law framework affords comprehensive policies and supports for workers in companies at risk of closure via three broad pillars:

(1) *saving jobs and productive capacity* via the formation of worker cooperatives;
(2) a *priority right (or right-of-first refusal) for employees* seeking to buy out companies in crisis that are undergoing liquidation or bankruptcy procedures; and
(3) a *collaborative approach to the creation of new cooperatives* via workers' own entrepreneurial initiative and resources (including the possible use of *lump-sum payments of appropriate unemployment benefits* to employees intending on converting a business to a worker cooperative) and matching contributions to workers' share capital investments via public funds channelled through institutional investors such as CFI that *minimize undue burdens to state coffers*.

Italy's WBOs tend to emerge out of economic downturns

Macro-economic downturns or market difficulties, as the literature on LMFs predicts, open up the possibilities for WBO cases. Such is the case in Italy, as well. WBOs tend to be countercyclical – cases of WBOs increase in times of crisis and stabilize or diminish in times of economic stability (see Figures 10.2 and 10.3). The ample evidence we found for this trend in our findings converges our research with the literature on the emergence of LMFs and cooperatives (for instance, Ben-Ner, 1988; Burdín, 2014; Burdín and Dean, 2009; Fontanari and Borzaga, 2013). As we outlined in this chapter, the overall Italian economy over the past 20 or so years has witnessed a steady decline. This has especially had a negative impact on smaller, more volatile and lighter industrial and craft-based firms, particularly in the SME-based Made in Italy manufacturing regions. Moreover, more and more Italian workers have been affected negatively by the increased loss of workers' rights and job security after the neoliberal labour and economic policies of the 1990s and 2000s, evidencing also a marked rise in temporary, contingent, and contract work and, in more recent years, a deepening of structural unemployment. Collectively, these macro-economic factors make WBOs more attractive to workers facing unemployment, especially given the rising socio-economic barriers to finding alternative work in Italy (Salvatori, 2012; Spattini, 2015; Tridico, 2012).

Italy's WBOs tend to emerge within some degree of inter-firm and territorial networks

Given the right socio-economic and -political contexts, there is an increased propensity for SMEs to convert to cooperatives when they are situated to some degree within *inter-firm networks*, such as those in the tightly networked Made in Italy industrial districts. SMEs in geographic situations found in the Made in Italy regions seem to be more prone to consider the WBO option when other known firms in their territory or networks have done so, which has also been noted of the *empresas recuperadas* in Argentina and Brazil, and WBOs in Canada, which also tend to cluster (Chedid Henriques, 2014; Quarter and Brown, 1992; Ruggeri, 2010). What we have termed 'WBO business clusters' in Italy can be found, for instance, in the provinces of Florence, Ancona, Rome, Padua and in a corridor between the provinces of Parma and Bologna. In agreement with Ben-Ner (1988), this familiarity with other known instances of WBOs 'enhances the possibility that [worker-owned firms] will be considered an option . . . and reduces . . . establishment costs related to the [otherwise] scarcity of the [worker-owned] form of organization' (p. 22).

Italy's WBOs tend to emerge in labour-intensive sectors

WBOs tend to emerge in *labour-intensive sectors made up of high-skilled workers* rather than capital-intensive ones with a low-skilled workforce (Ben-Ner, 1988). Such too is the case with Italy's WBOs. Their 'small size, simplicity of the production process and ability to follow a product through completion are prominent' and reduce the need for large amounts of capital which further lowers entry costs (*ibid.*, p. 24). As articulated in this chapter, labour-intensive SMEs appear to be an appropriate firm size for conversions to worker cooperatives, especially relevant later on when worker-members of the cooperative need to respond quickly to production or market fluctuations by, for instance, varying salaries or adjusting production inputs and outputs. Indeed, this size factor taps into the competitive advantage of the SME-sized cooperative, enabling these firms to be nimble enough to quickly alter production decisions should they need to, such as in situations of market or financial troughs when the solidarity of the workforce must be drawn on to reduce salaries or change product lines. The survey and case study evidence from our research work begins to point to this trend in the WBOs we followed. This trend also aligns with similar findings in research on Argentina's *empresas recuperadas* (Ruggeri and Vieta, 2015; Vieta, 2010, 2012, 2013, 2014).

Italy's WBOs tend to emerge with workers having relative geographic and sectoral situatedness

WBOs will tend to form with a *workforce profile of relative geographic and sectoral situatedness*. Again, the Made in Italy regions are known for their firms' labour-intensive, craft-based, inter-connected, and skilled production processes, usually consisting of dedicated workers with specific skill-sets that are not easily transferable to other jobs outside of their economic sector and with long-held commitments and social embeddedness to their local territories, where most workers also live (Becattini *et al.*, 2003). Thus, workers in WBO firms in Italy tend to have low-mobility propensities and strong commitments to their localities and existing social networks, making workers more receptive to the idea of a WBO. These characteristics are typical for Made in Italy firms, where they are often situated within smaller parts of an intricate inter-firm production process, and located within industrial districts consisting of tight networks of SMEs. This is the case, for instance, with WBOs that have emerged in the footwear and leather goods manufacturing districts of the Province of Ancona, the metallurgical shops of the Province of Padua, the varied specialty manufacturing firms of Tuscany and Emilia-Romagna, or in the services-intensive SMEs found in Rome (Vieta *et al.*, 2017, Chapter 4). In these craft-based occupations, workers tend to have low-mobility propensities and strong commitments to their localities and existing social networks (Amatori *et al.*, 2013; Lazerson and Lorenzoni, 1999; Piore and Sabel, 1984), suggesting that workers in these scenarios might be more receptive to the idea of a WBO. In other words, WBOs appear to be attractive to workers with careers heavily invested in these types of occupations and sectors, and with lives strongly rooted in the localities where they live and work. These are factors that, again, outweigh the risks for engaging in a WBO.

Italy's WBOs tend to emerge with some degree of intra-firm social networks

Recent case study work further suggests that WBOs tend to emerge within *strong intra-firm social networks* with a workforce that has forged strong bonds of solidarity on shop floors (Vieta *et al.*, 2017, Chapter 5). SMEs are small enough to have fostered workplace solidarity amongst members considering a WBO and to best 'meet members' demands for participation' (Ben-Ner, 1988, pp. 23, 25). In turn, member participation is stimulated by the camaraderie that emerges within the workforce from having gone through crisis moments together (Vieta, 2014). Indeed, these bonds are further entrenched during the process of conversion and thereafter as the firm matures as a cooperative. Employees that form a WBO from moments of shop floor struggle in a SME solidify their solidarity through 'internalization of the conflict,' which eventually merge into more democratic reconceptualizations of 'the functions of work, control, risk-bearing and capital ownership' (Ben-Ner, 1988, p. 21; see also Vieta, 2014). The strong take-up of democratic governance structures at Italy's WBOs underscores this characteristic (Vieta *et al.*, 2017, Chapter 5).

Italy's WBOs are resilient

Finally, Italian *WBOs are resilient*, witnessing relatively *long lifespans* and *robust survival rates* linked to the age of the firm and when the firm was founded. While the average lifespan (i.e., age) of all active and inactive WBOs in our database was 13 years, and 13.9 years for all active WBOs, almost half of WBO-generated firms that were still active as of 31 December 2014 had existed for 16 years or longer. Further, 23 per cent of the oldest WBOs in our database (i.e., having emerged 16 or more years ago) were still active as of 31 December 2014, while 26.21 per cent of all WBO firms in our database had existed for over 20 years. Moreover, Italy's WBOs were surviving the economic crisis very well. Between 2002 and the end of 2014, 81 new WBOs had emerged in Italy, mostly over the seven years since the beginning of the global economic crisis in 2008. The resilience of Italy's WBOs is further underscored in that, as of 31 December 2014, there were only 10 complete closures of the 81 new WBOs that had emerged since 2002, an almost 88 per cent survival rate. And newer WBOs have been emerging throughout 2015–18, including the storied Italian newspaper of the left *il manifesto* (Il Fatto Quotidiano, 2016; Vidal, 2014).

Parting thoughts

Conversions of conventional business to labour-managed firms were rehearsed in earlier periods of Italy's history and perfected as WBO-generated worker cooperatives over the past three decades, especially in the 'Made in Italy' regions. And today in Italy, still in the thick of lingering economic and financial crisis, new cases of WBOs continue to emerge. The Italian road to creating worker cooperatives from WBOs sees these labour-managed firms emerging counter-cyclically during economic downturns, in the process of saving jobs and preserving or enhancing the productive capacities of communities. Their counter-cyclical character is connected, in no small way, to the positive externalities of workers' control and ownership of enterprises (Vieta *et al.*, 2017, Chapter 6). Indeed, cooperatives generated from WBOs, similar to other labour-managed firms, contribute to the prevention of the 'desertification' of regions and act as 'shock-absorbers' for the socio-economic needs of communities (CECOP CICOPA-Europe, 2012, 2013). Together with the favourable enabling environment created by the Marcora Law framework in Italy, these factors help explain the sharp rise in WBOs since 2008 and the resilience of the WBO solution in Italy for over three decades.

In parting, we would like to suggest that the findings presented in this chapter begin to offer strong evidence for encouraging and enhancing policies for WBO formation in other countries. Such policies can go a long way in fostering enabling environments for the creation of community- and worker-led cooperatives that serve to defend against and overcome the ill effects of socio-economic crises on local communities. Indeed, Italian WBOs have been showing for decades now that workers are more than capable and willing to revive failing or depleted firms and that, therefore, WBOs that establish new worker cooperatives should be actively supported by national and regional governments, unions, and cooperative movements.

Notes

1 The project was a collaboration between the author's home research centre, the Centre for Learning, Social Economy and Work (CLSEW) (formerly the Social Economy Centre) at the University of Toronto, the European Research Institute on Cooperative and Social Enterprises (EURICSE), and other key organizations in the Italian cooperative movement. For the full report, including details of the methodology used for gathering data and analysing the database of Italy's worker buyouts, compiled between 2012 and 2014, see Vieta *et al.* (2017).

2 See Table 10.1 for the administrative regions that make up Italy's five major geographic areas. Here we rely on the geographic area categories used in EURICSE's reports on Italian cooperatives, based on the European Union's first-level Nomenclature of Territorial Units for Statistics (EURICSE, 2011, 2013, 2015).

3 '*Provvedimenti per il credito alla cooperazione e misure urgenti a salvaguardia dei livelli di occupazione.*'

4 Our research to date has identified 257 confirmed worker-recuperated enterprises in Italy that emerged from experiences of WBOs between the early 1980s up to 31 December 2014 . Most of these conversions have been facilitated by the Marcora Law framework. We have also found a small number of WBOs and worker-recuperations that were not financed by Marcora Law provisions via other cooperative movement sources and journalistic accounts, verifying all WBO cooperatives in our dataset with the Italian Chamber of Commerce's data. Detailed in our report (Vieta *et al.*, 2017), our WBO database is thus emergent. While there have been other WBOs in Italy, our database captures most of the country's known worker-recuperated firms up to 31 December 2014 and is representative of trends in WBO formation that have existed in the country since the early 1980s.

5 An exception to the Marcora Law process has been the Trentino-Alto Adige region of Italy. The WBOs in that region in our database, all from the Province of Trento, are affiliated to its cooperative federation, the *Federazione Trentina della Cooperazione*. Due both to the region's autonomous status and the region's traditional independent approach to legislation from Rome, Marcora Law provisions explicitly exclude Trentino-Alto Adige (see various Articles of L. 49/1985). Instead, in the Province of Trento the *Federazione Trentina della Cooperazione* has directly worked with these WBOs and workers have used their savings and favourable loans from the *Cassa Rurale di Trento* to buy out their firms without directly appealing to the Marcora Law framework.

6 Geographic categorization follows EURICSE's reports on Italy's cooperatives (EURICSE, 2011, 2013), which is based on the European Union's first-level Nomenclature of Territorial Units for Statistics for Italy: Nord-Est = Northeast; Nord-Ovest = Northwest; Centro = Centre; Sud = South; Isole = Islands.

7 Using well-accepted birth and mortality rate calculations for firms (following Ben-Ner, 1988), we calculated birth and death rates of WBOs by dividing new formations and closures of WBOs respectively by the mean number of WBOs in existence during a period of one calendar year. For birth rates we divided the number of new WBO openings during a given year by the mean number of WBOs in existence in a given year (i.e., the average of the number of active WBOs at the beginning of the year and the number at the end of the year). Similarly, death rates were calculated by dividing the number of exits during the year by the mean number of WBOs in existence during that year. The growth rate, in turn, was calculated by subtracting the number of active WBOs at the end of the year from the number at the beginning of the year, which gives the change of WBOs (positive or negative) during the year, and then divided this change by the number of WBOs at the beginning of the year.

8 Similar patterns of surges in worker-recuperated firms are in evidence in other national contexts, such as Argentina (see Ruggeri and Vieta, 2015).

9 For instance, according to the Italian Chamber of Commerce's *InfoCamere-Movimprese* database (2014) and based on our own calculations of the raw data, in December 1995

there were 639,100 manufacturing firms in Italy. By December 2013 there were roughly 596,200, a drop of 42,900 firms in almost 20 years. Most alarming, the *InfoCamere-Movimprese* database shows, there has been a widening gap between business closures and start-ups in the manufacturing sector since 1995 (see Figure 10.3). While in 1995 there were almost 50,400 closures of manufacturing firms and 49,700 openings – a difference of only around 700 firms – by 2013 there were more than 35,100 business closures and only 18,000 openings, a difference of more than 17,000 firms.

10 As of 31 December 2014, just over 57 per cent of all Italian WBOs were affiliated with Legacoop, just over 18 per cent with Confcooperative, almost 5 per cent with AGCI, just over 4 per cent with the *Federazione Trentina della Cooperazione*, around 1 per cent with UNIT, and almost 15 per cent having no direct affiliation with a cooperative federation (Vieta *et al.*, 2017, Chapter 3).

11 See Vieta (2016) and Vieta *et al.* (2017, Chapter 2) for a review of three major forms of worker-recuperated enterprise (WRE) present throughout the world today. In short, these include: labour conflict WREs (where conversions happen via workplace takeovers by workers and other scenarios of conflict between employees and exiting owners), negotiated WREs (where conversions occur within more structured and institutionalized processes), and partial WREs via initiatives such as employee share-ownership plans (where employees purchase an ownership stake in their companies but do not, in most cases, take on administrative responsibility).

12 Either due to market failure, bankruptcy, strategic downsizing, or owner retirement.

13 For various beneficial legal and tax reasons, in Italy most WBO projects form into new worker cooperatives. For specifics, see Vieta *et al.* (2017, Chapter 3).

14 That is, from workers' *Trattamento di fine rapporto* (TFR). The TFR is severance pay given to employees upon termination of the employment contract. It is based on a percentage of deferred salary at source and is managed by private sector employers by law on behalf of employees.

15 Besides using their personal savings and TFR, employees who will be or have become redundant due to company crisis, restructuring, or closure can contribute to the initial start-up capital of a new work-related cooperative by tapping into their cash transfer-based unemployment benefits. This is an innovation of the Marcora Law framework that has been, in recent years, replicated in Spain's *pago único* model for funding WBOs (CECOP-CICOPA Europe, 2013; Vieta, 2016; Vieta *et al.*, 2017).

16 '*Fondo di rotazione per la promozione e lo sviluppo della cooperazione.*'

17 '*Fondo speciale per gli interventi a salvaguardia dei livelli di occupazione.*'

18 '*Sezione speciale per il credito alla cooperazione*' (see BNL, 2009).

19 The involvement of Italy's administrative regions in co-managing Foncooper in conjunction with BNL emerged out of the broader process of decentralizing public policy to the regions in the late 1990s (Mori *et al.*, 2002, pp. 79–80).

20 Both types of financial investors, *socio sovventore* and *socio finanziatore*, now exist in Italian cooperative legislation. The *socio sovventore* (subsidizing member), originally established by Article 4 of L. 59/1992, now constitutes a particular type of *socio finanziatore* (financing member), the latter introduced in 2003 with the Civil Code cooperative law reforms (Fici, 2013, p. 482). Both designations (with some exceptions) may be granted to an internal cooperative member or external person (physical persons) or to external agencies, firms, or their consortia (legal persons). In a nutshell and most generally, a *socio sovventore* usually contributes funds or know-how for the technological development, restructuring, or consolidation of a cooperative, while a *socio finanziatore* contributes funds towards share capital.

21 Due to this gap in the emergence of WBOs in Italy, and the legal changes to the Marcora Law framework of 2001, we can divide Italy's WBOs of the past four decades into three periods: 'Pre-Marcora Law' (WBOs established before 1985), 'Marcora Law I' (WBOs established between 1985 and 2001), and 'Marcora Law II' (2002–present) (see Table 10.1). For the ensuing quantitative analysis, we group Pre- and Marcora Law I WBOs together. Note that most of the WBO firms that emerged before 1985 in our database

were in subsequent years financed retroactively under the Marcora Law I provisions (i.e., the original L. 49/1985).

22 The Made in Italy regions are known for their 'industrial districts' of SMEs collaborating in small-batch, specialty, and inter-firm production processes and situated within tight social networks of familial, social, and associational bonds (Bagnasco, 1977; Becattini and Dei Ottati, 2006).

23 For analysing and discussing the economic activity of WBOs in Italy, we follow the ATECO2007 (2007) classification system. This is the system used by ISTAT (Italy's National Institute of Statistics) to minutely categorize the landscape of economic activities carried out by Italian firms and is deployed almost universally by economists, sociologists, policymakers, and planners looking at Italian businesses.

24 As Morone and Testa (2008) confirm, drawing on ISTAT figures: '[SMEs] play a major role in the Italian economic system. They account for nearly 99 per cent of national firms and, among them, the micro-enterprises (those with less than 10 employees) represent the wide majority ... represent[ing] 95.2 per cent of the Italian entrepreneurial system and account for more than 30 per cent of its overall turnover' (p. 311). Italian WBOs, however, buck this overall trend for Italian SMEs in that they tend to be much larger than the majority of Italian SMEs.

25 Note that definitive employee data for firms is difficult to calculate due to fluctuating employee numbers over time. Figures here are calculated based on the latest AIDA-Bureau Van Dijk, Italian Chamber of Commerce, and CFI employee numbers available as of 31 December 2014.

References

Amatori, Franco, Matteo Bugamelli and Andrea Colli. Italian firms in history: Size, technology and entrepreneurship, *Quaderni di storia economica* (Economic History Working Papers), no. 13. Rome: Bank of Italy, 2011.

Bagnasco, Arnaldo. *Tre italie: La problematica territoriale dello sviluppo italiano*. Bologna: Il Mulino, 1977.

Banca Nazionale del Lavoro (BNL). *Finanziamento 'Foncooper'*. Rome: Banca Nazionale del Lavoro, 2009.

Becattini, Giacomo, Marco Bellandi, Gabi Dei Ottati and Fabio Sforzi. *From industrial districts to local development: An itinerary of research*. Cheltenham: Edward Elgar, 2003.

Becattini, Giacomo and Gabi Dei Ottati. The performances of Italian industrial districts and large enterprise areas in the nineties, *European Planning Studies* 14, no. 8 (2006): 1147–1170.

Ben-Ner, Avener. Comparative empirical observations on worker-owned and capitalist firms, *International Journal of Industrial Organization* 6, no. 1 (1988): 7–31.

Bentivogli, Chiara and Eliana Viviano. Le trasformazioni del sistema produttivo italiano: le cooperative, *Questioni di Economia e Finanza* (Occasional Papers), no. 113. Rome: Bank of Italy, 2012.

Birchall, Johnston. *Rediscovering the co-operative advantage: Poverty reduction through self-help*, Geneva: ILO, 2003.

Birchall, Johnston and Lou Hammond Ketilson. *Resilience of the cooperative business model in times of crisis*. Geneva: ILO, 2009.

Burdín, Gabriel. Are worker-managed firms more likely to fail than conventional enterprises? Evidence from Uruguay, *ILR Review* 67, no. 1 (2014): 202–238.

Burdín, Gabriel and Andrés Dean. New evidence on wages and employment in worker cooperatives compared with capitalist firms, *Journal of Comparative Economics* 37 (2009): 517–533.

CECOP-CICOPA Europe. *CECOP position on EC's Green Paper: Restructuring and anticipation of change: What lessons from recent experience?* March 2012, Brussels.

____. *Business transfers to employees under the form of a cooperative in Europe: Opportunities and challenges.* June 2013, Brussels.

Chedid Henriques, Flavio. *Autogestão em empresas recuperadas por trabalhadores – Brasil e Argentina.* Florianópolis: Editora Insular, 2014.

Dandolo, Francesco. *L'industria in Italia tra crisi e cooperazione: La partecipazione dei lavoratori all agestione d'impresa dall'autunno caldo alla legge Marcora (1969–1985).* Torino: Bruno Mondadori, 2009.

Erdal, David. Employee ownership is good for your health, *Journal of Cooperative Thought and Practice* 1, no. 1 (2012): 3–6.

Estrin, Saul. The role of producer cooperatives in employment creation, *Economic Analysis and Workers' Management* 19, no. 4 (1985): 345–384.

____. Workers' cooperatives: Their merits and their limitations. In *Market socialism*, edited by Julian Le Grand and Saul Estrin, 165–192. Oxford: Clarendon, 1989.

European Research Institute on Cooperative and Social Enterprises (EURICSE). *La cooperazione in Italia. Primo rapporto EURICSE.* Trento, 2011.

____. *La cooperazione italiana negli anni della crisi. 2o rapport EURICSE.* Trento, 2013.

____. *Economia cooperative. Rilevanza, evolution e nuove frontier della cooperazione italiana.* Trento, 2015.

Eurostat. *Data: Database: Economy and finance: National accounts (including GDP).* European Commission, November, 2014. http://ec.europa.eu/eurostat/data/database

Fici, Antonio. *Italian co-operative law reform and co-operative principles,* EURICSE Working Paper 02 | 10). Trento: EURICSE, 2010.

____. Italy. In *International handbook of cooperative law*, edited by Dante Carcogna, Antonio Fici, and Hagen Henrÿ, 479–502. Heidelberg: Springer, 2013.

Fontanari, Eddi and Carlo Borzaga. La funzione anticiclica delle cooperative italiane, *La cooperazione italiana negli anni della crisi: 2o rapport EURICSE.* 87–104. Trento: EURICSE, 2013.

Gallino, Luciano. *La scomparsa dell'Italia industrial.* Torino: Einaudi, 2003.

Il Fatto Quottidiano. *Il manifesto,* i giornalisti ricomprano la testata: Siamo tornati padroni di un giornale indipendente e autogestito. July 15, 2016. http://www.ilfattoquotidiano. it/2016/07/15/il-manifesto-i-giornalisti-ricomprano-la-testata-siamo-tornati-padroni-di-un-giornale-indipendente-e-autogestito/2908778/

InfoCamere-Movimpresa. *Dati totale imprese 1995–2014.* July, 2014. Roma: La Società di Informatica delle Camere di Commercio italiane.

Instituto nazionale di statistica d'Italia (ISTAT) *Employment and unemployment.* August, 2014. Roma: ISTAT). http://en.istat.it/dati/microdati/

Jensen, Anthony. Saving companies worth saving: Spain pioneers a sustainable model of democratic corporate governance, *Economic and Industrial Democracy* 32, no. 4 (2011): 697–720.

____. *Insolvency, employee rights, and employee buy-outs: A strategy for restructuring.* Unpublished PhD dissertation, University of Sydney, Sydney, Australia, 2012.

Lazerson, Mark H. and Gianni Lorenzoni. The firms that feed industrial districts: A return to the Italian source, *Industrial and Corporate Change* 8, no. 2 (1999): 235–266.

Malanima, Paolo and Vera Negri Zamagni. Introduction: 150 years of the Italian economy, 1861–2010, *Journal of Modern Italian Studies* 15, no. 1 (2010): 1–20.

Menzani, Tito and Vera Negri Zamagni. Cooperative networks in the Italian economy, *Enterprise and Society* 11, no. 1 (2010): 98–127.

Mori, Pier Angelo, Giovanni Belletti and Martina Cioni. *L'impatto economico dei finanziamenti pubblici sui principali settori del sistema Toscano delle cooperative: Evoluzione e valutazione.* Florence: L'Osservatorio dall'Assessore Regionale all'Artigianato, P.M.I, Industria, Innovazione, Promozione e Internazionalizzazione del Sistema Produttivo e Cooperazione, Ambrogio Brenna, 2002.

Morone, Piergiuseppe and Giuseppina Testa. Firms growth, size, and innovation: An investigation into the Italian manufacturing sector, *Economics of Innovation and New Technology* 17, no. 4 (2008): 311–329.

Oakeshott, Robert. *Jobs and fairness: The logic and experience of employee ownership.* Norwich: Michael Russell, 2000.

Organisation for Economic Co-operation and Development (OECD). *Unleashing innovation in firms: Entry and exit.* Paris: OECD, 2010.

Pérotin, Virginie. Entry, exit, and the business cycle: Are cooperatives different? *Journal of Comparative Economics* 34, no. 2 (2006): 295–316.

———. Worker cooperatives: Good, sustainable jobs in the community, *Journal of Entrepreneurial and Organizational Diversity* 2, no. 2 (2014): 34–47.

Piore, Michael J. and Charles F. Sabel. *The second industrial divide: Possibilities for prosperity.* New York: Basic Books, 1984.

Quarter, Jack and Judith Brown. Worker buyouts in Canada: A social networking analysis, *Economic and Industrial Democracy* 13 (1992): 95–117.

Ruggeri, Andrés. (ed.) *Informe del tercer relevamiento* de empresas recuperadas por sus trabajadores: *Las empresas recuperadas en la Argentina, 2010.* Buenos Aires: Programa Facultad Abierta, Facultad de Filosofía y Letras, Universidad de Buenos Aires, 2010.

Ruggeri, Andrés and Marcelo Vieta. Argentina's worker-recuperated enterprises, 2010–2013: A synthesis of recent empirical findings, *Journal of Entrepreneurial and Organizational Diversity* 4, no. 1 (2015): 75–103.

Salvatori, Gianluca. *La cooperazione ai tempi della crisi,* EURICSE, Working Paper, 37|12. Trento: EURICSE, 2012.

Sforzi, Fabio. Il contributo dei distretti industriali al cambiamento del'economia italiana, *Economia Italiana* 1 (2007): 79–104.

Smith, Stephen C. and Jonathon Rothbaum. Co-operatives in a global economy: Key issues, recent trends and potential for development. In *Co-operatives in a post-growth era: Creating co-operative economics* edited by Sonja Novkovic and Tom Webb, 221–242. London: Zed, 2014.

Soulage, François. France: An endeavour in enterprise transformation. In *Beyond the crisis: Cooperatives, work, and finance: Generating wealth for the long term,* edited by Alberto Zevi, Antonio Zanotti, François Soulage and Adrian Zelaia, 155–196. Brussels: CECOP Publications, 2011.

Spattini, Silvia. Gli ammortizzatori sociali nel Jobs Act, *BollettinoAdapt.it,* 2015. www. bollettinoadapt.it/gli-ammortizzatori-sociali-nel-jobs-act/

Theorell, Töres. (2003) Democracy at work and its relationship to health. In *Emotional and psychological processes and intervention strategies: Research in occupational stress and wellbeing,* Vol. 3, edited by Pamela L. Perrewe and Daniel C. Ganster, 323–357. Greenwich: JAI, 2003.

Tridico, Pasquale. *Italy from economic decline to the current crisis.* Working Paper N. 5/2012. Rome: Associazione Study & Ricerche Interdisciplinari sul Lavoro, Università degli Studi Roma Tre, 2012.

Triglia, Carlo and Luigi Burroni. Italy: Rise, decline and restructuring of a regionalized capitalism, *Economy & Society* 38, no. 4 (2009): 630–653.

Unioncamere-Tagliacarne. Imprese, occupazione e valore aggiunto del mondo delle cooperative. In *Rapporto Unioncamere 2010*. 431–459. Roma: Insituto Guglielmo Tagliacarne, 2010.

Vidal, Dominique. Historical paper of the Italian left fights back: Buying back 'il manifesto'. *Le monde diplomatique*, 2014. http://mondediplo.com/2014/12/15ilmanifesto.

Vieta, Marcelo. The social innovations of autogestión in Argentina's worker-recuperated enterprises: Cooperatively organizing productive life in hard times, *Labor Studies Journal* 35, no. 3 (2010): 295–321.

____. From managed employees to self-managed workers: The transformations of labour at Argentina's worker-recuperated enterprises. In *Alternative work organisations*, edited by Maurizio Atzeni, 129–157. Houndmills: Palgrave Macmillan, 2012.

____. *The emergence of the empresas recuperadas por sus trabajadores: A political economic and sociological appraisal of two decades of self-management in Argentina*, EURICSE Working Paper 55/13. Trento: EURICSE, 2013.

____. Learning in struggle: Argentina's new worker cooperatives as transformative learning organizations, *Relations Industrielles/Industrial Relations* 69, no. 1 (2014): 186–218.

____. Workers' buyout. In *Impresa cooperative: Parole chiave / Cooperative enterprises: Key words*, edited by Andrea Bernardi and Salvatore Monni. Rome: Il Mulino / Università Roma Tree Press, 2016.

Vieta, Marcelo, Sara Depedri and Antonella Carrano. *The Italian road to recuperating enterprises and the Legge Marcora Framework: Italy's worker buyouts in times of crisis*, A EURICSE Report. Trento: EURICSE, 2017.

Whitford, Josh. The decline of a model? Challenge and response in the Italian industrial districts, *Economy and Society* 30, no. 1 (2001): 38–65.

World Bank. *Data: Economy and growth: GDP growth (annual %): Italy*, November, 2014. http://data.worldbank.org/country/italy

Zamagni, Stefano and Vera Negri Zamagni. *Cooperative enterprise: Facing the challenge of globalization*. Cheltenham: Edward Elgar, 2010.

Zanotti, Antonio. Italy: The strength of an inter-sectoral network. In *Beyond the crisis: Cooperatives, work, and finance: Generating wealth for the long term*, edited by Alberto Zevi, Antonio Zanotti, François Soulage and Adrian Zelaia, 21–100. Brussels: CECOP Publications, 2011.

Zevi, Alberto. The financing of cooperatives in Italy, *Annals of Public and Cooperative Economics* 61, no. 2–3 (1990): 353–365.

____. *President of CentroStudi, Legacoop and former President of CFI*, Personal interview conducted by Marcelo Vieta, March 29, 2012.

Zevi, Alberto, Antonio Zanotti, François Soulage and Adrian Zelaia, *Beyond the crisis: Cooperatives, work, finance: Generating wealth for the long term*. Brussels: CECOP Publications, 2011.

11

COOPERATIVES OF INDEPENDENT WORKERS IN FINLAND

A unique forum for self-employment

Anu Puusa and Kirsi Hokkila

Introduction

Classifying or defining cooperative types is not without challenges. In Finland, cooperatives are typically classified into four categories: producer cooperatives, consumer cooperatives, service cooperatives and small cooperatives (Troberg, 2014). The latter have distinctive features which gave birth to a new cooperative movement (Troberg, 2009, 2014). These cooperatives, called in Finnish '*uusosuus-toiminta*', which, translated into English, reads 'new worker cooperatives',[1] can be regarded as being different in comparison with the international definition of worker cooperatives (see CICOPA, 2005). Hence, in this chapter we refer to our case cooperatives as cooperatives of independent workers in order to distinguish them from conventional worker ownership. In worker cooperatives, work and management is carried out jointly (*ibid.*), whereas the function of cooperatives of independent workers is more to act as an intermediary for individual professionals' work (Troberg, 2000; Puusa *et al.*, 2016).

According to researchers, in Finland the cooperatives of independent workers which emerged in the 1990s can be partly considered to be a self-help solution to the mass unemployment that followed the recession (Troberg, 2014). Many laid-off people established them or joined one in order to employ themselves. According to Pättiniemi and Immonen (2002), the trend to form worker cooperatives in the 1990s can also be considered as a movement of experts to liberate themselves from the necessities of ordinary employment, such as outward directed goals and tasks of the company. Currently in Finland, cooperatives of independent workers are rapidly emerging in new sectors, particularly in knowledge-intensive sectors and, for example, in the fields of arts, culture and media, where permanent employment relationships are scarce (Tainio, 2009; Troberg, 2008; Pättiniemi, 2007). In these fields, the work is usually carried out in projects through which professionals are often required to have a company through which they can invoice their allocated services from the customer. Hence these cooperatives of independent workers can be seen as a useful tool for the modern self-employed (Puusa *et al.*, 2016).

After examining the existing literature on self-employment in general and through cooperatives, we will present the specificities of the Finnish model of cooperative of independent workers. In the next section, based on case studies about three Finnish cooperatives of independent workers, we will identify six core motivational factors of which three are universal needs identified in self-employment literature and the others are specific features of a cooperative form of business, and explain certain conflicts between these factors. We will conclude with some final remarks.

Self-employment through cooperatives

Blanchflower (2004) suggests that the majority of the workforce in Western industrialized countries has a latent desire to be self-employed. Douglas and Shepherd (2002) state that the lower the risk-aversion but the greater the need for decision-making autonomy, the greater the potential to be self-employed. However, Blanchflower (2004) concludes that only a small proportion of the current workforce would prefer running their own business to actually act out their entrepreneurial aspirations. One obvious impediment is the entrepreneurial risk. For example, Puusa and Hokkila (2014) found that many Finnish students would be reluctant to take the entrepreneurial risk because they evaluate their business competence to be inadequate. In addition, many associate the business life in general with cold and hard values. The Finnish youth's reluctant attitude towards entrepreneurship might be partly explained by their experience of the 1990s recession, when many of them saw their entrepreneur parents lose their businesses and run into economic difficulties.

Financial capital constraints too have been extensively discussed in entrepreneurship literature (Blanchflower and Oswald, 1991; Evans and Jovanovic, 1989). Blanchflower (2000) claims that 'one possible impediment to entrepreneurship is lack of capital'. However, liquidity constraints seem to be one of the main factors that correlate positively with self-employment practised through cooperatives. There is no clear consensus as to whether unemployment rates affect overall (all business types) self-employment rates (*ibid.*), but in Finland it has been demonstrated that the number of cooperatives tend to increase with unemployment rates (Kalmi, 2013). When there are fewer resources or stable jobs available, cooperatives seem to be a more attractive option for entrepreneurship by offering a possibility for equal sharing of resources, as opposed to other forms of enterprise (Díaz-Foncea and Marcuello, 2015; Pérotin, 2006). In precarious situations, the community of peers can provide a self-employed person with various kinds of support for their employment (Puusa *et al.*, 2016; Tainio, 2009). In addition to lower financial investments, business competence requirements are not seen to be as high as in cooperative settings because the members can support and assist each other in tasks related to running and administrating the business, which can also be a valuable asset of cooperation in terms of risk-aversion (Puusa *et al.*, 2016).

Based on the above, becoming an entrepreneur can be based on a necessity but also on a desire. Many of the characteristics of the new workforce, especially the need for independence and autonomy in addition to an ability to have influence on one's work, are characteristics that have traditionally been related to entrepreneurial personality traits (Benz and Frey, 2008; Mescon and Montanari, 1981; Van Gelderen and Jansen, 2006). Another pull factor that makes self-employment a desired option is the current turmoil of work values and expectations towards work life among the new generation of workers. This generation, often referred to as Millennials, who will soon occupy the majority of the workforce, is said to have a fundamentally different approach to career and work-related goals. They are tolerant to diversity and are characterized as a group-oriented generation in their work. They prefer flexibility in their work schedules, expect to have a meaningful job as well as the ability to maintain a good work–life balance (e.g. Kultalahti and Viitala, 2015; Smola and Sutton, 2002). However, it is often said that entrepreneurs must work long hours (Hyytinen and Ruuskanen, 2007) and sacrifice their personal life for their venture. Blanchflower (2004) states that, despite being happy with their lives on the whole, self-employed persons are less satisfied with the hours they work and report more feelings of stress than employees. Self-employment through a cooperative, however, has been proved to offer the entrepreneurs vast possibilities to have control over their workload and working hours to meet their personal preferences (Puusa *et al.*, 2016).

Douglas and Shepherd's (2000) utility-maximizing career choice model suggests that people choose to become self-employed if the total expected utility of self-employment is greater than the expected utility from their best employment option. The expected utility can be measured in terms of income, independence, risk-bearing, work effort, and other prerequisites associated with self-employment. In the light of the previous research, it is obvious that the perceptions and the nature of the greatest utility are profoundly changing from economic benefits to 'softer' and human values, which may increase the favour of self-employment, and especially that of self-employment through a cooperative. Hence, modern self-employment can be a consequence of a situation where there is a lack of other job prospects (Biehl *et al.*, 2014; Svaleryd, 2015) but also a reflection of a changing value climate and aspiration to have more influence on one's work.

Thus, a cooperative seems to be a suitable option for modern self-employment for various reasons. Cooperatives can be described as being value-based and human rather than financial-based organizations (Davis, 2001). Cooperatives' operational principles and ownership structure are distinctively different compared with those of investor-owned companies. Somerville (2007) argues that the unique values and the institutional form stemming from the distinctive ownership and democracy principles are the differentiating features of cooperatives. According to Inkinen (1997), solidarity, particularly with regard to the ownership philosophy, distinguishes cooperatives from other forms of economic organizations. Member participation is the backbone of member contribution and thus a prerequisite for the success of a cooperative (Nilsson, 2001; Spear, 2000). Participation is related to the member needs which form the motivation for joining or founding a cooperative, and in the case of the studied cooperatives of independent workers, the motivation is creation and support of self-employment.

Despite the growing trend, there is in practice a limited amount of research concerning these cooperatives of independent workers' fundamental characteristics and their interpretation (Pättiniemi and Tainio, 2000; Pencavell, 2015). Especially entrepreneurship in the cooperative context has received limited attention in academia (Cook and Plunkett, 2006; Pérotin, 2006). To ensure member motivation and contribution, we claim that it is of utmost importance to recognize the diversity of motivations to be a part of a cooperative community. Deeper understanding of the motivation for self-employment through cooperatives in different contexts can have vast institutional effects. The need for deeper understanding of cooperative venture creation is also supported by the European Commission's objective to support cooperatives as a means to increase the economic influence of SMEs and as a means of entrepreneurial initiative (European Commission, 2004).

The unique Finnish model of cooperatives of self-employed workers

In relative terms, Finland is the most cooperative country in the world when measured in cooperative sales revenues relative to GDP and the number of cooperatives relative to population (Jones and Kalmi, 2009). Finland has a long tradition of consumer, agriculture and infrastructure cooperatives, but cooperatives of independent workers became common only in the mid-1990s. Finland suffered a severe economic recession and mass unemployment during the early 1990s, after which particularly worker cooperatives rapidly became a common approach to new job creation. These cooperatives were established to complement the services provided by the state-owned labour offices. The latter seemed unable to fulfil their tasks any longer, when they were faced with the sudden and extensive mass unemployment (Pättiniemi and Tainio, 2000). Finnish cooperatives more than doubled in number during the period 1995–97, as opposed to other companies, which declined in their numbers during the same period (Kalmi, 2013; Pättiniemi and Solhagen, 1999). One reason for their growing number, both following the recession and today, is that according to Finnish legislation, the basic principle is that if there are more than seven members in a cooperative and thus each member's share represents less than 15 per cent of the whole capital, a member can be entitled to an unemployment allowance (Jakonen and Silvasti, 2015). Basically, by owning less than 15 per cent of a company, a person is regarded in the eyes of the law as having the status of an employee, not an entrepreneur (Koskinen, 2013).

According to Pättiniemi and Immonen (2002), the new cooperatives emerging in Finland were also a reflection of the discussions on workplace democracy in the 1970s. Unemployed people were pursuing two goals at the same time: they wished to have steady earnings from a job and to have an opportunity to influence their own work. While striving for full-time employment, cooperatives of independent workers adopted a strategy of placing their members in other enterprises and developing a service where the enterprise in need only paid a lump sum in one bill, covering all the costs of the placed worker (salary, taxes, insurance, office costs, etc.). This strategy proved to be successful (Pättiniemi and Immonen, 2002). At the same time, these cooperatives proved to be an attractive alternative for those who, for various reasons, had difficulties being employed within the conventional labour markets. In the so-called protected labour market, the terms of employment take these challenges better into consideration, thus, e.g., meeting the terms of employment of disabled workers (Savtschenko, 2003). However, at the end of the 1990s these post-recession cooperatives started to transform themselves from multi-sectoral actors with the purpose of work integration into more focused communities of professionals (Troberg, 2000), which nowadays is the dominant nature of these cooperatives of independent workers.

As mentioned, statistics show that in recent years, there has been a growing trend in the establishment of cooperatives of independent workers, particularly in occupations that do not have established positions in the traditional industries but require high professionalism in emerging sectors (Pättiniemi, 2007; Tainio, 2009; Troberg, 2008). Many of these kinds of knowledge-intensive sectors employ a high rate of temporary workforce, freelancers and project workers. In 2015, the national cooperative register of Coop Center Pellervo[2] included 885 worker, service and professional cooperatives. As opposed to worker cooperatives, which normally employ wage-earning workers, the members of cooperatives of independent workers usually have their own acquainted customers to whom they provide services and work with and invoice their allocated services individually. Because of this operational model, these cooperatives can be described to be more like entrepreneurs' cooperatives than worker cooperatives (Puusa *et al.*, 2016). This kind of activity can also be perceived as joint entrepreneurship (Laukkanen, 2000). In this sense, the cooperative is a tool, not to organize work for the member, but to organize the services needed for members to organize their work. The motivation to join these cooperatives is usually to sell the member's own personal competence, capabilities and experience through the cooperative because it offers a low-risk and flexible possibility for it (Troberg, 2000, 2009). Often the cooperative can be used as a 'stepping stone' to entrepreneurship in terms of testing one's business idea and gathering a customer base.

The cooperatives of independent workers are a new kind of economic self-help organization, where not only the economic goals but also the social aims and goals are important (Troberg, 2009, 2014). Ideally, control is democratically distributed, membership is not restricted and the benefits obtained with invested capital are predetermined (Pättiniemi and Immonen, 2002). Members are in control of managing their own work, but also responsible for controlling and managing the mutual operations of the community according to the 'one member, one vote' principle (Pättiniemi and Tainio, 2000). Indeed, Kalmi (2013) describes cooperatives as the fullest expression of democracy in business, because their members are simultaneously subject to and in control of the cooperative's authority.

Alongside economic interests, Finnish cooperatives of independent workers are found to be able to offer social support, which serves as a positive incentive for entrepreneurs while also serving as a practical tool to organize self-employment (Puusa et al., 2016; Sivonen and Saukkonen, 2014; Tainio, 2009). Hence, a cooperative of independent workers is able to cater for a variety of needs: provide members with social connection in practising their occupation, distinctive freedom and flexibility of work, and bringing extra income or, on the contrary, serving as the only source of employment and earnings (Puusa et al., 2016; Tainio, 2009; Troberg, 2000). When the motivations and needs of the members are balanced and complement each other, a cooperative of independent workers seems to provide an ideal work community for modern entrepreneurs. In order to function successfully, cooperative members need to contribute equally to creating a working environment that is democratic, empowering and fruitful (Puusa et al., 2016). The unique possibility to attain unemployment benefits gives the members of the cooperative of independent workers flexibility and financial security during the times when there is less work to be done or in the beginning of the self-employment, for example when the customer base is still inchoate (Sivonen and Saukkonen, 2014).

Ideally, cooperatives are said to form a coherent social group where the interaction is characterized by trust and membership is based on both rational and emotional motives (Henzler, 1960; Spear, 2000). However, studies conducted among Finnish cooperatives of independent workers have revealed problems in organizing and managing successful cooperation (Pättiniemi, 2009; Pötry, 2009; Puusa et al., 2016; Troberg, 1997, 2000). These problems often stem from differing views, motivations and needs among members, lack of informed management and poor understanding of cooperative principles and unique business model. For example, variation in the expectation of work hours and, thus, income between members affects members' commitment and effort in managerial issues and may easily lead to inefficiency of business actions, member passiveness and thus weak financial status (*ibid.*).

Motivations to choose the cooperative form of self-employment

In this section we will describe the findings based on multiple case studies (Yin, 2003) that we conducted. We familiarized ourselves thoroughly with three Finnish cooperatives of independent workers. Two of the studied cooperatives are established multi-professional cooperatives that were founded after the recession and originally were worker cooperatives, but over the years have transformed themselves into entrepreneurs' societies and nowadays can be described as cooperatives of independent workers. The third one is a relatively new cooperative, which employs media, art and education professionals and has functioned as a cooperative of independent workers from the beginning.

Our data consists of 13 open individual, pair and group interviews including a total of 16 interviewees. We used a qualitative content analysis to analyse the rich transcribed interview data. Our aim was to understand why the studied people selected a cooperative as their form of business. In addition, due to the inherently distinctive nature of cooperatives, we wanted to explore the extent to which this unique quality had relevance in the process of choosing a cooperative as the instrument for self-employment. We are interested in whether the cooperative's features matter in the entrepreneurial process related to joining a cooperative or if becoming a cooperative entrepreneur is just one option among others. This section focuses on interpreting the motivations for choosing a cooperative as a business form for self-employment by reflecting how a cooperative of independent workers meets the needs of the self-employed.

Based on our analysis, we identified six core motivational factors that describe a cooperative as a business form in the context of self-employment. According to our interpretation, three of these reflect the universal autonomy needs identified in self-employment literature: empowerment, self-management and freedom. We propose that the other three are unique features of a cooperative form of business, which stem from the established cooperative principles: safety, diversity and communality. Whereas the former features are common to individual self-employed persons, the latter features make the studied cooperatives a distinctive and unique forum for self-employed members. In many respects they are the appealing features, the essential drivers of self-employment through cooperatives and make self-employment in these cooperatives different from other business models. However, we also found that once combined with the autonomy features, there are certain conflicts between them which result in a negative impact on cooperatives' and members' activities. Below, we will describe each feature in more detail.

Personal autonomy features

Empowerment

According to the data collected, the interviewees became cooperative members based on a highly rational motive: to employ themselves. In addition to this rational economic-related justification, we also identified an emotional one: self-employment enhances people's self-esteem by providing a feeling of being a valuable individual and useful member of society, who is in control of their own life. According to Laurinkari (2004), being employed is a central value for a Finn. It is a way to integrate into the society and to avoid exclusion. Marginalization and exclusion enhances inequality and thus employment can also be perceived as a means to maintain and foster equality. Laurinkari (2004) argues that becoming a member of a cooperative of independent workers has proven to be an effective tool in preventing exclusion. It might be an important point of reference and guiding light for an unemployed person, an impetus to find a self-help spirit. In our data, the process of establishing and developing a cooperative was often referred to with a sense of pride in having been able to create something from scratch and developing it into a functioning business. At best, it allows a person to do meaningful work on one's own terms, making one feel good and self-competent in a responsible manner. Responsibility was associated with a clear distinction between operating in the informal economy or being a registered entrepreneur paying appropriate taxes. We conclude that rational and emotional empowerment resonates with the entrepreneurs' need for achievement and internal locus of control (see e.g. Carlson *et al.*, 2007).

Self-management

Interviewees strongly emphasized self-responsibility. It was collectively interpreted that a cooperative entrepreneur is the master of their own destiny, despite the possible assistance and support from others. The specified cornerstones of cooperative work emphasized self-sufficiency, personal initiative and individual activeness. They are responsible for seeking work, keeping the customers and getting new orders. There is no outsider to monitor the performance but each member carries the responsibility themselves. Interviewees recognized this to be highly different from salaried positions. They stated that cooperative entrepreneurs must be independent, active, competent, customer-oriented and able to manage themselves: in other words, they must be an entrepreneurial type. As Benz and Frey (2008) have noted, the ability to decide how daily work is organized and the procedural aspects of work are important for a self-employed person and thus in the centre of locus of control and the need to be one's own boss.

Freedom

A cooperative seems to be a form of business that provides highly flexible opportunities, which, according to the literature, is regarded as the most significant driver for self-employment. Employees' satisfaction has been proved to increase when they are given greater autonomy and independence and, consequently, the self-employed are widely reported to be more satisfied with their jobs than employees in salaried positions (Benz and Frey, 2004; Blanchflower, 2000; Hundley, 2001). In fact, a wide range of literature states that the most significant identified motivator for self-employment is the desire 'to be one's own boss'.

The culmination of this theme seemed to be the ability to employ oneself in a way that meets the individual's needs, hopes and values. The members did not necessarily want regular full-time work as money was not their key motivation, and also because, in a Finnish worker cooperative setting, project and freelance work is possible due to the unemployment benefits when there is no full-time employment. Becoming wealthy was not regarded as important. Instead, the interviewees valued a flexible way of working and the opportunity to do project-type work, thus leaving enough room for other aspects of life.

A balance between free time and work was of the utmost importance. In this sense, self-employment through cooperatives is distinctive from the self-employment reported in the literature (see Hyytinen and Ruuskanen, 2007), as the interviewees did not mention long hours or a heavy workload. Therefore, self-employment through cooperatives does not seem to require a particularly high tolerance for work effort. Instead self-employment through cooperatives seemed to offer a certain kind of freedom that enhances a sense of self-fulfilment and overall life satisfaction that is possible due to the unique labour law existing in Finland. The interviewees stated that being able to arrange one's work in a manner that suits one's schedule and other areas of life, independently and on one's own terms, was one of the key reasons why they became self-employed. However, this is not to be conflated with laziness.

Communal features

Safety

Based on our analysis, we identified three features regarding cooperative safety: financial, rational and social. The financial viewpoint is linked to the fact that a cooperative can be established without major initial capital or investments. The main motivation to establish a cooperative is that it offers a safe way to become self-employed, due to the shared financial risks between the members and entitlement to unemployment benefits, which significantly reduces the financial risk for Finnish cooperators. The rational viewpoint refers to an entrepreneur's possibility to focus on their own strengths in a cooperative while other members can provide assistance in other tasks, for example administrative issues. As Karjalainen (1996) points out, this allows members to actively affect their own job content in a cooperative. The social viewpoint was linked to the communal nature of a cooperative, which at its best can provide strong mental and professional support. It can therefore be stated that rational and social security contributes to the feeling of self-efficacy (see Bandura, 1997). Based on these, we can surmise that safety is the most important motivation in selecting a cooperative form of business, as the interviewees stated that they would not be at ease with taking the entrepreneurial risk alone.

Diversity

According to the data there seems to be no limits to the structure of a cooperative, which leaves a great deal of room for diversity. It allows combining a variety of skills, knowledge and experience. The case cooperatives had members with different kinds of backgrounds and states of their career as well as a wide range of different life situations, interests and expectations. In addition to this, the members' personal job opportunities seem to be very wide-ranging in terms of the work itself as well as the contexts in which the work took place. Douglas and Shepherd (2002) state that people differ in their attitudes and tolerance towards work effort and, in the case cooperatives, there was considerable diversity in members' expectations regarding work effort and an appropriate level of compensation. Work effort refers to the amount of physical and mental effort while working, e.g. working hours and working intensity. We conclude that diversity and variety are the core characteristics of cooperatives of independent workers, as the interviewees seem to, in many ways, consider them as a kind of a starting point for a cooperative business. The reported permissive atmosphere honours diversity and leaves room for everyone to arrange their own employment in a diverse and personally suitable and meaningful way.

Communality

According to the data, the surrounding member community and cooperation between members was a very significant motivational factor for joining or establishing a cooperative, especially for younger entrepreneurs. Cooperative communality provides both mental and practical support for members, which touches on the themes of safety and diversity. Members can provide each other with advice and tangible help by sharing the workload and responsibility, or by recommending each other to potential clients, assisting each other in getting more work. The opportunity to work together provides learning opportunities, wide-ranging experiences and professional support, for example by enabling joint projects between members with different qualifications. Some also described how others had helped and encouraged them to try out new things, thus eventually increasing their competence and self-confidence.

The communality theme also included other psychological motivations, such as the feeling of being an equal part of a group and mental support from others. The interviewees described how it is important to have peers that can personally identify with one's situation and share the feelings of being an entrepreneur. Moreover, team spirit and the feeling of solidarity generated from mutual responsibility for the jointly owned enterprise's success was deemed important. The group validates emotions and offers the members a feeling of empowerment, as they reported being motivated and encouraged by other members or through the example set by others. Communality might turn out to be an abstract sense of team spirit between the members, which manifests itself as a higher degree of solidarity and culture of trust. In this case, it can appear as a 'one for all and all for one' type of attitude. Indeed, a cooperative appears as an emotionally embedded entrepreneurial model in which behaviour of entrepreneurs moderate cooperation between the actors and its outcomes (Biniari, 2012).

Cooperative features vs. self-employment needs

According to our findings, communal features of safety, diversity and communality make self-employment jobs through the cooperative model a distinctive and, in many ways, viable alternative to individual self-employment. As said above, ideally, these features result in a variety of benefits that lower the barrier of entrepreneurship. However, we also identified some problematic consequences of member behaviour when these cooperative features are combined with basic self-employment needs, which might partly explain the problems that have been identified in the literature concerning Finnish cooperatives of independent workers (Pättiniemi, 2009; Pötry, 2009; Puusa et al., 2016; Troberg, 1997, 2000).

The freedom provided by both the flexibility of the cooperative structure and Finnish labour law seems to be a clear and unique benefit of the studied cooperatives at the individual level and respond to the needs and expectations of the self-employed. However, when it was examined at the community level and linked to member diversity, it can potentially bring about negative consequences in a cooperative context. The variety of members' personalities, hopes and expectations might also result in highly diverse motives and ways of participating in the cooperative activity. Consequently, these diverse expectations and the idea of voluntariness can easily make people indifferent or passive.

The principle of democratic member control, however, requires active member participation in the decision-making and administration of a cooperative (Spear, 2004). It is based on the principle of one vote per member, which was the approach used in the cooperatives studied. However, in practice, the members were reported to be quite passive in exercising this right. For example, the data revealed difficulties in organizing management, as the members are partly reluctant to take part in joint affairs and activities. Participation and influence did not seem to be matters of great importance for the members. Instead, voluntary liability seems to be relevant in this context, provided that it benefits the member personally.

The level of involvement seemed to be meaningful in terms of conducting mutual errands and responsibilities, but also general atmosphere, feelings of equality, fairness and justice, as well as in terms of the fair use of resources. The interviewees stated that, although they welcomed diversity, disparity could become a problem. Variety in social groups that possess different resources creates better possibilities for cooperation and the creation of social capital (Ring et al., 2010), but, according to our findings, it is also a problem if the starting points and expectations are highly varied. As these cooperatives are communities of special-interest groups, their functions are expected to be based on particular, but consistent, member needs (Mori, 2014). In line with this presumption, many authors (Cechin et al., 2013; Hansmann, 1996; Romero and Pérez, 2003; Ruben and Heras, 2012) before us have noticed that employee ownership is more effective when the owner group is homogenous. Our study elaborates on this by stating that conflicts caused by people's varying interests and subsequent precarious levels of activity and commitment might break out in a cooperative, occurring more easily due to the lack of hierarchical structures and positions of power. In the Finnish context this is further enabled by the unique possibility to receive unemployment benefits, which seems to be one of the factors that distinguishes the Finnish model of cooperative of independent worker from the worker cooperative model.

Another conflict between ideal and practice was the state of cooperation between the members. Ideologically, the interviewees valued the presence of the group. However, in practice, it could be interpreted that cooperation was quite infrequently used as a benefit of the business structure so that its full potential was not in use. Instead, it was treated as a desired possibility for gaining individual benefits, i.e. getting work and income with the help of others. It was not considered as their social aim, as the traditional concept of cooperative dual nature suggests (Pättiniemi and Tainio, 2000). The interviewees hardly referred to the idea of mutual act in the sense of togetherness, communality or a sense of providing work opportunities for the whole community, as is the case in the cooperatives that normally are referred to as worker cooperatives. This can be perceived as the culmination of the difference between the case cooperatives and worker cooperatives. Instead of the traditional idea of collective action, work in the case cooperatives seemed more like an individual act, involving obtaining it, performing it and benefiting from it. It aims at individual financial well-being rather than that of the whole group.

Final remarks

In summary, we conclude that it seems that the persons we interviewed are not worker cooperative members in the sense of CICOPA's *World Declaration on Worker Cooperatives*, nor are the studied cooperatives worker cooperatives as defined in the international literature. It rather seems that the studied individuals are more like self-employed entrepreneurs because the Finnish labour law and the features of the cooperative model allows it. In other words, the ideological basis of the cooperative movement is not a driver to choose a cooperative as a form of business. The motivation to choose a cooperative is its features of safety, diversity, communality and freedom. It seems to provide a safe and flexible and thus meaningful way to employ oneself for modern cooperators.

We claim that in the Finnish context, a cooperative of independent workers provides its members with even greater freedom to work compared with other types of self-employment. Because of the extensive rights to unemployment benefits, it is possible for a member to occasionally refrain from working and concentrate on other areas of life. This can be an important factor for people in many different kinds of situations. It can be an attractive alternative to individuals who are faced with financial constraints, are somewhat risk-averse, have low self-efficacy or tolerance for work effort, for example in cases involving physical or mental disabilities. Furthermore, individuals working in professions or sectors that require combining various kinds of expertise are likely to find a cooperative a suitable structure for entrepreneurship. It can also be an appealing means of self-employment for individuals who possess highly collective and social personal values, as the cooperative structure enables a collective way to work and cooperate among members.

From a business standpoint, the studied members were quite loosely linked to each other and lacked keen interest in developing the cooperative as a collective enterprise. The main concern seemed to be maintaining an economic activity level that is adequate to provide the necessary services for individual employment functions, such as invoicing and other administrative services. According to the traditional idea of cooperative members bearing mutual responsibility for the continuity of the economic activity of their company, the cooperative members would be interested in securing not only their own, but also their peer members' employment in the future. In these cases, members hardly gave consideration to the communal aspects of the enterprise.

We therefore claim that the needs of self-employed people are not unquestionably compatible with the features of a cooperative mission nor the values and principles of it. Individuals' aspirations might also conflict with the common good. Individual desires and aspirations of freedom, autonomy and self-management, which are central to the modern self-employed person, do not contribute to the collective needs of a cooperative community (Puusa *et al.*, 2016). The cooperative community requires active and equal participation of all members, out of a sense of mutual responsibility and obligation, not solely for an individual incentive. And from a self-employed person's standpoint, it seems that, without genuine communality, a cooperative is not able to realize its full potential to benefit the members. Agirre *et al.* (2014) also argue that it is crucial for a cooperative to find a balance between individualism and collectivism by protecting the equal realization of organizational coordination mechanisms and aspects of individual freedom, autonomy and responsibility.

It is our conclusion that the Finnish cooperatives of independent workers form an entrepreneurial business model which corresponds well to the self-employed person's expectations and values of freedom and self-fulfilment, leaving possibilities to be active and develop oneself in others parts of life. However, we suggest that a cooperative of independent workers is a business community model that has unique needs of its own that would need more careful attention among the members that the cooperative structure would be able to serve their needs and expectations in the most effective way. Therefore, our concern is that, although the Finnish model of cooperative of independent workers seems to be a viable option for the self-employed, it entails characteristics that might end up functioning against itself, meaning that its highly valued aspects like the unique freedom of the structure might threaten the success and survival of these cooperatives.

The authors wish to thank the European Social Fund (ESF) for the financial support for this research and Hyungsik Eum and Bruno Roelants for insightful and valuable comments during the review process.

Notes

1 According to Sivonen and Saukkonen (2014), the term '*uusosuustoiminta*' was taken into use to describe cooperatives that operate in new sectors and to allow separating these cooperatives from the ones operating in more traditional fields and ways.
2 Coop Center Pellervo, a member of the International Co-operative Alliance (ICA), is a service organization for Finnish cooperatives and a forum for cooperative activities aiming at making the cooperative business model more known to the public. Coop Center Pellervo strives to influence the legislative work and the economic and financial policies in Finland and Europe to accommodate the cooperative business model as well as to promote the cooperative model as a competitive alternative for those thinking about starting a business.

References

Agirre, Izaskun, Pedro Reinares and Amaia Agirre. Antecedents to market orientation in the worker cooperative organization: The Mondragon Group, *Annals of Public and Cooperative Economics* 85, no. 3 (2014): 387–408.

Bandura, Albert. *Self-efficacy: The exercise of control*. New York: Freeman, 1997.

Benz, Matthias and Bruno S. Frey. Being independent raises happiness at work, *Swedish Economic Policy Review* 11 (2004): 95–134.

___. Being independent is a great thing: Subjective evaluations of self-employment and hierarchy, *Economica* 75 (2008): 362–383.

Biehl, Amelia M., Tami Gurley-Calvez and Brian Hill. Self-employment of older Americans: Do recessions matter?, *Small Business Economics* 42, no. 2 (2014): 297–309.

Biniari, Marina G. The emotional embeddedness of corporate entrepreneurship: The case of envy, *Entrepreneurship Theory and Practice* 36, no. 1 (2012): 141–170.

Blanchflower, David G. Self-employment in OECD countries, *Labour Economics* 7, no. 5 (2000): 471–505.

___. *Self-employment: More may not be better*, No. w10286, National Bureau of Economic Research, 2004.

Blanchflower, David G. and Andrew Oswald. *Self-employment and Mrs Thatcher's enterprise*, CEP Discussion Papers dp0030, Centre for Economic Performance, LSE, 1991.

Carlson, Neil R., William Buskist, C. Donald Heth and Rod Schmaltz. *Psychology: The science of behaviour*, 4th Canadian ed. Toronto: Pearson Education Canada, 2007.

Cechin, Andrei, Jos Bijman, Stefano Pascucci, Decio Zylbersztajn and Onno Omta. Drivers of pro-active member participation in agricultural cooperatives: Evidence from Brazil, *Annals of Public and Cooperative Economics* 84, no. 4 (2013): 443–468.

CICOPA. *World Declaration on Worker Cooperatives*, Approved by the ICA General Assembly in Cartagena, Colombia, on 23 September 2005, 2005.

Cook, Michael L. and Bradley Plunkett. Collective entrepreneurship: an emerging phenomenon in producer-owned organizations, *Journal of Agricultural and Applied Economics* 38, no. 2 (2006): 421–428.

Davis, Peter. The governance of cooperatives under competitive conditions: Issues, processes and culture, *Corporate Governance* 1, no. 4 (2001): 28–39.

Díaz-Foncea, Millan and Carmen Marcuello. Spatial patterns in new firm formation: Are cooperatives different?, *Small Business Economics* 44, no. 1 (2015): 171–187.

Douglas, Evan J. and Dean A. Shepherd. Entrepreneurship as a utility-maximizing response, *Journal of Business Venturing* 15, no. 3 (2000): 231–252.

____. Self-employment as a career choice: Attitudes, entrepreneurial intentions, and utility maximization, *Entrepreneurship Theory and Practice* 26, no. 3 (2002): 81–90.

European Commission. *Comunicación de la Comisión al Consejo, al Parlamento Europeo, al Comité Económico y Social Europeo y al Comité de las Regiones sobre fomento de las cooperativas en Europa,* 2004. Accessed 14 August 2016. www.uv.es/cidec/documents/bibliovirtual/comunicacion_2003_18.pdf.

Evans, David S. and Boyan Jovanovic. An estimated model of entrepreneurial choice under liquidity constraints, *Journal of Political Economy* 97, no. 4 (1989): 808–827.

Hansmann, Henry. *The ownership of enterprise.* Boston: Harvard University Press, 1996.

Henzler, Reinhold. *Osuuskunta yritysmuotona ja jäsentensä tukena,* Helsingin Yliopiston osuustoimintainstituutti, 1960. (Original: Henzler, Reinhold. *Die Genossenschaft eine fördernde Betriebswirtschaft,* 1957).

Hundley, Greg. Why and when are the self-employed more satisfied with their work?, *Industrial Relations* 40, no. 2 (2001): 293–316.

Hyytinen, Ari and Olli-Pekka Ruuskanen. Time use of the self-employed, *Kyklos* 60, no. 1 (2007): 105–122.

Inkinen, Kari. Charles Giden solidarismi kansantaloudellisena oppisuuntana In *Sanastosta sanomaan – Osuustoiminnan ideologiasta ja arvoista,* edited by Sauli Puhakka, 17–33. Helsingin Yliopisto, Osuustoimintainstituutti, 1997.

Jakonen, Mikko and Tiina Silvasti. *Talouden uudet muodot,* Helsinki: Into Kustannus, 2015.

Jones, Derek C. and Panu Kalmi. Trust inequality and the size of the cooperative sector: Cross-country evidence, *Annals of Public and Cooperative Economics* 80, no. 2 (2009): 165–195.

Kalmi, Panu. Catching a wave: The formation of cooperatives in Finnish regions, *Small Business Economics* 41, no. 1 (2013): 295–313.

Karjalainen, Jari. *Työosuustoiminta työllistämisen välineenä,* Labour Policy Studies no. 154. Helsinki: Ministry of Labour, 1996.

Koskinen, Seppo. Työosuuskunnan kautta työtä suorittavan status työttömyysturvassa, *Edilex,* 2013. Accessed 19 June 2016. www.edilex.fi/artikkelit/9436.

Kultalahti, Susanna and Riitta Viitala. Generation Y: Challenging clients for HRM?, *Journal of Managerial Psychology* 30, no. 1 (2015): 101–114.

Laukkanen, Jarmo. Osuuskunta yhteisöllisenä yrityksenä. In *Enemmän kuin yritys – yhteisöllisen yrittämisen menestystekijät,* edited by Tapani Köppä, Jarmo Laukkanen and Jaana Santala, 99–151. Helsinki: Oy Edita Ab, 2000.

Laurinkari, Juhani. *Osuustoiminta – Utopiasta Kansainvälisen Yrittämisen Muodoksi.* Kuopio: Suomen Graafiset Palvelut Oy, 2004.

Mescon, Timothy and John R. Montanari. The personalities of independent and franchise entrepreneurs: An empirical analysis of concepts, *Journal of Enterprise Management* 3, no. 2 (1981): 149–159.

Mori, Pier Angelo. Community and cooperation: The evolution of cooperatives towards new models of citizens' democratic participation in public services provision, *Annals of Public and Cooperative Economics* 85, no. 3 (2014): 327–352.

Nilsson, Jerker. Organizational principles for co-operative firms, *Scandinavian Journal of Management* 17, no. 3 (2001): 329–356.

Pencavell, John. The labor supply of self-employed workers: The choice of working hours in worker coops, *Journal of Comparative Economics* 43 (2015): 677–689.

Pérotin, Virginie. Entry, exit and the business cycle: Are cooperatives different?, *Journal of Comparative Economics* 34, no. 2 (2006): 295–316.

Puusa, Anu and Kirsi Hokkila. *Osuustoiminnan tunnettuus ja houkuttelevuus yrittäjyysvaih-toehtona-hankkeen loppuraportti,* 2014. Accessed 8 November 2015. www2.uef.fi/documents/1174654/2393643/Loppuraportti.pdf/ae631418-8208-47bc-97c7-3717bd8b9840.

Puusa, Anu, Kirsi Hokkila and Antti Varis. Individuality vs. communality: A new dual role of cooperatives?, *Journal of Cooperative Organization and Management* 4, no. 1 (2016): 22–30.

Pättiniemi, Pekka. Yhteisötalous Suomessa. In *Yhteisötalous: johdatus perusteisiin,* edited by Juhani Laurinkari, 93–120. Helsinki: Gaudeamus, 2007.

____. Yhteisyrittäjyys ennen ja nyt. In *Henkilöomisteinen yritys – yhdessä yrittämällä menestykseen,* edited by Merja Hiltunen, Jarmo Hänninen, Jaakko Ossa, Pekka Pättiniemi, Jukka Pötry, Jukka Tainio and Eliisa Troberg, 23–33. Helsinki: Tietosanoma, 2009.

Pättiniemi, Pekka and Niina Immonen. *National profiles of work integration social enterprises: Finland,* Working Papers Series, no. 02/10. Liège: EMES European Research Network, 2002.

Pättiniemi, Pekka and Sauli Solhagen. *Finland,* CIRIEC report, 1999. Accessed 2 February 2015. www.uv.es/uidescoop/TSE-DGV-FINLAND%20report%20-%20English.pdf.

Pättiniemi, Pekka and Jukka Tainio. *Osuustoiminnan periaatteet kilpailueduiksi. Työosuuskuntien kehittäminen demokraattisina ja osallistuvina.* Kansan sivistystyön liitto. Vantaa: Hakuprint, 2000.

Pötry, Jukka. Yhteisesti omistetun yrityksen erityisongelmia. In *Henkilöomisteinen yritys – yhdessä yrittämällä menestykseen,* edited by Merja Hiltunen, Jarmo Hänninen, Jaakko Ossa, Pekka Pättiniemi, Jukka Pötry, Jukka Tainio and Eliisa Troberg, 121–127. Helsinki: Tietosanoma, 2009.

Ring, J. Kirk, Ana Maria Peredo and James J. Chrisman. Business networks and economic development in rural communities in the United States, *Entrepreneurship Theory and Practice* 34, no. 1 (2010): 171–195.

Romero, Antonio J. and Miguel Pérez. Organizational culture, individual differences and the participation system in cooperativism of associated workers in Andalusia, Spain, *Annals of Public and Cooperative Economics* 74, no. 2 (2003): 283–320.

Ruben, Ruerd and Jorge Heras. Social capital, governance and performance of Ethiopian coffee cooperatives, *Annals of Public and Cooperative Economics* 83, no. 4 (2012): 463–484.

Savtschenko, Victor. *Disabled people in the labour market of the information society: Discussion paper.* STAKES, Themes 1/2003, 2003.

Sivonen, Outi and Pasi Saukkonen. *Taide- ja kulttuurialan osuuskunnat Suomessa.* Cuporen verkkojulkaisuja 22. Kulttuuripoliittisen tutkimuksen edistämissäätiö, 2014. Accessed 19 June 2016. www.cupore.fi/fi/julkaisut/cuporen-julkaisut/outi-sivonen-ja-pasi-saukkonen-taide-ja-kulttuurialan-osuuskunnat-suomessa.

Smola, Karen Wey and Charlotte D. Sutton. Generational differences: Revisiting generational work values for the new millennium, *Journal of Organizational Behavior* 23, no. 4 (2002): 363–382.

Somerville, Peter. Cooperative identity, *Journal of Cooperative Studies* 40 (2007): 5–17.

Spear, Roger. The cooperative advantage, *Annals of Public and Cooperative Economics* 71, no. 4 (2000): 507–523.

____. Governance in democratic member-based organizations, *Annals of Public and Cooperative Economics* 75, no. 10 (2004): 33–59.

Svaleryd, Helena. Self-employment and the local business cycle, *Small Business Economics* 44, no. 1 (2015): 55–70.

Tainio, Jukka. Johdanto. In *Henkilöomisteinen yritys – yhdessä yrittämällä menestykseen*, edited by Merja Hiltunen, Jarmo Hänninen, Jaakko Ossa, Pekka Pättiniemi, Jukka Pötry, Jukka Tainio and Eliisa Troberg, 11–14. Helsinki: Tietosanoma, 2009.

Troberg, Eliisa. *Työosuustoiminnan erityispiirteet ja niiden vaikutukset osuustoiminnalliseen yhteisyrittäjyyteen*, Turun kauppakorkeakoulun julkaisuja Series D-71997, 1997.

____. Knowledge intensive business sector and the cooperative form: A study of Finnish knowledge intensive cooperatives, *Journal of Rural Cooperation* 28, no. 2 (2000): 161–176.

____. Co-operatives: Flexible form of self-employment in competence-based business, *International Journal of Co-operative Management* 2, no. 1 (2008): 28–39.

____. Yhteisyrittämisen menestystekijöitä. In *Henkilöomisteinen yritys – yhdessä yrittämällä menestykseen*, edited by Merja Hiltunen, Jarmo Hänninen, Jaakko Ossa, Pekka Pättiniemi, Jukka Pötry, Jukka Tainio and Eliisa Troberg, 253–269. Helsinki: Tietosanoma, 2009.

____. *Osuustoiminnan idea*. Helsinki: Pellervo-Seura, 2014.

Van Gelderen, Marco and Paul G. W. Jansen. Autonomy as a start-up motive, *Journal of Small Business and Enterprise Development* 13, no. 1 (2006): 23–32.

Yin, Robert K. *Case study research: Design and methods, Vol. 3.* Thousand Oaks, CA: Sage Publications, 2003.

12

LABOUR TRANSFORMATION AND INSTITUTIONAL RE-ARRANGEMENT IN FRANCE

A preliminary study of a business and employment cooperative

Mélissa Boudes

Introduction

Globalization and digitalization are some of the recent changes that destabilize labour and the institutional arrangements regulating it. New forms of work emerge between employment and entrepreneurship (Cappelli and Keller, 2013) creating what is called the 'grey employment zones'.

In a context of high and lasting rates of unemployment, these new forms of work are growing. However, they are located beside welfare institutional arrangements and are characterized by precariousness. Thus, in order to maintain good working conditions, these 'grey employment zones' call for regulations, and new institutional arrangements.

The present chapter shows how, in such a context, a new type of cooperative – business and employment cooperative (*coopérative d'activité et d'emploi*) – is creating a new institutional arrangement. The first part presents the evolution of labour in France and how this affects the extant institutional arrangement. Second, business and employment cooperatives and the method used to study them are presented. The third part shows how this new type of cooperative is creating a new institutional arrangement. Finally, as a conclusion, the main insights for the cooperative movement are presented.

Labour in France

Disruption of welfare state institutional arrangements and the grey employment zones

After the end of the Second World War, under the effect of economic growth and the development of the welfare state, employment became the work norm. The typical work form became the open-ended and full-time employment relation with a unique employer (Fourcade, 1992; Méda, 2010).

This norm highlights our ambivalent relationship to labour. On the one hand, French case law characterizes employment by subservient relation or, in other words, labour submission to capital. On the other hand, employment links people to a political community through access to national social protection. Indeed, the French social system relies on a Bismarckian model where workers' contributions ensure protection for themselves and their family.

Until the end of the 1960s, the welfare state institutional arrangement relied on Fordist regulation or, in other words, on massive workforce and union–employer bargaining.

However, the socio-economic evolutions of recent decades – globalization, growing service economy, digitalization, etc. – have profoundly disrupted this institutional arrangement. Global competition increases market flexibility, leading to growing worker insecurity, whereas the welfare state appears unable to (re) create appropriate/efficient solidarity links. Thus, since the first oil crisis, France has experienced high unemployment rates, which disrupt the equilibrium of the welfare regime. Since 1984, the unemployment rate has never fallen below 7 per cent of the workforce, reaching 9.8 per cent in 2013, according to the ILO. Moreover, according to the National French Statistics Institute, an additional 1.3 million people are not included in the statistics as they are looking for a job but are not available immediately, do not want a job or are discouraged from looking for one. As fewer workers are making contributions and a growing number of unemployed receive social benefits, the welfare budget is continuously in deficit (9.7 billion euros in 2014).[1]

The labour market has gradually split, with on one hand 'insiders', namely people with long-term employment contracts and the related social benefits, and on the other hand a growing number of 'outsiders', namely jobless people or people with precarious contracts (self-employed, short-term and/or part-time workers, etc.). The increasing gap between the two groups creates tensions. Whereas the former try to preserve their security and working conditions, the latter are tempted to consider them as the privileged few who are blocking the balancing mechanisms in the labour market.

To tackle unemployment, policy makers have developed specific legal statuses and adapted tax rates to encourage people to set up their own business. These incentives, combined with the willingness of corporations to outsource some tasks and people's desire of autonomy at work, led to the increase of self-employment (Kunda et al., 2002).

Consequently, a large range of work forms have developed between entrepreneurship and employment in what is labelled the 'grey employment zones'. A myriad of new organizations has emerged within these zones to allow self-employed people to access clients, to train, and to share means and/or risks. They have taken different forms, ranging from web platforms to co-working spaces through cooperatives and employers' associations (de Vaujany et al., 2016; Jang, 2017; Lorquet, 2017).

These new forms of work and organizations located at the margin of the welfare state institutional arrangement raise questions about working conditions. In these grey employment zones, how can new institutional arrangements favouring good work conditions be created? As one possible answer, we focus on a new type of cooperative that has emerged in France: the business and employment cooperative.

The case of business and employment cooperatives

The first business and employment cooperative (BEC) was created in 1995 in the French city of Lyon by a group of public and private for-profit and not-for-profit organizations. Recognizing the inefficiency of the measures encouraging people to set up their own businesses (entrepreneurs' loneliness and lack of skills, economic risk, poverty, etc.), they decided to create a new organization that aims to support people in their entrepreneurial journey.

The objectives were:

- To reduce economic insecurity for individual project holders by allowing them to integrate their micro-projects and know-how with work collectives with access to broader business opportunities;
- To make professional pathways more secure by fostering, organizing and accompanying mutual apprenticeship within the work collectives;
- To enable, via work collectives, a better economic integration of micro-entrepreneurs within local economic dynamics, and real wealth production for the territory;
- To allow the emergence of a new economically efficient form of enterprise, exclusively dedicated to a social project, the professional fulfilment of its salaried members (Report – Evaluation of the mutualization devices within Coopaname – Plein Sens Consulting Group).

Interestingly, Elisabeth Bost, who managed the first BEC and later the first BECs network, inspired by other experiences, chose the cooperative status 'to become a full-fledged stakeholder of the enterprise project that we share with the entrepreneurs' (Bost, 2011). BECs are cooperatives relying on the cooperative principles, aiming to allow their members to self-fulfil their needs, through a not-for-profit and democratic organization. Choosing the cooperative organizational form was choosing an approach that diverged from other forms of enterprises and provisions for support to entrepreneurs that rely either on a for-profit or on a public service basis.

Concretely, BECs offer their members a three-stage path mixing entrepreneurship, employment and cooperation. First, when entering the BEC, people sign a mentoring contract, which allows them to build and strengthen their projects through meetings, workshops, trainings and support by a personal advisor. While developing their project, people can keep their former status and rights. For example, an entrepreneur who works part-time as an employee or who receives unemployment benefit can combine the different incomes (up to a ceiling amount for social benefits).

Although the entrepreneurs propose their own expertise and canvass clients for their own products, they do not have to create a legal structure as it is the cooperative that invoices the clients. Thus, after the first product sale or service delivery, entrepreneurs sign an employee contract. The turnover generated is then transformed into a salary by the cooperative's shared departments (accounting, management, etc.), staffed by what are known as 'permanent employees'. Each entrepreneur has their own accountancy within the BEC and their salary is smoothed according to their anticipated turnover.

In a third phase, the employee-entrepreneurs, like the permanent staff, can participate in the share capital, acquiring cooperative shares and getting involved in cooperative governance.

Thus, BECs bring together entrepreneurs with various skills who work independently but within an enterprise with shared tax, administrative and accounting departments. They can develop collective entrepreneurial projects and become decision-makers. Thus, BECs (re)create solidarity between self-employed people.

This new type of cooperative presents a hybrid status and economic structure. The entrepreneurs are accountable for their own activities; they finance their salaries and social security contributions with their turnover. A share of the turnover (on average around 10 per cent) is used to finance the shared support services ('permanent staff'). As BECs also offer a public interest service by giving advice and help to all those with an entrepreneurial project who contact it, they receive public funds (European funds, local administration funds, etc.).

Although BECs are formally registered as worker cooperatives, they differ from conventional worker cooperatives. Within BECs, each entrepreneur develops their own business; workers do not work together on a single production. Moreover, BECs have a high level of turnover due to people entering to test their project.

It is important to mention that this new form of cooperative developed without any specific legal framework until the Social and Solidarity Economy Law voted in July 2014. After more than 20 years of experimentation, this law offers a legal recognition to the BECs and the employee-entrepreneur-cooperators. However, BECs did not wait for this legal recognition to spread throughout the country and there are now around 200 BEC establishments in France with 7,000 salaried workers and 3,000 project holders with a support contract.[2]

The analysis in the following sections is based on a single holistic case study (Yin, 2003) of a Parisian BEC, Coopaname. This cooperative was established in 2003 and is now one of the biggest BECs in France, with more than 800 members (entrepreneurs with support contract, employee-entrepreneurs, 'permanent staff', etc.), 253 of whom participate in the share capital, and a turnover of 8 million euros. Data were collected through three main sources: interviews, focus groups and non-participative observation. Moreover, the cooperative provided open access to its intranet and more than 70 files were collected, comprising annual reports, newsletters, PowerPoint presentations, meeting minutes, press and academic articles, pictures and books. BEC network actors were also interviewed, observed and provided secondary data. The data analysis followed an abductive approach consisting of shuttling back and forth from theory to dataset (Corbin and Strauss, 2008).

A new-institutional analysis

From a new-institutional approach, BECs rely on three different institutional orders: the market, the state and the social economy.

Institutional orders are:

> different domains of institutions built around a cornerstone institution that represents the cultural symbols and material practices that govern a commonly recognized area of life. Each institutional order represents a governance system that provides a frame of reference that preconditions actors' sensemaking choices.
>
> *(Thornton et al., 2012, p. 53, inspired by Friedland and Alford, 1991)*

Table 12.1 offers a simplified analytical reading of the three institutional orders upon which BECs were built. Each order encompasses symbolic components – myth and meaning – which are embodied by material components – practices and instruments.

Each order relies on a myth or ideal supported by specific meaning linking the myth to human basic needs. The myth underpinning the state is that of a solid national community responding to the need for protection. The market myth is a natural trading equilibrium responding to the need for autonomy. The social economy relies on the myth of emancipation and the need to be and feel part of a collective. These symbolic components are activated by practices and instruments. The social economy ideal of emancipation is embodied by the creation of not-for-profit organizations (more formal ones, such as non-profit or mutual organizations and cooperatives; and less formal ones, such as social movements, collectives, internet communities, etc.) resulting in various forms of cooperation. The ideal-type

TABLE 12.1 BECs institutional orders

Institutional orders		Institutional arrangement Welfare state		Social economy
		Market	State	
Symbolic components	**Myth**	Market equilibrium	National solidarity	Emancipation
	Meaning	Need for autonomy	Need for protection	Need to be part of a collective
Material components	**Practice**	Entrepreneurship	Employment	Cooperation
	Instrument	Contract	Labour law and national social insurance	Not-for-profit organizations

Source: Author's own elaboration

of practice promulgated is cooperative work, free of any subordination. We can observe that this order also includes a part of volunteering to ensure democratic governance. The market ideal regarding labour is embodied in entrepreneurship. All people, as the entrepreneur of their life (time, workforce and capital) are considered free to engage in the market to set up a business or to offer labour and/ or capital to an existing enterprise. The ideal type of practice is flexible labour based on the mechanisms of supply and demand. Finally, the state ideal in terms of labour is embodied by employment relationship, where the work contract involves mutual rights and responsibilities to guarantee workers a certain level of security.[3]

At societal level, whereas the social economy order has remained marginalized regarding work regulation, both the state and the market have developed under the welfare regime institutional arrangement.[4] The latter provides frameworks and infrastructures for trade to develop and the necessary protection/assets (education, health care, etc.) to ensure good working conditions for employees. Whereas, at first sight, the market and state orders may seem contradictory, the welfare state makes them complementary and interdependent, so that the orders reinforce each other, representing an institutional arrangement (Smets and Jarzabkowski, 2013).

However, as presented in the first section, with the socio-economic changes of recent decades, labour has undergone profound changes, destabilizing this welfare regime arrangement. Overall, the economic evolutions have transformed it: from being an institutional arrangement bringing together the state and market orders, it has become a complex environment characterized by competing demands (flexibility versus security), inefficiency (deficit of the national social insurance) and a lack of legitimacy (non-adapted national rules).

Neo-institutional scholars have studied how people and organizations deal with complexity (Greenwood et al., 2011; Pache and Santos, 2010; Smets and Jarzabkowski, 2013). They have identified a range of actions, ranging from passive adaptation to active strategizing. One of the major evolutions in this theoretical path is the shift from considering complexity as a threat to considering it as a potential resource (Durand et al., 2013; Zilber, 2011). The multiple components of the institutional orders, considered as united in settled times, are perceived in unsettled times – when inefficiency, maladjustments, conflicts of interest, and crises of legitimacy occur – as potential assets for institutional change (Seo and Creed, 2002; Swidler, 2011).

In these changes of institutional orders, how do actors create new institutional arrangements to face the disruption of the extant ones?

Selective coupling and new institutional arrangements

Selective coupling

Driven by a desire to offer new solutions to what are now called 'grey employment zones' comprising all the precarious forms of work between employment and entrepreneurship that do not benefit from genuine social protection, Coopaname relies on three institutional orders: the state, the market and the social economy. However, the cooperative does not rely on each of them in the same way. The BEC has developed what Pache and Santos (2013) call a 'selective coupling' of the different components of the institutional orders. In other words, it chooses among the different institutional order components to build an original arrangement. This section presents how the BEC selectively couple the three orders.

The state

Coopaname relies on the state order to provide its members with some security. Thus, the BEC adheres to the need for protection. However, it has a pragmatic use of the myth of national solidarity and labour laws; in other words, it uses these institutional order components to achieve its goal (secure entrepreneurial path) while being aware of their limits. More precisely, although Coopaname is aware that the myth of national solidarity is vanishing and that labour laws have failed to adapt to the new socio-economic conditions, it relies on them because, even though they are far from perfect, they provide some security. Finally, Coopaname uses an existing employment form but also advocates for emancipated work relations released from subordination. Therefore, by using the existing employment form while trying to transform it, the BEC is manipulating this institutional order component. The quote below illustrates this complex relationship to employment:

> Worker cooperatives in the 19th century were built upon a call to end sub-missive employment, thought of as an expropriation of the working tool. At Coopaname we consider ourselves as part of this history and endeavour to go beyond an alienating type of relation to labour, which is alienating, dumb, violent, and seems to us to be completely incompatible with the necessary evolution of the economy. While we are awaiting and calling for this evolution, we paradoxically are completely committed to salaried employment, being still the only framework where we can find social protection, rights, and real solidarity [. . .]
>
> *(Coopaname Welcome booklet)*

Table 12.2 summarizes the evolution of the state institutional order in society as a whole and the way Coopaname uses its symbolic and material components.

The market

The BEC also relies on the market order. It recognizes people's need for autonomy so that entrepreneurs deliver their products or services under their own brand, and their salary depends on their turnover. However, Coopaname is highly critical of the myth of market self-balance and the 'heroic' approach of the entrepreneur as a self-made (wo)man. This approach, which is largely disseminated in society and is linked to the need for autonomy, sometimes takes the form of an injunction. One of the

TABLE 12.2 State institutional order, societal evolution and how Coopaname uses these concepts

State institutional order			Societal evolution	Coopaname use
Symbolic components	Myth	National solidarity	Inefficiency and decreasing legitimacy	Pragmatic use
	Meaning	Need for protection	In movement: national and local mechanisms	Adherence
Material components	Practice	Employment	Transformation and diversification of statuses (grey employment zones)	Manipulation
	Instrument	Labour law and national social insurance	Only small incremental changes – lack of adaptation	Pragmatic use

Source: Author's own elaboration

most symbolic forms of this injunction in France is the new status of '*auto-entrepreneur*' (self-entrepreneur), established to encourage jobless people to create their own job by setting up their own business. Whereas this status facilitates procedures (simplified administrative tasks, tax advantages, etc.), it does not provide the new entrepreneurs with the necessary skills and does not protect them against isolation.

Thus, Coopaname relies on the need for autonomy by using entrepreneurship and contracting but in a manipulative way with the intent to transform them. The aim of the cooperative is to move from an individualized and risky approach to entrepreneurship to a more collective and less precarious one, as illustrated by the following quote:

> The generalization of political decisions to support entrepreneurship, led by policy-makers towards increasingly smaller projects, held by people who are less and less prepared socially, professionally and financially to succeed in their enterprise constitutes a solution to unemployment only in as much as it pushes an increasing number of people out of the employee category. [. . .] the micro entrepreneur appears, beyond the myth, as a new emblematic figure of precariousness: his/her micro-enterprise allows him/her to earn a micro-income that allows him/her to reimburse his/her micro-credit and to access micro social protection. . .
>
> *(article written by Coopaname members and published in academic journal)*

TABLE 12.3 Market institutional order, societal evolution and Coopaname use

Market institutional order			Societal evolution	Coopaname use
Symbolic components	Myth	Market equilibrium	Increasing legitimacy and use	Criticism
	Meaning	Need for autonomy	Increasing legitimacy and use	Manipulation
Material components	Practice	Entrepreneurship	Increasing legitimacy and use	Manipulation
	Instrument	Contract	Development and diversification (e.g. 'auto-entrepreneur' status)	Manipulation

Source: Author's own elaboration

Table 12.3 summarizes the societal evolution of the market order and how Coopaname uses it.

The social economy

Finally, the BEC relies on the social economy order. It adheres to the myth of emancipation through labour. Thus, all members can develop their own skills according to their aspirations, combine different professions, etc. The cooperative also adheres to the need to be part of a collective through cooperation. It develops a strong community culture through friendly events, such as potlucks, or with a specific and humoristic vocabulary: for example, members call themselves 'Coopanamians'.

Cooperation among members takes diverse forms. The entrepreneurs mutualize the support activities (accounting, etc.) but they are also encouraged to create groups to share advice or even set up collective businesses. Furthermore, the BEC develops many tools and events to spread information and offers appropriate training to allow members to speak out and take part in debates, be they cooperators or not yet.

As a cooperative, Coopaname relies on the cooperative principles as per the 1995 *Statement on the Cooperative Identity* of the International Cooperative Alliance. However, the BEC appears very critical of the cooperative movement and more broadly of the social economy movement. In fact, Coopaname deplores the fact that the social economy has acquired economic recognition but has failed to construct a unified political movement. When the new French social economy bill was being debated in parliament, Coopaname welcomed the news with an opinion column in a national newspaper calling for the social economy 'of good causes' to be replaced by the social economy 'of struggle'. For the authors,

> what is at stake is not the size or institutional recognition, but the disastrous lack of a political project shared by social economy organizations to sustain the whole economy. [. . .] We must replace the issue of employment by that of labour: we have to assume that the mission of the social economy is not simply to create employment, but to develop new forms of labour that will provide a bigger contribution to developing tomorrow's society than a thousand social integration firms.

Behind this sentence, one has to remember that the government has used social economy organizations (mainly with charitable status) greatly to enforce job creation policies through funding, specific contracts or a new organization status. From the Coopaname viewpoint, this *instrumentalization* to create new jobs or foster entrepreneurship seems to have separated the material components of the social economy – not-for-profit organizations and cooperation practices – from its symbolic components – the myth of emancipation and the need to be part of a collective.

Therefore, the BEC appears to have a manipulative use of the social economy instruments, as stated here by the former co-director of Coopaname:

> I think that, within five years there will be no more old-style BECs. I think tomorrow's question is: how will completely new types of social organization be born within the grey employment zones. The BEC is preparing the ground. Such organizations do not have to be cooperatives; they could be mutuals or unions.

Table 12.4 summarizes the relations Coopaname developed with the social economy order.

Building a new institutional arrangement

Facing the disruption of the welfare institutional arrangement, BECs aim to build a new one providing the growing number of self-employed people with a secure collective framework and democratic economic relationships. To do so, they are building a new institutional arrangement through the selective coupling of three institutional orders: the market, the state and the social economy. The case of Coopaname highlights different ways of selectively coupling institutional order components, ranging from adherence to criticism through pragmatic use and manipulation. Two main transversal dimensions play a key role in the building of the new institutional arrangement: the meso-level social innovation dynamic and the cooperative principle of education, training and information.

TABLE 12.4 Social economy order, societal evolution and Coopaname use

Social economy institutional orders			Societal evolution	Coopaname use
Symbolic components	Myth	Emancipation	Increasing	Adherence
	Meaning	Need to be part of a collective	Increasing	Adherence
Material components	Practice	Cooperation	Development of some new uses (e.g. collaborative economy)	Adherence
	Instrument	Not-for-profit organizations	Increasing legitimacy but still marginal	Manipulation

Source: Author's own elaboration

A meso-level social innovation dynamic

By combining the components of three different institutional orders, the cooperative entails a social innovation dynamic: a process aiming at improving social conditions and generating institutional changes that involves a diversity of stakeholders in an empowerment approach (Bouchard *et al.*, 2015; Mulgan *et al.*, 2007; Terstriep *et al.*, 2015; Westley *et al.*, 2014).

Indeed, as the following quote highlights, it is more than a new organizational form; the BEC is a dynamic:

> [. . .] there is a project that is utopian, there is a structure that is in constant evolution but is still unfinished.
>
> *(Former co-director)*

The meso- or intermediary level of the dynamic, between people's needs and aspirations at micro-level and the disruption of welfare state at macro-level, is highly important. Indeed, at this level, the cooperative can experiment with the institutional orders available in an innovative and pragmatic way, which appears legitimate to both workers and policy makers.

To reach this position Coopaname has built partnerships with other cooperatives sharing the same objectives, as stated in the following quote:

> [. . .] our interest is to have a cooperative group of structures working in the field of grey employment zones. [. . .] The general idea behind it is: what united us, as cooperatives, is the notion of social protection, general protection; when we say social protection, we mean mutuality.
>
> *(Former co-director)*

Education, training and information

Another important dimension of the creation of the new institutional arrangement is the cooperative principle of *education, training and information*. Indeed, the social innovation dynamic relies heavily on this principle and Coopaname develops numerous times and spaces to foster it.

The BEC and its partners have publicized their social innovation through public talks, press interviews and even research papers. Quite early after its creation, the cooperative has created a group of research action. This group, which first gathered members who had more or less experience with research, gave birth to partnerships with different scholars and laboratories developing projects to improve and theorize social innovation dynamics (economic model, mutual entrepreneurial support, gender equality, and so on).

Moreover, the cooperative does not consider reflexivity to be reserved to a small number of its members. Therefore, according to the fifth cooperative principle, it has developed multiple tools to encourage its members to take an active part in the social innovation process: annual universities, internal training sessions bringing together all members to discuss the cooperative's latest concerns, set of documents presenting the cooperative, its history and specific vocabulary in a very instructive and humorous way. Thus, the cooperative spreads what can be called a 'critical economic culture'.

Figure 12.1 summarizes the process through which the BEC is building a new institutional arrangement with the top–down – welfare regime disruption – and bottom–up – people needs and aspirations – pressures.

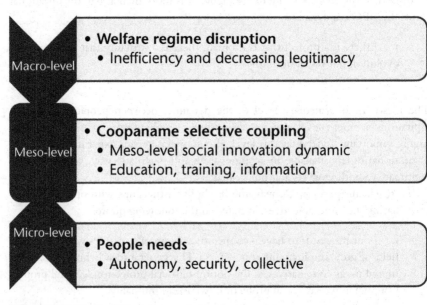

FIGURE 12.1 The building of a new institutional arrangement

Source: Author's own elaboration

Conclusion

The study of the Coopaname case highlights how, in a context of institutional arrangement disruption, a new arrangement can be created by selectively coupling different institutional orders. This resonates and completes new institutional research showing that institutional orders, or logics at field level, can represent strategic resources (Durand *et al.*, 2013).

This case also presents interesting insights for the cooperative movement.

First, it highlights the crucial role played by the fifth cooperative principle of education, training and information – a principle quite overlooked by scholars, who tend to focus prevalently on cooperative governance and economic structure. More than just a means or a principle to conform to, this principle is the cornerstone of the BEC project. Coopaname enacts this principle through dedicated training and specific times for debate, such as the annual universities or research groups. All these tools enhance critical thinking and aim to improve the institutional arrangement under construction. This represents an interesting insight for cooperatives, as one of their pressing issues is to preserve their social goal and democratic functioning over time in a context dominated by for-profit organizations (Cornforth, 1995; Draperi, 2012). Furthermore, people's motivations for entering the BEC are very diverse – better life balance, flexibility, autonomy, etc. – with some of them facing 'personal hardship' – long-term unemployed, difficult career change, etc. Although the BEC offers a new form of work, the latter is no panacea; however, the culture of constant and democratic reflexivity appears to strengthen the trust and confidence that workers have in their BEC.

Second, whereas worker cooperatives mainly focus on a single production, BECs rely on diversity, opening their doors to all occupations, as long as they are not submitted to specific regulations. This is an interesting feature in a context of deep transformation of labour, where workers have multiple jobs, different employers/clients and even different statuses. Thus, production no longer appears to be the catalyst gathering people who simply contract on a project mode. This raises questions about the definition of the enterprise – be it a cooperative or not – and why/how people create new collectives. In the BEC case, people come together because they share common needs and aspirations: the willingness to build professional projects within a flexi-secured framework.

Third, by opening their doors almost unconditionally, BECs serve the interests not only of their members but also of society as a whole. Exceeding their organizational boundaries by positioning themselves as servants of society or 'supra-configuration missionaries' (Malo and Vézina, 2004), the BECs offer to rethink the economy. The boundaries between the public and private economy blur to give rise to a 'collective economy', where enterprises work 'through economic democracy to the public interest' (Draperi, 2012).

To sum up, this new cooperative form calls for a renewal of cooperation among working people by (1) reconsidering cooperatives not just as organizational forms but as social innovation instruments; (2) going back to the initial political project of emancipation through education and self-organizing; and (3) blurring the boundaries between collective and public interests.

Notes

1 Commission des comptes de la Sécurité sociale, June 2015, quoted in *Les Chiffres clés de la sécurité sociale 2014*, Direction de la Sécurité Sociale, 2015.
2 These numbers are an estimation by the French network of worker cooperatives. As BECs can take diverse forms, it is difficult to have accurate statistics.
3 Here we are not referring to the civil service, which represents only one particular form of salaried work, but to the approach to labour promoted by the public authorities within society.
4 However, it is important to highlight that state and market agents develop many partnerships with actors of the social economy. Thus, some public policies would probably never have developed without the support of the social economy.

References

Bost, Elisabeth. *Aux entreprenants associés. La coopérative d'activités et d'emploi*. Valence: Editions Repas, 2011.

Bouchard, Marie J., Adalbert Evers and Laurent Fraisse. Concevoir l'innovation sociale dans une perspective de transformation, *Sociologies Pratiques* 31, no. 2 (2015): 9–14.

Cappelli, Peter and JR Keller. Classifying work in the new economy, *Academy of Management Review* 38, no. 4 (2013): 575–596.

Corbin, Juliet and Anselm Strauss. *Basics of qualitative research: Techniques and procedures for developing grounded theory*. Thousand Oaks, CA: Sage, 2008.

Cornforth, Chris. Patterns of cooperative management: Beyond the degeneration thesis, *Economic and Industrial Democracy* 16 (1995): 487–523.

de Vaujany, François-Xavier, Amélie Bohas, Julie Fabbri and Pierre Laniray. Nouvelles pratiques de travail: La fin du clivage entrepreneuriat-salariat? Rapport de recherche 1, Research Group on Collaborative Spaces, 2016.

Draperi, Jean-François. *La république coopérative*. Brussels: Larcier, 2012.

Durand, Rodolphe, Berangere Szostak, Julien Jourdan and Patricia H. Thornton. Institutional logics as strategic resources, *Research in the sociology of organizations* 39 Part A (2013): 165–201.

Fourcade, Bernard. L'évolution des situations d'emploi particulières de 1945 à 1990, *Travail et Emploi*, no. 52 (1992): 4–19.

Friedland, Roger and Robert R. Alford. Bringing society back in: Symbols, practices and institutional contradictions. In *The new institutionalism in organizational analysis*, edited by Walter W. Powell and Paul DiMaggio, 232–263. Chicago: University of Chicago Press, 1991.

Greenwood, Royston, Mia Raynard, Farah Kodeih, Evelyn Micelotta and Michael Lounsbury. Institutional complexity and organizational responses, *Academy of Management Annals* 5, no. 1 (2011): 317–371.

Jang, Jongik. The emergence of freelancers cooperatives in South Korea, *Annals of Public and Cooperative Economics* 88, no. 1 (2017): 75–89.

Kunda, Gideon, Stephen R. Barley and James Evans. Why do contractors contract? Experience of highly skilled technical professionals in a contingent labor market, *Industrial and Labor Relations Review* 55, no. 2 (2002): 234–261.

Lorquet, Nadège. *Rôle et fonctions des intermédiaires du marché du travail sécurisant les transitions professionnelles.* Liège: HEC Liège, 2017.

Malo, Marie-Claire and Martine Vézina. Gouvernance et gestion de l'entreprise collective d'usagers: Stratégies de création de valeur et configurations organisationnelles, *Economie et Solidarités* 35, no. 1–2 (2004): 100–120.

Méda, Dominique. *Le travail. Une valeur en voie de disparition.* Paris: Flammarion, 2010.

Mulgan, Geoff, Simon Tucker, Ali Rushanara and Ben Sanders. *Social innovation. What it is, why it matters and how it can be accelerated.* The Young Foundation – Skoll Center for Social Entrepreneurship, 2007.

Pache, Anne-Claire and Filipe Santos. When worlds collide: the internal dynamics of organizational responses to conflicting institutional demands, *Academy of Management Review* 35, no. 3 (2010): 455–476.

___. Inside the hybrid organization: Selective coupling as a response to competing institutional logics, *Academy of Management Journal* 56, no. 4 (2013): 972–1001.

Seo, Myeong-Gu and W. E. Douglas Creed. Institutional contradictions, praxis and institutional change: A dialectical perspective, *Academy of Management Journal* 27, no. 2 (2002): 222–247.

Smets, Michael and Paula Jarzabkowski. Reconstructing institutional complexity in practice: A relational model of institutional work and complexity, *Human Relations* 66, no. 10 (2013): 1279–1309.

Swidler, Ann. *Talk of love: How culture matters.* Chicago: University of Chicago Press, 2011.

Terstriep, Judith, Maria Kleverbeck, Alessandro Deserti and Francesca Rizzo. Comparative report on social innovation across Europe, Deliverable 3.2 of the project *Boosting the impact of SI in Europe through economic underpinnings (SIMPACT)* – European Commission 7th Framework programme, 2015.

Thornton, Patricia H., William Ocasio and Michael Lounsbury. *Institutional logics perspectives: A new approach to culture, structure and process.* Oxford: Oxford University Press, 2012.

Westley, Frances, Nino Antadze, Darcy J. Riddell, Kirsten Robinson and Sean Geobey. Five configurations for scaling up social innovation: Case examples of nonprofit organizations from Canada, *Journal of Applied Behavioral Science* 50, no. 3 (2014): 234–260.

Yin, Robert K. *Case study research: Design and methods.* Thousand Oaks, CA: Sage, 2003.

Zilber, Timmar B. Institutional multiplicity in practice: A tale of two high-tech conferences in Israel, *Organization Science* 22, no. 6 (2011): 1539–1559.

13

MULTI-STAKEHOLDER COOPERATIVES AS A MEANS FOR JOBS CREATION AND SOCIAL TRANSFORMATION

Sonja Novkovic

Introduction

This chapter offers a discussion of the multi-stakeholder cooperative (MSC) form, with particular attention given to MSCs with workers as a member category. Most of the literature on MSCs highlights their relatively recent appearance as an independent legal form (see Vézina and Girard, 2014, for example). The chapter widens the discourse to point out that MSCs are not a new phenomenon, and are much more prevalent than implicated by the focus on a specific legal form. Particular attention here is given to cooperatives with roots in labour association (i.e. worker ownership),[1] with membership, and therefore a role in decision-making, extended to other types of stakeholders.

The purpose of this chapter is to highlight the importance and raise some of the key relevant issues and research questions, associated with formation, purpose, and governance of MSCs. It does not, however, do justice to the vast diversity of forms of multi-stakeholder cooperation, nor does it produce an exhaustive account of the literature or practice. What it does attempt to illustrate is that there are cases of cooperatives with roots in social justice issues and labour emancipation who innovate to include other stakeholders when faced with complex problems; in need of diverse resources; in solidarity with other stakeholders; or for community development purposes.

The term 'multi-stakeholder cooperative' used in the literature has been contested by many in the cooperative movement, and is therefore in some instances used interchangeably with 'solidarity cooperative'[2] (see Novkovic and Miner, 2015, p. 12). Both terms indicate cooperatives with multiple types of members, but the misgivings about the MSC term are rooted in the understanding of a 'stake' as a personal interest, rather than a part of the collective good reflected in multi-stakeholder governance. Since the term dominates the literature, we continue to use it here.

Development of multi-stakeholder cooperatives

Historical consideration

Cooperatives are attributed multi-stakeholder (as well as multi-purpose) beginnings, from the early developments in Rochdale,[3] or in earlier cooperative experiments in Europe and elsewhere (Battilani, 2014). Over time, they evolved into entities with single member type, often reinforced by legal frameworks that emphasized a single-stakeholder structure. Twentieth-century developments, in particular globalization and deregulation in market economies, also placed unprecedented competitive pressures on cooperative enterprise, often resulting in isomorphism and degeneration as cooperatives were emulating structures and behaviours of the ubiquitous investor-owned businesses (Spear, 2004). New trends countering these isomorphic pressures emerged with new needs developing out of crises, such as the neoliberal push for a reduced provision of welfare services by states under austerity budgets, and engagement of multiple stakeholders in the delivery of social services, for example. Also notable for cooperative development are new industries such as renewable energy where multi-stakeholder and community cooperatives play a prominent role, but also other complex social changes that require flexibility and involvement of diverse stakeholder groups (Vézina and Girard, 2014).

Over recent decades, MSCs have been increasingly institutionalized across the world and, therefore, they can be identified through legal frameworks in increasing numbers of countries. Without a suggestive legal framework, detecting these cooperative forms is a case-by-case task, but they are pervasive, indicating the ability of cooperatives to resort to innovative organizational approaches in order to satisfy particular needs in diverse environments. In some jurisdictions where single stakeholdership is mandated by law, a worker cooperative may establish a sister cooperative, such as a consumer or community cooperative, as needs arise.[4] Where law is less restrictive, cooperatives can venture into multi-stakeholder organizational form more freely.

Theoretical consideration on advantages of multi-stakeholder cooperatives

MSCs integrate multiple types of members into cooperative ownership and governance.[5] This added heterogeneity in governance is counter-intuitive in the framework of the transactions costs literature (Dow, 2003; Hansmann, 1996), yet in practice this model comes about either as a way to integrate labour into a consumer/user cooperative, or a way to internalize governance and management externalities by inclusion of outside stakeholders in decision-making. According to new-institutional economics, different patrons of firms have specific, often conflicting, goals depending on the type of transactions with the enterprise (Hansmann, 1996): workers seek higher pay, consumers lower prices, suppliers high prices for inputs they supply, investors the highest return on investment, and so on. Ownership by a homogeneous group of patrons/stakeholders is therefore considered least costly, while heterogeneity increases governance costs as it encompasses trade-offs. Heterogeneous members are thought to contribute to inefficiency in governance and eventually cause cooperative degeneration (see Cook, 1995; Cook and Burress, 2009).

In reality, individuals 'wear many hats' and may simultaneously engage with the cooperative as: workers, users of services, consumers, suppliers/producers, community members (Leviten-Reid and Fairbarn, 2011; Lund, 2011). Translated to inclusion in governance in MSCs, and therefore a voice in decision-making within the organization, there seems to be more advantages to multi-stakeholder governance than the transactions costs literature would suggest,[6] particularly with regards to motivations for MSC ownership and control. Advantages of multi-stakeholder cooperatives, understood to imply distributed ownership and control among diverse stakeholders, may outweigh the increased costs of decision-making. Distributed control and governance may reduce costs of information asymmetries and manage complexity in a more effective way (Turnbull, 2002). In addition, positive externalities produced by multi-stakeholder cooperatives may also outweigh the increased costs of governance and explain why this form of enterprise is on the rise, particularly in the sphere of social services, work integration, community development, and production and distribution of renewable energy, among others.

Empirical research has been conducted in order to validate these theoretical considerations. Borzaga and Depedri (2015) find that multi-stakeholder social cooperatives in Italy attract significantly larger number of volunteers (both members and non-members) compared with single-stakeholder social cooperatives. This finding can partly support the claim that access to resources increases in MSCs, although more research may shed some light on other types of resources accessible to diverse member groups. Regarding multiple objectives, Campi et al. (2006) find no evidence that goals differ between single-stakeholder and multi-stakeholder organizations among work integration social enterprises in their study, indicating homogeneity of purpose among seemingly heterogeneous stakeholders. They also confirm the findings in Quebec and elsewhere that multi-stakeholder governance is not as costly as transactions costs literature suggests (Leviten-Reid and Fairbairn, 2011), or that its benefits have not been fully accounted for in the literature.

Beyond short-term cost–effect perspectives which focus on multiple constituents' concerns for preservation and management of the commons, we can find some more normative arguments which emphasize solidarity as the root of social relationships in a number of MSCs. Diverse members do not necessarily represent a particular interest group, but engage in solidarity with others for a common purpose (Novkovic and Miner, 2015). Lund terms this feature 'solidarity as a business model', arguing that stakeholders in MSCs build long-term relationships to encourage transformation, rather than engage in purely transactional relations:

> Another way to understand the multi-stakeholder cooperative model is to consider the different time horizon inherent in the solidarity approach.

While a traditional price-driven business model (whether cooperative or not) may be seen as primarily transactional, the multi-stakeholder cooperative enterprise is often focused on being more transformational.

(Lund, 2011, p. 5)

In this sense, Lund points out that the prevalent understanding of cooperative entry as a result of market (or government) failure (see Cook and Burress, 2009, for example) needs to be modified as MSCs enter industries in response to social injustice, or 'a rejection of the quality of an important good or service as it is presented in a conventional investor-driven or government-controlled marketplace' (Lund, 2011, p. 5). Indeed, fair pricing, wages and wealth distribution are the core principles of engagement of multiple-stakeholder groups. Particularly, labour inclusion, which is the focus of this volume, is important in that it also reflects uses of multi-stakeholder form of governance for purposes of labour self-determination as a tool for social transformation.[7]

Labour inclusion as a core motivation of multi-stakeholder cooperatives

Among different interpretations of the meaning of worker ownership, a view in support of labour inclusion in ownership and governance as a right to self-management and labour sovereignty is typically motivated by an ethical standpoint or tradition, rooted most notably in the Catholic social doctrine, as originally in Mondragon; socialist aspirations at the root of worker cooperative developments in Italy and elsewhere, as well as in some socialist economies; or labour movements seeking social justice[8] through labour empowerment and economic democracy, as in Latin America, or within the food cooperative movement[9] in the US (Lund, 2011). European social economy tradition is also about 'giving precedence to people and labour over capital [. . . implying they] will tend to preserve employment and quality of service to their members and customers even at the cost of reducing their margin of profit' (Borzaga *et al.*, 2014, p. 6).

Theoretical justification for labour sovereignty can be found in the labour theory of value (Ricardo, Marx) institutionalized in socialist contexts, and more recently in the labour theory of property (Ellerman, 1984, 2016). Ellerman presents a more fundamental argument in favour of worker ownership, arguing that workers are de facto legally responsible for their actions, and should also be the legal owners of the outcomes of their actions. The implication of this argument is:

The legal members of the firm as a legal party would then be the people working in the firm. After abolishing both the owning and renting of persons, private property would finally be founded on 'the principle on which property is supposed to rest'. Such a firm is a democratic firm and the private property market economy of such firms is an economic democracy.

(Ellerman, 2016, p. 34)

Another understanding of labour as a subject of free association, rather than a commodity subject to market exchange, is expressed by Polanyi (1944), who terms labour, money, and natural capital as fictitious commodities, not produced by people for the purpose of exchange.

More recently, De Peuter and Dyer-Witheford (2010) describe worker cooperatives as a form of labour commons. Labour in this framework advances the transformation of social relations and society, as its perception shifts from the object of capital's value practices ('a human resource'), towards a notion of labour power as a collectively and sustainably managed resource for the benefit of society (Azzellini, 2016).

From a more economic perspective, Borzaga and Depedri (2015) conjecture that workers are included in membership because work is difficult and costly to monitor in the social services sector, due to multitasking and its personalized nature that relies on human relationships. Monetary incentives (wages and benefits) trigger extrinsic motivations, but are not effective when intrinsic motivation is key to quality service in healthcare, education, elderly care, or other social services. It is therefore efficient in these cases to empower workers as members. An additional argument in favour of worker self-management in cooperatives is the increased demand for relational goods and customization of services in the new economy (Zamagni, 2014). Motivations for labour inclusion may therefore stem from the ethical stance of the founding members with respect to workers' rights and empowerment, as well as social inclusion through work, and labour's transformative potential.

These theoretical justifications might explain why some of the existing projects of self-management have expanded to multi-stakeholder ventures as the need arose to include a wider community. In other cases, non-worker stakeholder groups may extend ownership and control rights to labour, realizing its fundamental transformative role. While context and historical evolution of these ownership forms vary, evidence points out that workers are members in a significantly large numbers of MSCs in Italy,[10] France, Quebec, Portugal and elsewhere. Even in some jurisdictions such as collective interest cooperatives in France, type B social cooperatives in Italy, or initially in Quebec's solidarity cooperatives, worker membership is mandated by law. In other cases, workers are members because labour inclusion is the purpose and mandate of the cooperative – this may be job creation in general, or inclusion of marginalized workers into the labour force in particular. Italian data further indicate that intrinsic motivation and job satisfaction of workers in multi-stakeholder cooperatives is high and not diminished by the inclusion of other stakeholder groups, compared with worker cooperatives in the same sector (Borzaga and Depedri, 2015, p. 118).

Diverse development trajectories

Institutionalization of multi-stakeholder cooperatives

In recent decades, MSCs have been newly institutionalized through new legal frameworks, and also more recognized in the existing institutional settings. An emerging pattern for the new development of multi-stakeholder cooperatives in jurisdictions where single-member type has been the dominant form appears to be the government failure to provide goods/services, and/or increased engagement of the civil society and communities taking on entrepreneurial ventures for social and community development purpose. These include provision of goods and services and securing local jobs, with various stakeholder groups involved in different ways: from finance to services, consumers to workers.

Social cooperatives in Italy have been developing partly due to government failure to meet the expressed needs for social services, but also due to a growing demand for civil society's participation in the delivery of such services (Vézina and Girard, 2014). Although evolving since the late 1970s, social cooperatives did not fall under a specific legal framework until 1991, when two types of social cooperatives were recognized by law: type A, providing welfare services in specific sectors (social, health and educational services, later extended to other types of services of general interest), and type B, involved in work integration of disadvantaged persons. These social cooperatives were formed for a specific purpose to pursue the general interest of the community as a vehicle for social integration. Italian social cooperatives can include different types of members – workers, users of services, volunteers, finance providers, or legal entities (Borzaga and Depedri, 2014). The majority of social cooperatives include workers as members, with type B cooperatives required to do so by law. Italian law recognized the defining features of already formed social cooperatives: social purpose; collective, democratic, and multi-stakeholder nature of engagement by users and supporters (although not necessarily in governance – see Borzaga et al., 2011); and limitations on the distribution of profits (Borzaga and Depedri, 2014). These elements, together with other factors, provided an enabling environment for the phenomenal growth of this organizational form in subsequent years.

Unlike in Italy where social cooperatives functioned for many years without a law, the legal form for solidarity cooperatives in Quebec preceded practice. In Quebec, the impetus for solidarity cooperative law was given by community revitalization projects as government abandoned these and other local development services (Vézina and Girard, 2014), and by the need to create local, stable jobs. As in Europe, work integration for the marginalized population was also on the policy agenda. Quebec amended its cooperative law to allow for solidarity cooperatives with multiple stakeholders as members. The mandatory stakeholder groups were workers and users of services, with a third supporting member category including anyone with social or economic interest in the cooperative. This requirement was later relaxed to include any two categories of members (ibid.). Although no longer a legal obligation, majority solidarity cooperatives in Quebec do include worker-members. This legal development resulted from the economic summit in 1996 in an effort by the Quebec government, civil society groups, and social movements to create jobs and jumpstart the economy. With job creation high on the priority list, it is no surprise that workers were considered a key stakeholder group.

Collective interest cooperatives in France share similar beginnings. Government austerity and high youth unemployment led to the formation of the multi-stakeholder cooperative form, involving workers, local government, beneficiaries and supporters of the project. Workers are a mandatory member category in these cooperatives (Margado, 2004; Vézina and Girard, 2014).

It is worth mentioning that other countries have also introduced legal frameworks for social cooperatives, with or without provisions for multi-stakeholder governance, such as Portuguese social solidarity cooperatives in 1996 and Spanish social initiative cooperatives in 1999 (Münkner, 2004).

Other non-institutional multi-stakeholder cooperative developments

Whereas a lot has been written in the past couple of decades about the new MSC legal frameworks, less well documented are many cases of multi-stakeholder cooperatives in countries where cooperative law does not exist, or is not prescriptive about membership type. Besides new legal frameworks, MSCs are established under the existing cooperative laws when these are not prohibiting diverse classes of members, as is the case in Germany or Croatia; under the general company law as in Denmark; special laws for community benefit organizations in the UK; or social purpose companies[11] in Belgium (Münkner, 2004). In those instances, MSCs develop around specific concerns – social justice, advocacy, economic development, community development, and the like. Attention to labour self-governance often leads to MSC formation. Notable examples are found in the Mondragon network whose roots are in the Catholic social doctrine; socialist economies where labour sovereignty is paramount to their fundamental economic relations; and new cooperativist movements resisting neoliberal economic policies (among others, 'platform cooperativism' belongs to new types of multi-stakeholder solidarity movements raising against recent developments of precarious employment with digitalization of work due to new technologies (Scholz, 2016; also see Schneider, Chapter 14 in this volume)).

Mondragon cooperative group

Mondragon's founder father Arizmendiarrieta instilled a clear focus on the transformative power of work from the onset of the first cooperative established in 1956. Over the next half century the Mondragon network grew to some 120 cooperatives and 80,000 workers. The number of multi-stakeholder cooperatives in Mondragon also grew over time, as it was recognized that other stakeholder groups besides workers should have the voice in governance[12] of cooperatives established with multiplicity of goals and a different purpose from the initial industrial cooperatives. These include social services, consumer cooperatives, banking, research centres, and a university, to name a few. Therefore, many cooperatives in the Mondragon network today feature the multi-stakeholder governance form, giving voice to diverse stakeholders in a network governance structure (Turnbull, 2002).

The Mondragon story is usually told as a worker cooperative experience. It is important to also understand it from the pragmatic, multi-stakeholder engagement and governance perspective, in order to explore its evolution into today's power-house of networked cooperation. A few years after the first worker cooperative was established in Mondragon, the cooperative bank Caja Laboral was founded as the second-tier cooperative by the group of cooperatives 'comprised of Ulgor, Arrasate, and Funcor worker cooperatives and a consumer cooperative San Jose' (Whyte and Whyte, 1991, p. 52). The Caja Laboral Popular was the first multi-stakeholder, sec-ond-level cooperative of the Mondragon movement. The main purpose of the Caja was to link other cooperatives, finance their creation and expansion and provide technical support for 'community development through cooperativism' (Ormachea, 1993, p. 45). It also initially took on the role of a provider of social security since worker-members were not eligible for government benefits at the time, to later become a separate MSC, Lagun Aro. Similarly, a cooperative school system was devel-oped over time, starting with Eskola Politeknikoa in 1943 (turned into a cooperative in 1956), and it today encompasses education from nursery to the university level, provided and governed by multiple stakeholders, including the local government, students, parents, and cooperatives (Lezamiz and Sanchez Bajo, 2011; Ormachea, 1993). A cooperative employing students, Alecop, was also established as a way for students to earn an income while they also learn the skills on the job and engage in cooperative governance, with representation from three types of constituents: per-manent staff, students, and the contracting cooperatives (Whyte and Whyte, 1991). The first producer-worker MSC, Lana, was established in 1961. Worker-members were integrated into what was originally a producer cooperative. All these innovative forms of enterprise were accompanied by the creation of a research centre, Ikerlan. Its founders included the Eskola Politeknikoa (with its R&D unit), Caja Laboral, and a group of cooperatives. Some 15 research centres with a number of different roles engaged the whole community in later years; Garaia Innovation Centre, for example, includes local small businesses, local government, as well as the Mondragon cooperatives. Besides these developments, the group was creating industrial clusters with a spinoff growth model (Whyte and Whyte, 1991), as well as incubation by the bank and other methods (Lezamiz and Sanchez Bajo, 2011).

The focus on labour rights, and community development through cooperativ-ism that engaged the entire community of stakeholders, allowed the growth of the Mondragon network to today's complex and cohesive group of industrial enter-prises, social services, education, and innovation centres. All cooperatives include workers in their membership, highlighting the philosophical premise on which Mondragon was built.

Croatian cooperatives

Another illustrative case of multi-stakeholder governance with worker ownership as one of the membership types can be found in Croatian cooperatives. Croatian law does not prescribe the type of member relationship with the cooperative, and so long as they support the organization's purpose and mandate, members can patronize the cooperative as consumers, workers, investors, suppliers, community members, civil society or local government representatives. This development is a reflection of the history of cooperatives in the region and path dependence in their evolution. During the last 20 years of socialist self-management, cooperatives were a vehicle for association of independent producers working with their own capital, and self-managed labour in socially owned companies (Golja and Novkovic, 2014; Novkovic and Golja, 2015). Under the socialist institutional arrangements, labour sovereignty demanded a voice; cooperative membership therefore had to be extended to workers employed in cooperatives, besides the independent producers. At this time, cooperatives were predominantly formed by agricultural producers, artists and crafts makers, or independent trades-persons, and with workers as a member category they were multi-stakeholder in character. Current cooperatives in Croatia continue to develop along a multi-stakeholder or a single-stakeholder structure. The MSC form is prevalent in cases of community development, renewable energy, and agro-tourism, among others, with an important role played by various civil society associations. Some examples include PZ Vodnjan, a cooperative with producer members, community investor members, employees, municipal government and an association promoting agro-tourism in the region; Praksa, an urban planning cooperative with diverse members, spanning from urban planners and architects to journalists and community supporters; and Zadruga za dobru ekonomiju (Cooperative for the good economy), whose members are community supporters, an association promoting green economy activism, organic food producers, and a municipal government agency for local development, Mrav.

New cooperative types

In North America, Europe and around the globe, the digitalization of work and the subsequent precariat (Standing, 2011) are creating conditions that are mobilizing the civil society and workers fighting for labour rights and against worker exploitation. In response to these trends, the platform cooperativism movement is slowly gaining ground (Scholz, 2016, 2017):

> Platform cooperativism is a term that describes technological, cultural, political, and social changes. Platform cooperativism is a rectangle of hope. It's not a concrete utopia; it is an emerging economy. Some of the models [. . .] already exist while others are still imaginary apps. Some are prototypes, other are experiments; all of them introduce alternative sets of values.
>
> *(Scholz, 2016, p. 14)*

These new platform cooperatives are rooted in solidarity and engage various stakeholders, from platform developers and hackers, to workers, cooperative educators and activists. Like solidarity movements in Latin America (Laville, 2010; Ranis, 2016; Veltmeyer, 2018; Vieta, 2010), they too call for a system change from 'platform capitalism' promoted as the sharing economy, thriving on the exploitation of workers in precarious jobs and a lack of transparency regarding data ownership and transactions, to platform cooperativism actuating self-help. This has become a movement engaging multiple stakeholders in solidarity, in a push for labour protection and democratization of the digital economy.

Among other multi-stakeholder developments with labour inclusion is the FairShares Model (Ridley-Duff, 2014). Proponents advocate that each stakeholder group ought to participate in decision-making and in income distribution – the founders, workers, users, and investors. The model attempts to socialize power and wealth, moving distributional and decision-making rights from a single stakeholder (owners of capital in the case of investor-owned firms; or labour, producer or user in the case of cooperatives) to multiple stakeholders by issuing a separate class of shares depending on membership type.

Conclusion

In the last few decades more attention has been given to MSCs as cooperatives with a general benefit and socio-economic mandate, due in particular to development of the specific legal frameworks in Italy, Portugal, France, Quebec and elsewhere (Lund, 2011). While single-member cooperatives are criticized for being focused on members only, and degenerating into behaviours characteristic of investor-owned enterprises focused purely on financial return, MSCs explicitly address the internalization of externalities into the mission of the enterprise. MSCs are often involved in the provision of social services and other community services (education, health, culture, environmental services, etc.), although they can be identified in all types of activities. In the US, for example, multi-stakeholder governance is often present in food cooperatives, networked in a movement for local, organic food production with transparent distribution channels and coop-to-coop trade.

The focus in this chapter is to highlight the type of multi-stakeholder cooperative in which labour is one member category among others, with solidarity as a shared value informing the governance structure and goals of the organization. A review of some more recent trends in the formation of MSCs highlights the critical role of labour association for their transformative potential. Such MSCs are formal cooperatives that may arise from single-membership-type cooperatives extending membership to other stakeholders, or ventures starting anew as MSCs. The source of labour participation in ownership and self-management in MSCs may be the engagement of the labour movement or other solidarity movements as a stakeholder (labour focus), or community/policy makers' concern with work integration and provision of stable jobs. More recent concerns with precarious work and digitalization of labour is giving rise to new forms of multi-stakeholder cooperatives acting in solidarity. Another way of looking at MSCs with worker-members is that MSCs can provide a safe negotiating space between workers and/ or producers on the one hand, and other types of stakeholders such as the users, local government representatives or NGOs involved in the MSC project, on the other. Solidarity, reciprocity and a common general purpose typically allows this process to take a more benevolent, rather than necessarily adversarial, form.

An important distinction between different MSCs is that some of these developments, although possibly having a social aim, are about filling the gap left by austerity governments or simply providing a better service/access to resources, while 'new cooperativist' movements (Vieta, 2010) around the world are about social justice and call for a system change that typically includes labour struggles. As such, they may adopt significantly different paths and exhibit different lifecycles.

Regardless of diverse motivations in the global MSC evolutions, this organizational form defies the economic logic built on neo-institutional assumptions where agency costs and decision-making costs increase in a democratic enterprise with heterogeneous members. This costly governance practice is expected in theory to result in a change of ownership structure, i.e. demutualization. Evidence of MSC longevity, growth and endurance seems to suggest that the purpose of these organizations is more cohesive than thought, and that multiple stakeholders engage through reciprocity and solidarity, rather than competing interests. Further, Turnbull makes a case that in the face of increased complexity, multi-stakeholder network governance has competitive advantages for all types of organizations, compared with unitary boards where access to information is at best limited. Mondragon's pragmatic approach also illustrates the transformative potential of multi-stakeholder governance.

Beyond governance issues, advantages of multi-stakeholder engagement are many. Integration of various stakeholders provides access to resources, and to diverse voices and concerns. Solidarity at the heart of social cooperatives, and in particular those who view labour as a vehicle for social transformation (or, a social asset), gives MSCs the needed motivation for social innovation. Multi-stakeholder governance, however, may be costly and ineffective if governance structures enforce the differences between constituent groups, rather than a common purpose (Girard, 2015). A careful and deliberate design for a fair engagement of multiple voices needs to be given due attention.

Notes

1 This is the term in English, used by CICOPA members to describe the worker-member type of cooperative membership. In Spanish this is referred to as *trabajo asociado* and in French *travail associé* ('associated work' or 'associated labour', similar to the expression 'labour association' used here). I use labour association to mark the difference between employee ownership of capital shares (e.g. an ESOP) from 'user' (here work) share.

2 Multi-stakeholder cooperatives in Quebec are termed solidarity cooperatives, for example.

3 see http://ica.coop/en/whats-co-op/history-cooperative-movement

4 An example is Just Us! Cooperative in Canada, with Judes development association and an investor sister cooperative.

5 While stakeholder engagement may fall outside the sphere of ownership or governance (see Borzaga and Depedri, 2015, p. 111), we are concerned with diverse categories of members in MSCs who, by definition, are implicated in ownership and control of the enterprise.

6 Borzaga and Sacchetti (2015) argue that social costs ought to be included in the transactions cost calculation. When they are, the multi-stakeholder option may prove less costly than homogeneous member governance. In particular, they discuss democratic deliberation by multiple constituents as a solution to social issues. When social costs of exclusion are high, multi-stakeholder governance is more likely to fulfil stakeholder-specific and societal needs.

7 See the quote by Arizmendiarrieta in Herrerra (2004).

8 One of the principles in the *Declaration of Philadelphia* (*Declaration concerning the Aims and Purposes of the International Labour Organization, adopted at the 26th session of the ILO, Philadelphia, 10 May 1944*), the foundation of the International Labour Organization, is that labour is not a commodity. This principle is also cited in the ILO's Recommendation 193 of 2002 *on the Promotion of cooperatives*.

9 Examples of multi-stakeholder food cooperatives in the US include Weaver Street Market, North Carolina; Central Coop, Washington; FEDCO Co-op Seeds, Maine; Fifth Season Coop, Wisconsin.

10 'Distinction by types of governance shows that one out of three cooperatives is multi-stakeholder – i.e. it is governed by different classes of patrons, such as employees, volunteers, other institutions and clients of the organization (although clients are involved only in the membership of one out of ten organizations). Another 30 per cent of cooperatives are hybrid organizations, where the membership also comprises other stakeholders, but only workers are members of the board of directors. The percentage of single-stakeholder cooperatives where workers constitute the entire membership is lower (21.2 per cent), although workers are always involved in the membership and are, therefore, the most represented class of patrons' (Borzaga *et al.*, 2011, p. 288).

11 Although only some of the social purpose companies in Belgium are cooperatives, this and other similar examples serve as an illustration of the MSC developments that earned limited attention in the literature. A more careful mapping of these cooperative forms requires more research.

12 It was also the other way around – producer and consumer cooperatives joining the Mondragon group were asked to include the worker-member category in order to maintain the '[...] fundamental principles of [Arizmendiarrieta's] philosophy of cooperatives' (Whyte and Whyte, 1991, p. 55).

References

Azzellini, Dario. Labour as a commons: The example of worker-recuperated companies, *Critical Sociology* (2016): 1–14.

Battilani, Patrizia. Features and determinants of cooperative development in Western countries. In *Cooperative innovations in China and the West*, edited by Caroline Gijselinckx, Li Zhao and Sonja Novkovic, 11–28. London: Palgrave MacMillan, 2014.

Borzaga, Carlo and Sara Depedri. Cooperatives providing welfare services: The case of Italian social cooperatives In *Cooperative innovations in China and the West*, edited by Caroline Gijselinckx, Li Zhao and Sonja Novkovic, 126–142. London: Palgrave MacMillan, 2014.

Borzaga, Carlo and Sara Depedri. Multi-stakeholder governance in civil society organizations In *Civil society, the third sector and social enterprise: Governance and democracy*, edited by Jean-Louis Laville, Dennis R. Young, Philippe Eynaud, 109–121. New York: Routledge, 2015.

Borzaga, Carlo and Silvia Sacchetti. *Why social enterprises are asking to be multi-stakeholder and deliberative: An explanation around the costs of exclusion*, EURICSE Working Paper n. 75|15, Trento: EURICSE, 2015.

Borzaga, Carlo, Riccardo Bodini, Chiara Carini, Sara Depedri, Giulia Galera and Gianluca Salvatori. *Europe in transition: The role of social cooperatives and social enterprises*, EURICSE Working Paper n. 69|14, Trento: EURICSE, 2014.

Borzaga, Carlo, Sara Depedri and Ermanno Tortia. Testing the distributive effects of social enterprises: The case of Italy. In *Social capital, corporate social responsibility, economic behaviour and performance*, edited by Lorenzo Sacconi and Giacomo Degli Antoni, 282–303. New York: Palgrave Macmillan, 2011.

Campi Sara, Jacques Defourny and Olivier Grégoire. Work integration social enterprises: Are they multi-stakeholder and multiple goal organizations. In *Social enterprise: At the crossroads of market, public policies and civil society*, edited by Marthe Nyssens, 29–49. London and New York: Routledge, 2006.

Cook, Michael L. The future of U.S. agricultural cooperatives: A neo-institutional approach, *American Journal of Agricultural Economics* 77, no. 5 (1995): 1153–1159.

Cook, Michael and Molly J. Burress. *A cooperative life cycle framework*, Graduate Institute of Cooperative Leadership (GICL), University of Missouri, 2009.

de Peuter, Greig and Nick Dyer-Witheford. Commons and cooperatives, *Affinities: A Journal of Radical Theory, Culture, and Action* 4, no. 1 (2010): 30–56.

Dow, Gregory. *Governing the firm*. Cambridge: Cambridge University Press, 2003.

Ellerman, David P. Theory of legal structure: Worker cooperatives, *Journal of Economic Issues* 18, no. 3 (1984): 861–891.

___. The labour theory of property and marginal productivity theory, *Economic Thought* 5, no. 1 (2016): 19–36.

Girard, Jean-Pierre. Governance in solidarity. In *Cooperative governance: Fit to build resilience in the face of complexity*, edited by Sonja Novkovic and Karen Miner, 127–134. Brussels: ICA, 2015.

Golja, Tea and Sonja Novkovic. Determinants of cooperative development in Croatia. In *Cooperatives' power to innovate: Texts selected from the international call for papers*, edited by Lou Hammond Ketilson and Marie-Paule Robichaud Villettaz, 15–26. Lévis: International Summit of Cooperatives, 2014.

Hansmann, Henry. *The ownership of enterprise*. Cambridge: The Belknap Press, 1996.

Herrera, David. Mondragon: A for profit organization that embodies catholic social thought, *Review of Business* 25, no. 1 (2004): 56–68.

Laville, Jean-Louis. *The solidarity economy: An international movement*, RCCS Annual Review #2, 2010.

Leviten-Reid, Catherine and Brett Fairbarn. Multi-stakeholder governance in the social economy: Toward a new framework for research?, *ANSERJ Canadian Journal of Nonprofit and Social Economy Research* 2, no. 2 (2011): 25–36.

Lezamiz, Mikel and Claudia Sanchez Bajo. The Mondragon cooperative group. In *Cooperatives, territories and jobs*, edited by Bruno Roelants, Valerio Pellirossi and Olivier Biron, 169–181. Brussels: CECOP-CICOPA Europe, 2011.

Lund, Margaret. *Solidarity as a business model: A multi-stakeholder cooperative manual*. Cooperative Development Centre, Kent State University, 2011.

Margado, Alex. A new cooperative form in France: *Société Coopérative d'Intérêt Collectif* (SCIC). In *Trends and challenges for cooperatives and social enterprises in developed and transition countries*, edited by Carlo Borzaga and Roger Spear, 147–163. Trento: Edizioni 31, 2004.

Münkner, Hans. Multi-stakeholder cooperatives and their legal framework. In *Trends and challenges for cooperatives and social enterprises in developed and transition countries*, edited by Carlo Borzaga and Roger Spear, 49–82. Trento: Edizioni 31, 2004.

Novkovic, Sonja and Tea Golja. Cooperatives and the civil society: Potential for local cooperative development in Croatia, *Journal of Economic and Organizational Diversity* 4, no. 1 (2015): 153–169.

Novkovic, Sonja and Karen Miner. (eds.) (2015) *Cooperative governance fit to build resilience in the face of complexity*. Brussels: ICA, 2015.

Ormachea, José Maria. *The Mondragon cooperative experience*, Mondragon: MCC, Otalora, 1993.

Polanyi, Karl. *The great transformation: The political and economic origins of our time*, Boston: Beacon Press, 1944 (3rd edition 2001).

Ranis, Peter. *Cooperatives confront capitalism: Challenging the neoliberal economy*, London: Zed Books, 2016.

Ridley-Duff, Rory. New co-operativism and the FairShares model, *Stir Magazine* 7 (2014): 12–14.

Scholz, Trebor. *Platform cooperativism: Challenging the corporate sharing economy*. New York: Rosa Luxemburg Stiftung, 2016.

___. *Uberworked and underpaid: How workers are disrupting the digital economy*. Cambridge: Polity Press, 2017.

Spear, Roger. From cooperative to social enterprise: Trends in European experience. In *Trends and challenges for cooperatives and social enterprises in developed and transition countries*, edited by Carlo Borzaga and Roger Spear, 99–114. Trento: Edizioni 31, 2004.

Standing, Guy. *The precariat: The new dangerous class*. London and New York: Bloomsbury Academic, 2011.

Turnbull, Shann. *A new way to govern*, NEF Pocketbook #6. London: New Economics Foundation, 2002.

Veltmeyer, Henry. Cooperativism and development: Latin American dynamics of a social and solidarity economy. In *Cooperativism and local development in Cuba: An agenda for democratic transformation*, edited by Sonja Novkovic and Henry Veltmeyer. Leiden: Brill publishers, 2018.

Vézina, Martine and Jean-Pierre Girard. Multi-stakeholder cooperative model as a flexible sustainable framework for collective entrepreneurship: An international perspective. In *Cooperative innovations in China and the West*, edited by Caroline Gijselinckx, Li Zhao and Sonja Novkovic, 64–78. London: Palgrave MacMillan, 2014.

Vieta, Marcelo. The new co-operativism (editorial), *Affinities: A Journal of Radical Theory, Culture, and Action* 4, no. 1 (2010): 1–11.

Whyte, William Foote and Kathleen King Whyte. *Making Mondragon*. Ithaca: ILR Press, 1991.

Zamagni, Vera. The cooperative enterprise: A valid alternative for a more balanced society. In *Cooperatives in a post-growth era*, edited by Sonja Novkovic and Tom Webb. London: Zed books, 2014.

14

AN INTERNET OF OWNERSHIP

Democratic design for the online economy[1]

Nathan Schneider

On 18 March 2016, at a press conference with US Secretary of Labour Thomas E. Perez on his right and a platform user named Ty Lane on his left, Managed by Q CEO Dan Teran announced, 'Over the next five years, Managed by Q will give 5 percent of the company to the operators working in the field.'[2] On the backdrop behind them, Managed by Q's logo – a futuristic, sans serif grey Q repeated over a black background, much like Uber's *U* – evoked the company's status as one of the many trying to be 'the Uber for *x*' – in this case, the Uber for office cleaning. But Teran's announcement represented a departure from Uber's notorious disavowal of employment responsibility for its drivers, whom it seems impatient to supplant with self-driving cars. In addition to full-time jobs and benefits, Managed by Q was welcoming the platform's worker-users as genuine co-owners.

Co-ownership has mostly been missing in the implicit social contracts of the online economy – the internet-enabled platforms that employ networked forms of connection and transaction to transform industries, workplaces, and livelihoods (Parker *et al.*, 2016). The principal owners of platforms, along with founders, have been the investors who inject capital in expectation of generous returns. Technology companies may offer stock options to early employees; users, in contrast, have been treated like external customers. Yet in many cases they don't pay the company any money while contributing essential content (e.g. virtually everything one encounters on platforms like Facebook or Reddit), or they entrust to the platform their personal data and their livelihoods. Platforms train users to think of themselves as participants in 'peer production' (Benkler, 2007) and a 'sharing economy' (Schor, 2014). But the online economy's ownership structures habitually fail to reflect either the platforms' stated aspirations or their social realities.

Managed by Q's directors, however, recognized that its office cleaning 'operators' were a class of users that served as the company's face to the office-owning clients who provided revenue; co-ownership, therefore, seemed like an appropriate way to incentivize operators to take their responsibility seriously. The announcement also made for good press.

Canonical notions of corporate structure and governance, even when a company serves a wide variety of stakeholders, tend to affirm the practice of granting ownership and control to investors, since they bear direct financial risk (Jensen, 2000; Monks and Minow, 2008; Parmar et al., 2010). But when platforms hold near-monopoly status and wield control over urban transportation networks or data about intimate relationships, their risk profile is more complex than a share price. Platforms increasingly act as infrastructure, enabling productive activity among users – from individuals to large organizations. They're not just a means of production but a means of connection. These webs of dependency, however, have not reached the platforms' boardrooms. Managed by Q's experience, together with a growing body of research on cooperative models, suggests that platform builders may be missing out on opportunities shared ownership could present – from retention, loyalty and diversity among their users to untapped potential for financing and public benefit (Albæk and Schultz, 1998; Davidson, 2016; Hueth, 2014; Molk, 2014; Pérotin, 2016).

The platforms now vying for dominance have tended not to maintain high labour standards, even bending the law in the process (Scholz, 2016b; Slee, 2016). Platform-based workers typically lack the expectation of coverage for illness, injury and retirement. The allure is real, as platforms offer the possibility of independent livelihoods, a departure from the drudgery and discipline of an old-fashioned job. But platform owners enjoy the far more lucrative benefits of having a fluid workforce without a large, fixed payroll. Since the investor-owners generally aren't themselves dependent on income from platform labour, they have little to lose and much to gain from sidestepping the conventional responsibilities of employment.

Less visibly, the mismatch between the interests of platform owners and users presents itself in the realm of data. Ubiquitous platforms like Facebook and Google, as well as others that operate more discreetly, gather reams of data about internet users and offer it as a product. This data supplies a growing surveillance economy based on targeted advertising and pricing, which, intentionally or not, easily bleeds into discrimination of already marginalized populations (Bernasek and Mongan, 2015; Couldry, 2016; Pasquale, 2015). Although a platform like Facebook may insist that users retain ownership of their data, immense and illegible service agreements grant the platform such sweeping rights over that data as to render user ownership close to meaningless. Additionally, the prospect that one's online activity might affect a credit rating, or find its way into the database of a spy agency, has already dampened the free speech that the internet once promised.

As the platform economy reorients how industries operate, it should also challenge taken-for-granted corporate ownership models. Cooperative ownership not only shares wealth more equitably among participants, but it also unlocks efficiencies by reducing the costs of transacting and contracting with an enterprise's essential stakeholders (Bogetoft, 2005; Hansmann, 2000; Hueth, 2014; Molk, 2014; Taylor, 2015). Online platforms have yet to enjoy the value and benefits of this model.

The time seems especially ripe to take up the challenge that Marjorie Kelly (2012) has described as 'ownership design': what ownership structures are appropriate, competitive, and just for an economy orchestrated through platforms? How can corporate structure better align the feedback loops of actual online sociality?

One collective effort to address these questions has come to be called 'platform cooperativism'. As well as a rhetorical insurgency, this initiative has opened a space of experimentation in online ownership design, taking inspiration from the legacy and ownership designs of the mostly offline cooperative movement. This chapter will present and analyse here some of the ways platform cooperativism has begun to generate ownership designs that may serve the platform economy of the future better than have the investor-owned structures that currently prevail.

'The next sharing economy'

Cooperative economies of some kind have probably existed as long as human economies in general. But in parallel with the rise of industrial capitalism, they have formed a distinct and transnational series of niches, with shared values and business practices of its own. From local food and housing cooperatives to vast cooperatives of farmers, retail stores, or electric utilities, this sector generates over US$2.2 trillion in turnover worldwide, often in ways that serve needs unmet by investor-owned businesses.[3] It's a part of the global economy widely relied upon yet overlooked, a 'sharing economy' before Silicon Valley adopted the term.

The prospect of platform cooperativism is at once new and old among the cultures surrounding the internet. Early software and hardware hackers employed certain cooperative-like practices as they assembled the rudiments of the personal computer and the means of networking them. They shared source code; they developed structures of democratic governance across great distances; they resisted corporate enclosure in the process (Benkler, 2007; Coleman, 2012; Kelty, 2008). Small groups of software developers have formed successful worker cooperatives.[4] Some of tech culture's innovations deserve to be studied more closely by the offline cooperative movement, as they demonstrate the plausibility of, and some proven techniques for, highly distributed and productive self-management; many cooperatives emerging among young people today are organized around tech culture's flexible, networked forms of connection rather than recreating industrial-era jobs and membership societies. Platform cooperativism, therefore, is not starting from scratch in tech culture.

Still, true cooperative business models have been almost entirely absent from the online economy. One can at least speculate about the reasons why. The disruptive efficacy of the venture-capital financing mechanism has rendered it a go-to blueprint to the exclusion of other approaches. The technological sophistication necessary to build online enterprises has also proved prohibitive for the often-marginalized communities that tend to adopt cooperative strategies. And until recently the internet could be considered an optional realm of activity; cooperatives tend to appear when people have an unmet need, not to furnish a mere accessory or curiosity. But it is becoming harder and harder, around the world, to secure a livelihood without taking part in the online economy. Perhaps this is why, in the past few years, recognizable platform cooperatives have begun to appear.

The Spanish collective Las Indias distinguished platforms as one type of cooperative in a 2011 blog post (de Ugarte). In 2012 the Italian confederation Legacoop promulgated a manifesto for 'Cooperative Commons', stressing the need for cooperative business models to manage the growing stores of data that users feed to online platforms.[5] Stocksy United, a stock photo platform owned by its photographers, went online the following year. By 2014, Janelle Orsi, founder of the Sustainable Economies Law Center in Oakland, was calling for 'the next sharing economy'[6] – the sharing of cooperative ownership – and was helping to design the bylaws for Loconomics, a gig platform owned by its workers. Dedicated documentation of such projects began in collaboration with the online newsletter *Shareable* (Schneider, 2014); meanwhile, drawing on the lessons of his Digital Labour conferences at The New School, Trebor Scholz coined the term 'platform cooperativism' as an alternative to the systemic abuses of investor-owned platforms (Scholz, 2014, 2016a). Consultation with labour organizations and platform workers led to the 2015 Digital Labour conference, 'Platform Cooperativism: The Internet, Ownership, Democracy', and a subsequent book, *Ours to Hack and to Own* (Scholz and Schneider, 2016). People around the world trying to develop online platforms through democratic ownership and governance began to coalesce their scattered efforts into a new economic ecosystem.

This study derives from the development of the Internet of Ownership,[7] the most exhaustive directory to date of the platform cooperative ecosystem. The directory includes not only 'platform cooperatives' (which adhere to the International Co-operative Alliance's standards for cooperative identity) and various tools and organizations that support them, but also 'shared platforms' (like Managed by Q) that practise shared ownership or governance with platform users, at least in part.

Platform cooperativism can likewise be taken to mean a broad invitation to a fairer online economy through shared ownership and governance; platform cooperatives, however, are strictly those platforms that are also bona fide cooperatives by widely agreed-on standards (Sutton *et al.*, 2016).

Most of the cooperative principles resonate somewhat with the social contracts of the platform economy. 'Voluntary and open membership' is a default practice among platforms, which typically enable anyone (with access to requisite technology) to create an account; 'autonomy and independence', too, is a value that platform owners often assert while disrupting incumbent industries, even while proclaiming a well-meaning 'concern for community'. There is much 'cooperation' among platform companies as well, such as through API protocols and standards-setting organizations like the World Wide Web Consortium. Practices of 'education, training and information' often happen on platforms through much the kind of mutual education – in online forums and in-person meet-ups – that cooperatives encourage among their members.

The resonance, however, only goes so far. Principles two and three – democratic governance and ownership, crucially – are almost wholly absent from the platform economy. Online user-experience design often seeks to divert users' attention from matters of governance and ownership, such as by rendering opaque the processes of revenue generation through apparently 'free' services. Consultation with users on changes to features or policies is, at best, superficial.

Democracy itself has taken on a new meaning online. A web search for 'democratize internet' or the like reveals that in tech culture 'democracy' has come to signify merely an expansion of 'access' to various tools and resources, rather than the collective governance and joint stakeholdership to which the word, in other contexts, refers. That old kind of democracy is illegible to the internet's dominant ownership designs. The contention of platform cooperativism is that the design of platform businesses, and thus of the online economy generally, can and should allow for democracy in the fullest sense. There is no one-size-fits-all solution, and cooperation won't necessarily produce the appropriate response to every design challenge. But these kinds of designs are worth at least considering far more than they have been in the online economy thus far.

Ownership designs

The following sections introduce some of the design patterns (Alexander *et al.*, 1977) that have so far arisen in the experimentation of platform cooperativism and related undertakings, drawing from published material on the projects' websites and conversations with their participants. Most of the projects referred to can be found in the Internet of Ownership directory, as well as the 'showcases' in *Ours to Hack and to Own*. While nearly all are too early-stage for a thoroughgoing evaluation, the patterns they embody at least trace the outlines of a new palette of options for ownership design in the online economy.

Work: value creators as value owners

Amazon's Mechanical Turk platform, which enables posting and carrying out piece-work tasks (tag some images, transcribe a recording, fill out a survey), gets its name from an 18th-century curiosity in which a human chess player sat discreetly inside a machine, dazzling the public and contemporary notables alike with its apparently mechanical intelligence. The reference is too apt for comfort; the human beings working on Mechanical Turk appear through the platform almost as if they were just another algorithm. Starting in 2014, these workers mounted a widely publicized email-writing campaign called 'Dear Jeff Bezos', alerting the Amazon CEO to the fact that 'Turkers are not only actual human beings, but people who deserve respect, fair treatment and open communication.'[8]

Workers on Mechanical Turk, for instance, enjoy no minimum wage or ability to rate the behaviour of the pseudonymous employers who meanwhile rate theirs. And while this case is egregious, it is not unique. In 2016, as many as 24 per cent of US adults reported earning income on platforms (Smith, 2016). The prevailing platform business model is to achieve scale while reducing labour costs and interference in management, automating tasks wherever possible.

Platform cooperativism inclines towards a different approach, one in which the people contributing value co-own the platforms and help decide to what ends they operate. The aforementioned Loconomics, for instance, is a platform cooperative for short-term gigs whose freelancers are also co-owners; unlike 'Turkers', who rarely receive replies from Amazon when they submit complaints, Loconomics is designed to benefit from worker participation in governance. Its member-owners invest in the platform through periodic dues. The stock photo platform Stocksy United, incorporated as a Canadian cooperative, has found that including the photographers as members (alongside staff and founders) is a way of recruiting more talented contributors than might otherwise be possible, and of prioritizing artistic quality over ruthless expansion. Stocksy United includes around 1,000 artist-members, based in dozens of countries, and their work grossed more than US$10 million in revenue during 2016. Through an online forum, they discuss the business of the platform with the day-to-day employees, who are members of the cooperative as well.

Part of securing fair work-lives on platforms is the development of 'portable benefits' that don't rely on any one employer, but that better suit the promiscuous connectivity of a platform economy. This, too, is a job well suited to cooperative models – hearkening back to the cooperatives and mutuals that gave birth to the modern insurance industry. The Freelancers Union in the United States and SMart, a network of cooperatives across Europe, have delivered benefits to many thousands of independent workers, relying heavily on online tools. This kind of model, often in cooperative forms, is proliferating rapidly (Conaty *et al.*, 2016).

The storied successes of 20th-century worker cooperativism – such as the Mondragon Corporation in the Basque Country and the Emilia-Romagna region of Italy – sought to secure full-time industrial jobs. But many in the latest generation of cooperatives seem designed to free their members from the need for a job altogether. Prime Produce, for instance, is a cooperative co-working space in New York City that prefers the language and ethic of 'craft' over 'work'; the New Zealand-based cooperative network Enspiral aspires to redefine work as 'stuff that matters'. 'Open companies' (such as Gratipay, a crowdfunding platform) or 'open value networks' (such as Sensorica, which develops scientific instruments) seek to rely on no fixed payroll at all, but to create products by rewarding the contributions of participants through a distributed platform. In Barcelona and the surrounding region, the Catalan Integral Cooperative draws member-owners in first by facilitating freelance work, and then by enabling them to obtain food, housing and services through internal trade and mutual credit rather than relying on earned euros. Some of its members have been involved in creating FairCoop, which proposes to do much the same on a global scale by connecting local 'nodes' through online tools, including a cryptocurrency called FairCoin (Schneider, 2015b).

Platforms need not regard those who contribute value through them as temporary stand-ins for algorithms. By orienting their business models around such contributors, platforms can provide not only decent livelihoods, but also a means of bypassing dependency on employment relations altogether.

Data: treat it like it's someone's stuff

Much as Mechanical Turk disguises value-contributing workers behind a platform, business models based on so-called 'big data' often seek to disguise the fact that they're capturing value from those contributing it. Facebook, for instance, provides extensive privacy controls by which users can customize what other users see about them – few of which affect, however, what Facebook itself sees, records, and claims licence to monetize. The economic power and promise of large pools of human data depend on the relinquishment of certain ownership rights by the humans involved, such as through opaque service agreements. These pools, in turn, can become outsourced repositories for government intelligence and law enforcement agencies.

What would less duplicitous ownership designs for data look like? Commodify. us, for instance, has prototyped a model by which users can download a copy of their data from Facebook, then re-upload it, selecting which licence they would like to apply to each data set – allowing them to monetize their data on their own terms. A more developed version of that general idea is TheGoodData, a London-based cooperative, which allows users to monetize their browsing data with a browser extension and donate the proceeds to charitable causes. Meanwhile, under the aegis of MIT and the Qatar Computing Research Institute, an ambitious initiative called Solid ('social linked data') proposes a framework for a new species of social applications based on modular, consensual data-sharing agreements, granting users granular control over what they share.

Given the centrality of trust and ownership in matters of data, particularly highly personal data, cooperative business models may be especially well suited to building data economies that are both transparent and competitive. Starting with highly sensitive medical data, the Swiss platform MIDATA.coop is developing a business model for personal data storage based on cooperative ownership and governance, together with secure open-source software. In the United States, meanwhile, out of the longstanding legacy of farmer cooperatives has come AgXchange, a farmer-owned platform for agricultural data.

A further use for data cooperatives is in practising the sixth cooperative principle of cooperation among cooperatives. Already, established cooperatives like Ringlink Scotland (which supports agricultural business development) facilitate data-sharing among their members. Newer projects, such as the US-based Data Commons Cooperative and CoopData.org, seek to provide platforms for data-sharing among cooperatives that can help them find each other and work together. The promise of big data need not depend on ambiguous or duplicitous ownership arrangements.

Finance: rent capital, don't be rented by it

Some assume that cooperatives are incompatible with large-scale financing, that they must forego the growth and innovation that investor ownership enables. A glance at the global cooperative sector, however, belies this. It is true that cooperatives cannot cede the powers of governance and ownership that investors typically expect, but in areas where cooperatives have flourished, they have formed quite formidable financial institutions – such as credit unions and cooperative banks – to hold capital and make it available to the sector for growth. José María Arizmendiarrieta, founder of the Mondragon Corporation, insisted that cooperatives have a responsibility to capitalize: 'A cooperativism without the structural ability to attract and assimilate capital at the level of the demands of industrial productivity is a transitory solution, an obsolete formula' (2013).

Rather than ruling out the possibility of financing, cooperative models require a different kind of ownership design in their financing schemes than businesses that invite investor control. Thus far, however, the online economy has relied on a venture capital investment model based on granting considerable rights to early investors, followed by an eventual 'exit' through either selling the company to another company or trading shares on speculative markets. For platform cooperativism to take hold as a live option for enterprises, other designs are needed.

Loomio is a New Zealand-based worker cooperative that produces a popular online decision-making platform. Venture capital was not an option, and the team members considered adopting non-profit status, but found it incompatible with their ambitions for scale. By early 2016, however, they had raised a round of US$450,000 from investors who supported their mission and regarded their worker-owned structure as adequate assurance. The investors purchased non-voting, redeemable-preference shares, assuring a return based on the company's revenue without compromising its cooperative model. While the investment remains a modest one by Silicon Valley standards, it beckons toward more sizable promise.

Cooperatives were, in a sense, the original crowdfunding, allowing communities to self-fund enterprises that served them. And while online crowdfunding has been an effective enabler of new initiatives, it lacks the shared ownership of cooperatives. New platforms want to bring that back. Seedbloom is building a blockchain-based equity crowdfunding tool, enabling contributors to become co-owners of the projects they support; it has already helped enable the development of Resonate, a cooperative music-streaming platform owned by fans, musicians, and labels. Open Collective, while not a cooperative, is a crowdfunding tool that enables groups to form online cooperatives and manage their budgets without need for formal incorporation or a bank account. Tools like these can help significantly lower the barriers to cooperative formation.

A vibrant platform cooperative sector will require a variety of financing mechanisms. Based in Barcelona, Sharing Accelerator is developing a model for supporting early startups in ways conducive to cooperative ownership. Purpose Capital is an emerging investment firm designed from the start to specialize in 'self-owned', 'purpose-driven' companies that seek sustainable growth, not a rapid exit; as the companies grow, their success enables new companies to join a mutually supporting ecosystem. FairCoop is attempting to create a global cooperative financial system with several concurrent mechanisms, including its own cryptocurrency, a mutual-credit network, a savings service, and a variety of mission-driven funds.

An opportunity for platform cooperative investment that often goes overlooked is the existing offline cooperative sector. While some large, well-capitalized coopera-tives have begun investing in platforms, they often face a learning curve in doing so. Just as the tech sector is still learning how to develop online cooperatives, the coop-erative sector must learn how to apply its financial resources and know-how online.

What unites these various forms of cooperative-friendly financing is how they reverse the conventional corporate model, in which capital rents workers' time and seeks to extract profit from customers. In cooperatives, online and off, participants find capital when they need it and rent it on their own terms.

Policy: local value for local benefit and control

Confronting the platform economy's onrush of disruptions, policy makers have found themselves in the position of trying to say 'no', in various and sometimes futile ways, as they attempt to retain appropriate control over their economic infrastructures. Ride-sharing platforms destabilize structures for taxi regulation, and room-renting platforms unsettle tourism policies. Both bypass established compromises in labour relations. Industries that were once more or less locally governed and owned are now orchestrated from the platforms' headquarters far away – and those platforms' inves-tors insist on taking a sizable cut. Platform cooperativism gestures towards a new set of options to consider, towards something policy makers can say 'yes' to.

Cooperatives have long represented this kind of constructive alternative, and in many parts of the world their flourishing has been made possible through proactive policy. In the United States, for instance, the Department of Agriculture provided grants and loans for the creation of electric utility cooperatives in rural areas that investor-owned companies opted not to electrify, starting in the 1930s; today, federal agencies have begun helping some of those same cooperatives offer user-owned broadband service. Cooperatives are a tool not only for meeting needs that capital markets fail to meet, but for doing so justly, in a way that keeps wealth among the constituencies that create it. To this effect, Michel Bauwens and others have theorized the 'partner state' as a framework for governments that enable, but do not control or direct, the flourishing of cooperative and commons-oriented enter-prise (Kostakis and Bauwens, 2014). The city of Barcelona has taken early steps to enshrine platform cooperativism into its economic strategies. And in August 2016, UK Labour Party leader Jeremy Corbyn issued a 'Digital Democracy Manifesto' that included 'platform cooperatives' among its eight planks.

In her statement for the 2015 Platform Cooperativism conference,[9] New York City Council member Maria del Carmen Arroyo wrote, 'Worker cooperatives offer a viable method to address the long-term challenge of reducing the num-ber of chronically unemployed and underemployed residents and the number of workers trapped in low-paying jobs.' To this end, she had already supported legislation to fund worker-cooperative development in the city, as well as steps toward preferential treatment for cooperatives in city infrastructure contracting. She added that platform cooperativism 'can put the public in greater control of the Internet, which can often feel like an abyss we are powerless over'.

Taking the example of the accommodation-rental platform Airbnb, Janelle Orsi has proposed three kinds of cooperative alternatives, outlining a distinct role for government in the ownership design of each (Schneider, 2015a). What she calls 'Co-bnb' would be a cooperative owned by the renters of rooms in a given area; 'Munibnb' would be owned and operated by cities as a public good, enabling them to set controls and caps on short-term rentals; similarly city-managed, 'Allbnb' would add the principle of redirecting the profits from the platform back to residents as dividends, recognizing the fact that, when visitors come, their hosts are all the city's residents, not just those from whom they rent a room.

Such municipal ownership models have been pioneered by so-called 'sharing cities' such as Seoul, South Korea, which has restricted certain platforms while promoting the development of local alternatives. Municipal ownership is not strictly cooperative – it violates the cooperative principle of 'autonomy and independence', among others – but this approach recognizes that, as stewards of common infrastructure, governments are essential stakeholders in the platform economies that rely on such infrastructure to operate. And cities may prefer the accountable autonomy of cooperative models to municipal control; after Uber and Lyft stopped doing business in Austin, Texas, the city government seeded the development of a taxi cooperative and non-profit ride-sharing platform to take their place.

When a platform serves the role of organizing and enabling the transactions throughout an entire sector of the economy, it should be regarded as a public utility. Just as the monopolies of connective railroads inspired the US antitrust laws of a century ago, a recognition is growing that new strategies of enforcement, and perhaps new laws, are needed to regulate the emerging online utilities (Khan, 2016). Enabling transitions to more democratic ownership designs may be a way to help these platform utilities better self-regulate, rather than inviting more stifling regulatory regimes.

Ownership transitions

What would it take to have an economy in which a can-do entrepreneur with an idea for a platform – the kind of person who wants nothing more than to create something new and excellent and receive some fair compensation for succeeding – will conclude that their best way to proceed is by practising democracy? The answer, of course, is that it would take a lot of things at once. Ownership design is best considered a process of open-ended choices, based on patterns that we test and apply iteratively (Alexander *et al.*, 1977). Integral to the designs themselves, therefore, are the processes for instantiating them.

Offline, there are two basic kinds of cooperative development: startups and conversions. Startups that begin as cooperatives from their inception have the chance to hard-wire cooperative values into their structures and cultures; they typically rely on the widespread recognition of an unmet need. Conversion, meanwhile, involves transitioning an existing enterprise to democratic ownership and governance, combining a proven business model and its existing momentum with a structure better aligned to serve the people who rely on it.

Startups might come in several forms. Some will be bootstrapped – drawing on existing communities of users to finance and populate a platform that meets their needs, perhaps through equity crowdfunding. Along these lines, venture capitalist Brad Burnham of Union Square Ventures envisions a new generation of less risky 'skinny platforms' that deliver lower returns to investors and higher returns to labour. He told Shareable in 2015, 'We can generate a return participating in that, and we think that's what we should be doing' (Geraci, 2015). Other kinds of startups, meanwhile, might spin off from existing cooperatives, online or off, perhaps retaining an association through a federation or other forms of ongoing cooperation. For instance, the German cooperative marketplace platform Fairmondo is spreading to the UK through the aid of two existing cooperatives – Fairmondo itself and Worth Cooperating in the UK – with the intention of creating a freestanding multi-stakeholder cooperative.

Conversions, too, can come in various forms. One is a mature-stage transition. Especially when a product is unproven or lacks a ready community of users, a cooperative structure may not be the appropriate ownership design early on; it makes sense, then, that forward-thinking founders and investors should hold the risk, as well as the opportunity, for reward. Once a community of users forms, however, the nature of the business changes, and cooperative ownership models become more appropriate – such as to govern labour policies or the use of personal data. A loyal and active community can provide the founders with a fair return for their early innovation and investment; shared ownership, meanwhile, can help keep that community loyal and active and interested in their platform's success. Another kind of conversion – more speculative and challenging, to be sure – could take place once a platform has achieved the sort of ubiquity that makes it, in essence, a monopoly-utility.

For instance, as former Harvard Library director Robert Darnton contends (2009 and elsewhere), Google Books has created a unique and essential information commons by scanning and making available documents that may never be scanned again; a company whose chief responsibility is shareholder profit, however, does not seem to be the appropriate steward for an archive of such immeasurable value. A new generation of antitrust law might finance and aid a transfer of ownership to those who depend on them. Cooperative models are both proven and adaptive enough to merit consideration as we design and adopt – so far with too little foresight – the platform utilities of the 21st-century economy.

Despite the one-way determinism that often characterizes tech culture's 'futurist' speculations, the rise of platform cooperativism offers the corrective that a range of ownership designs are possible besides the presently dominant ones. These designs can result in better alignment between platforms and their users, as well as fairer distributions of value among those who create it and the communities that enable them to do so. But such designs, like the current dispensation, are not inevitable. They are choices.

Notes

1 This chapter stems from an ongoing collaboration with Trebor Scholz, and while he is innocent of my oversights, I am indebted to his insights. The following has also benefited from the input and feedback of Devin Balkind, Josef Davies-Coates, Enric Duran, Daniel Hu, Brent Hueth, Tim Kuhn, and Keith Taylor, in part through an open review process at https://ioo.coop. It is adapted from an essay first developed for the *Sociological Review*.
2 https://vimeo.com/159580593.
3 http://ica.coop/en/facts-and-figures.
4 A directory of North American examples is available from https://techworker.coop.
5 http://cooperativecommons.coop/index.php/en/manifesto.
6 https://youtube.com/watch?v=xpg4PjGtbu0.
7 https://ioo.coop.
8 http://wearedynamo.org/dearjeffbezos.
9 http://platform.coop/2015/participants/maria-del-carmen-arroyo.

References

Albæk, Svend and Christian Schultz. On the relative advantage of cooperatives, *Economics Letters* 59, no. 3 (1998): 397–401.

Alexander, Christopher, Sara Ishikawa and Murray Silverstein. *A pattern language: Towns, buildings, construction*, Oxford: Oxford University Press, 1977.

Arizmendiarrieta, José Maria. *Reflections*. Mondragon: Otalora, 2013.

Benkler, Yochai. *The wealth of networks: How social production transforms markets and freedom*. New Haven, CT: Yale University Press, 2007.

Bernasek, Anna and D. T. Mongan. *All you can pay: How companies use our data to empty our wallets*. New York: Nation Books, 2015.

Bogetoft, Peter. An information economic rationale for cooperatives, *European Review of Agricultural Economics* 32, no. 2 (2005): 191–217.

Coleman, Gabriella. *Coding freedom: The ethics and aesthetics of hacking*. Princeton, NJ: Princeton University Press, 2012.

Conaty, Pat, Alex Bird and Philip Ross. *Not alone: Trade union and co-operative solutions for self-employed workers*. Manchester: Co-operatives UK, 2016.

Couldry, Nick. The price of connection: 'surveillance capitalism', *The Conversation*, 22 September, 2016. https://theconversation.com/the-price-of-connection-surveillance-capitalism-64124.

Darnton, Robert. Google and the future of books, *New York Review of Books*, 29 February, 2009.

Davidson, Adam. Managed by Q's 'good jobs' gamble, *New York Times Magazine*, 25 February, 2016.

de Ugarte, David. Tipologías de las cooperativas de trabajo, *El Jardín Indiano*, 18 September, 2011.

Geraci, John. Interviewed: Venture capitalist Brad Burnham on skinny platforms, *Shareable*, 22 June, 2015. http://shareable.net/blog/interviewed-venture-capitalist-brad-burnham-on-skinny-platforms.

Hansmann, Henry. *The ownership of enterprise*. Cambridge, MA: Belknap Press, 2000.

Hueth, Brent. Missing markets and the cooperative firm. In *Conference on Producer Organizations,* Toulouse School of Economics, 5–6 September, 2014.

Jensen, Michael C. *A theory of the firm: Governance, residual claims, and organizational forms.* Cambridge, MA: Harvard University Press, 2000.

Kelly, Marjorie. *Owning our future: The emerging ownership revolution.* Oakland, CA: Berret-Koehler Publishers, 2012.

Kelty, Christopher M. *Two bits: The cultural significance of free software and the internet.* Durham, NC: Duke University Press, 2008.

Khan, Lina. How to reboot the FTC, *Politico,* 13 April, 2016. http://politico.com/agenda/story/2016/04/ftc-antitrust-economy-monopolies-000090.

Kostakis, Vasilis and Michel Bauwens. *Network society and future scenarios for a collaborative economy.* New York: Palgrave Macmillan, 2014.

Molk, Peter. The puzzling lack of cooperatives, *Tulane Law Review* 88, no. 5 (2014): 899–958.

Monks, Robert A. G. and Nell Minow. *Corporate Governance,* 4th ed. London: John Wiley & Sons, 2008.

Parker, Geoffrey G., Marshall W. Van Alstyne and Sangeet Paul Choudary. *Platform revolution: How networked markets are transforming the economy – and how to make them work for you.* New York: W. W. Norton & Company, 2016.

Parmar, Bidhan L., R. Edward Freeman, Jeffrey S. Harrison, Andrew C. Wicks, Lauren Purnell and Simone de Colle. Stakeholder theory: The state of the art, *Academy of Management Annals* 4, no. 1 (2010): 403–445.

Pasquale, Frank. *The black box society: The secret algorithms that control money and information.* Cambridge, MA: Harvard University Press, 2015.

Pérotin, Virginie. *What do we really know about worker co-operatives?* Manchester: Co-operatives UK, 2016.

Schneider, Nathan. Owning is the new sharing, *Shareable,* 21 December, 2014. http://shareable.net/blog/owning-is-the-new-sharing.

____. 5 ways to take back tech, *The Nation,* 27 May, 2015a. https://thenation.com/article/5-ways-take-back-tech/.

____. Be the bank you want to see in the world, *Vice* 22, no. 4 (April, 2015b): 80–92.

Scholz, Trebor. Platform cooperativism vs. the sharing economy, 2014. https://medium.com/@trebors/platform-cooperativism-vs-the-sharing-economy-2ea737f1b5ad.

____. *Platform cooperativism: Challenging the corporate sharing economy.* New York: Rosa Luxembourg Siftung, 2016a.

____. *Uberworked and underpaid: How workers are disrupting the digital economy.* Cambridge: Polity, 2016b.

Scholz, Trebor and Nathan Schneider. (eds) *Ours to hack and to own: The rise of platform cooperativism, a new vision for the future of work and a fairer internet,* New York: OR Books, 2016.

Schor, Juliet. Debating the sharing economy, *Great Transition Initiative,* 2014. http://greattransition.org/publication/debating-the-sharing-economy.

Slee, Tom. *What's yours is mine: Against the sharing economy.* New York: OR Books, 2016.

Smith, Aaron. *Gig work, online selling and home sharing,* Pew Research Center, 2016. http://pewinternet.org/2016/11/17/gig-work-online-selling-and-home-sharing.

Sutton, Maira, Cat Johnson and Neal Gorenflo. A Shareable explainer: What is a platform co-op?, *Shareable,* 16 August, 2016. http://shareable.net/blog/a-shareable-explainer-what-is-a-platform-co-op.

Taylor, Keith. Learning from the co-operative institutional model, *Administrative Sciences* 5, no. 3 (2015): 148–164.

CONCLUSION

Bruno Roelants

Cooperatives significantly contribute to the world of work: they make up 10 per cent of the global employed population (see Eum, ch. 5). This figure does not take into account the impact on numerous persons who, as members of credit cooperatives, have obtained productive loans to start or consolidate an economic activity (Kornginnaya, ch. 7) or who, as members of an insurance cooperative, have obtained critical risk coverage, or those who, as members of an energy cooperative, have had access to electricity to launch a business in remote rural areas. Considering that a large part of the estimated 1.2 billion cooperative members are either producer-members, worker-members or user-members who obtain key inputs to start and consolidate a business, cooperative work and cooperative-supported work represent by far the largest movement of work organized jointly by citizens. The wider social and solidarity economy (which also includes mutuals, non-profits, foundations, worker-owned enterprises, socio-economic associations, social enterprises, etc.), of which cooperatives are the main pillar, represents an even more impressive share of the world's employed. Cooperatives also represent a strong model for SME clustering, as recognized by the ILO, thus spinning a wide and complex web of self-defined employment relationships in the world of work.[1]

Yet, for much that these quantitative estimates may be impressive, there is a cooperative feature which is even more relevant to labour, and evident in the contributions to this book: the capacity of cooperatives to constantly invent, generate and spread innovative solutions when facing the challenges of the changing world of work (Schwettmann, ch. 2): practical ways to move away from the informal economy (Eum, ch. 5; Dias and Ogando, ch. 8) and poverty (Ya-Bititi *et al.*, ch. 6; Kornginnaya, ch. 7), specific methods to organize freelancers in cooperatives (Puusa and Hokkila, ch. 11; Boudes, ch. 12), the practice of workers restructuring and saving the enterprises in which they work (Vieta, ch. 10), the empowerment of women within the enterprise (Ya-Bititi *et al.*, ch. 6; Kornginnaya, ch. 7;

Dias and Ogando, ch. 8), the combination of various interest groups within the same enterprise including the workers themselves (Novkovic, ch. 13), adherence to and advancing decent work standards (Eşim *et al.*, ch. 3), or the creation of democratically controlled online platforms, also often among different stakeholders (Schneider, ch. 14). In these efforts, cooperatives simply do what they have been doing since their emergence in the early 19th century, when they started helping the emerging proletariat survive with affordable daily provisions, and the small farmers organize and sell their produce: reinvent themselves when new needs and aspirations emerge. Indeed, cooperatives are oriented towards meeting these needs and aspirations and, since they are constantly changing, cooperatives are bound to innovate continuously.

In this drive for innovation, we observe a strive towards creating jobs and economic activities, but also towards making these more sustainable and resilient, moving towards more formal arrangements with better social protection (Eum, ch. 5; Kor nginnaya, ch. 7; Dias and Ogando, ch. 8; Puusa and Hokkila, ch. 11), improved people's knowledge through training (Kor nginnaya, ch. 7; Boudes, ch. 12), improved financial means by acting as intermediaries (Ya-Bititi *et al.*, ch. 6; Schneider, ch. 14) or directly providing loans to support the real economy (Kor nginnaya, ch. 7), organizing data for producers/freelancers (Schneider, ch. 14), offering better transport conditions to go to work or deliver one's production (Ya-Bititi *et al.*, ch. 6), adherence to decent work standards (Eşim *et al.*, ch. 3) or better connectivity (Schneider, ch. 14), create a better income balance within the family and better work–life balance (Kor nginnaya, ch. 7; Ya-Bititi *et al.*, ch. 6; Puusa and Hokkila, ch. 11).

To a large extent, the engine of this innovation drive is the internal governance system of cooperatives, corresponding to the second part of their international definition, being jointly owned and democratically controlled enterprises. One of the first effects of democracy, be it in an enterprise or in a country, is that it lays bare all the tensions, anger, frustrations, injustice and inequalities existing among that community of persons, and brings to light the existence of different interest groups and types of stakeholders. Such emergence creates the possibility to make an inventory of the existing problems, then try to solve them. This book lays particular emphasis on gender, with three chapters dedicated to that dimension (Ya-Bititi *et al.*, ch. 6; Kor nginnaya, ch. 7; Dias and Ogando, ch. 8), because women play a fundamental role in the world of work. Along these three chapters, we can observe that the process towards adequate representation of women's specific interests within cooperatives gradually brings about more equality at work, in terms of remuneration, treatment, working conditions, and so on, and that, in the end, this is in the interest of men as well, as women's improved income has a strong impact on the stability of the family income. It is probable that this increased stability allows families to invest in their children's education, and thus in the future of their children's work as well.

The same process of reduction of tensions and inequalities takes place among other types of stakeholders within a cooperative, provided, of course, that democratic control is properly carried out: among 'blue collar' and 'white collar' workers in an industrial enterprise being restructured into a cooperative (Vieta, ch. 10) and in which the voting rights do not depend on the colour of one's collar; among different types of producers and freelancers who join a cooperative where members pursue their own professional activities (Puusa and Hokkila, ch. 11; Boudes, ch. 12); among various types of stakeholders (including workers and producers) who join a multi-stakeholder cooperative (Novkovic, ch. 13), a cooperative platform (Schneider, ch. 14) or a cooperative value chain (Schwettmann, ch. 2).

In spite of cooperatives' achievements so far, the ongoing wave of transformation of the world of work is only beginning to surge, and cooperatives are faced with big challenges in order to ride it. Here are some of the main challenges ahead:

- Myriad isolated small-scale agricultural producers with no access to business scales or negotiating power find themselves increasingly powerless in the face of global competition; at the same time, we observe a vertiginous increase of self-employed people in the secondary and tertiary sectors, also lacking business scales and negotiating power; this reality presents a massive challenge for the cooperative movement to support them in organizing common services together.

- Compliance to labour standards (Eşim *et al.*, ch. 3) and social protection levels (Eum, ch. 5) are becoming increasingly unequal, not only among countries but increasingly within countries, and in particular between workers with employment status and those with self-employed status. In many countries today, worker-members of worker cooperatives can only have a self-employed status (García Jiménez, ch. 4), including those who restructured their enterprise and previously enjoyed an employee status with the corresponding social protection. At the same time, independent producers and freelancers in some countries are organizing themselves in cooperatives partly in order to optimize their social protection (Puusa and Hokkila, ch. 11), obtain a full-fledged employee status (Boudes, ch. 12) or simply find occasional jobs through a kind of cooperative interim agency that provides them with some level of social protection (Eum, ch. 5). However, these new experiences are still numerically insignificant in comparison with the growing needs in this field.

- Whereas SMEs are the main employers in many countries, large numbers of them are disappearing each year for a number of reasons: they may be family businesses without successors and are not sufficiently attractive to external investors; they may have suffered internal management problems, or a lack of proper industrial policies, or they are part of a business group that wants to delocalize the activity to another country, etc. These trends are bound to accelerate. Cooperatives have experience in successfully restructuring such businesses through worker buyouts, in particular in the midst of traditional industrial clusters (like in central and northeast Italy, see Vieta, ch. 10) and in directly clustering SMEs (like the Mondragon group in the Spanish Basque region). But the needs in the fields of restructuring and clustering are accelerating, and cooperatives should keep pace with this need.

- As Schwettmann (ch. 2) rightly points out, while large multinationals have gained control of entire global chains of production and distribution, cooperatives are still by and large confined to national boundaries. The examples of cooperative value chains which he evokes in his chapter are very interesting and bode well for the future, but are still a drop in the ocean in terms of contribution to international trade. An expansion of the cooperative movement in this field is fundamental to help determine fairer prices, and therefore better remuneration and social protection to millions of individual producers.

There are three main avenues to meet the above-mentioned challenges: (1) reinforce the meso level among cooperatives; (2) create and strengthen alliances and networking with other actors; and (3) engage in advocacy for conducive policy and legislative environment:

1) The whole fabric of local, national, continental and global federative structures among cooperatives has been fundamental in achieving the level of identity and structuring which the cooperative movement has attained today, a century or more after the beginning of such process. However, cooperatives still suffer from vulnerability and isolation, and the 'meso' dimension needs to be strongly reinforced.

    - A first component of this meso dimension is training and education, including exchanges of experience. Although training and education are part of the cooperative principles and although cooperatives often dedicate more efforts to it than other enterprises and economic organizations on average, the weakness of cooperative training is still a worldwide problem. Training and education are fundamental to the democratic control component of cooperatives, not to mention their need for professional re-skilling and multi-skilling. Education cannot remain at the individual cooperative level only. This is the key role that needs to be played by federations and networks, as the examples in this volume illustrate, namely cooperative members from the Indian state of Karnataka visiting the Amul cooperative group in the Indian state of Gujarat (Kornginnaya, ch. 7), or the Brazilian cooperatives learning from housing cooperatives in neighbouring Uruguay (Dias and Ogando, ch. 8).
    - Such exchanges have been fundamental in shaping the cooperative movement since the 19th century, and an acceleration of exchanges can be observed today thanks to the modern means of communication. These efforts should be further encouraged considering their proven efficacy in terms of training and reinforcement of cooperative networks.
    - The meso level directly deals with all the developmental instruments of the cooperative movement, such as financing tools, entrepreneurial advisory services, clusters and consortium strategies, etc., and which can also negotiate the policies and legislation that will promote such instruments.

- The meso level is where the monitoring of labour standards can be done through a series of procedures, like the French cooperative auditing system (*révision coopérative*). Tools to develop the concrete application and monitoring of the labour standards, and in particular the Fundamental Principles and Rights at Work (FPRW), should be devised at national and international levels as part of the federations' work (Eşim *et al.*, ch. 3).

2) The cooperative movement then needs to create and strengthen alliances and networks with other actors.

- A first fundamental type of alliance is with the trade unions. Kurimoto (ch. 9) and Vieta (ch. 10) illustrate the potential of actions promoted jointly by the cooperative movement and trade unions. In Japan's case, this is through the establishment of consumer, insurance and worker cooperatives that have benefited a large portion of workers and their families, to such a point that the ratio of cooperative membership to the population is much higher than the level of unionization in that country (Kurimoto, ch. 9). In the case of Italy, this is demonstrated through the establishment of a financial and legal system to process sustainable worker buyouts (Vieta, ch. 10). However, in the case of Japan, the two sides have gone through diverging trajectories since the Second World War; and in the case of Italy, the potential of a stronger alliance between the two sides is much bigger than what has been attained so far. This observation can be extended to many countries and to the international level. Far more should and can be done in this field (Schwettmann, ch. 2).
- Beyond the trade unions, we find a wide spectrum of social movements with which the cooperative movement should create alliances in the promotion of decent work (Schwettmann, ch. 2), and as illustrated by the example of the national waste picker movement in Brazil (Dias and Ogando, ch. 8). In particular, alliances with informal workers', women's, fair trade and environmental movements would be very beneficial to the cause of cooperatives and their members.
- Even more obvious but not necessarily easier is to build alliances with other actors of the social and solidarity economy, a concept born in France and extended throughout Europe (in particular through specific laws) and the rest of the world, and which is also being promoted at the ILO and UN levels as well. The other social and solidarity economy actors share many common causes and principles with cooperatives.
- Governments themselves, at local or national level, can be partners in working alliances with the cooperative movement in jointly agreed agendas in order to reach the status of what Schneider (ch. 14) calls the 'partner state', without compromising the fourth cooperative principle of autonomy and independence. The growing management of services of general interest by cooperatives, and in particular social cooperatives, increasingly calls for such partnerships.

- At the global level, the reinforcement of the epistemic community between the ILO and the cooperative movement (Sanchez Bajo, ch. 1) is also fundamental. The existence of this epistemic community has provided a very important contribution to the identity of cooperatives worldwide (particularly through the ILO Recommendation No. 193), and a further reinforcement of this dimension is a historical opportunity that should not be missed.

3) The strengthening of the meso level and the building of strong alliances, are, in turn, fundamental bases for the enhancement of the advocacy work in favour of policies and legislation conducive to the promotion of cooperatives.

    - Cooperative enterprises still suffer from a low level of legal recognition, both in its general and in its specific forms. It is even more impacted by the lack of active policies for the promotion of this type of enterprise and corresponding meso-level organizations described above. It should also extend itself to obtaining satisfactory levels of social protection and adherence to labour standards, and of recognition of the specific working status of worker-members.
    - Last but not least, the advocacy work should promote the achievement of the United Nations 2030 Development Agenda and its Sustainable Development Goals (SDGs) as an indivisible whole, calling for policies that combine economic growth, social, health and peace considerations, as well as the promotion of all measures to protect the environment, such as in the fields of carbon emissions, the production of clean energy or the protection of natural spaces. Apart from the enormous untapped potential for jobs in social and environmental services, where the cooperative mode of organization is particularly well adapted, compliance with the SDGs and other intergovernmental instruments such as the 2015 Paris Climate Agreement are the only way to ensure both balanced socio-economic growth and the environmental salvation of this planet, a necessary condition for the survival of humankind and thus for any future of work at all.

However, this triple approach (reinforcing the meso level, establishing alliances, and advocating conducive policy and legislation), even if it was applied on a much larger scale than it is today, would, *per se*, not suffice to activate the full potential of cooperatives' contribution to the future of work. More is needed.

For this purpose, we need to rediscover the cooperative identity, namely the definition, seven operational principles and ten underlying values included in the *Statement on the Cooperative Identity* approved by the 1995 International Co-operative Alliance Centenary Congress in a new light.

Indeed, the cooperative identity should no longer be seen in isolation but should, instead, be consciously and explicitly considered as being fully embedded in an even wider and more universal set of standards that have gradually become a world consensus in the aftermath of the Second World War, with the *United Nations Universal Declaration of Human Rights* providing the basis, and the large set of texts (declarations, resolutions, conventions, recommendations, etc.) that have built on it in the UN system, and in particular the ILO's Fundamental Principles and Rights at Work (FPRW) and Decent Work concept (Eşim *et al.*, ch. 3).

Since the cooperative identity prescribes that cooperatives must translate their values into practice through concrete tools, cooperatives should also put into practice the wider set of universal standards of which their own identity has now become part and parcel. In this regard, it seems relevant to underline the growing commitment of the cooperative movement worldwide to the United Nations' 2030 Development Agenda and its Sustainable Development Goals (SDGs), including the principle of Decent Work enshrined in SDG 8. The chapters of this book also provide us with diffuse elements showing that, in today's world, cooperative principles and values are indissociably connected to the larger body of universal standards in the fields of human rights, social justice and decent work.

The commitment of cooperatives to this wider set of standards should be translated into concrete tools to be designed and installed in their institutional environment and organizational structure, in order to guide their daily practices and thinking. An example of these tools is the multi-stakeholder governance structure, which could be adopted in the governance of many cooperatives whose mission is to combine various stakeholders' interests, including those of the workers or producers of the cooperative (Novkovic, ch. 13). This tool could also be applied to online platform-based cooperatives (Schneider, ch. 14) in order to create a power balance among IT technicians, financial investors and workers so that workers' voice and rights could be explicitly recognized. Through the dissemination of such tools, cooperatives could then produce forms of work and employment that are innovative and, at the same time, better comply with the Fundamental Principles and Rights at Work and the Decent Work concept.

In order to bring about, in all cooperatives' daily practice, the link between the cooperative identity on the one hand and the wider body of universal standards in which this identity is now embedded in an irreversible way on the other, a strong effort in the field of awareness-raising, and in particular through education and training, will probably be needed. This effort would certainly bring positive results because, at the end of the day, this wider dimension is bound to provide a multiplying factor to cooperatives, in terms of transformational capacity, including a decisive step forward in their contribution to the improvement of the world of work.

Note

1 ILO. *Small and medium-sized enterprises and decent and productive employment creation*, 104th Session of the International Labour Conference. Geneva: ILO, 2015.

INDEX

Page numbers in *italics* denote a figure, **bold** a table, n an endnote